In memory of my father . . .
For Kate
And for Donna

Who shall put his finger on the work of justice and say, "It is there." Justice is like the kingdom of God; it is not without us as a fact; it is within us as a great yearning.

GEORGE ELLIOT

The whole case agianst me consists of suspision and if theres any justice in this world somthing will be done. However I am begining to have serious doubts as to weither or not there is any such thing as justice.

Letter from the death cell
ROBERT RAYMOND COOK

THE WORK OF JUSTICE

THE TRIALS OF

Robert Raymond Cook

The Story of the Last Man Hanged in Alberta

J. Pecover

Reread from
Forward to 24
where family buried
1 mile north of Hanna
anyway?

Greg Mockford, Publisher

WOLF WILLOW PRESS
EDMONTON

Published by

Wolf Willow Press
6932A-104 Street NW
Edmonton, Alberta T6H 2L7

GMOCKFRD@PLANET.EON.NET

Design, Production Editing and Typesetting by
Greg Mockford

Printed and Bound in Canada by
Friesen Printers, Manitoba

Canadian Cataloguing in Publication Data

Pecover, J. (Jack Ferris), 1928-
    The Work of Justice: The Trials of Robert Raymond Cook
    The Story of the Last Man Hanged in Alberta

ISBN 1-55056-423-4

    1. Cook, Robert Raymond, 1937-1960.
    2. Trials (Murder)--Alberta--Stettler.
    3. Murder--Alberta--Stettler.
      I.Title

HV6535.C33S74 1996 364.1'523'0971233   C96-900175-4

TABLE OF CONTENTS

FOREWORD

At the present historical moment, if one may use such a phrase, the "rudely muted voice" of Robert Raymond Cook, rising like a ghost from Jack Pecover's transcription of a letter Cook wrote to the Solicitor General of Canada in 1960, would seem to have a particular relevance. The letter, composed two weeks after the Supreme Court of Canada had dismissed what was to be the final appeal in *Regina v. Cook*, calls into question not only all absolute and relevant presuppositions, to use R. J. Collingwood's useful but controversial distinction, but also any other perilously balanced dichotomy including the not inconsequential and often substantiating distinction between the seductively alliterating terms *fiction* and *fact*. "I respectfully put it, Sir," Cook wrote, vesting his phrase in the civil respect due to constituted authority, "that when the facts replace the unanswerd questions and infernce, the err of this confiction will be proved."

As Cook, the condemned, and to all intents and purposes the functionally illiterate defendant, translates speech into visible ink, the slippage of a consonant from 'v' to 'f' has a devastating effect. In a momentary flash it illustrates the provocative questions posed by Pecover's skillfully constructed text - its overlapping chapters, its shifting juxtaposition of archival documents, psychiatric conjectures, police photographs and other photographic simulacra, charge sheets of recorded infractions of penitentiary regulations, in one instance as disingenuously trivial as the theft of a piece of pie.

To further ramify his text, Pecover weaves into its fabric his own selected interviews with witnesses or potential witnesses at the time of the trial and retrial of Cook, the suspect in the mass murder of his father, his stepmother and his five half-siblings. A final complication, as Pecover the lawyer fully realizes, is his own disaffected intervention in the case of *Regina v. Cook* , as he explores the strategy, to use Michel Foucault's phrase, of bourgeois legality in a system still haunted (even as empire is transforming into commonwealth) by the judicial theology of the Middle Ages.

To honor the visit of Queen Elizabeth when, accompanied by Prince Philip, she and President Eisenhower arrived in Canada, a general amnesty was proclaimed. It was, then, this magnanimous gesture which on June 23, 1959 released Cook, twenty-two days short of his twenty-second birthday, and about sixty other eligible prisoners, from Saskatchewan Penitentiary in Prince Albert into the body of the general public.

What followed occurred, as the events in James Joyce's haunted and haunting *Ulysses* do, "in a very short space of time through very short times of space." The time is that between Cook's release on the morning of June 23 from the Saskatchewan penitentiary and the evening of June 25 or the early hours of the following day; the distance - however devious the paths implicated in its divagations - was the distance between Prince Albert, Edmonton and Stettler, Alberta.

From the confines of such evasive parameters, the optic impressions emanating from abandoned articles of clothing, exhibited at both Cook's trials under restlessly changing numeric signifiers, assume a phantasmagoric life of their own. It is, however, the cheap penitentiary-made "robin's egg blue polyester suit with a silvery-pink thread woven through it" that finally dominates the screen as the judge in the second trial, with unequivocal abruptness as he instructs the jury, focuses their attention on the incriminatory garment. As irony compounds irony, it is perhaps not surprising that the foreman of the second-trial jury was "a well-known clothing salesman named Henry Singer" - a fact noted by Pecover without comment.

If irony, as it was once defined in the first quarter of the present century, is "the opportunism of the disinherited", then the abandoned clothes and other discarded and misplaced articles among the police exhibits assume lives of their own in a mental economy in which "the scales of justice", since the metaphor persists, are caught in the spiraling counter-movements of an obsolescing metaphysics and a burgeoning metapsychology. At this point of juncture the economy of the rebellious body seems to have become a cultural obsession in a war of conflicting proprietary interests and a "multiplicity of scientific discourses" which, according to Michel Foucault, the system of penal justice "is still unable to control."

As recorded, with or without any delegated authority, in the early days of August, 1991, members of the Tory Convention at Toronto "who ranged from cabinet ministers to party rank and file" narrowly called for bringing back the death penalty. "We believe there is an incredible cost saving to be had by bringing back capital punishment", one delegate is reported to have said. "There's no need to keep murderers in jail for life when they can be executed quickly." At the same time the site of a federal penitentiary of evil repute on the banks of the Fraser River had been dismantled and was being reformed by real estate developers into what has been subversively called elsewhere "an enclave of class criminals"of a different stripe.

In the fall of 1986 the previously hemmed in grounds of this maximum security fortress were already being advertised as a retirement park or "garden apartment units on the most prime land in the Royal City" *aka*, as Pecover would say, New Westminster. "Although the walls are down", the developers boasted at the time of its dismantling, "the penitentiary gatehouse, the original 1878 jail and one guard tower will be retained." Whether the history of this invested space has been written I did not know when I first read Pecover's text. However, to one who lived during the ten years before 1920 in the provincial mental hospital (MHI or #9) because one's father was the medical superintendant at the time, any reference to the federal penitentiary separated as it was from the mental institution only by its high walls with their armed guards and by a narrow ravine familiarly known as "the dump" Pecover's reconstruction of the trial, the retrial and the execution of Robert Raymond Cook spoke with an evocative and strangely disturbing force.

Perhaps it should be noted now that in 1994 George Bowering in his novel *Shoot!* has attempted to recreat, not as Pecover does, but in a intricately constructed novel, the conditions and events which led to the execution of fifteen year old Archie McLean, his brother Alan, both of mixed Scottish and Salish blood and their side-kick the half French-half Indian Alex Hare at the site of what I knew as the federal pententiary in New Westminister which in 1878 was known as the 'Colonial Jail'.

The closing of the federal penitentiary in New Westminster is referred to only in a footnote appended to the main text. It is not to the ambiguous symbols retained in a transformed economy of enclosure by the real estate developers of an exclusive complex of garden apartment units that Pecover turns the attention of his reader. It is to the transformation of the drygoods storage room for the nearby prison kitchen in Fort Saskatchewan Provincial Gaol in 1954 into what was known as the Execution Chamber when the retired "Senior Staff Sergeant, second in command of the Lethbridge Subdivision of the RCMP, was asked by the Attorney General of Alberta to take on a new career as Superintendent of Prisons for the province." It was his decision then that transferred the site of execution from the exercise yard, or "Courtyard II" as it was designated, from under the eyes of prison inmates to its new site in the kitchen store room from which a boilerplate trapdoor opened down into the empty Autopsy Room below and the Death Pit beneath.

It is finally, however, the newspaper photograph of twenty-four anonymous toured or touring bodies gathered together in the abandoned storage space, now identified as the "Hanging Room", that Pecover asks the reader to contemplate. They are, one supposes, the journalistic symbol of the public body into which, many feared, Cook had been released like a deadly virus by a quasi-divine gesture. Among these figures, four faces, Pecover notes, seem to be the focal center of the camera's gaze, those of two women and that of a man in a baseball cap, apparently "beaming at the noose", and the obviously puzzled face of the small child they have in tow. What they are staring at, Pecover observes, is a rough similacrum of the looped rope which had dropped Robert Raymond Cook from the floor of the storage room into a pit not unlike the pit into which the violated bodies in Stettler had been deposited near where the cheap prison made suit with the silvery- pink thread woven through it, abandoned for a pair of liberating "strides" had been carelessly or deliberately left to bear witness against him.

Through the interstices of Pecover's text the ghosts of discarded archetypes, shifting signifiers, and obdurate etymologies can be glimpsed as they confront the apparition of catchall phrases and emergent banalities like the image of the baseball cap on the head of the anonymous spectator. At what time, one is left to speculate, and by what chance circumstances, could the cap and face made visible beneath it be transformed into a potentially dangerous mug-shot in the hands of any one of a host of unidentified complainants, neighborhood watchers, or realtors trained by the RCMP like tracking hounds to become "eyes for the police", as a local paper reassures a public made nervous by reported thefts of "macaroni and hair shampoo", carpentry tools, Nintendo games, ghetto blasters, VCR's, CD players, and other objects like motor vehicles, of uncontrolled and insistently induced desire.

Whether or not Pecover reads the appearance of the baseball cap in the press photograph as "a class inscription" limiting "the scope of his lived subjectivity" by marking the wearer as "a member of the working class", as John Biln in a recent article in the journal *Assemblage* (16) does in another context, his noting of its presence on one of the heads in the pale of the now vacated Execution Chamber in the old Fort certainly indicates the possibility of such a reading with all its ambiguous connotations. The attention Pecover pays, however, to another type of headgear, the black hood, which drawn over Cook's head muffled his voice before the pull of the lever abruptly interrupted the final phrases of the Lord's Prayer Cook was reciting at that decisive moment, implicates the reader in an undertexture of restless signifiers which it is difficult to ignore.

After Robert Raymond Cook was led from his death cell in the basement of Fort Saskatchewan Provincial Gaol to his execution on the gound-level floor his body, as Pecover records, was taken down and examined by the six coroner's jurors as part of "An Inquisition taken for our Sovereign Lady the Queen at the House of the Provincial Gaol" and the lifeless and the soon-to-be eyeless body was taken to the Anatomy Department of the University of Alberta for use as a teaching cadaver.

The eyes Cook himself had already donated to the eye bank as he had donated his body to the Anatomy Department. As irony compounds irony Cook himself, and for reasons ultimately known only to himself, gave back to the state with a eucharistic gesture the youthful body which had been liberated not long before, with a horde of others, by royal authority from diminishing confinement merely into a society which eventually in the name of the same Crown was to take away from him the very life of that body itself.

ACKNOWLEDGMENTS

The reader will learn in the Introduction that in researching the *Cook* case I interviewed some 200 people. All of them were unreserved in their willingness to talk about Cook, about the trials or about his time in various prisons. It was true at the outset and it remains true today that those who can remember the case and particularly those who were involved either in Cook's life - and death - or in the trials are not at all hesitant to talk about it, and indeed are often anxious to do so. It is not too much (nor is it all that original) to say that the case haunts us still. In only three instances was I rebuffed: once by a newspaperman anxious to protect the image of Stettler; once by a former RCMP officer who cannot have been proud of his part in the manhunt; and once by a trial witness who declined to be interviewed. To be fair, the trial witness did not reply to a letter asking for an interview, so perhaps it wasn't a rebuff so much as mere indifference.

The 200 or so will understand my not listing their names here, and I trust they will accept my sincere thanks for providing me with the thousand and one pieces without which Cook's story could not have been told - for the letters, photographs, recollections and memories which permitted me to try and vest a man with the personality which was an unknown quantity to all of us who remember the unforgettable events of 1959-60.

I wish to extend thanks no less sincere to The National Archive of Canada, The Penitentiary Service of Canada, The Legal Archives Society of Alberta, The Provincial Archives of Alberta[1], The Provincial Museum of Alberta, the Departments of the Solicitor General of both Canada and Alberta, the office of the Clerk of the Court of Queen's Bench of Alberta and the libraries of both The Edmonton Journal and The Calgary Herald for their cooperation in making available to me the documentary material still preserved 35 years after the events it records. I thank as well The Canada Council and express the hope that it will see its generosity as justified.

[1] *The use of plates 25-31 courtesy of the Provincial Archives of Alberta is acknowledged with thanks.*

Friends who were asked for advice on early drafts deserve an apology for the imposition and they have earned the right - and then some - to be gratefully acknowledged here together with others, friends most of them, some only acquaintances, who provided assistance in particular ways. To these too my sincere thanks: June Anderson, Gordon E. Arnell, Elizabeth Atherton-Reid, Clara Behuniak, Dennis N. Bell, Cliff Bingham, Mel Brooks, Sharon Butala, Don Campbell, Jennifer Campbell, Gerald A. Cone, John H. Cone, Maurice F. V. Doll, Chris Evans, Victoria Fielding, Bette Fuhrmann, Floyd Halls, Dr Charles Hellon, Judeen Hendrickson, Joyce Heyliger, Audra Hollingshead, Lila Howse, Alan Hustak, John Hustwick, Her Honor Judge Dolores Hutton-Hanson, Margaret Jacobs, Larry S. Knight, The Honorable Mr Justice Ernest A. Marshall, Professor Robin Matthews, Dennis Minion, Greg Mockford, Helen O'Connor, Hank O'Handley, Jim O'Sullivan, Rosalyn Prauner, Mel Pyper, the late Reverend George Rode, His Honor Judge Dwayne W. Rowe, Gail Sadauskas, Susan Sharpe, June Sheppard, Ted Simmermon, Jean Smellie, Nick Solowan, Leif Stolee, Gwen Therrien, Nellie van de Ligt, Jim van Domselaar, Dr Wilfred Watson, Darlene Woods and Chris Zobel.

Finally, two friends deserve singling out for special mention and special thanks: Sandra Mallett who knows the language and the handling of it as well as anybody and better than most, who made many valuable suggestions on textual matters, and who struggled valiantly and in vain to teach me why the active is to be preferred to the passive voice, and Dr Sheila Watson for her Foreword. Her presence here gives me a pretext for mentioning her novels, *Deep Hollow Creek* and *The Double Hook*, classics of Canadian letters, and their mention within its pages, and her presence, honors *The Work of Justice*.

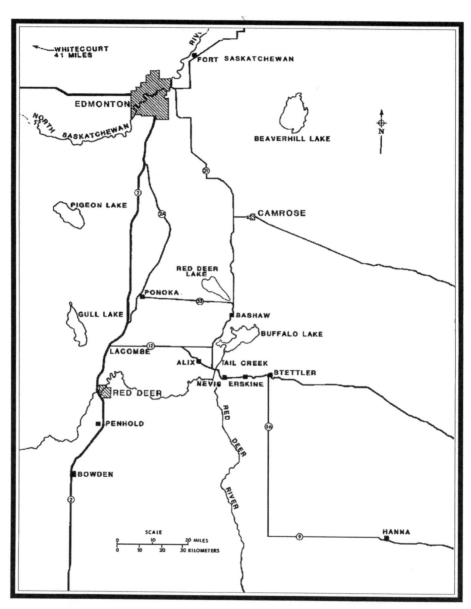

WHITECOURT
41 MILES

RIVER

FORT SASKATCHEWAN

EDMONTON

NORTH SASKATCHEWAN

BEAVERHILL LAKE

N

PIGEON LAKE

CAMROSE

RED DEER
LAKE

PONOKA

GULL LAKE

BASHAW

BUFFALO LAKE

LACOMBE

ALIX   TAIL CREEK

NEVIS   ERSKINE   STETTLER

RED DEER

PENHOLD

RED

DEER

RIVER

BOWDEN

SCALE
0   10   20 MILES
0   10   20   30 KILOMETERS

HANNA

Gerald A. Cone

xvi

INTRODUCTION

At midnight on Monday, November 14, 1960, Robert Raymond Cook was led from his death cell in the basement of Fort Saskatchewan Provincial Gaol to the execution chamber on the ground-level floor. Four minutes after midnight he was hanged, and at 12:18 a.m. he was declared dead by the attending physician. His body was taken down and laid on a stretcher where it was examined by the six coroner's jurors, as part of "An Inquisition taken for our Sovereign Lady the Queen at the House of the Provincial Gaol." It was then carried up a flight of stairs and out into the cold night to a waiting green panel truck which delivered it to the Anatomy Department of the Faculty of Medicine of the University of Alberta in Edmonton. There it was placed in a zinc tub and someone made an incision in the left thigh in preparation for its use as a teaching cadaver. The eyes, which Cook had donated to the eye bank (as he had donated his body for medical research) were removed and flown the following morning to Vancouver for transplant of the corneas. Their recipient was not informed that his new corneas had belonged to a man convicted of the largest mass murder in the history of Alberta.

Cook was 23 when he died. Nothing so befitted his rudely abbreviated life as the way he faced its being taken from him. In the still vivid memory of people who witnessed his death, he died quietly and bravely. Two Lutheran pastors, who had given him spiritual counsel during his last months and communion an hour earlier that night, were with him as he walked down a long pipe filled underground corridor toward the execution chamber. He entered it and walked without hesitation or faltering toward the far end of the 15 by 21 foot room, where a rope hung motionless from the ceiling directly over the waiting trapdoors. Waiting for Cook were a half dozen officials and five times as many observers, most of them policemen, most of whom had had no connection with the case and seem to have been there for the same reasons as those that used to bring festive crowds to the Tyburn Tree. Those who had come - and some of them had - expecting to be entertained by Cook's death, found their expectation quelled by the predominant mood: fear. The room was pervaded by it: Cook's to be sure, but also that of the witnesses.[1]

---

[1] *The memory of fear was predominant in the accounts of witnesses who had attended other executions at the 'Fort' and were thus able to compare earlier reactions with those experienced at Cook's. They ascribed it to the fact that prior to Cook, executions had taken place on an outdoor gallows, where Cook was the first - and only - man to be put to death on the new indoor facility. For each of the earlier executions, a wooden gallows was erected in the exercise yard onto which a small window in each of two death cells looked. A condemned man was thus afforded the diversion from death cell routine of being able to watch the construction of the instrument of his coming death.*

There was in the witnesses a palpable sense of forced confinement, which owed nothing to the prison setting. They were a captive audience rooted to where they stood by the unfolding of an event bloody out of mind, and no more capable of escaping it than was Cook, wrists strapped behind his back and in the grip of two guards whose size - for which they were chosen - was the guarantee of Cook's not keeping his audience waiting should he attempt to do so. Intensifying the sense of confinement, the witnesses crowded at one end of the room, seeming to draw as far away as possible from the terrible apparatus and paraphernalia at the far end: the black steel trapdoors, the release lever and eight or so feet of rope neatly coiled above the noose and tied with a light string to the bight that rose to the concrete ceiling.

There the rope was made fast to a ceiling device[1]. The rope was three-quarter inch manila hemp purchased that afternoon at a local hardware. A black hood hung on a nearby wall reminding one observer desperate for any distraction no matter how incongruous of Moore's "stockings hung by the chimney with care." But this was no night for the benevolent elf. It belonged rather to the angel of death just as half the well-lit ground-floor room (the procession had had to mount ten steps leading up from the basement corridor) belonged to Cook and his handful of tense attendants. A fearful stage was set for the death of a man in the prime of his life.

There was no eleventh hour confession, but there were some 'last words.' As the hangman swiftly strapped Cook's ankles Cook said, in the hearing of both pastors, "Father, forgive them." As the hangman was about to slip the hood over Cook's head the pastors began the Lord's Prayer and Cook joined them. The recitation continued with Cook's voice now muffled by the hood as the hangman carefully set the knot under the left ear and slipped the slack out of the noose - an act facilitated by the noose and knot being heavily smeared with Vaseline. Positioning the knot thus would ensure that the clockwise turn the rope makes before being brought up short in the split-second drop would bring the knot under Cook's chin rather than the back of the neck as would have happened had it been placed under the right ear. The difference is one of death resulting instantaneously from a severing of the spine between the second and third cervicæ, rather than from slow strangulation. A third and somewhat disconcerting result - decapitation - sometimes occurs wherever the knot is placed, but the mode of death seems immaterial to the heart, which beats on for several minutes in a forlorn attempt to maintain life.

[1] *I was reliably informed that a granny knot was employed.*

xviii

When the well-rehearsed preparations were completed, the hangman motioned away the two guards who flanked the condemned man on the trapdoors. He then stepped quickly from behind Cook towards the lever and, in a smooth motion, pulled it. The prayer on the lips of the three men abruptly gave way to silence and shock. The pastors were left to struggle with the disappearance of a man for whom they had formed a profound respect and affection in the preceding months.

There is no question that Cook knew the balance of Christ's dying absolution, and its omission can be read by advocates of his innocence as bearing out his insistence that far from their not knowing what they were doing they knew very well indeed - or could have known had they taken the trouble to find out. They had, Cook said again and again, carelessly guessed him into a death sentence, but the guess was wide of the mark since he was innocent. But even he would not have denied that on the face of the evidence he looked guilty and that the guess they made, if guess it was, seemed reasonable enough. But he would say that, and the question is, the conundrum at the heart of this book is can a perfectly rational man (as Cook appeared to be to all those whose job it was to determine whether he was or not) be guilty and genuinely believe in his innocence? The reader will not find the answer here.

Whether forgiveness was his to afford or not, we may marvel conditionally at a quality that would be strained in most of us. It is one thing to be able to forgive one's transgressors when they act merely out of mistake, however well-intentioned. It is quite another where, as in Cook's view of the *Cook* case, they act - although he would not have known the words - out of fear, negligence, dull-wittedness or sloth all leavened by malice.

***

He was, he said, innocent, but of course, in one way of viewing these things, it was not true. Cook had been tried twice in the Trial Division of the Supreme Court of Alberta and twice convicted. Both convictions had been appealed to the Appellate Division of that Court; the second conviction was then further appealed to the Supreme Court of Canada. The first conviction, it is true, was overturned by the Appellate Division, but on a point of law which in the second trial proved to be immaterial to the question of guilt or innocence. The second trial was ordered because the judge presiding at the first had made a mistake; the second showed that, had he not done so, the result would have been the same. The evidence at both trials was substantially identical, and it was sufficient to permit two juries to convict him. It is fair to say therefore that only a small minority of criminals are tried more thoroughly than Cook was, and twice over he was proved guilty of murder beyond all reasonable doubt. It is difficult to be proved much guiltier than that.

Cook was charged with and convicted of only his father's murder, but in a loose and non-technical sense he was convicted as well of the murder of all the remaining members of his family: his step-mother and his five half brothers and sisters - the eldest nine, the youngest three. The least of murders is savage enough in one sense or another, but the annihilation of the Cook family was savage beyond ready description. The adults were shot from close range with a double-barreled shotgun as they lay in bed. One of them also was clubbed in the head - probably with the butt of the shotgun and probably before being shot.

The five children were bludgeoned to death by the same gun that had been used to shoot their parents. In the maniacal fury of the clubbing, the shotgun had disintegrated into a dozen or more pieces. Wooden gun stocks will fracture and pieces of mechanism will fly off with the application of a moderate enough amount of force when a gun is used as a club - an employment for which shotguns are not designed. But the force required to bend laminated steel barrels - either being swung against a child's skull, as the Crown suggested, or, more probably, against the steel cot the child slept in - was almost a matter of disbelief.

By any measure it was the most spectacular murder in Alberta's history and for that among other reasons - to be examined here - the case gripped the imagination of Albertans in a way that had never been rivaled. One measure may be seen in the fact that *The Red Deer Advocate* issued an 'extra' - for the first and only time since the Second World War - carrying the news of Cook's conviction. The first trial was held in Red Deer. While it lasted, nothing else was of very much account.

***

Cook was steadfast in maintaining his innocence, but a protestation of innocence, even on the gallows, is not necessarily evidence of it any more than is the fact that a man has narrow-set eyes and cannot face down the foreman of the jury evidence of guilt. Still, we expect a guilty man about to be hanged to confess at the last. There is, heaven knows, reason enough for not doing so earlier, but we hope that someone who was guilty will find the courage to admit it when there is no longer any chance of one more lie turning the tide. We would not have our consciences troubled by vague possibilities if all it takes is a confession, made at no cost, to secure their quiescence. But Cook would not accommodate us.

His own advocacy was not surprising, particularly if he was innocent. What is surprising is that he was not alone in it, either then or now. In researching the case, I interviewed some 200 people, all of whom fell into one or both of two categories: either they had known Cook or members of his family or both, or they were involved in the aftermath of the murders - as investigators, manhunters, trial witnesses, lawyers and judges, court and jail officials, medical officers, his spiritual advisors, witnesses of his death. I talked casually to half as many again, at a guess, who remember a case not easily forgotten.

At some point in the interviews or casual conversations, I would ask for an opinion as to Cook's guilt or innocence, or would where an opinion had not already been volunteered, usually in emphatic terms. Almost without exception the opinions were on one side or the other: he was innocent; he was guilty; there were few shades of doubt. Of the people who talked to me, those who think he was innocent outnumber the 'guilties' by a ratio of just over six to one. The ratio is difficult to ignore (apart from the fact that it tended to shore up my own predilections), and it tends to pose some insistent questions.

6 Innc
1 guilty

Assuming - admittedly a large assumption - the validity of extrapolating from the results of my quite unscientific straw poll to the population of Alberta at large, one question is why the painstaking proof of Cook's guilt failed to persuade about 85% of Albertans that the verdict squared with the truth. While justice may indeed have been done, those forming the majority were not prepared to concede it, and thought they saw a particularly draconian injustice being done: the judicial condemnation and judicial murder of an innocent man - itself a heinous enough crime although not one proscribed by the Criminal Code. The contrast between what appears almost to have been self-evident to Cook's jurors, and the seeming fact that to a majority of their fellow citizens it was anything but, invites the question why? Had the jurors seen and heard something denied to the rest of us?

The answer of course is that they had. They had seen and heard the damning totality of the evidence against Cook. They had watched and listened as the Crown prosecutor paraded his witnesses to the stand and, through them, carefully constructed a circumstantial edifice of guilt. The jurors had examined the blood- and brain-spattered parts of the broken shotgun, and they had looked on as garments saturated in dried blood were held up in fastidious fingers for identification by RCMP investigators. They had looked at police photographs of torn bodies and had probably, like the rest of us drawn in spite of ourselves to the sight of violent death, subjected them to rather closer scrutiny than their evidential value merited.

Above all, they had watched Cook himself as he reacted to the Crown's witnesses, and they watched and listened to him with single-minded intensity as he took the stand in his own defense and sparred with the prosecutor in the deadly game. The fact that he stumbled frequently was not lost on them.

All this was denied to everyone outside the courtroom, forced to rely on newspaper accounts of the previous day's evidence. The accounts were accurate within the limitations imposed by the medium[1], but they could not convey anything transcending the spoken word, nor could they impart the impact of the exhibits heaped in sickening array on the exhibit table. The written word cannot reproduce the defiant cadence of truth or suggest the faltering step of perjury; it never reflects the nervous gesture, the too-glib or too-hesitant reply, the evasive glance that causes jurors to look on reflectively. Witnesses must be heard and seen in order to assess the truthfulness of their testimony. Appeal courts are therefore rightly reluctant to reverse trial verdicts when the ground of appeal is an allegation that the "triers of fact" (the jurors in Cook's case) have come to an erroneous finding of what the facts were and, therefore, to the wrong verdict.

---

[1] *In one case inordinately so. In what must be one of the few such instances in the practise of criminal law, the harried defense lawyers in Cook's first trial relied heavily on the reports appearing in* The Red Deer Advocate *in preparing their final arguments to be made to the jury. They needed as comprehensive a compendium of the 11 days' evidence as was available. The shorthand reporter's transcripts would not be ready for some few weeks. Their own notes, made in the press of examination and cross-examination, were unavoidably sketchy. They turned without hesitation - and without much choice - to* The Advocate, *which thus found itself in the heat of advocacy in a way its founders undoubtedly had never contemplated.*

But most newspaper readers are not appellate judges, and they are not overly concerned with niceties of law, among them such arcane matters as perverse findings of fact. Particularly not when those niceties seem to get in the way of justice. Something in the newspaper accounts of the Cook trials suggested to readers that justice - and Cook along with it - was having a tough time of it. In a departure from the norm ("They are there; they must know more than we do"), the readers decided that, on this occasion at least, it was immaterial that they were not as fully informed as the jurors; they would nevertheless reach their own conclusion. In doing so, they were impliedly putting the jurors on trial, in the court of public opinion. Nor were they prepared to give the jurors the benefit of any doubt, reasonable by definition had there been any since doubt is unreasonable only when harbored by others.

This was an echo of the problem in the courtroom. Neither were the jurors in possession of all the facts or all the answers - a rather sweeping indictment of the investigatory and trial processes which awaits substantiation here. The gaps were made evident to the newspaper readers, who could not escape the conclusion that the damning totality of evidence was neither as damning as it undoubtedly appeared on its face, nor was it a totality. They could not escape the conclusion, however visceral, that Cook was innocent.

The newspaper accounts raised large questions. If answers to them were provided in later testimony, then the reporters missed them. But the answers of course would have been commensurate with the importance of the questions and, thus, unlikely to be missed. In fact, they were not reported because they were not provided. Questions were prompted by the evidence against - and, for that matter, for - Cook, and when the legal rhetoric had died on the stale courtroom air, they were seen, or felt, to be still airborne.

It was not surprising to learn that some people - mostly inhabitants of the town where the murders occurred - preferred that the bones of the Cook case not be disinterred. It was, they said, a long time ago. The murders had done little to enhance the image of the town. The victims were buried in a common grave in a cemetery near a distant town, largely forgotten except as part of the ineradicable memory of the case itself. Cook, who had not graced the town when he was more or less growing up in it, had been caught, tried, convicted and executed. Why stir up events this long after their savage quietus? The dissenters suggested, often enough with a note of belligerence, that while nothing much was to be gained by stirring them up, there was much to be lost with the revival of disturbing memories, of divisive argument, of a discreditable attempt to bring the administration of justice into disrepute - the last a hobby horse to be ridden by the author, it was implied, until the last dog was hung. Cook was hanged; best to let sleeping dogs lie.

Perhaps. Except that the *Cook* case has never fully been put to sleep. It has been somnolent at times, but then along comes a book, a play, an opinion piece, a series of newspaper articles, a radio phone-in show, someone wanting to do a television dramatization, and the case stirs fitfully and the ugly questions are raised again.

Some of them. The purpose of what follows is to ask once more all the questions that were asked in the courtroom and, where answers were provided, to examine them, to suggest alternatives and to invite comparison. Often enough there were questions for which no answers were attempted during the trials, even tentatively - motive for one, although the law does not require that motive be established - and answers for these questions will be suggested. The reader will decide how plausible they may be.

More important than the courtroom's failure to provide answers was its frequent failure to ask questions. Some of these will be asked here for the first time, and it will be argued why it was crucial that they be asked, when doing so would have had a bearing on the case.

All of this may or may not persuade the reader that the *Cook* trials deserve yet another analysis. She will form - or have confirmed - her opinion as to Cook's innocence. Proof of it is beyond the scope or competence of this study. Calling into question the adequacy of the judicial system's proof of his guilt - not the same thing as proof of innocence were it shown to be inadequate - is not.

My purpose is not to second-guess the jurors; they concluded what they did based on the evidence they heard. Nor is it to criticize those who investigated or those who tried the case - although some such criticism - occasionally severe - will be found here. Rather, it is simply to present the complexities of the case, allowing readers an outsider's view of how and why a man was sent to death by his community. Readers will be left to decide for themselves whether his guilt was clearly established.

CHAPTER 1

THE STORY: I

The name Prince Albert conjures a number of images: for historians, the Prince Consort and his grieving sovereign; for wardrobe mistresses, frock coats; for pipe smokers - a vanished breed - pipe tobacco. But for most of us it means a small city in north-central Saskatchewan which itself conjures a powerful image, that of John Diefenbaker. So powerful indeed that there is reason for supposing that the city barely existed independently of Diefenbaker; that it would have occasioned little surprise had it evaporated as a figment of The Chief's runaway egomania when he was gathered to his fathers.

For some of us however, particularly if we happen to be in serious trouble with the criminal law, the name Prince Albert summons the image of the federal penitentiary on the western outskirts of the city. Officially it is Saskatchewan Penitentiary, but few would call it that even if they knew it. The city and its landmark institution have merged in one name: Prince Albert or, more commonly, PA.

The salient feature of the penitentiary's geographical setting is the North Saskatchewan River - a dark-brown god dominating the scene. The river sweeps past the walls of the institution in a broad curve and on through the heart of the city, figuratively dividing this part of Canada into two dissimilar countries. To the north lies what remains of Captain Butler's great lone land: the boreal forest which, giving the abrupt lie to its seeming endlessness, ends at the tundra's precise southern limit. To the river's south lies the livid scar of civilization - the legacy of those who, Cæsars-come-lately, saw the wilderness as enemy and conquered it. That their descendants should build a prison here fits the ethos of that particular form of progress.

In the usual case, scenery is the last thing in the world on the mind of a prisoner being driven from the city center or the airport to the penitentiary. The distraction of what awaits him could be expected to blind him to something as commanding as the sweep of the Himalayas were they to flank the two-mile route. How much more oblivious then to what is after all an ordinary enough river, deity though it may be to someone not destined to live months and years within sight of it without being able to see it. But it is there, and see it or not, its slow-flowing power will mock the shackled prisoner's weakness as the penitentiary looms before him, and its timelessness will underscore the precise block of time which now delimits his existence.

Canada's old penitentiaries were built in a time when there were no degrees of security - minimum, medium and maximum. In a less frivolous time, there was no-nonsense security. Men entered them, served their time, and left, and if they happened to be rehabilitated in the process, that was a by-product, welcome if fortuitous. The penitentiaries' builders builded better than they perhaps knew; nothing, it seems, is more indestructible than a penitentiary once constructed. New penitentiaries seldom replace old ones; they are merely added to the growing number. Nearly all of these fortress-like structures survive[1], now as Canada's maximum security institutions. Some of them, predating Confederation, seem as old as the Canadian Shield and a good bet to outlast it.

And they are all of them a foul and pestilent congregation of vapors - a muggy ambrosia made up of the smells of old paint (if stone walls will not a prison make nor iron bars a cage, eighteen coats of Department of Public Works paint will do it), of men in confinement, of food prepared for six hundred men which invariably smells of turnips, and would even if that night's menu offered nothing but lemon chiffon pie. The nostrils are assailed and the spirit is assaulted by the smells of a penitentiary.

There is more. There is an ambience to penitentiaries made up of bitter elements: despair, hopelessness, arrogance, brutality, perversion, death. Of the work of justice contaminated by injustice and of privacy denied; for the prisoners there is no time or place in which they can escape being watched. Hatred of those who deny them privacy is an ingredient added to the witches' brew.

There is withal an outward serenity, a muffled quiet, but the serenity is that of a quiescent volcano and the quiet a premonitory hush. There is

---

[1] *British Columbia Penitentiary is now closed - an exception to the rule.*

not a penitentiary that hasn't known violence and death in the past, and none that does not foretell their coming again; it is merely a question of time - the elongated form of it peculiar to prisons. Time is the stuff of imprisonment, and the prison can afford to wait for the next riot, the next suicide, the next knifing of one prisoner by another while the prize, the 'kid' after whom both lust, looks on in fear or indifference.

Saskatchewan Penitentiary is a maximum security prison in the classic mold. The ancient complex of buildings, surrounded by 18-foot red brick walls, is set back a quarter of a mile from the southern shoreline of the river. Stepping at last through the main gate on the day of his release, the river is the first thing the prisoner will see. It is doubtful however that scenery is any more on his mind on that day than it was on the day of arrival. Freedom is what matters, and if a river happens to be an aspect of the world outside the hated walls, it is at most an undifferentiated one.

***

Little reason then to suppose that one Robert Raymond Cook, being released from Prince Albert on the morning of Tuesday, June 23, 1959, was aware of the majestic river, or that he dwelt on the mild coincidence that 370 miles upstream it also flowed past another penal institution: the Fort Saskatchewan Provincial Gaol. Nor could he foresee that 512 days later he would gain yet another release from that other institution. The events of concern in this book had not yet taken over his life, but they were about to.

The agency of Cook's release from Prince Albert was more benign than the death which brought his deliverance from Fort Saskatchewan. He had been sentenced to PA for three years for breaking and entering and car theft. His term was set to expire on October 11, 1959, but in June of that year the Queen and Prince Philip were due to arrive in Canada where, with President Eisenhower, they were to open the St Lawrence Seaway. In the tradition of honoring a visiting sovereign, a general amnesty had been declared for certain classes of offender. Cook, along with 120 or so other inmates, was fortunate enough to be included in one of the classes.

3

On his release he was 22 days short of his 22nd birthday, and no stranger to prisons in which by then he had spent about a third of his life. He had served his first federal term in Stony Mountain (more properly Manitoba) Penitentiary, two years for what was by then the usual: breaking and entering and car theft. He had completed an earlier term in Prince Albert, again for the usual, and was now being released from his second.

Cars, and in particular the theft of them, were his life. From an early age he had proved himself extraordinarily accomplished in his ability to get into any locked car, 'hot wire' it and drive off, all within seconds. Gordon Russell, now an athletic program director in Edmonton, was the junior half of a two-man police force in Hanna, Alberta - Cook's birthplace - when Cook was growing up there. Russell remembers Cook well, and would even had Cook not attained his later notoriety, recalling with rueful admiration Cook's offbeat combination of talents, among them the gift - inspiring awe in Russell - of being able to make a car, any car, his own. When Russell saw another car being driven off at breakneck speed, the pint-size driver barely visible as he strained to peer over the wheel, the investigation was complete before the chase began. A weary Russell would prepare a now routine police report: "Car theft. Cook again."

But the time came when the diminutive bandit was diminutive no longer. Where, in Cook's pre-teens, his father had been able to intercede to have his son's latest escapade written off as merely another instance of boyish high-jinks, as Cook began to expand his horizons beyond Hanna's, he found that the RCMP was not so avuncular and forgiving as Russell had been. The law began to call Cook to account. What had been the borrowing of cars, school buses, even tractors, for a little carefree joy-riding, now became the theft of them. The law's attitude hardened apace with the development of Cook's behavioral pattern, and before it was all over, a reformatory, a provincial jail twice, two penitentiaries on three occasions between them and a set of trapdoors had opened to receive the young offender who found his life's rut early and never veered from it.

While car theft and B&E violate property, they are nevertheless non-violent crimes in the eyes of the law which look only for the laying on of hands, real or threatened. Yet they formed the sum of Cook's criminal career until he committed, at least allegedly and perhaps in fact, the most violent of all crimes: mass murder[1]. He graduated twice from one degree

---

[1] *All future references to guilt or innocence will assume one or the other as the particular context requires in order to avoid awkward constructions such as this. In a given instance they are not to be taken as the book's point of view which, overall, is that his trials mocked the concept of proof beyond a reasonable doubt,*

of criminality to the next. The first was in the normal progression of things: from juvenile joy-riding to car theft with which breaking and entering went almost as an occupational adjunct. The presumed second promotion however had the quality of a quantum leap. The least demanding of theories of the way a criminal mind develops, the way misdemeanors will lead on to felonies and worse, would be strained to find a causal progression from theft of a dismally unimaginative kind to murder unique in Alberta in its magnitude and ferocity.

Perhaps; but it seems a safe assumption that murder was not on his mind on a morning made lambent by the prospect of liberty, any more than was the North Saskatchewan River which greeted him as he stepped at last through the main gate. Nothing so rare as a day in June unless it be a day in June on which a convict is being released 110 days earlier than he had had any reason, two months earlier, to anticipate. And so Cook, along with about 60 other prisoners scheduled for early release on June 23, was led out to the bus which was waiting to take them to Saskatoon from which they would disperse to the four winds. The fact that the winds would blow about 70% of them back into one or another penal institution could not have been of less moment. For years freedom was all that mattered to them, and freedom was now theirs including the freedom to do whatever it took to ensure that most of them would once again be deprived of it.

Preparation for his release had begun when he received a memorandum from the Warden's office addressed with fine institutional impersonality to "7185 Cook" informing 7185 that "We are now starting release procedures on all those being released on June 23...and request your cooperation in supplying the following information: (a) destination; (b) preference as to mode of transport." In all his jail and penitentiary years Cook had never been anything but a near-model prisoner. The request for cooperation was in no danger of being denied and Cook filled in the blanks on the memorandum with Edmonton as his destination, preferably by bus.

For release he was issued a two-piece prison-made suit of indifferent cut for which he had been fitted in the prison's tailor shop. He was given a pair of black oxfords, also prison-made, and he wore a pair of yellow socks and a red tie sent him by his stepmother for wearing on the great day. Completing the ensemble were prison-issue white shorts and as well a white shirt which was also from penitentiary stores. We will see

and that while there are two or three severely troubling indications of guilt, if more was known they would be dealt with in such a way as to satisfy all but the most diehard skeptics.

5

that clothing littered the landscape of the Cook murders both literally and figuratively. Clothing given, borrowed, traded, discarded and stolen. Clothing rained on, stained, strewn, torn, ironed and left unironed, packed and left unpacked and maybe neither and maybe both. Clothing identified, ignored or wrongly identified, and all of it, its location and condition, at least interesting and at most suspicious in some degree. Not alone did it do so, but here the apparel seemed oft to proclaim the guilty man when the time came to piece together proof of Cook's guilt not now of his nth B&E and car theft, but of patricide, matricide and fratricide.

That time however lay in a dark future foreseen by no one. Not certainly by the PA officials who, had they thought of it, would have seen Cook as nothing more than a cinch bet to be back within a few months at most with that nth B&E and car theft and, with the routine raising of the ante, with three-and-a-half or four years. Nor, it seems certain, by Cook himself, not in this best of times: the shining morning of his release, a morning made even sunnier by the simultaneous release of his friend, Jimmy Myhaluk of Edmonton, another beneficiary of the amnesty.

Cook and Myhaluk were buddies - Myhaluk's term - and each saw the other as a 'good thief'- the highest compliment one B&E man can pay another. They now boarded the bus for Saskatoon, and during the trip put the finishing touches on the plans formulated by them during the interminable months inside. What the plans lacked in subtlety they made up in verve. Myhaluk and Cook were a team - of desperadoes, brigands, outlaws, who knew? Or cared for that matter; the name was not important. They knew only that there could be no stopping them.

In their inception, penitentiaries were designed to induce penitence, hence the name. It is a function in which they have not always succeeded, penitence, as in the case of Myhaluk and Cook, taking the form not of regret for past sins, but for carelessness, nothing more, in getting caught in the commission of them. Never again for these incipient bandits. They had identified all their mistakes ensuring that they would not repeat them nor of course would they make any new ones. They acknowledged that the law might throw up a few trifling barricades between them and the objects of their exuberant ambition, but these they would storm with invincible elan. They failed to see that they would be brought low by their even more invincible naivete, and so they sallied forth, a couple of blind Bourbons who, having learned nothing, had forgotten nothing. Hope and Crosby off down the light-hearted Road to Recidivism.

Seventeen years later, again in prison, Myhaluk remembered that halcyon time. His eyes alight, partly in recollection of the golden days of their freedom, partly in the wry and self-mocking humor often found in the makeup of five-time losers, Myhaluk reminisced. As he did so, the cruel concrete and steel of the interview cubicle in British Columbia Penitentiary seemed to crumble away. Myhaluk was again on the bus, his buddy Bobby beside him, bound for Saskatoon and the boundless future beyond. "In those places," he said, forgetting for the moment that he was sitting in one of those places, speaking by monitored telephone through shatter-proof glass, "you dream, you plan. . . . Boy! We were going to terrorize the country, open cans, kick in joints . . . . We'd get this car. High-powered. There was no way they were going to stop us. God, there was no way!" Not the most sophisticated and best-laid of plans perhaps, but a plan, which got as far as Cook getting the car, and as far as Cook at least terrorizing the countryside, although rather more radically than Myhaluk, for one, had envisioned. Myhaluk had not included slaughter as part of a campaign of kicking in joints and then fleeing the scenes of their good-natured crimes in the high-powered car, followed by the RCMP, a pack of angry wolves trailing helplessly in the wake of the two ebullient terrorists. But there is terror and there is terror.

Arriving in Saskatoon, the pair found they had a long wait before making the bus connection to Edmonton. Not surprisingly, this was taken as a signal to slake thirsts that had gone unquenched for the past couple of years apart from occasional shots of moonshine distilled in endlessly inventive ways in obscure corners of the joint. So Cook and Myhaluk set off on a mid-morning tour of Saskatoon's downtown hotels. It was a tour that spanned the afternoon and stretched into the evening, and it went without incident until a chance beer parlor meeting with one Oliver Durocher.

'Stuttering Oliver' Durocher was one of the few men, inside the penitentiary or out, who did not get along with Cook; who in fact hated him with an intensity which exploded in violence during the afternoon of Wednesday, April 1, 1959 when, in a sneak attack in a cellblock corridor, Durocher bludgeoned Cook on the back of the head with a steel pipe. Cook had been set up for it by friends of Durocher who enticed Cook to join a card game in the corridor. While Cook was not a loner, he was a private man who seems to have found his own company acceptable and to have enjoyed that of only a handful of close friends. He socialized infrequently - sitting in on a card game happened rarely - but he was not anti-social nor shy, so that no one was more than mildly surprised when Cook agreed to join in. He suspected nothing.

Durocher intended to kill Cook. The effects of the assault could have been more serious. Cook was taken to the prison hospital where 15 stitches were required to close four scalp wounds. He remained hospitalized for two weeks before being returned to the general prison population. The x-rays showed nothing beyond a severe concussion. He was both tough and lucky.

Stuttering Oliver was merely lucky. Had he killed Cook, then rather than being removed to the Segregation Unit - the 'Hole' - for a term of concentrated penitence, he would have faced life either in a federal penitentiary or - a more truncated form of it -in the death cell of a provincial jail awaiting execution. Bearing in mind a natural tendency to inflate Goliath's statistics when comparing them to David's, Cook was nevertheless no match for Durocher in terms of height, weight, or reach; they were an unequal match. But because of Cook's reputation as a fighter[1] Durocher lived in fear of him. For his part, Cook feared no one and not certainly Durocher who was, if anything, nothing more to him than proof of the maxim that the bigger they are, the harder they fall. But he bore Durocher no particular enmity, and would have been content merely to have a man he saw as ungainly and oversized keep his respectful distance. With the corridor ambush that changed.

Durocher's fear of Cook was evident in two encounters between them. Both survive in word-of-mouth accounts of those who witnessed the encounters. The first occurred in the immediate aftermath of the assault. A good story can be expected to grow, change and improve in the repeated telling of it, but several descriptions of the corridor attack corroborate each other with surprising consistency, leading one to think that the impact of the event was such as to fix it indelibly in the minds of the men who saw it - men seasoned in violence and normally indifferent to it when it is merely happening to someone else. The facts were what they were, their accounts seemed to say, nor would they be improved by embellishment.

Those facts were simple enough. The blow from the pipe had knocked Cook sprawling to the floor, stunned, the major wounds on the right temple and the "rt. [and] Left supra-auricular[s]" briefly white before a profuse on-rush of blood. Cook had had some experience in forcing himself to his feet in response to the count of a fight referee, and he now drew on this experience to respond to the grim imperative of survival. In gaining his feet he defied belief, most of all Durocher's who watched as if witnessing the resurrection of Lazarus. Cook then began an

[1]   *He was not a street fighter - a different animal. His reputation as a fighter will be examined in Chapter 3.*

agonizingly slow advance on Durocher who, still armed with the pipe, retreated before Cook down the length of the corridor. Feinting faintly, unable to find an opening, unable to exploit it had he found one, Cook collapsed from shock and loss of blood. Not for the last time, something in Cook's life had stood out in the memories of those who observed it, but few more than this episode. They had seen a display of savagery and cowardice in one man which would have caused them to turn away in embarrassment had they not been transfixed by the preternatural courage of the other.

The second, and less traumatic, of the two encounters stemmed from the first. Spotting Durocher in a Saskatoon beer parlor, Cook again went for him and would have been revenged for the corridor attack had he not been restrained by friendly hands long enough for Durocher to beat a politic retreat out of the beer parlor and out of Cook's life. What then is the purpose of breaking this lumbering butterfly on the wheel since it can be stated here that he had nothing to do with the Cook murders? Only that he did have something to do with the *Cook* trials and with a current of opinion about those trials which is still extant, and for those reasons he has been introduced here. We will return to him in a later chapter.

***

Cook and Myhaluk arrived in Edmonton in the early morning of Wednesday, June 24, and took a taxi from the bus depot to the city's south side where Myhaluk's parents lived. A few blocks short of the Myhaluk house, Cook left the taxi and checked into the Commercial Hotel where he slept a few hours before visiting, in the early afternoon, a nearby car dealership. There he discussed the purchase of a new Impala convertible displayed on the showroom floor, informing the salesman that should he decide to make the purchase, he would intend to trade in a station wagon he owned. It was, he said, waiting for him in Stettler, his home town, and with that he left the dealership. It was 1 pm.

What happened in the ensuing five-hour interval, before he arrived at Jimmy Myhaluk's home at 6 pm, cannot be stated with certainty. In his trials, Cook described the events of the five hours but, without offering an alternate account, the Crown disputed Cook's in its entirety, and here emerged the first serious divergence between the prosecution and defense cases. The better part of a later chapter will be devoted to an examination of Cook's version of the five hours.

After supper with the Myhaluks, Cook left for downtown Edmonton to search in the second-rate restaurants and hotels which are part of every city's core for whomever he might know from shared penitentiary time. Ex-cons have a way of easing the policeman's lot by congregating in places where they can readily be (and know they are being) watched, and so it wasn't a search so much as a certainty that he would find someone in one of the standard haunts. So it proved; a group of eight or ten were gathered in the Selkirk Hotel, then a landmark of Edmonton's main intersection, when Cook found them.

What was destined to become an all-night drinking party was well launched when Cook joined it. The party was interrupted by the hotel's closing and resumed at a second-rate motel nearby, the Pan American. On the way, three of the celebrants including Cook bought enough liquor to fuel the party.

The party flowed until the morning of Thursday, June 25, when Cook decided it was time to go home to Stettler, 130 miles southeast of Edmonton. For the trip, he borrowed a panel truck from Eddie Read, a celebrant by then lost to the now-sputtering merriment, and together with Walter Berezowski, another celebrant, Cook drove to Stettler, arriving about noon.

***

The 'material time' to be identified in a criminal trial is the time span which encompasses every occurrence which bears in greater or lesser degree on the question of guilt or innocence. In the Cook case, the time extended from his penitentiary release on Tuesday, June 23, to the evening of his arrest on Saturday, June 27. It can be divided into six distinct periods. During three of them (release to Wednesday noon; 6 pm Wednesday to Thursday noon; 8 am Friday to the time of his arrest - 8 pm Saturday) his movements and actions were observed by enough Crown witnesses to accurately account for them in trial. Nothing occurring in these three periods was seriously in issue. But for two of them (1 pm to 6 pm Wednesday and 9 pm Thursday to 8 am Friday), there were no witnesses found credible by the jurors able to say where

Cook went and what he did. In a sense of course, Cook was a witness to what he did, but he could scarcely have been found less credible, and thus the jurors were thrown back on inference to provide their own account of the lost hours.

The sixth period - noon to 9 pm Thursday shared with each of the other two groups a characteristic of each. Thus while there was no lack of Crown witnesses able to describe in plentiful detail his movements during the nine hours following his arrival in Stettler, there was no explanation for them by any rational measure. For the fact was that it took Cook that length of time following arrival to make the first contact with a member of his family, leaving the defense with the daunting problem of explaining to understandably skeptical jurors why, after an absence of two years, and after his arrival in a town which could be walked across in ten minutes, in nine hours he never managed to make it to the front door of his father's house and announce the return of the prodigal son.

As a general rule, when someone is charged with the murder of his family, every man, woman and child of it, while it does not act as a defense, it helps to be able to show that far from hating them to the point of murder, there was in fact a warm and loving relationship. But as if it were not enough for the hard-pressed defense lawyers to have to explain away the nine hours in which Cook went everywhere in Stettler but the one place most of the rest of us would be inclined to go - home - they were not able to show that he went home at all. For the further fact was that rather than meeting any member of his family on his own volition, it was left to one of them, Cook's father Ray, to seek him out. Ray Cook was seen at 9 pm to drive up to his son standing on the main street and to drive off with him.

Yet the infamous nine hours presented the prosecution with its own problem, since its burden would be eased if it could show premeditation. But on the face of them, Cook's well-observed movements around Stettler were anything but those of a man edging towards murder - the construct the Crown could automatically invoke to explain the nine hours of foot-dragging. To the handful of people who saw him, he seemed to be moving amiably from place to place in the town, to be wandering about rather aimlessly on a pleasant summer afternoon. Faced with such observations (which of course were not conclusive of anything), the best the Crown could have done (although in the end it did nothing, preferring to let the nine hours speak for themselves) would have been to suggest Cook's action were an audacious gambit designed to implant the image of innocence in as many of the townspeople as possible. Whether or no, Cook may have succeeded in doing precisely that. Long after the murders, the town remains divided into two camps on the Cook question, and in that they were part of a province-wide phenomenon.

***

With the meeting of father and son, the key period was about to begin. Sometime during the next ten or so hours, seven members of the eight-member Cook family were killed, and their bodies dumped in the greasepit located in the floor of the lean-to garage attached to the rear of the Cook house. The greasepit was then covered over. The period ended at 8 am, Friday, June 26 when Cook showed up at a second Edmonton car dealership, driving a station wagon which was to be proved to have belonged to his father. Cook appeared to the salesman to whom he spoke to be moderately disheveled and tired, but otherwise normal.

Leaving that dealership he made two visits to yet another, following the second of which he drove away a white Impala convertible, showroom-new and highly eye-catching. He and Myhaluk (who was with him on the first of the two visits) now had their high-powered car, and all that remained was to target some joints and then to kick them in. But that was intended for later. For the moment, Cook had managed the car deal by passing himself off as Ray Cook, for the purpose employing papers from his father's wallet which he was carrying.

After a few routine enquiries in South Edmonton as to the whereabouts of a friend, Gene Cebryk, Cook (no longer accompanied by Myhaluk) drove to Camrose, then a town but now a small city 50 miles southeast of Edmonton where he knew Cebryk to have lived at one time. Considering the events of the early morning hours in Stettler, and his presumed knowledge of them, he foolhardily invited the attention of the Camrose police by making a U-turn on the main street. Nothing loath, the police were quick to respond. Constable Jack Bell stopped Cook and asked him to produce his driver's license. Cook extracted his father's license from his father's wallet. Bell, not the most observant of police officers (a factor which was to have a bearing on what Bell saw or might not have seen in another area of the evidence) failed to notice that the license produced by Cook showed its bearer to have been born in 1907. Satisfied, Bell cautioned Cook on the insalubrity of U-turns in his town and bade him go and sin no more.

Leaving Bell and continuing on the main street, Cook spotted two teenagers having the improbably Tarkingtonian names of Ricky Feth and Homer Teeple. Both were strangers to him. Pulling up, he asked them if the knew Cebryk. They did, and offered to drive with him to Cebryk's apartment. They stopped first outside the York Hotel where they were joined by 15-year old Lorraine Beasley, a friend of Teeple's and Feth's. It was learned that Cebryk was probably in Whitecourt, a town in the diametrically opposite direction from Edmonton, 190 miles from Camrose. Cook decided to go to Whitecourt and asked his three new-found acquaintances if they wanted to accompany him. They accepted with alacrity; the red-upholstered convertible was inducement enough as was the fact that the invitation came from a pleasant man not appreciably older than them who was obviously well-heeled and a spender. One of the teenagers suggested that first they go to a wedding dance at the Avenroy dancehall four miles east of Camrose. Cook threw in with the suggestion as readily as they had accepted his invitation to Whitecourt, and added one of his own. He would buy a couple of cases of beer, which he did.

At the best of times Cook had an off-handed attitude towards the law. Since by any normal measure consistent with his guilt, the best of times was behind him and the worst of times threatened on the near horizon as soon as the crime in Stettler was discovered, as inevitably it would be, his cavalier attitude towards observance of the law was incomprehensible. The attitude is evident in the beer purchase - a contravention of provincial regulations prohibiting the supply of liquor to minors. Any invitation to the police to look at him even sideways was an invitation to disaster. At the least they could be expected to be looking for him shortly if only to break the news that someone had wiped out his family, and at the most there would be an all-points-bulletin instructing that he be picked up so that he might be asked a few questions. A U-turn, giving beer to teenagers, anything which would give the police a fix on his whereabouts was either stupidity of the most profound sort, or insouciant daring which cannot help but excite admiration of a sort as one thinks back on the youthful killer. There is a third possibility of course: his actions were consistent with innocence.

***

There were two minor incidents at the dance in character with all three possibilities. First, Cook became involved in a minor altercation and second, one of the Cook party stripped - 'stole' is a better word for it - a streamer of paper rosettes from one of the wedding cars and tied it to the Impala's aerial from which it still hung, now rather sadly, when the car was photographed on the tarmac behind RCMP headquarters in Stettler. Trivial incidents to be sure, but the first of them (perhaps in conjunction with the possession of beer) may have been enough to cause the party to be reported to the police.[1]

Even Cook, oblivious as he was to his mounting peril, or as unconcerned, could see that the four unwelcome wedding guests had outstayed their self-extended invitation, and the decision was made to chuck it and to resume the search for Cebryk[2]. They drove back through Camrose and on to the highway to Edmonton. Four miles west of town they stopped at Junction Service, an all-night coffee shop where, unexpectedly, they were joined by Constable Bell.

Jack Bell was a sort of man for all seasons - he was to appear in the preliminary inquiry and in the second trial as a Crown witness, and in the first trial for the defense. Earlier that evening he had been a no-nonsense police officer warning against U-turns, but now he was a police officer cruising in a police car four miles outside his jurisdiction, presumably in his off-hours, joining the object of his earlier official attention for a casual coffee. Moreover, while Bell knew Feth and Teeple, insofar as he knew Cook, he knew him as Ray Albert Cook whose driver's licence showed him to be a youthful 52 years old. As well, insofar as anything

---

[1] *Caused which offense committed by whom to be reported by whom to which police force remains one of the unsolved mysteries with which the case abounds, a mystery deepened by the possibility that no offense was reported to any police force by anyone. No one involved in the Camrose interlude still alive during the research for this book, including the three Camrose police officers involved (the RCMP may have been involved as well) can remember clearly. The questions raised here will receive expanded examination in Chapter 7.*

[2] *Cebryk was the second and, in the context of the evidence, lesser of the two mystery figures appearing, by reference only, in the* Cook *trials; the other was Durocher. There was some confusion as to name. On occasion Cebryk appears in the transcripts as "Seabrook" and "Siebert" which may have been merely reporters' errors although internal evidence suggests neither the defense lawyers nor the prosecutor had a clear idea of Cebryk as Cebryk; that the defense lawyers hadn't grilled their client closely enough (for example he appears in Dunne's notes as "Seabright") and the prosecutor was aloof from the RCMP - one of whom sat at Anderson's right elbow throughout both trials.*

Why was Cook looking for him? Another mystery. The RCMP theory (never voiced at trial) was that Cook sought Cebryk in order to kill him. They pressed Beasley -

on the driver's license had registered with Bell, he knew Cook as "Ray" where, if Cook's new-found acquaintances referred to him by his first name at all (which is perhaps unlikely) it would have been as "Bob." Still, the coffee klatsch had some of the attributes of a Mad Hatter's tea party.

The four departed for Whitecourt. In prison the sustaining dream for most men is of freedom, and so for Cook who, however, expanded the dream to include *the* car. He now had both. For the first time three elements converged to permit Cook to vaunt in his youthful sap at the pinnacle of his ambition: he had an empty paved highway stretching in front of him; he had three impressionable companions to whom he could show off his unquestionable driving skill - his desire to do so was not diminished by the fact that one of them was an attractive girl; and he had the high-powered car. The call was irresistible and he answered it by driving the 190 miles to Whitecourt at speeds hovering around 100 mph, apparently unconcerned with the fact that such speeds have a way of inviting a second look by RCMP patrols, even at four o'clock in the morning. His luck held however and the four arrived in Whitecourt without incident.

After breakfast they searched briefly for Cebryk without success. They decided to return to Camrose, but a few miles from Whitecourt the Impala's transmission began emitting noises indicating all was not well with it. The car was less than 24 hours old and the odometer had yet to register 700 miles, but any new car - the best of them - will not take the kind of breaking in Cook was giving the Impala. He had not reduced speed on what was then a gravel highway, and while the transmission whined in protest, his three passengers sat silently, fearing now for their lives.

she told me; she too was never called as a witness - to admit that Cook was carrying a revolver in the Impala's glove compartment. He wasn't, so far as Beasley knew.

Informed of the RCMP theory, Cebryk laughed, somewhat drily remembering the closeness of their friendship in the penitentiary, and the fact that they had parted friends when Cebryk was released a few months earlier than Cook. Cook had taken Cebryk under his tutelage in the prison boxing program and had attempted, not without success, to make a boxer of him. With evident pride Cebryk produced to me a dog-eared snapshot which, by then, he had carried in his wallet for 17 years. It showed Cook and him in a standard boxing pose, squaring off against the camera. It is perhaps too much to read affection into the snapshot - but not much too much given Cebryk's memory of Cook who, for Cebryk, was innocent of murder. But he still had no idea why Cook was looking for him. Here we leave Cebryk, the mystery intact.

15

Cook stopped at a small garage to have the transmission looked at, and Beasley, Teeple and Feth seized this as on opportunity to leave Cook, informing him, not that "you're going to kill us all", but that since it appeared he was going to be delayed, maybe it would be better if they hitchhiked back to Camrose, particularly since none of them had informed their parents that they would be gone for the night. All things considered, including the fact that there was a man showing some of the attributes of a madman behind the wheel, maybe they should be getting home now. Before leaving him, they observed him to fly into what the prosecution was later to try to make out as a murderous rage. So incensed was Cook with the failing Impala that he kicked at an unfortunate beer bottle with such force that a shoe flew off and into some nearby bushes. While Cook hobbled after it, his late friends left him, offering up thanks to St Christopher, the patron saint of teenage joyriders.

The three hitched a ride without difficulty but it was good for only ten miles or so and they were again standing on the side of the highway when Cook pulled up. The garage had been too busy to look at the transmission. Cook offered to drive more moderately if they would rejoin him and surprisingly, remembering the fate of the beer bottle and his unrestrained driving to that point, they did so without hesitation so persuasive and friendly was he, and so anxious to make amends for the distress he had caused them - this at least is how all three remembered it years later. Either because the transmission had not been repaired or because Cook was genuinely contrite, or both, he was as good as his word; the remainder of the trip back to Camrose was uneventful in terms of the excesses of the trip to that point.

But it was not without minor incident which assumed a significance in the prosecution's case seemingly out of proportion to its actual importance. Cook decided to have the transmission looked at in Edmonton. Ricky Feth made the not unreasonable suggestion that given the car's mileage and that the worst of new-car warranties is normally good for at least 24 hours, Hood Motors, where Cook had bought the car, was as good a place as any to take it. For his own reasons, which he did not disclose to Feth, Cook decided against Hood Motors even though, earlier, he had expansively volunteered the information that Hood Motors was once owned by his father. True, Ray Cook did own a garage of sorts, but it was a shabby lean-to tacked onto the back of the Stettler house, and he lay mouldering in its greasepit while his eldest son careered around central Alberta bragging of his prospective patrimony.

The transmission was ultimately repaired in Edmonton by the replacement of a mount bolt (the trial evidence is murky as to the nature of the repair and by whom it was done), and Cook then permitted first Feth and then Beasley to drive the remaining distance to Camrose. On arrival at 4 pm Saturday, to their surprise they were flagged down by Bell who was waiting for them on the sidewalk in front of the Camrose police station. A fuller examination of this perplexing stage of Cook's odyssey has been promised; for the moment it is enough to note that the Camrose officers (Bell having been joined by Charlie Starcheski and Duff Franklin) concluded their rather indecisive questioning of Cook - about what no one involved in the *Cook* trials ever learned - by telling Cook to get out of town and go home to Stettler.

This, he told them, was his intention in any case, and for their part the police informed Cook that someone would be down to Stettler later to serve him with a summons to appear in court on some unnamed offense. It seemed to be a rather casual police investigation; indecisive was the word for it. Remembering that we are squarely in the middle of the 'material time' surrounding the Cook murders, it occasions some surprise that of the eight or more people involved in the entire Camrose-Whitecourt-Camrose episode, five of them, Beasley, Starcheski, Franklin, Cebryk and some unidentified transmission repairman, were not called to give evidence. Beasley particularly and Cebryk to a lesser extent would have proved valuable to the defense as character witnesses, although a testimonial from a man of Cebryk's checkered background might have been considered a mixed blessing by the defense. The evidence of the other three might well have helped dispel the fog which settled in over the Camrose-Whitecourt segment of the saga which remains there yet.

Everything Cook did after the murders must be seen and interpreted in the light either of guilt or innocence. If the former, then most of the things he did must be characterized as either monumentally rash or of a degree of stupidity which deserves being codified in the Criminal Code in its own right as being only slightly less culpable than murder. Thus with his decision, encouraged by the Camrose police, to return to Stettler. The fact that he now had good reason to anticipate a visit from the police more or less at the scene of the crime would, one would have thought, operated as an invitation to make tracks for Murmansk.

But not for Cook who was quick enough to make up invitations to himself (as, for example, to the wedding dance), but slow to accept those proffered by others when, to a normally intelligent murderer bent on distancing himself from his crime, such invitations would not need to be engraved and handed to him on a silver salver. His previous encounters with the police, now three in number, had been of the chance variety. Now however the element of chance was almost absent; he was going back to Stettler to hang around the scene of mass murder, supposing that the police were going to show up sooner or later albeit in connection with another matter.

He had a reason for going back to Stettler which lay at the heart of the story he stuck to from the first time he told it: within three hours of his departure from Camrose. He had come home about an hour before he first related the story to Sergeant Roach, he said, only because he expected to receive a phone call from his father in the coming week. His family had left for BC on Friday to look for a garage business to buy. Before Cook left his family to return to Edmonton on Thursday night, he and his father had agreed that Ray would call and let Cook know where in BC the family was so that Cook might drive out and bring them back to Stettler. Prior to his leaving Stettler, his father had handed him his wallet, all papers intact, for use by Cook in dealing on a new car. As well, he had given him the keys to the family car, a 1958 Chevrolet station wagon, to be traded on the new car. The truth of what he told Roach, told here in skeletal outline only, was central to Cook's defense, but it had about it the ineluctable smell of falsehood. Some things about Cook were not easy. He was not an easy man to get to know, and he was not about to present his lawyers with an easy defense.

Cook arrived in Stettler from Camrose at about 7 pm and went home where he spent about an hour. He then drove to Stettler's main street, two blocks distant and had begun to cruise it when he was flagged down by an RCMP patrol car. Would he mind coming to the Detachment to answer a few questions about the car? Without hesitation he agreed to do so. At the Detachment office he was asked to come inside. Except when he escaped custody and eluded capture for about 90 hours, Cook was never free again in his lifetime.

CHAPTER 2

THE STORY: II

By early Sunday afternoon the contents of the greasepit had been discovered and Cook was informed by the police that he was now to be charged with murder where, from the time he was picked up on Main Street the previous evening, he was held first on the suspicion and then the charge of false pretenses. At 10 am on Monday, June 29, he was brought before a magistrate who remanded him for psychiatric examination at the Provincial Mental Hospital (PMH) at Ponoka.

Whatever sense of security Albertans may have enjoyed from the knowledge that the prime suspect had been apprehended and was in maximum security was short-lived. The only way Cook could become more notorious than he was was to escape from the PMH which he did at about midnight on Friday, July 10-11. Ninety hours later he was captured. The psychiatric examination conducted before he escaped had determined he was fit to stand trial. A plea of not guilty was entered and he elected to be tried by judge and jury. The Criminal Code did not give him the option of going directly to trial. Rather, a preliminary inquiry had first to be held before a magistrate to determine whether there was enough evidence against him to justify committing him for trial.

The preliminary inquiry opened before Magistrate G. W. Graves on August 24, 1959. The Crown prosecutor, H. F. (Scotty) Macdonald called 43 witnesses, most of whom were cross-examined by S. Giffard Main, QC of Edmonton, the senior lawyer on the two-man defense team. Junior to him was David P. MacNaughton, a Stettler lawyer Cook had retained when he thought he faced nothing more than the charge of false pretenses. The preliminary inquiry took four-and-a-half days, and at the end of it Graves was satisfied there was sufficient evidence against Cook, all of it circumstantial as it is in most murder trials, to commit him to trial. Cook appeared at the criminal arraignments before the Trial Division of the Supreme Court of Alberta[1] on September 21.

The charge was read: "*Robert Raymond Cook, you stand charged that you did at the Town of Stettler, in the Province of Alberta on or about the 25th day of June, 1959 unlawfully murder Ray Cook contrary to Section 206 of the Criminal Code.*" "How say you to the charge?" the Clerk intoned in the archaic and stately periods by which the law seeks to preserve veneration and awe. Cook listened impassively, a demeanor he was to preserve throughout his remaining days in court (with a minor exception), and entered a plea of not guilty. He elected to be tried by "a court composed of a judge and a jury of six."

Whether Cook knew precisely the blunt and chilling wording of the section of the Code to which unlawful murder is contrary, he certainly knew the gist of it: "Every one *[sic]* who commits murder is guilty of an indictable, offense and shall be sentenced to death." The law is not always so free of ambiguity. There was no scope here for a haggle of lawyers to argue nuance. If Cook was found to have murdered someone, he would hang.

At the September arraignments Mr Justice Peter Greschuk committed Cook to stand trial at the sittings of the court scheduled to begin on November 16 in Red Deer, but on that date Main was hospitalized with a minor heart attack and a special sittings of the court was scheduled for November 30. It was a difference of only an additional 12 days but Main, somewhat weakened, was ready to go. J. Wallace Anderson, QC, as chief prosecutor in the Attorney General's Department, took over the prosecution from Scotty Macdonald who continued on, now as Anderson's junior.

The trial took place before Mr Justice Greschuk and a six-man jury, then standard in Alberta. It lasted almost 11 days. Thirty-six Crown and seven defense witnesses were called, among them Cook himself who spent two days on the stand, divided roughly equally between being directly examined by Main and cross-examined by Anderson. The Crown produced 84 exhibits, the defense one. The jurors listened to the arguments of counsel and an exhaustive review of the evidence by the

[1] *Now The Court of Queen's Bench.*

trial judge. They deliberated for 90 minutes and returned with a verdict of guilty.

Cook heard the verdict without being seen to flinch, but in a letter to Main written from Fort Saskatchewan, he disclosed something of the feeling he had managed to conceal: "Must admit that my knees buckled when I heard that foreman say guilty. I used to think it was up to the crown to prove a person guilty. After that I belive differnt. Mr Main I know that they cannot prove me guilty for in all truth I am not. I've been guessed into a death sentence."

Before passing sentence, Mr Justice Greschuk commanded "Cook" (where previously he had been Mr Cook) to "stand up!" (the exclamation point is the reporter's). He was then asked whether he wished to say anything before sentence was passed "in due course and according to law", as if to make known to the weak-kneed Cook that the sentence was not necessarily Greschuk's choice in the matter.

The reason for a man about to be condemned to death being invited to say anything at that singular moment, when whatever he might say cannot have the slightest effect on what is to come next, is as obscure as is any statement unavailing, but the law's not to reason why, nor Cook's, and he chose to speak. *The Ottawa Evening Citizen* reported that "The young mechanic replied 'All I have to say, sir, is that I am not guilty. I couldn't have done this thing and I didn't do it.' His voice was calm and steady." *The Winnipeg Tribune* added that "He stood with his hands clasped behind his back as he spoke."

Mr Justice Greschuk heard out the denial - perhaps a stock denial in the circumstances - and then pronounced sentence (which he erroneously referred to as a judgment): "I now pronounce the judgment of this court upon you. You will be taken from here to Fort Saskatchewan Provincial Gaol at Fort Saskatchewan, Alberta, and there you will be confined until the 15th day of April, 1960, on which day you will be taken to the place of your execution and there you will be hanged until you are dead."

Appeal was automatic. Main filed the appeal on January 4, 1960, a part at least of his Christmas season having been given over to the mounting fight to save Cook's life. Buried inconspicuously in the Notice of Appeal among the 23 grounds advanced was the single ground upon which the Appellate Division of the Supreme Court of Alberta[1], in a 3-2

---

[1] *Now the Court of Appeal.*

split, saw fit to allow the appeal and order a new trial. In the opinion of the majority, the trial judge had erred in refusing Main's request to call Ricky Feth as a defense witness when Feth had previously given evidence for the Crown, and as such had been cross-examined by Main. Main had had the right to ask the trial judge to exercise his discretion and order that Feth be produced for further cross-examination (that is, that Feth be brought forward again as a Crown witness), but Main did not want to run the risk of being turned down by Greschuk when Feth would then have been lost to him for good. He therefore decided that even though Feth had given evidence for the prosecution, there was no reason in principle why he couldn't as well give evidence for the defense.

The situation stemmed from some information Feth had given Main in a courthouse hallway *after* Main had cross-examined him as a witness adverse to the defense, information which Main decided was so favorable to Cook that it was important that Feth now give evidence as a defense witness. The situation appeared to be without precedent in common law. Neither Main nor Anderson were able to cite any decided cases for or against, and Greschuk adjourned the trial until the following day to permit the legal teams the opportunity to work through the night to try and find something. They failed to do so, and the next morning, in the absence of authority one way or the other, Greschuk decided Main's contention was groundless. Feth was allowed to leave.

In the more ample time they had to prepare for the appeal, both sides again had at the problem and again failed to come up with a single case upon which the court of appeal could hang its collective hat. The opinion is unavoidably somewhat subjective, but in reading the court's majority judgments it is difficult to avoid the conclusion that the court wanted a less contentious ground of appeal but, finding none of merit, fixed on this single ground (which it could as persuasively have decided the other way) as the best of a bad lot[1].

The real reason, one thinks, for allowing the appeal was that by reading between the lines of the transcripts the majority of the court of appeal judges could see - as Ottawa later saw - that all wasn't quite as it should have been in the trial of Robert Raymond Cook; "guessed" into a conviction was not a bad way to put it.

In a word, it was not up to the court of appeal to ask all the questions defense counsel should have asked, nor to provide the answers the RCMP would have provided had they been asked the right questions -

[1] *But see p. 153 ff*

22

and of course had they had the answers. But it was up to someone, and the court therefore sent it back for re-trial on the supposition that the omissions would be rectified the second time through. The court did not - nor was it required to - reckon with the undercurrents running in *Regina v. Cook.*

On being informed of the result of the appeal, Main wrote his client to tell him the good news - which doubtlessly Cook had already heard on the prison grapevine. Main's letter is reminiscent of the stilted style one lawyer will employ when, say, informing another of the terms of a mortgage. There was no hint in it of the relationship growing between Cook and Main which was to go well beyond that of lawyer and client, and none of the elation Main felt at the - almost adventitious - success of his effort:

Dear Sir: We are pleased to advise you that we have today been advised that the Appellate Division of the Supreme Court of Alberta have *[sic]* allowed your appeal against your conviction on a charge of murder. The decision was three judges in favor of a new trial and two judges in favor of dismissing the appeal.

"It remains now a question of whether or not the Crown will appeal the decision to the Supreme Court of Canada. If the Crown decides not to appeal to the Supreme Court of Canada, your new trial will probably be held at Red Deer commencing the week of April 18th. We will discuss this matter with Mr McNaughton *[sic]* and with the Crown Prosecutor and will keep you advised."

Cook replied on March 29:

"I recived you're letter to-day and wish to express my apreciation for the work and skill put into the appeall. Certainly nobody can be happyer than a condemned man who is given back a chance for his life. I have some things I would like to talk over with you that may be of importance in a new trial.

"I of course understand that the Crown may appeall I can only hope not. I have taken it for granted that on a new trial wed have a differnt Judge, however as to were and when the trial should be held is up to you. As I have said I have complete confidence in you're ability and what you think is best I am behind all the way.

"Thank you."

He signed the letter "Sincerly, Robert R. Cook", omitting on this occasion the scroll - a jaunty horizontal two-curve flourish trisected by two diagonal strokes - with which he sometimes sealed his letters.

Sometime before the date set for the second trial - June 20, 1960 - the decision was taken by Main to step down in favor of his partner Frank Dunne. Dave MacNaughton continued as junior counsel. The first move of the new defense team was to apply for a change of trial venue, and after some confused skirmishing during which one judge granted an order changing the venue at the same time another judge was contemplating the drafting of his order denying the application for a change, Edmonton was settled upon since among other reasons, as Main deposed in an affidavit prepared for him by MacNaughton, "news coverage caused wide-spread alarm and terror throughout the judicial district of Red Deer."

Once again the witnesses were summonsed, the exhibits readied, the jury list drawn up. The second trial opened on Monday, June 20, again as a special sittings of the court which was now presided over by Mr. Justice Harold W. Riley. In the first trial, when spectators at the morning sessions left for lunch, their places were quickly taken for the afternoon by people who had lined up on the sidewalk. Second-trial seats were also at a premium. *The Edmonton Journal* of June 21 reported that "The courtroom was packed and more than the usual number of RCMP constables were evident. Two officers guarded the accused; normally only one is used. Another uniformed constable stood near the public entrance...and several plainclothesmen were seated among the spectators." No chances were being taken with Cook nor, judging from the sprinkling of plainclothesmen, with anyone else.

Once again Cook took the stand for the better part of two days, once again the opposing lawyers made their final arguments and once again the judge summed up the evidence for the benefit of the jury, calling its attention to all the points made by the defense and once again, after six-and-a-half days, the jury retired to consider all that it had heard, returning about a half-hour later with its verdict: guilty.

For the second time no recommendation for mercy was made. Again Cook was ordered to stand up. *The Calgary Herald* of June 29 reported that "[when] the accused had the death penalty pronounced on him [the] crowd gasped but Cook did not move a muscle". The execution was set for October 11, and even as Cook was being led from the courtroom, Riley, barely pausing for breath after sentencing Cook, crisply thanked the jurors and upped their *per diem* from $6 to $21 for a job well done. Cook was returned to the death cell which by then had been home for about 106 days and sat back to await the result of the second appeal.

On September 16, the same five-man court which had heard the first appeal unanimously turned down the second. The next step was an appeal to the Supreme Court of Canada, but prior to it Dunne applied to the Supreme Court of Alberta for an order postponing the execution date from October 11 to November 15 to permit the appeal in Ottawa to be heard in timely enough fashion for it to do some good should it go in Cook's favor.

On October 4, Wally Anderson arrived in Ottawa prepared to argue for the Crown, but rather than Dunne arguing Cook's side, he retained Arthur Maloney, QC, now deceased but then one of Canada's most respected criminal lawyers and later ombudsman for the province of Ontario. The court heard Maloney first, and decided that so pronounced was the lack of merit in the points raised by him that it did not need to hear Anderson in reply. Recalling the appeal 15 years later, Anderson paid tribute to Maloney's competence, and remembered that even as late as during the course of Maloney's argument, he had no clear idea of what he was going to say to counter it. It was therefore with profound relief he heard the court say, "We won't need to hear from you Mr Anderson." The sensation is well-known to lawyers, as is the apprehension with which it is mixed, since one cannot know until the court pronounces its decision whether the reason the judges have decided against hearing both sides is because nothing the second side can say can offset the persuasiveness of the first, or because nothing the first side has said is worth answering.

It is never the first reason, as it happens; it just feels that way. Nothing Maloney had said had caused four of the judges on the five-man court more than a moment's pause. The appeal was dismissed the following morning from the bench, Mr Justice Cartwright, not surprisingly given that he was one of the better judges in Canada's judicial history, dissenting.

So much for the Supreme Court of Canada, and now, unless the Diefenbaker cabinet exercised the royal prerogative of mercy, Cook had 41 days to do whatever a man does to steel himself for the ordeal of living through those days, and against the increasingly certain prospect of being led from his cell at the end of them in order to be killed.

Shades of the prison-house begin to close
Upon the growing Boy

WORDSWORTH, *Ode:Intimations of Immortality.*

CHAPTER 3

THE SUSPECT

In 1936, Hanna, Alberta was a vertex of the prairie dustbowl, a desolate, wind-scoured wasteland, alive to hope springing eternally if feebly, but dead to any realistic expectation of things ever getting any better. Drought and the Depression had combined to devastate it and to make of it a disaster area where disaster was the norm for ten successive years. But love blooms in the most arid of deserts, and on November 7 of that year, Josephine Grover, born in Halkirk, Alberta, the 18 year-old daughter of Earl Clinton Grover and Delia Josephine Grover, married Raymond Albert Cook[1], the 28 year-old son of William F.Cook and

[1] *Cook's father used the diminutive 'Ray' throughout his life. Albertina Cook (nee Porret) is shown on Ray's and Josephine's Registration of Marriage as "Elbertine Port" - the first of about a dozen variations in proper names in a case in which names seemed to lead lives of their own. As well as "Elbertine", Albertina appears on various documents as "Albertine" and her son Ray shows up in four distinct variations - "Rae Albert", "Albert Raymond" and so on. Ray's second wife Daisy May surfaces as "Daisy Mae", and her father, Christopher Nicholas Gasper as "Christ* [sic] *Nick Gasper. Ray's five children by his second marriage had three aka's among them, and his only son by his first marriage served a complete penitentiary term registered as "Albert Raymond Cook".*

All this is mildly diverting and of no significance until one comes to examine the birth certificate of Robert Raymond Cook when it is discovered that he was registered at birth (and he was christened) as "Robert Rae Cook." Law is a profession to which one looks for a modicum of accuracy, and horror stories abound where commercial empires have fallen on the misplacing of a single comma in an agreement. It now appears the legal system devised by that profession arrested, charged, tried, convicted and hanged a man it would have been flustered to learn did not exist in any narrow legal sense.

Albertina Zelena Cook of High River, Alberta. They were married in the United Church in Hanna where their first and only child who the world was to come to know as Robert Raymond, born July 15, 1937, was christened.

If the times were not auspicious for marriage, there was nevertheless some promise for theirs. Ray and Josephine came from similar backgrounds and they seem to have shared the standard dream: the house, a car of sorts - probably a 1928 Chev - and a small family. The marriage certificate identified their occupations as hair dresser and drayman - the latter summoning up remembrance of things past although Ray was to become a self-taught mechanic - a good one - and Josephine an attendant in a Hanna dress shop until the birth of their son. The marriage was set on a familiar path.

Whatever its modest promise, the marriage was not successful. The ten year difference in ages may have operated as a May-December factor, one more rock on a path which became strewn with accusations of philandering and threats of divorce by Josephine, and a trial separation which ended in a trial reconciliation shortly before Josephine's death from natural causes in September, 1946. Divorce threatened came close to becoming divorce realized: Josephine sought advice from a friend's mother who counseled in favor of divorce only, to her surprise, to hear Josephine decide against it in order, she said, "to make Ray suffer." But for her perversity, it might have happened that when students of the *Cook* case came to enquire into the sources of her son's homicidal bent, they would have had as a starting point a broken home - always promising ground in which to dig for the roots of psychopathy.

But a home riven by divorce is frequently a more salutary environment in which to raise a child than one in which the parties cling together in the eye of a marital storm - a truism not lost to psychiatry. Although one of the psychiatrists charged with the responsibility of determining whether Cook was fit to stand trial for murder was not looking for reasons why he had killed his family, he was, nevertheless, naturally curious. He asked Cook a handful of questions concerning his life prior to the death of his mother, and his report reflects Cook's recollection of it: happy and filled with love. Another psychiatrist asked him whether he thought he had been spoiled by his parents. He replied, "Yes, that's possible - well, I got disciplined a couple of times I can remember - ordinary things that kids do, but I can't remember them." It was an ordinary childhood, and as might be expected therefore from an

ordinarily self-centered child, Cook was hazy as to the date and cause of her death.[1]

The probing went no further. The latter psychiatrist noted in his report that "Of course I was somewhat puzzled about how little he remembered about his real mother and her people, unless of course, as he claims, his second mother was a real mother to him." This was the last anyone was to hear of Josephine except in the second trial when, as an afterthought, Frank Dunne asked him "When did your mother die, approximately?" Approximation was all he could expect from Cook who answered, "About nineteen fifty...no, about 1948."

His birthdate, July 15, 1937, gave food for what passes for thought in students of astrology. One earnest soul wrote Giffard Main pleading with him to inform her of the exact minute of Cook's birth so that she could cast a horoscope from which he would be able to chart a complete defense strategy. But casting Cook's horoscope for Main would have been like casting pearls before swine. He appears not to have appreciated the beauty and power of the instrument and did not reply.

If he was a normal child, it would have been unusual for a researcher to find very much in his formative years memorable enough to impress itself on the minds of the handful of people who can remember him from those years. But there were snippets. Victoria Fielding of Calgary knew the family well and retained a vivid memory of Cook in Hanna: "He was a great lover of pets, but he didn't have any of his own because of their living in an apartment. He was always bringing home stray dogs and cats. Bobby never even played cops and robbers as a child. All he did was go out and pick up animals. I don't remember that child ever playing with a gun. He wasn't brought up to violence. Both Jo and Ray were very mild. Bobby was exceptionally fond of kids; he was very good with children. He was always looking after mine who were both younger than him."

---

[1] *She had contracted rheumatic fever at 14 and her heart was permanently damaged; she was warned by her obstetrician that further child-bearing would probably cost her her life. The warning was heeded; she did not attempt to have a second child although she and Ray discussed adoption - a prospect at which her son was reported to have been both excited and pleased. She died on the operating table in the aftermath of an operation for a twisted bowel. Cook was 9 when she died. He informed one of the fitness-to-stand-trial psychiatrists that he was 10, and the following day told another he was 11. During his term in Manitoba Penitentiary he told the chaplain that he was "orphaned" when he was 13. In their investigations, the RCMP came up with 8, 11 and 12. The field was blanketed but no one managed to zero in on 9.*

29

It was necessary to guard against the possibility of Fielding's picture of Cook being colored by her conviction of his innocence, but its broad outlines accorded with the memories of others. Meagre in number though the interviews were, two things surfaced in them: that he indeed was "very good with children" and that, true to his memory of it, he had been spoiled by his parents although there is no reason to suppose that it went much beyond what normally befalls an only child. The first squares with a lasting impression he made on acquaintances of his later years: whether or not of all kids, he was almost inordinately fond of his half brothers and sisters. The second provides a possible clue as to why he went so dramatically wrong.

If there is a paucity of evidence from the early years, the later years provide an abundance - tempting one to work backwards to draw a portrait of the child. It was found that as he matured, the qualities which came across most often to those who encountered him were good manners and politeness, self-containment and a sanguine and even-mannered disposition. But - the reverse side of a black and white coin - we will see that he became an inveterate thief, and that at least where prison officials and the police were concerned, truth was a commodity to be shaped to the exigencies of the moment. We will see also that he had an ingrained sense of honor rare among thieves, and above all we will learn, not to put too fine a point upon it, that he was likable. Not only liked but well-liked - a fitting son for Willy Loman.

The only available picture of Cook in childhood is that reproduced as Plate 1. It shows him at about age seven as part of a birthday party group in front of a Hanna theater. To attempt to read anything into it, to draw any conclusion from it, is to run the risk of not being able to see past the mark of Cain which is presumably indelibly inscribed on it. No assessment, no comparison with other faces in the group is possible without the realization that this is the counterfeit presentment in boyhood of a man who ascended his private Calvary at the same time as the others were descending into anonymity. The picture cannot be examined in the absence of what we think we know about Cook.

That acknowledged, it nevertheless is by far the most interesting face in the party. He - and the cause of objectivity - would be disserved by calling him angelic; he was no cherub, not then and not, if it needed to be said, when he was embarked on a full-time criminal career. But there is an appealing quality to the self-possessed and well-groomed little boy. All children are appealing at one time or another, just as all babies look like Winston Churchill, but Cook, depending I suppose on one's taste in these things, more than average. There is a striking contrast, for example, between him and the Teutonic little chap on his right. One warms easily towards Cook but looks at his companion with faint distaste.

The appeal may lie precisely in the fact that underlying the somewhat off-putting attributes of sweetness, there is mischievousness. And of the nine children depicted, Cook is the only one giving a sense of being withdrawn, of being somewhere else, entirely his own man. Four of the children face the camera in the delightful attitudes of abashed self-consciousness with which children have their pictures taken. Four have had their attention drawn towards someone on the photographer's right - probably someone turning cartwheels in a convulsive effort to make them laugh for the photographer to whom they are lost. Even the sappy visage of George Formby is at home in the gathering. But Cook has something more than mischievousness pursing his mouth and playing in his eyes. He alone is in the group but not of it. He alone appears to be listening to a distant drummer or perhaps to a pied piper.

***

On September 16, 1946 Josephine died, a week before Ray's 38th birthday. Her son was not allowed to attend her funeral, a decision taken by his father and his mother's family. Cook's Aunt Lucy (Ray's sister-in-law) told me she thought it was a mistake that he was not allowed to see his mother "laid out", but if so it seems not to have affected him in any overt way. He rarely spoke of her, and then only when asked. One of the few times he volunteered any information about her was on the night before his execution when he reminisced with his spiritual advisers, recalling her death and the presents he opened on Christmas morning which she had wrapped just before she died. Unlikely as it is that she was wrapping Christmas presents in September, Cook seems to have remembered it that way, perhaps exaggerating the loss of her as a way of gaining for himself the sympathy his present terrible circumstances demanded. He could not ask for it, nor did he.

Unlikely too that her death affected him beyond normal grief, although the RCMP, like the psychiatrists trying to get a handle on their 21-year old murder suspect by dissecting the child, were told that he stood on the lawn screaming at Ray when informed of the death of Josephine. Maybe so; but nine-year-old boys are as resilient as they are given to melodrama, and the evidence of the next three years of his life suggests that he survived her death without lasting scarring. He might not have done so had his relationship with his father been strained before Josephine's death, but it was not. Close before his father became a widower, the father-son relationship became even closer afterwards, and it is probably here that the seeds of Cook's destruction were sown. If he was spoiled by both parents, he was set up for a fall by the surviving one who now doted on him.

As early as Cook's seventh year, his father had set him on the path of a lifelong passion for cars. Under Ray's tutelage he learned to drive at that age. Cars were most of what his father knew, but he knew them well and he had in his son an apt and eager student. For three years following Josephine's death, Cook went with him night after night and on weekends to the garage where Ray worked (and which Cook was to later break and enter) to work with him and to bask in his exclusive attention while the love of cars entered his flesh like blood.

***

On July 7, 1949, eight days before Cook's 12th birthday, his father married Daisy May Gasper, a Hanna girl who had been one of Cook's grade-school teachers. Just as he had not attended his mother's funeral, he did not attend the wedding which was solemnized in a nearby town. It has been suggested they stole away to avoid having to be married under Ray's son's disapproving eye. It remains a matter of speculation but the wedding seems as good an event as any as marking the start of the time when it all began to come apart for Cook for whom it may well have seemed that the funeral-baked meats had coldly furnished forth the marriage table. At all events, shortly after the wedding he stole his first car as distinct from merely borrowing them for some innocent joyriding - perhaps a distinction without much of a difference so far as irate owners were concerned - knowing he would soon be stopped. For the purpose and for the first time he ventured afield, travelling out from Stettler to which the family had moved soon after the wedding. An

RCMP report of January 4, 1960 refers to the incident: "At the age of 12 years he took a car belonging to Mr. E. Hart of Botha, Alta. Was eventually stopped by a Police road block. He had been operating the car at a high rate of speed, and apparently was not particularly concerned with his behavior."

The report does not say what the consequences to Cook were, and in general the record is spotty for the next year or so although it is known that he stole his father's car in order, he said, to "visit his relatives in Stettler" (he may have meant to say Hanna since they now lived in Stettler), that he stole a school bus in Hanna and that he stole at least one car from his father's employer, McTaggart Motors in Stettler. In September, 1951 he enrolled in Grade 9 but he did not graduate since, by December of that year, he had graduated instead (after a short term in a provincial reformatory from which he escaped) to the bigs. In the space of 27 days starting on December 27, 1951, he was sentenced four times in courts in Edmonton, Banff, Red Deer and Calgary on a succession of charges of theft, breaking and entering, car theft and dangerous driving, for combined sentences of 18 months less remission time in Lethbridge Provincial Gaol. He was not yet 15 when jail gates closed behind him for the first time.

The pace quickened: December 24, 1953, Winnipeg, car theft, one year, Headingly Provincial Gaol (and restitution ordered), but he was saved from Headingly since, on December 28, 1953 he was sentenced to two years in Manitoba Penitentiary on three charges of breaking and entering and theft. It becomes a dreary recital: August 19, 1955, Hanna, two charges of breaking and entering and theft, two years, Saskatchewan Penitentiary; May 21, 1957, Vegreville, Alberta, two charges of breaking and entering and theft and car theft, three years, Saskatchewan Penitentiary; June 3, 1957, Edmonton, three charges of breaking and entering and theft, three years concurrent to the Vegreville sentence, Saskatchewan Penitentiary.

Nineteen offenses in all. Cook told the RCMP that he had committed five offenses for every one for which he was sentenced. He may have been bragging about a not wildly successful criminal career, but if not then 95 or so crimes are indicated between 1951 and 1957. It would not have taken much prescience on his part to observe (as he did in a letter from prison to his father) that unless he straightened out, he would end by being declared an habitual criminal with an indeterminate sentence. He already was one; the declaration would have followed as a matter of course. But *why* was another problem. He recognized the problem, but was at a loss to know what to do, assuming - the facts don't much warrant the assumption - that he genuinely wished to. But the recognition was there. He admitted to the chaplain in PA that he was at a loss to understand why he had been in trouble continuously since the age of 12.

During his early teens, between jail engagements, he earned a reputation for his skill as a driver which was talked about long after his death. Gordon Russell, whom we have met, remembers his ability to drive large tractor-trailers around the streets of Hanna, coached by his father, when he was so small he couldn't be seen from the ground. He remembers as well a high-speed chase: "One night he stole a car from Stettler. I was at Castor at the time, my Dad was there, the town cop was there and a Mountie. We got a call to put up a road block; a stolen car was coming down the highway from Stettler. Dad went out to stop him and he swerved at Dad and took off. The Mountie said, 'Christ! There's nobody in that car!' We chased him into a coulee near Castor. Dad went up to the car and said, 'All right, get out!' but he had abandoned the car and gone up into some trees. He disappeared completely. We hunted for him till about 5 am but we couldn't find him. We were standing by the hotel and somebody hollered, 'There he is!' He was stealing another car off a used-car lot across the street. We grabbed him."

Arnold Filipenko was a contemporary of Cook's. His memories are as vivid as Russell's: "We were not really in the same gang, but we used to do a little 'car driving' together as young bucks will do. He was really a phenomenal driver. I don't believe he ever rolled a vehicle[1]. I remember that I had a demo that belonged to Dad and Cook had a '40 Chevy. We were dragging and I was quite a bit ahead. All of a sudden this green truck loomed up ahead of me, and I had to do a skidding, broadside stop. The dust was flying, the gravel was flying, and you couldn't see anything, but Cook pulled up alongside me through the dust braking from about 80. The dust, my God! He had nerves of steel. Nothing frightened him when it came to a vehicle."

Spoiled perhaps, good with children, a lover of pets, an accomplished driver of stolen cars, a "good thief" in Jimmy Myhaluk's view, if not a notably successful one, likable - whatever it is that adds up to the composite picture of a murderer, these don't do it. There is of course more, and the enquiry must be extended into his relationship with his victims. I propose however to leave that until a later chapter, and to conclude this one by looking at Cook as he 'did time', and by looking at him through the eyes of those who knew him in his final years.

---

[1] *He rolled at least one; see Chapter 5.*

There are worse things than being sentenced, at 14, to 18 months in a provincial jail. At that age Steven Truscott was scheduled to be hanged two days, as it happened, before Cook heard the sentence of death pronounced on him for the first time, and the fact that Truscott's life would eventually be spared was by no means assured when the sentence was passed. Until commutation, Truscott sweated out a harrowing ordeal compared to which Cook's 18 months was a term he could serve 'standing on his head ' - the phrase they employ, defiant in their ears, pathetic in ours, to make light of the coming darkness. It was a trifle particularly if one wished to reflect on the 77 years total he could have received for the offenses which sent him to Lethbridge.

Almost inevitably, Lethbridge operated as a finishing school for juvenile criminals, and when Cook emerged, his future was as if inscribed in stone: prison, then a few days of freedom in which to commit the offenses which mandated prison again. The record is ineffably sad: in the 3247 days between December 27, 1951 and the date of his death, he was out of prison a total of 243 of them.

Prisons have much to answer for but not for all of it by any means. There are good men in prison administrations doing their best by such lights as society is prepared to hand them. In reading Cook's prison records, I was impressed again and again with the conscientiousness brought to difficult tasks in impossible situations with intractable men; with the care expended on someone who, in Cook's case, was just one more number, in order to accord him as fair an assessment as possible. The Manitoba Penitentiary classification officer's report of May 9, 1955 - "This young man...has failed to improve sufficiently to warrant a parole. His general conduct and attitude towards his work is not too good. He is still quite the smart Alex *[sic]* type with big ideas of getting even sooner or later" - was, in a sense, to praise him with faint damnation as some prison assessments go, but it was in any case offset by a CTI report of the same date which recorded that "This man is a quiet, inoffensive worker, tries hard, does the best according to his ability. His instructor advises that he is a good worker. This young man appears to be a good risk re a ticket of leave." The classification officer however had recommended against parole, and the Remission Service in Ottawa elected to go with him. For someone with big ideas of getting even sooner or later, later it was going to be.

Again, on June 27, 1957, a Saskatchewan Penitentiary classification report stated; "Cook has been in attendance [in vocational education] 43 days so far this term[1]. His work, especially in math, is good, He isn't

---

[1] *The "43 days" is an error since Cook had been only been back 21 days.*

35

particularly interested in English subjects, but is nevertheless doing fair work in this subject. He is cooperative, reacts to kindness, and had never given any trouble in class. He has the ability and is capable of learning any shop math he will require."

If, like Blanche Dubois, he reacted to kindness at 20, how much more susceptible might he have been at 14 in Lethbridge. We cannot know. But we do know that a humane magistrate in Winnipeg, D. G. Potter, extended the hand in December, 1953 when on the warrant of committal he wrote: "I strongly recommend that the accused be transferred to Saskatchewan Penitentiary as a first offender. He is just 16 years of age, and although he has quite a record, I feel that PA will be better for him so that he can learn a trade and be of more use to himself and to the community when his time expires." Judges' recommendations are ignored more often than they might think, and Cook served his first penitentiary term in Stony Mountain as a third offender rather than in PA as a first.

He was employed in the carpentry shop and on the farm for the whole of his Stony Mountain term and, during the Prince Albert terms, in the cleaners, the garage, the machine shop and once more on the farm - his first love among the limited vocational opportunities a prison has to offer. The reports on his work performance remained favorable: "Cook has worked on the tractors for the past eight months and has become a very dependable inmate." "Cook will do good work in the shop of his choice." "Doing well in the carpentry shop, but would prefer garage when there is a vacancy." "Quiet, inoffensive worker, tries hard, does the best according to his ability, a good worker."

These were reports one could easily have taken home to one's parents, but there were exceptions. We have looked at the classification report of May 9, 1955, and we may add to it a written request by Cook for a transfer from the machine shop to one of the farm teams because "I like that type of work and think I'll be of more use out there." The classification officer tersely disagreed, writing on Cook's request, "This inmate has done nothing for this department." Despite the officer's demur - or perhaps because of it - Cook got the transfer to the farm team where he contentedly remained driving a tractor until he got a note from the Warden advising him that "We are now starting release procedures on all those being released on June 23...."

He was an apt enough student: "He is now attending school and I am informed that his work is very good. He is a good student and interested in mathematics." He took a special education course, completed it successfully, and was awarded a Saskatchewan Grade 8 certificate, appearing to have duplicated some Alberta work since, as we have seen, he advanced as far in Alberta as to have enrolled in Grade 9. He never advanced beyond that level. His attendance at prison chapel was spotty; when he did go it was undoubtedly rather less out of conviction than as a means of enhancing a parole application. But God was not mocked, nor was the chaplain - "It is felt that he is merely putting in time" - nor, as we have seen, was the Remission Service[1].

***

An inmate's charge sheet - the record of his infractions of prison regulations - is to him undoubtedly the most important of the half-dozen or so records - health, education, religious observance, work habits and so on - which are closely kept on him by his keepers. Should he apply for parole it will be looked at first, and in calculating his release date, his 'good time' earned in remission of his sentence will be reduced in direct proportion to the number of entries on the charge sheet.

For the five years and three months he served in penitentiaries, Cook's three sheets, one per term, carried eight charges: four during the first term and four during the last. For a three-week period in his tenth month in Stony Mountain he became mildly fractious. The sheet shows that he fought with another prisoner and "failed to comply with an order to stop"; that he left his place of work without permission; that he was idle at work; and that he was "talking in a loud manner after silence signal given." It was not exactly an Attica riot in the making, but it must have seemed to Cook to be not worth the candle, and he settled down for the balance of his first term. No further entries appear.

The whole of his second term was without incident - he could take pride in a clean charge sheet - but by the twentieth month of the third he had decided to test the limits again. In the span of a few weeks he was charged with using "improper", then "insolent", then "indecent"

[1] *A Saskatchewan Penitentiary Conduct Sheet prepared during his last term shows "Religious training: S.S. as a child. Religious example of family: poor. Practise of religion before convictions: none since childhood."*

language "to or in the presence of an officer." Worse, he was caught "attempting to take an extra piece of pie for lunch." He denied it but was not believed; the entry was made. There would be no others. Once again he settled down to await release, once again a model of courtesy - a demeanor he was to display memorably when, in another prison and in more trying circumstances, he awaited death.

By current standards, Cook's transgressions seemed hardly worthy of notice to Archie Ellis, Prince Albert's Assistant Director of Offices and Administration at the time of our interview. Ellis, who had not known Cook, scanned his charge sheet and smiled. "Those were the days. That's a good charge sheet. Most guys now with three years...." He left it hanging. It was not necessary to spell out the difference between, say, taking pie and taking hostages.

Had he been inclined to do so, Ellis would not have had to go far afield for an example of what the penitentiary world had come to. His own institution, which its administrators regard with pride as one of the most smoothly run in Canada, is not immune from incident. At the same time as Ellis was reading Cook's charge sheet in the administration office, investigators were inside the walls seeking the solution to a murder of the night before. An inmate had been stabbed 38 times with one-half of a pair of hedge-trimming shears with which, finally, his lifeless body had been pinned to the floor. The murder had taken place in a hallway outside the prison theater in which a group of inmates were watching a movie. The movie completed, the inmates trooped out past the corpse tracking through a rivulet of blood, their minds presumably still on a celluloid drama more real to them than the death of someone who probably deserved it.

The next night, while Ellis was discussing Cook's charge sheet with the author, and the investigators were poring over a list of the 526 surviving inmates, a call came from a Regina radio station for the Director of the penitentiary, James O'Sullivan. Would the Director care to make a statement about the murder? O'Sullivan, who has the black and wicked sense of humor of the Irish, would be glad to: "The victim is in hospital [which was true, the morgue being located in the prison infirmary] and we have the suspect firmly in custody." Seemingly with no clear idea of whether the murder victim was dead or alive and none as to who the suspect was or how they'd managed to capture him, the reporter seemed satisfied, thanked O'Sullivan and rang off. His news editor's reaction is not known.

***

Early in Cook's Manitoba term, he was identified as "a rather frightened youth and immature in his thinking" - a condition which hadn't changed much when, six years later, his last ever pre-release report stated "For his age, subject has a long criminal history. Expresses good intentions towards the future, but is well on the way to becoming an habitual criminal. Adjustment to the institution is fair. Did little to improve himself and failed to complete vocational training when selected for it. Very unstable prison-wise, and not a hopeful prospect for rehabilitation." The promise of earlier reports had come to nothing.

There was however one field of endeavor in which Cook was a hopeful prospect - one which would not find its way into a prison report. He was a prison-trained boxer. That naked fact says little since before boxing was banned in federal institutions, prison pugilists were a dime a dozen. The ring provided a better opportunity than most places in the joint for the controlled release of violence, and boxing was by far the most popular part of the athletic program for both spectators and participants[1].

One more boxer among dozens, but the thing that set Cook apart is that by all accounts, without exception, he was the best of them. It appeared to people claiming knowledgeability - those who fought him, trained him, managed him, watched him through ring-wise eyes - that he had what it takes to become the welterweight champion of the world. He was (the phrase recurs in interview notes) "one *hell* of a fighter, a natural." Nor were they unaware of the fact that punch-drunk pugs who shuffle down the pike touted by promoters and managers as future world

---

[1] *From both sides of the wall in both cases; both spectators and participants came in from outside for a given card. Cliff Bingham remembers "Those cards were a big thing. Six or seven weeks in advance they were speculating as to who was going to fight who and laying down bets. So many guys wanted to come in from the outside that maybe only 40 inmates could get seated. The rest couldn't get out of their cells, so we hooked up a p.a. system and piped it in blow-by-blow. Maybe it wasn't no Don Dunphy, but they'd describe it as best they could."*

As does Alex Wilson: "We had a program there that even the administration was interested in, and outside guys - they were coming in. We used home-made gloves at first and we stole the lumber to make a ring. Everything was stolen. Alex Turk [a Manitoba MLA] was interested, even the Winnipeg police who gave us a whole bunch of gloves and bags. We were jockeying around for a long time trying to get facilities and then we just went ahead and stole the lumber and made our own ring. When the guards walked in, everybody was busy, everybody was working out. We ran it well. Prior to that we got three-quarters of an hour of exercise a day. We'd had to wangle our way into the gym, and then they began to give us half a day here, half a day there.

champions are also a dime-a-dozen. But Cook was not one of those. He was one hell of a fighter, a natural.

While he learned what he knew of boxing in prison, he had had his first brush with it in childhood. Gordon Russell has devoted his life to young boxers, going back to his Hanna years. When he first knew Cook, he knew him only as a likely suspect when the most recent crime bore a juvenile stamp, and he thought that boxing might give Cook a sense of direction which his widowed father was showing himself unable to provide. Cook wandered into Russell's gym one night and Russell took him in hand:

"I encouraged him because I thought he could use it. He seemed to me to be troubled; emotionally there was something wrong with Bobby. He was beating up on kids 13 and 14; when he got them down he would take the boots to them. He was a mean, small kid. Perhaps he did it because of his size, I don't know, but he was tough. Yet none of the guys he beat up seemed to bear him any grudges. They all liked him.

"The second night in the gym, he went home with a black eye. Ray came down to the gym and told me he was taking him out of there. I tried to get him to change his mind. I said, 'I think it is better for him to be in here than running the streets.' Ray said, 'When you have kids of your own, you can look after them. In the meantime, I'll look after mine.' That was the end of it. I think that if he'd been allowed to stay, he wouldn't be [dead] today. Even then I could see he was a natural. They don't come along like him more than once in ten years. He was a natural, a good puncher, a rough type of kid. He would have made a good pro."

"Everybody was happy with the program and what we were doing, and I like to believe it kept a lot of guys out of trouble. A lot of guys did good when they got out. One of them fought Blair Richardson for the Canadian middleweight championship - Richardson had fought Wilfy Greaves. Some guys abused it. A couple of guys got out and got into a fight with the cops, but not many. It paid off. We had weights in there. Guys were blowing off steam. Some guys got real strong. And it spread across the country.

"When I got to PA it was there. And then in PA one day, 'No more boxing', just like that. 'That's it.' Right off. 'You've got one more card, you can hold that and then that's it. It's not us, it's Ottawa.' With our program, kids were behaving themselves, no knives, they were sleeping at night, no drugs. And then they cut us off! Christ! they were as nutty as thirty-three left shoes. "

And, as Russell stated, that was the end of it until Cook was 16 and sentenced for the first time to a penitentiary. As he had in Hanna, he wandered again into a gym, Stony Mountain's, where Steve Bolenchuk was part of the boxing program. Bolenchuk, who used to fight semi-pro, was training a group of fighters when he noticed Cook: "He sat around and watched and I asked him whether he was interested in trying it. He said he'd like to, so I gave him the equipment and he got in the ring. Right from the beginning I could see it. Watching his reaction with others, I could see the heart and other things this boy had. I could see a lot of things. He could take punishment, but he could hand it out. Later, when we put him on the cards, if he had a guy he would turn to the referee. Like if he had a guy in trouble, a man with a lot of staying power, rather than pound and pound at the guy he would turn to the referee. He was no sadist. He had a sort of code of the west, a sort of 'do unto others.'

"I remember he took on a heavyweight one time for the same reason that led to the Durocher incident. This guy said to Bobby, 'I'll take you apart.' Bobby knocked him on his ass. The guy was a heavyweight! Bobby was a good one. He had tons of potential. He had a punch. He could take a man down if he wanted to.

"He was the champion of his division in the pen and he could fight in heavier classes. But he lost a few decisions. What comes to mind: anyone who outpointed him, he would pester me until he got a return match."

Bolenchuk was not alone in recognizing in the early stages of Cook's career the qualities which marked him as a comer. For 40 years Alex Turk was the boxing and wrestling promoter in Winnipeg. He knew and had seen them all: Marciano, Dempsey, Ketchell, Zale, Graziano, Tunney, Louis, Cohen - he was the Canadian incarnation of Nat Fleischer, a compendium of the lore of that world. In his later years he used his eminence as a member of the Manitoba Legislative Assembly to gain access to Stony Mountain. He adopted Stony, and for years single-handedly underwrote a major part of the athletic program, providing equipment, encouragement, outside competition. He was also a one-man halfway house and John Howard Society. A man being released from Stony knew he could go to Turk for a meal, a loan or help in finding a job.

Turk was a gentle man, an anomaly from the world of stylized brutality. Did he remember seeing Cook in Stony Mountain?

"Yeah, I remember that kid, he was a hell of a fighter, a welterweight, a natural fighter. This kid could have been one hell of a fighter. I saw a lot of bouts in Stony. Campbell was the warden at that time and I used to tell him I saw better shows in Stony than I saw in Chicago. I invited Cook to contact me when he got out. I had the 420 Club and he could train there. He got in touch with me. I had the Grange Hotel at that time, I had connections in Minneapolis and I worked with Danny Spunt in Chicago who was with Jim Norris, the big fight promoter. I sent several fighters to Spunt. I may have sent Cook to Chicago or Minneapolis, and it's probable I sent him to Sioux City which was on that circuit. Maybe to Izzy Klein, the matchmaker for Truman Gibson.

"I know he was aggressive and a hard puncher, but the way I remember him was more because he was a *fighter* rather than because of his ability. There weren't that many fighters around. He might have gone to the top.

"He was a pretty fair kid, a likable sort of a kid, pretty reasonable. I can't remember what happened to him. He drifted away, just sort of disappeared. Maybe not to him, but I've seen it happen. They get punchy.... He could be hit; they can all be hit - look at Clay. Someone broke *his* jaw. I know them all; they're walking on their heels. Too many hits to the chin. It's like a bucket of ice cubes: you hit it, they all rattle around in there. But he was a hell of a fighter."

Thus Turk who knew one when he saw one. So did others, and in interviews they too told well their recollections of Cook:

Bruno Link: "Just to watch his moves.... He fought the best in PA, even the outside guys. The Fiddlers from Prince Albert...he fought them all. He could have gone far. He was young enough and had the stamina. He could have made a hell of a good living at it. He was a hooker - he could belt you and tear your goddamned head right off."

Jimmy Kaylor: "Cook could have been number one or number two in the world in the welterweights. He was a natural; you could see it. He had all the moves...could hit.... Gene and Del Flannigan in St Paul wanted to buy his contract off Turk, but Turk wouldn't sell. If the people from the States had got ahold of him, they would have made him number one or number two. I wasn't close to him but I liked him. Everyone liked him."

Ron Westad: "Cook was well-rated as a fighter - very smooth."

Cliff Bingham: "Steve Bolenchuk told me that Bobby could take a punch as good as anyone he ever saw. Alex Wilson - a hell of a good fighter - said that Cook was as good a fighter as he ever hoped to train. There was a tremendous number of fighters in there, and to be respected you had to be good. Bobby was respected."

Bob Tryska: "In prison there are very few guys who mind their own business and are also approachable. Cook was one. He was also one of the best boxers in the history of PA."

Gene Cebryk: "Cook could be hit but you couldn't hurt him. But he could hit like a son of a bitch. A mule kick. He was the toughest guy I ever saw in my life. Rick Haywood - Cook fought him. He could have decked him, but he packed him. Cook was a good fighter...fought along the lines of Cassius Clay. He would back away from punches and they would glance off his shoulders. He could take a good punch himself, but he was not a one-punch artist. He was a good boxer.

"Cook was the kind of guy who was conscientious about the young guys he was training. He trained me and we used to spar quite a bit. I often thought I could take him if we got serious, but now I don't think so. He was a tough son of a bitch. He fought Tommy Wagner one card. Tommy was a hell of a fighter. Trained steady. Cook had him hurt three or four times but held him up. But not out of meanness, not because he wanted to inflict more punishment. He could change his style. I don't think I could have whipped him in a street fight because of his ability to change his style.

"Cook was a hell of a nice kid. He wasn't the kind of guy to take advantage of his fighting ability. How the hell do you say it? Some people would say he had soul; that he had human feelings. No, that's not what I'm trying to say. His heart was good; he had a hell of a good heart for people. He wasn't a mean person. He didn't have to prove anything to anybody. I never saw him pick a fight with anybody."

John Smith[1]: "He could have been middleweight *[sic]* champion of the world. I knew Wilf Greaves. He was twice as good as Wilf Greaves. He would take on guys 240 pounds and never back down. Tough. I thought he was such a good boxer...."

John Brown[1]: "He was one of best fighters I ever saw in my life. He could punch like a bloody mule, good boxer, good reflexes. But no way

---

[1] *These names are changed on request. Both knew Cook and both at the time of the interviews were successful businessmen on the West Coast.*

was he vicious. That whole thing [the murders] was against his nature. If he had had a straight life, he could have been a world champion. He was like Gene Fulmer in style, a slugger who could be a boxer. A husky build, but could be a dancing type of boxer."

***

I have left the summing up to Alex Wilson. Wilson first met Cook in Stony Mountain where he shared credit with Steve Bolenchuk for the creation of the boxing program. He was in the gym when Cook wandered in for the first time and, quickly recognizing a prospect, he became Cook's chief trainer, a role he resumed later when they both made their separate ways to Prince Albert, although he was to claim there was not much more he could teach Cook by that time. Like Bolenchuk, he had been a fighter having fought semi-pro in Sudbury, Sault Ste Marie and Toronto.

I knew Wilson's reputation as a fighter in advance of interviewing him and, not having fought seriously since Grade 2 and having forgotten most of what I had learned, I anticipated difficulty in framing a question much more intelligent than the one I asked: "What kind of fighter was he?" It was enough. The question started Wilson who was soon carried away in the enthusiasm of his recollection. The problem became one of trying to get it all down as Wilson, dancing, bobbing and weaving in the middle of his kitchen floor, demonstrated styles and re-fought Cook's fights, accompanied throughout by a rapid-fire verbal obbligato:

"He had all the makings of a champion. I thought he could have went all the way. He had the heart, the ability, and he loved to fight. But he was never out looking for trouble. He was quite likable.

"I met him in '54 when I got that fin in Stony and he had a deuce. He came in one day and was hanging around and Steve [Bolenchuk] asked him if he wanted to fight. He said, 'Yeah', so I worked out a program for him and he never looked back, If you told him something, he had it and he really worked on it. He was punctual; he was there. A born winner. You couldn't help but like him. He had all the makings.

"We had this card in Stony. Turk came to see me afterwards, told me it was a nice card. I was sort of the promoter of it. I know he liked what he saw in Cook, and Bobby did have an opportunity with him when he left Stony. He was going to hook up with Turk and Pincus [phonetic] and those guys. They had a circuit between Winnipeg and St Paul, but I never heard nothing about him in Winnipeg. But I know they liked him. Other people propositioned him too, tried to get him.

"He put me in mind of Tony Zale. He could fight and he could take it. He worked harder in the gym than he ever did in any fight. He didn't have to work in the ring; fighting for him was just a joke. In the gym he worked out of his class. It was the only way he could get any work. But in a fight he was hard to match. Not everyone wanted to get in there with him.

"He never got careless, never lost his pattern, his style. To see him in street clothes you'd never think he had the heart he had. To me he was never awkward. A lot of boys, you show them how to hit the bag, but hitting the bag and hitting a guy are two different things. They can hit the bag, they think they know it, but Bobby never made that mistake.

"You show them how to use their feet first. He learned to punch really good, and as he went along he got confidence. He was hard to hurt. He was well-liked, especially when we broke him away from LaFerriere and those guys. He was a good, tough kid. He trained other kids. At his best he fought at maybe 152, 154, somewhere in there.

"He'd go for the k.o. He was a hooker. He had a pattern of his own. He wouldn't take that many shots. He could be jarred, but you give him a chance and he'd get you with a two, three, four, five combination. Yeah, he'd go for the k.o. That was the name of the game.

"I got in the ring with him one time, told him, 'I'm going to hold you in the corner and I won't use my hands. You don't use yours and see if you can get out.' I forearmed him, pulled back, ducked and so on, and he couldn't do anything. He was so goddamned mad, frustrated, he had to try and get out of that corner just using his forearms, the top of his head. He got the idea 'I'll hit this guy with one shot and that will do it', but it didn't work that way. He couldn't touch me. I told him, 'There you are, you blew your cool.' He learned the lesson. He didn't make no mistakes, not many mistakes.

"He had good personal self-control. He was always set in the ring, waiting, and if you made a mistake he was ready. Jab, uppercut! God! he could do it. He never took that many shots, but when he did it never kept him back from what he wanted to do. He gained, he learned. He relied at first on that one shot but later, if he hit you once, there were two or three more following. He didn't need help. He had a lot of natural ability.

"Cook was a hooker, not a boxer. He was more like a fighter in a heavier division. He kept cutting the ring down, cutting the ring down. He learned by experience. A hooker relies on power but not a boxer. A hooker has to know how to take a punch. A good hooker will have a ridge above the eyes. He has to have mobility, legs, and the desire to get inside. Boxers don't want to come forward. They'll circle, move clockwise, move counterclockwise, but a hooker moves up. Every time he misses a punch - maybe it goes around behind your neck or whiffs in front - he's cutting the ring down, moving inside. He has to know how to take a punch. He's harder to hit clean; his torso is always twisting, always moving. Bobby was a natural hooker. A hooker throws natural right off the bat, muscle behind it, shoulder behind it.

"He wasn't cocky, wasn't arrogant. He sure wasn't worried about fighting. He couldn't get in there quick enough to fight. He was happy in the gym. Nobody trained him when he got to PA; nobody knew enough. He'd learned all the fundamentals. He really did have it. He had all the guns. As far as crime goes - I didn't see how he could get involved in crime. And them murders. I never believed he done them."

***

In law the character of an accused becomes an issue only if the defense chooses to make it one. If it does, then it will round up as many witnesses as possible able to show that the accused may have a few minor faults, but then who doesn't? On balance, he is a prince among men. Once character is in issue, but not before, the prosecution may then proceed to prove that the accused is the second coming of the prince of darkness. But that is the risk the defense will run, and it will consider carefully what the Crown is likely to be able to dredge up before it decides to have anyone say anything good about its client.

In Cook's case the risk was minimal. Had Main or Dunne chosen to put Cook's character in issue, as much as the prosecution could have done was prove Cook's impressive criminal record and show that when Cook talked to the police, truth took on an elastic quality. But since the fact of a criminal record was essential to his defense, and since the defense was going to be able to tie Cook in knots on previous inconsistent statements whatever the defense chose to do or not to do (apart from keeping Cook off the stand which was out of the question), there was nothing to lose by calling someone - anyone - who might have had something good to say about the character of Robert Raymond Cook. There was more, but to start with he was a hell of a fighter, a natural, this happy hooker, and while that might not have much impressed the jurors, it was better than nothing - which is what Cook got - as a measure of his character.

As things developed, rather than his ability as a boxer and his character in the ring being used in his favor to the extent possible, rather than a progression of Cebryks, Browns, Binghams, Wilsons being called to give their enthusiastic testimony (and to run the risk of their criminal records being displayed to their discomfort), Anderson was able to exploit the defense lack of preparedness and use Cook's supposed boxing prowess against him with deadly effect:

"This being a boxer, are you a pretty good boxer?"

"Yes sir."

"Can look after yourself pretty well?"

"Yes sir."
....

"And then I believe you stated after that you went home to see your family and you saw some visitors?"

"I met my little brother Jerry on the way."

"I see, you met your little brother Jerry?"

"Yes sir."

"Then why didn't you go home with him?"

"Because as I say sir we were fooling around and got messed up quite a bit, and...."

47

"Well, how badly messed up did you get?"

"Well, how badly you get messed up if you're wrestling around like."

"Wrestling around?"

"Yes sir."

"On the ground?"

"Well, I don't remember being exactly on the ground, but...."

"This nine-year old boy?"

"Yes sir."

"And you are a fellow who tells us you are a pretty adept boxer?"

"I wasn't boxing with him sir."

"Your nine-year old brother messed you up that badly?"

"Well sir, you don't understand. I don't think...."

"Well, I'm trying."

"It is just a way you express emotion. I mean, you couldn't.... What could you do? You wouldn't shake hands with him or...."

The contrast between this perverse and heavy-handed cross-examination and the enthusiastic reminiscence quoted above, between the picture of Cook left by the Wilsons and the Kaylors and by Anderson's faintly sneering struggle to understand, does not require remarking. The question is, I suppose, what might the effect on the jury have been if, say, following Anderson's cross-examination, a Cebryk had been called to say that, in his opinion at least, Cook's heart was good; that he had a hell of a good heart for people, hit like a son of a bitch though he could?

The fact of a man's supposed ability to become "number one or number two in the world" is normally not all that germane to the issues of a murder trial, and to be a boxer is not normally to approximate to sainthood. One remembers the Sonny Listons and Mike Tysons for whom reformatories and penitentiaries were the dead ends in which boxing found them. On the other hand, there is always something to be said for the simple truth of a matter, and the truth here is that Cook was not the bullying braggart that Anderson succeeded in making him out to be, and as such all the more likely to have sought a rematch with "this nine year old boy" when, in the boy's bedroom and armed with a shotgun as an equalizer, Cook ensured the decision went in his favor.

Cook was flawed as a fighter. When he had an opponent in trouble and had not yet knocked him out, he would carry him or have the fight stopped rather than inflict needless injury - leading one to wonder perhaps what they were both doing in there in the first place. He did not, it seems, have the sadistic instinct to carve a man into pieces. John Brown recalls being in his corner: "I remember throwing sponges at him for Christ's sake! Hollering at him to keep on top of the guy, to give it to him, but he wouldn't." This is a serious enough flaw for someone aspiring to number one or number two, but Cook never did. Fighting was something for inside only. He recognized the flaw, and to him goes the last word on his boxing ability. In a letter to Dave MacNaughton dated shortly before the first trial, he wrote:

"I know I'm inocent and not capable of killing anybody, it's just something I couldn't do. I couldn't hit a person I even disliked with boxing gloves on when I had him helpless on the ropes. I remmber everybody yelling for me to finish him and I just couldn't. That happened in the Pen and could be proved. What Im trying to show you is that its just impossible that I could have done this. The sooner I can stand up in court and tell all I know and try and prove that I didn't and couldn't have done this awful thing, the better it'll be,"

But the absence of a killer instinct in the ring doesn't necessarily betoken its absence in other places, other times.

***

Important as may be the ability to knock someone senseless in a choreographed ritual, it is not normally the whole measure of its possessor. In an attempt to round him out, I will conclude this examination of the suspect by quoting at random from the recollections of those who knew or encountered him, most of them, apart from the boxing ring. It will be seen to be a mixed bag:

The penitentiary colleagues

STEVE BOLENCHUK, interview: "In my opinion, he was an outstanding young man, and I knew a lot of them in there. He was a simple, down-to-earth kid."

GENE CEBRYK, interview: "He wanted to go straight but didn't know whether he could or not. We were about the same age, but he sort of looked upon me as his protege because of the boxing thing. He stressed, 'Don't ever get in this place again.' He tried to straighten *me* out. That impressed me. It was a big factor in my thinking."

CURLY DUNLOP, interview: "He done his time by working hard - a hell of a good kid, polite, well-mannered. He never had a mean streak in his body. Cook was a hell of a nice kid."

JOHN SMITH, interview: "If you were a friend of his, you were a good friend, and there were damn few of those in there. But you had to pick and choose your words with him or he would cut you off. He was not a loudmouth, not a braggart. He was quiet, morose perhaps, and there were a lot of people in there who were afraid to cross him."

RON WESTAD, interview: "He was what we thieves call good people. He was not a stool-pigeon. He was a man about things; you were comfortable with him. I like to think that in spite of my lack of success I'm a professional criminal. Whatever you do, you do for money. That was the way with Cook; he did it for money. He was a pro. While Cook was waiting [in remand in Fort Saskatchewan], he'd get the paper and read it! He was well-informed; interested in what was going on; in other people. He didn't dwell on his own case. He was interested in everything that was going on in the world and he would talk about it. But not about his own case. He was soft-spoken, well-spoken. It struck me at the time how he could stay such good company in the jackpot he was in."

SONNY WILSON, interview: "In the RCMP bucket we were talking about some other kid's case before he went out for the last time [for the last day of the second trial.] He was not self-centered about his case; he did not revel in the publicity and notoriety. He conducted himself so well to the end. I heard he took the time to write people to say goodbye. 'I probably won't be seeing you again.' 'Good luck.' That sort of thing."

WALTER BEREZOWSKI, interview: "He wasn't the type of person to do [the murders.] Cook was a quiet guy, never used to bother anyone. I never saw him cut up a guy verbally in that guy's absence. He minded his own business. He wasn't hardened by doing time. He didn't impress me or anyone around me as being hard. He was a good guy, always cheerful, a happy-go-lucky kid. If he was doing hard time, he kept it to himself. It's pretty hard to do that in that setting."

EDDIE READ, interview: "To this day I can't believe [that he was guilty of murder.] I really liked Bobby. He was a straight, stand-up guy. There wasn't a mean bone in his body. He was always taking the side of the underdog. The inconceivable thing is those children. There was nothing could have turned him mean."

The pastors

REVEREND W. A. RUMSCH, interview: "The side I saw of this young man was polite, pleasant, courteous about the language he used around me. There was no gutter talk such as I hear from young people now. Someone said of him, 'He could have been a member of the young people's church group.' He left me with positive feelings. He was a gentleman; he was not coarse. He gave no impression of being violent, vengeful or spiteful."

REVEREND GEORGE RODE, interview: "I didn't follow the legal aspects, but he gave no indication of guilt to me. But he made no attempt to hide his other involvements. He opened up on so many things [on the night of the execution] - his father, his Christianity. It was all so genuine. I didn't feel...."

The psychologist

D. J. CRAUSE, report, Provincial Mental Hospital, Ponoka: "The subject was cooperative but showed some evidence of anxiety concerning test proceedings. The unstructured ink blots aroused intense anxiety. He began shaking visibly and held each card for only a few seconds then tossed it on the table, saying, 'I don't see anything there'.

"Such 'card shock' denotes avoidance of threatening or anxiety-provoking material. The subject's method of handling the cards suggests guardedness and evasiveness. Ordinarily such card shock would imply attitudes of suspicion with an acutely paranoid flavor. However, in view of the present circumstances in which the subject finds himself, there may be a deliberate conscious withholding of any meaningful material as a self-defensive mechanism.

"The...responses produced were generally crude and typical of an immature personality with limited personality resources in the way of creativeness. There appears to be some frustration of dependency needs with resulting hostility and 'chip-on-the-shoulder' attitude. There is evidence of marked feelings of inferiority which the subject attempts to cover up by a facade of bravado. In the realm of inter-personal relationships, the subject tends towards social isolation, withdrawing in a rather cold, schizoid-like way, despite his dependency needs. Some suggestion of narcissism was seen on one response.

"In view of the limited test protocol, it would not be possible to outline any definite personality type, or to find any real evidence of psychotic disturbance."

The psychiatrists

DR FRANK EDWARDS, report: "This patient...has caused no difficulty since admission [to Provincial Mental Hospital, Ponoka]. His manner has been, on the whole, sullen. He has taken his meals satisfactorily and has apparently slept well. There has been no abnormal behavior to date, nor has he expressed any ideas which could be considered bizarre. On interviews, he has given a fair amount of information, but does not care to elaborate too much on his early history. At all times, during interviews, he has been in good contact. There are no psychotic signs.

"Talk lacks spontaneity but this, I feel, is quite natural considering the circumstances in which he finds himself. Conversation is coherent. Answers to questions relevant. He gives the impression that he could impart more information, concerning his past, should he be inclined to do so.

"He made a statement to the effect that he felt upset by the whole situation and yet there was no clinical evidence of anxiety nor did there appear to be any depression. I felt that he adopted a superficial attitude to the whole affair. He maintained that he was innocent and that he hoped to prove this at his trial. He showed occasional mild irritability when pressed for certain historical information - chiefly relating to prior anti-social behavior."

DR J. B. S. CATHCART, report: "There was a long story at this point mostly volunteered by the prisoner in defense of his claim that police evidence that he had committed the crime was inadequate and could have been mistaken! I was beginning to wonder, in a different direction, was this young fellow with his story and natural smile the type to commit such a ghastly murder of his own family, and then stand up naturally under close scrutiny during hours on the stand in court and some five hours today?

"He said at one point, 'I'm afraid I'm getting rid of a lot of bitterness on you doctor.' It sounded off-hand like a pretty genuine comment.

"At most times, the prisoner seemed to act like a wholesome kid and particularly when he is discussing music and singing. Has several favorites on the radio.

" 'No, I don't have a bad temper. I don't hold grudges, but I get into a lot of arguments.' (Gosh, it's getting harder and harder to see this fellow [as] a wholesale murderer of his own folks.)"

The police

SERGEANT THOMAS F. ROACH, RCMP, interview: "He was a tragic figure."

Corporal Joseph L. Van Blarcom, RCMP, interview: "I never talked to Cook until after he was out in the Fort. Nobody I ever encountered was as cold as he was, but I fazed him once. I produced a picture of his father under his nose and that stopped him. I never saw such a cool, cold fish. When I went out to the Fort he wouldn't even talk to me. He had no feelings of any kind, no regret, about his father's death. Nothing at all."

CONSTABLE AL A. MORRISON, RCMP, interview: "I wanted to take a color shot of his father and show that to him, but they wouldn't let me. During the questioning by [Staff Sergeant] Beeching and [Sergeant] Roach, there was no reaction on his part over the deaths of anyone but Ray."

The peer group

RICKY FETH, interview: "He was a very pleasant person."

ARNOLD FILIPENKO, interview: "He was always a fighter but he was never that mean. I never figured him for what happened. I remember fights on the ice and he was not always on top, but he had his share of being on top, let's put it that way. But he never went out looking for fights. This is why I can't see it."

DILLON HOSKINS, interview: "Dad didn't like Cook but I did - he was a nice guy. I never knew him when he was in jail, and when he got out Ray wanted him to meet some better guys so he brought him over to our place. Dad said, 'This is Ray's oldest boy.' He was a perfect gentleman When Amelia [Giebelhaus] met him, she flipped right over him. He never even swore. How could he be a killer? My mother thought like me about him. He often came over for lunch. I slept with him in the same bed."

LORRAINE JOHANSON, nee Beasley, interview: "He was a real gentleman. When I was crying after we got stopped by the police, he put his arm around me and told me it would be okay. When we were coming in from the dance, I asked him to stop the car because I was going to be sick. Any guy who will stand there and hold you up while you're throwing up and tell you you'll be all right must have a lot of good in him. He was a real gentleman."

LILA HOWSE, nee Larson, interview [commenting on a picture of Cook she had not seen before]: "Yes, I recognize those eyes - always smiling. He couldn't have been more pleasant, more understanding. He performed all the tasks my parents asked of him cheerfully, and he never complained about anything. He was a very pleasant person."

The press

RON HAYTER, *The Edmonton Journal*: "I have never seen such cold eyes[1]."

The prison guards

PETE PATRICK, interview: " I used to bring his food down to him from time to time. He never gave me no trouble. He was always polite towards me. With some guys I've known in that fix, it was different. They would throw the food at me, swear, shout obscenities. With him it was always, 'Good morning.' A pleasant guy, asking for tobacco and so on."

WALTER BILTON, interview: "No one in [Fort Saskatchewan] would ever say anything bad about Bobby. I can speak for all the staff. He was the nicest kid I ever knew. Clean-cut, always polite, looked after himself,

---

[1] *Hayter's newspaper account of the execution was written as if he had attended it, but, if he did, he must have had his eyes closed since it started with the wrong location and went wildly from there.*

clean-shaven, his clothes were always neat. He was outstanding, the best prisoner I ever had. His death was the hardest thing I ever went through in my life. The last night, he asked to see me to say goodbye. I wasn't going to go down because I didn't think I could take it, but when he asked, I went. They had his arms strapped when I got there, and he asked them to take it off so he could shake hands with me. I *couldn't* take it. I got out of there. If he came through that door right now, I'd let him in, murderer or not."

I have left the last word for the men who trade in words: his lawyers. Both, seasoned criminal lawyers with many capital cases between them, were deeply affected by Cook's fate[1]. Giffard Main told me that Cook "was unfailingly polite to me throughout our association. He never called me 'Main' or 'Giffard', but invariably addressed me as Mr Main. He was polite, gentlemanly, good-humored, cheerful." Frank Dunne seconded Main and added, "I liked him very much. He was a courageous and gallant youngster. He had a lot of courage for a kid of 22, and he went like a man."[2]

***

An analysis of Cook's character awaits hands more skilled than mine, and as much as I have done is hand the reader the mixed bag to make of what she will. Of many answers to the carefully neutral interviewer's question What kind of a guy was he? the best of them in the sense of summing up what I had learned of Cook came from John Brown. He thought about it, tried a couple of answers that went nowhere and then said, "I'll put it to you this way. Have you met anyone yet who didn't like him?"

It was my turn to think about it, and the recognition dawned that, with a few exceptions, I had not; that in the years of the search for Robert Raymond Cook (if it may be put so pretentiously), where Diogenes had failed in his search for an honest man, I had succeeded in finding one about as rare: liked, respected, admired, loved is not too strong a word

[1] *Main died in January, 1969 and Dunne in October, 1970. Relatives of both have told me that the decline of each started with Cook's death.*

[2] *He was, as we have seen, 23. Sadly, Dunne's affection was not reciprocated.*

in some cases, by just about everyone who came in contact with him not excluding some members of the RCMP. He had had an effect, and it appeared clear that while he was remembered because of his notoriety where he might not have been had he, as he said "smartened up" and ended up as a parts man at Wal-Mart, there was more. To see a veteran prison guard and an experienced pastor in tears fifteen or twenty years after Cook's death as they struggled to describe the night of it, was to give one pause.

With an important exception, none of this greatly matters just as Cook didn't greatly matter. He had some unrealized potential in a direction not to everyone's taste, but short of realization, he was nothing more than another face in the crowd just as he had been when he shuffled in and out of courtroom dockets, and had he not died, he would have stumbled from arrest to conviction to release to arrest in a dreary and repetitive cycle until, at 50 or 55, he tired of it all and settled down on skid road with a bottle of wine. To be coldly realistic about it, the odds in favor of him making parts man at Wal-Mart were not good.

Or were they? Was the cycle's grip unbreakable? The road to his hell was paved with the same materials as are those of the rest of us, and each of his releases from each prison was accompanied by vows, eyes heavenwards, to go and sin no more - or at least to sin no more after the last big score which would set him up for life. Only insurance companies would suffer and they expected it. Just as often, within days he would be at it again in a series of very small scores. Hitherto there had been no discernible way out of the pattern. But death cells can have a cathartic effect, and it may be (he claimed as much in a letter from his) that if he ever got out of it, "things would be differnt."

And - the saddest words - they might have been. But should he have been in a death cell in the first place or should he have been denied what might have been his only chance at catharsis, however short-lived? What price redemption if there is no chance to capitalize on it because your neck is broken? It was a case of being damned either way, although Cook, had he been given the choice, would gladly have settled for the living hell of habitual criminality, which was in train, rather than the eternal damnation which resulted from the sentence of death which, paradoxically, might have saved him had it not killed him.

And thus the importance of the exception referred to. What mattered is that not a single word of the positive aspects of Cook's character ever reached his jurors. They knew him - everyone in Alberta knew him -

only from the headlines which had inspired terror in them: *Alleged Mass Murderer Escapes; Mass Slaying Suspect May Be Armed, Dangerous* and so on. They knew him from watching him on the stand fighting for his life - self-contained, asking no quarter and giving as little as possible. But they saw him again and again tripped up by the rules which the other side knew - and knew how to bend - and he did not. Too often, by the time his lawyers had come belatedly to his defense, the damage had been done. In tripping he looked bad. This was the only Cook the jurors saw and thought they knew. The image was not one to inspire belief much less admiration. A soupçon of admiration might have given *them* pause.

Character was not put in issue but, as things developed, the prosecution was able to have a field day destroying Cook's such as it was, making him out to be - which was true - both a liar when he was cornered and a petty thief and nothing more. It cannot be doubted that it might have made a difference if a rather more rounded picture of him had been attempted, even acknowledging that the evidence permitting a more balanced assessment would have come in large part from people - rounders most of them - who themselves could have used some favorable character evidence in *their* frequent turns before the courts.

The difference might only have been one of, say, keeping the second jury out an extra ten minutes - a 33% increase - in order to weigh the testimony of witnesses who could have said of Cook - and who would have been glad to have been asked to say of Cook - that he didn't do it because, knowing him, they *knew* he couldn't have done it. And they would have said it as fervently then as when they talked to me.

To be sure, "He just couldn't have done it" leaves something to be desired as proof in a murder trial, and will be dismissed by the Torvalds sitting on the average jury as feminine reasoning and, as such, unworthy of them and of the grave issues they are called upon to decide. Those issues, they are confident, will be decided only by bringing to bear the power of an awesome instrument: their ability to reason dispassionately. It is a conceit; the reality is otherwise. The railing of a jury-box is no barrier to all the sprawling illogic of life being brought into it, and it is quite within the rules of the game to exploit visceral responses knowing that they will occasionally tip the scales in favor of the client whose counsel knows how to elicit them.

To be equally sure, the annals of murder are replete with instances of murderers who, although incapable in the judgment of their neighbors of having done it, nevertheless done it. But are they any less replete with examples of men who were able to convince a jury that innate incapability was precisely that? If jurors retire to deliberate with nothing much more in favor of the accused than a gut feeling, it is sometimes transmuted into reasonable doubt, the evidence in the last analysis of it notwithstanding. Justice may be thwarted, but that's the system.

But justice is not denied where, as also happens, the evidence receives the unhurried analysis it might not get but for the fact that the man who started out as a *Mass Slaying Suspect* has been made out to be someone other than the headlines had him; has been endowed with some redeeming qualities which the headlines denied him as invariably they do and, one supposes, must. On occasion, unhurried analysis, even by six angry men, will reveal something concealed in the rush of certainty.

The name Robert Raymond Cook is entrenched in the collective memory of Albertans as an evocation of Stettler, the manhunt, the greasepit and the seven bodies, the execution unaccompanied by any overt rejoicing or even relief as Albertans pondered anew the infallibility of the courts and realized that at long last it was all over.

But he was never more than a name, and always all three parts of it as if the names he knew himself by - Robert Cook, Bob Cook (never Bobby - others called him that) - were not weighty enough to convey the high drama of the case. The attempt has been made here to impart some substance to the name which it never had in the days of its notoriety, and to invest its owner with the personality he was denied when he faced his accusers. We now turn to the victims, innocents all as victims invariably are when the merits of hanging are being urged, leaving Cook as a person remembered by his acquaintances with an unusual degree of fondness, and not yet convicted of much more than kicking in the doors of hardware stores, in favor of an examination of Cook giving his tense evidence knowing that the penalty for its failure would be his conviction and death.

That examination will be interrupted, in Chapter 10, long enough to examine his relationship to the family he was accused of killing. It may be that he saw it as having closed ranks against him, as having rejected him, and that therein lay the motive. Staff Sergeant Dave Beeching, the senior officer in the RCMP investigation, thought so but, finally, had to admit that he did not know. We shall then return to the trials and follow them through to their end when we will then look at Cook in his final role: as appellant in the confines of a death cell than which there are no confines more confining. We will see that the experience imbued him with extraordinary courage which may suggest what was finally of value in him.

Whatever he was, add to it that he was an example, stood on its head of Cæsar's legacy. Whatever good was in Cook has lived on in the memories of those who knew him, and to have found a permanent place there. It was the evil which was interred with his bones, or at least accompanied them to an anatomy laboratory. But what evil? The legally established fact that he killed seven people will serve for a start, which brings us to those seven people. We know they were innocent. What else were they? Who were they?

A simple child
That lightly draws its breath
And feels its life in every limb
What should it know of death?

WORDSWORTH, *We Are Seven*

CHAPTER 4

THE SEVEN

One mile north of Hanna a cemetery stands on a slight rise beside a rural road. Those interred there, the men and women who arrived around the turn of the century, rest in the peace of the countryside under the same wide skies which, while they lived, they had scanned anxiously for signs of the disaster or promise of the morrow. The sylvan quietness is disturbed from time to time by mammoth eight-tired tractors which rumble by and recede in the distance - plowmen homeward plodding their weary way in air-conditioned cabs. The sound dies and the cemetery is left to silence and to the shroud of diesel particulates which settles over it. An angelus should be heard here, but only ghosts and the elegiac muse stir on the ceaseless, soughing prairie wind. The lone and level prairies stretch far away. A light springs eternal - a pale flare over prairie marshes where the pungent slough grasses whisper to the seasons' change.

That the cemetery is a source of pride to its supporting community is evident from its landscaping and careful maintenance, and its purpose perhaps apart, it is a pleasant place. But like all of them - military burial grounds honorably excepted - the cemetery is possessed by something more gross and rank than mere weeds: plastic flowers. Purgatory itself is prefigured by these garish garlands, arranged in tasteless array in styrofoam urns - the tacky foster children of the petrochemical industry. The wind tears them loose, scattering them with rude indifference on graves where they are not welcome, and they make their rounds, rootless in the unreceiving earth, blooming in relentless, indestructible, faded splendor however dark the night or savage the blizzard knifing in from the Arctic Circle.

After a brief search, one finds here the headstone marking the common grave of Raymond Albert Cook, Daisy May Cook and their five children. One among hundreds, it stands out only because of its inscription: seven names, seven birthdates, one date of death repeated seven times in a sad dirge. Prior to my coming here, the Cook family had existed for me only as names surfacing periodically over many months in a sea of paper - newspapers, trial transcripts, appeal documents, estate documents, letters, interview notes. But here, in a manner of speaking, one was at last face-to-face with them.

Their names in a Surrogate Court document was one thing - names without substance, without faces - but their names chiseled in black granite seemed to be another. Their faces had become known to me by this time - generous friends had shared with me a wealth of old photographs and studio portraits - but now substance was lent by this imperishable record which brought home that all this was more than an intellectual exercise, a sort of spread sheet analysis of murder as it were where placing X at A at n o'clock meant one thing, but if B was substituted for A at $n+1$ o'clock, what highway speeds were required of X? The granite affirmed the reality of flesh and blood - inhumanly violated flesh and blood which once lived, felt dawn, saw sunset glow. No longer would it be possible to take them into account merely as tags showing on police photographs - "Body No. 4"; "Body No. 6" - or as pawns in the intellectual exercise. The time had come to extend the enquiry into their lives to see whether insight might be offered into their deaths, and more especially into the question At whose hand?

***

It was speculated - nothing more - by former friends of the Cooks that Ray met Daisy before Josephine's death, and that a relationship developed between them which was rather more than that to be found between a concerned father and his problem child's teacher. There is no firm evidence of it, and the fact is that three years intervened between

Josephine's death and her husband's remarriage which does not suggest a philanderer unexpectedly freed by the death of his wife to pursue the object of his illicit affections. Beyond possibly having had a wandering eye (if he did it came to rest in his second marriage) and a penchant for acquiring the property of others without the imprimatur of legality, which we will look at in a moment, nothing set Ray Cook apart from what could be identified as a type: a quiet, self-effacing father in the background of a boisterous family, content to play second-fiddle to the life swirling around him: steady, retiring, colorless especially when contrasted with his wife.

He was what a casting director would look for for the role of the little man, both figuratively and literally: he was five feet, eight inches tall and weighed 135 pounds. He was remembered as a man who rarely initiated conversation, and would participate only reluctantly in conversations initiated by others, but probably because of shyness rather than because of any anti-social bent. An exception occurred if the conversation turned to the service station he wished to buy in partnership with his son Bob; this he would discuss enthusiastically.

He was a non-drinker who would take a sociable drink, and a non-gambler who bought the odd Irish Hospital Sweepstakes ticket when it was illegal to do so; a Sweepstakes ticket was found in his wallet after his death. He was not noted for a pronounced sense of humor unlike Daisy who enjoyed a measure of renown for hers. He was a devoted family man remembered by one acquaintance for attending to the diaper requirements of one of the smaller Cooks when the family was enjoying an evening with friends, leaving Daisy free to socialize. Male chauvinism, it would appear, was not part of his makeup.

He was a small, wiry, tireless worker. His stepbrother Ralph Cudmore recalled he and Ray being offered a contract to stook 600 acres of wheat on a farm north of Calgary when he was 22 and Ray 21. The contract price was twenty-five cents an acre. They were called upon to keep up with four binders. Only the dwindling band of brothers who have stooked a field of wheat will appreciate their accomplishment in doing it in ten days. The $150 earned was paid to Ray who promised to send Ralph his half. Thirty-one years later Ralph was still waiting for his $75 when he heard the news of his stepbrother's murder.

He did not answer the call to arms in 1939, but spent the war years in Hanna as a self-taught car mechanic - his trade for the whole of his mature life. He excelled at it, both in Hanna and in Stettler to which he moved in 1950 to take a job first with McTaggart Motors and then for the Filipenko brothers in their Modern Machine Shop. He was employed at Modern Machine at the time of his death.

***

We will explore in Chapter 12 a key part of Cook's defense: his claim to have brought home a large sum of money - $4300 - on the night of the murders and to have given all but $200 of it to his father who took it knowing it to have been stolen. The prosecution countered by saying in effect that Ray Cook was not the kind of man to receive stolen money, and if Cook said he was, Cook was lying. Reluctant as he was to brand his father a criminal, Cook had no way out; establishing Ray's taking the money (knowing it was stolen; he could not have thought otherwise) was essential to the defense.

Cook could only struggle to put as good a face on it as possible when Anderson began to shred this part of his story. His father, Cook said, "no doubt knew where I got the money; he doesn't ask questions like that[1]." The money in any case had been "paid for", had been earned after the fact as it were by his having worked diligently through his last penitentiary term. The money, by Cook's singular lights, was no longer tainted by the questionable way it had come into his possession, and his father would have been prepared to see it that way and to have taken the money without more than fleeting, pro forma disapproval, if even that.

The issue was thus joined: was Ray himself a criminal in the far from trivial sense of being not averse to receiving property stolen by others knowing it to have been stolen? The problem for the defense was to tar Ray with the same brush used by the Crown to tar Cook; to prove that father and son were cut from the same cloth, and that Ray would have had no more qualms about receiving the money than Cook had had about relieving its rightful owners of it. Do that, and then at least one end of the money trail was tied down, and there remained only to get the money onto it. However the larger problem for the defense was that it failed to recognize it had a problem and accordingly it did nothing to show that Ray was a petty criminal in his own right if not in his son's league.

---

[1] *Long after his father's death, Cook continued to refer to him in the present tense, perhaps suggesting he was subconsciously having difficulty coming to terms with it.*

Showing that Ray would not have been reluctant to pocket stolen money would not of course have proved that Cook had given him any, but it was an essential first step on the road to that indispensable proof.

There was some evidence before the jurors from which they might have inferred something of the character (if not the flaws in it) of Ray Cook but in terms so broad, vague and inconclusive as to be virtually worthless. It was this: he was a mechanic holding the usual proficiency certificates; he renovated vehicles in his off-hours in a littered garage; he had a joint bank account with his wife in which there was $3500; he bought sweepstakes tickets; he went hunting from time to time and didn't shoot anything; and he had a satisfactory credit rating with GMAC.

That was it, *in its entirety*; nothing more than this was revealed in either courtroom about the head of the murdered family. The point bears emphasizing since those wisps of evidence were enough to permit Mr Justice Greschuk (who, like the prosecution, was wrestling with this part of Cook's story) to pose to the jurors the not entirely rhetorical question, "Would a person like Ray Cook accept stolen money?" to which the rejoinder, also not entirely rhetorical, might well have been on that evidence how could they possibly say?

Had the defense been ready with the evidence, the rejoinder would have been more incisive and it would have been that yes, as a matter of fact, a person like Ray Cook probably *would* accept stolen money. The question was what kind of person was Ray Cook when it came to the nuts and bolts of criminality? As it happens, there was evidence bearing on the question available to the defense.

Ralph Cudmore, for example, told me that "Ray was smart and he was light-fingered. Whenever we went to a dance he would always come away with his car full of gas. He'd never steal a car or that sort of thing, but would steal gas, parts for his car. I know his garage was filled with car parts after his death. He was a good chicken thief." Cudmore was called as a witness at the first trial only (to give evidence of having identified Ray's body), but Main did not examine him concerning his knowledge of Ray's larcenous proclivities. It can only be guessed that Main (and, in his turn, Dunne) failed to recognize that Cook's story had two essential parts - the handing over of the money, and Ray's receipt of it knowing its source - and that the credibility of the whole depended on the proof of each.

When Sergeant Tom Roach delivered Cook to the mental hospital at Ponoka, he told the admitting doctor that Ray Cook had been described to him as being "a very steady man...a very straight and upright man who would not touch stolen money" - a judgment Roach probably accepted otherwise why mention it? If so, the internal lines of communication in the RCMP were impaired since Roach's superior, Staff Sergeant Dave Beeching, told me that "Ray Cook was fixing cars using parts which he had taken from McTaggart Motors; we knew that. There's no question but that the father had a fair bit of knowledge about what young Cook was doing" including, one supposes, knowing that Cook was stealing as much money as he could get his hands on.

Did McTaggart Motors know anything about this? It turned out they did. George McTaggart told me what he would have been glad to tell the court had he been called as a witness: he had fired Ray Cook when he caught him stealing parts from the stock room. There was, it appeared, more to Ray Cook than met the wilfully blind eye: a moral laxity which permitted him to turn *his* blind eye to the want of rectitude in his son. One cannot help thinking that had Cook confined his criminal activities to a little shoplifting here, a little gas-siphoning there - innocent activities really - and managed to avoid getting caught at it even as Ray had managed to do (apart from losing his job at McTaggart), the relationship between son and father would not have spiraled out of control. It is one thing to lose a job because of minor stock room shortages; for one thing few people know of it. It is quite another to be sentenced three times hand-running to a federal penitentiary.

***

In Hanna she was "the red-headed schoolteacher." Hers was a more forceful and outgoing personality than that of her taciturn husband, and to Daisy May Cook's friends, this was almost a function of her hair. How could she not be who she was with such hair which, to Clara Behuniak, was her most striking feature: "She was the only redhead in the family. She had really red hair, gorgeous ringlets when she was younger, deep waves and naturally curly."

Mrs Behuniak continued her fond reminiscence: "Daisy was the nicest girl-friend I ever had - a barrel of laughs. When we were teenagers, just barely old enough, we used to hitchhike into Drumheller to drink. There was a pact between [Daisy's mother] and her daughter that Daisy would not go into bars in Hanna and that's why we used to hitchhike to Drum. The first time we got drunk, somebody had told us that the best way to start was on brandy, so we bought a mickey and drank it straight. God! were we sick!

"She was a very accomplished pianist. I remember she would play "Elmer's Tune" and I would tapdance. One day we walked by the RC church and she went in and played "Elmer's Tune" on the church organ. Either her mother or father was supposed to be RC, but she was not religious and was not brought up as one.

"We never knew in advance of her intention to marry Ray, but she had gone around with him for some time. She did not have anything to do with Ray's marriage breakup."[1]

Mrs Joe O'Reilly remembers a Rabelaisian streak: "She already had a boy and wanted a girl, so when the second little boy was born, she wrote me, 'Roses are red, violets are pink. Our little Kathy was born with a dink. So we named him Pat.'"

Daisy, Mrs O'Reilly continued, "was not pretty, but she had a good sense of humor and was fun to be with. After I moved away from Hanna, we wrote back and forth; I still have a letter from her. She was a really good pianist. They lived on a farm and she came into Hanna every Saturday morning for piano lessons."

Daisy was forever young in Marguerite Read's memory as she re-lived their time together when they left Hanna on the road to becoming teachers: "She was a real carrot-top. She went to Normal School with me in 1940-41. Just one year, no degree, no university, and then we were teachers. She was clever, witty, right on the ball. She was full of beans. The fun we had that year! She was a real wit; she had a keen sense of humor. She had a tremendous rapport with her kids at school. My husband Wally thought a lot of her. I remember when she bought that house in Stettler. We helped them paper it and move in. The house was very humble, but she was going to make the best of it. Cardboard boxes for dressers."

The accuracy of these memories was confirmed by Jo Inkpen: "Daisy played the piano. We'd get together for singsongs and she could play anything. She was a nice dresser. She had a pleasant, smiling face, but

[1] *We have seen that the marriage did not break up but survived to the death of Josephine.*

you wouldn't say that Daisy was a beauty in any way, not a great beauty. She had red hair, a nice figure, but she was shorter than I am and I'm five feet, seven and a half inches."

Teachers who run a no-nonsense classroom, as Daisy evidently did, are then and forever after 'crabby', and Daisy carried the sobriquet to the grave in the minds of some of her students who had run afoul of the crabby Miss Gasper. More generally however, she was cherished by her students. Add to this her friends' memories of her as someone they were always happy to be with - a state of affairs which doesn't obtain in every friendship - and a picture emerges of an attractive, easygoing, extroverted personality ready to make and maintain abiding friendships.

Sergeant Roach's investigation turned up that she was an efficient housekeeper - photographs of the interior of her house entered at trial show that she did well with little (although she might have considered slipcovers for the livingroom chesterfield - Plate 9) - and a thrifty shopper. Roach was impressed with finding that "that porch was full of kids' clothes" - evidence that she was a conscientious mother as well as a fecund one. Her role as stepmother awaits later examination, but as a mother can be dealt with briefly here. Nothing within her means was denied her children which is not to say they were over-indulged; that in any case would have difficult to manage on Ray's average monthly earnings as a piece worker of $180.

Dr Donald MacKay of the Well Baby and Immunization Clinic recalled her as a regular visitor to the clinic with her brood in tow for their regular shots against the thousand natural shocks childhood flesh is heir to. They did well by her. They are remembered by neighbors as being mannerly and polite - a credit to their parents - but normally high-spirited and mischievous. The photograph taken a week before their deaths[1] is poignant testimony to the happiness (and the mischief) which shines in it. They were well-cared-for and well-loved - the most a child's universe offers. The epitaph for an entire family, apart from its black sheep, is inscribed in the black granite of its tombstone: "Ever Remembered, Ever Loved." But there is a private epitaph for Gerry, Patty, Chrissy, Kathy and Linda, the affectionate diminutives by which they lived and which were chosen in a touching gesture to commemorate them in death. It is implicit in other words inscribed there which say more than a stock sentiment picked from a memorial manufacturer's catalogue, words synonymous with love at its fiercest: *Daisy 1922-1959.*

---

[1] *Plate 5*

I would not spend another such a night
Though 'twere to buy a world of happy days
So full of dismal terror was the time.

King Richard III, Act I, Scene iv

CHAPTER 5

THE STAGE - CENTRAL ALBERTA

The watershed year of Cook's life began eight days before his 12th
birthday, July 15, 1949, when without invitation something called a *maybe?*
stepmother invaded the inviolate conclave he and his father had held for
three years against all comers. Then, in February, 1950 a baby arrived
without permission - the second rival for what Cook saw as remaining of
his father's affection, leaving him only the dregs. In July, 1950, capping
a bad year, without consultation he had been uprooted from the only
home he had known and dumped rudely in some place called Stettler. It
was the last straw. His criminal career started about this time with
Stettler seeming to serve as an unwitting catalyst precipitating its most
infamous son, as he would become, into the underworld of petty crime.

Thus between July 1950 and the time of the murders, Stettler had been
home to Cook for nine years, but from the beginning it was a home in
name only. Over those years he was not to spend an aggregate of 12
months there, drifting back after jail and penitentiary terms to spend a
few days or weeks before being arrested again. The people of Stettler
really didn't get the opportunity to get to know him very well.

By the evening of Sunday, June 28, 1959 however, his name was a household word in his home town, and at 10 am on the following day his fellow citizens had packed the courthouse, and stood on the sidewalk in front of it, straining for a chance to put a face to the name which overnight had become an indelible part of their history. The criminal docket had been cleared to give Cook pride of place, and at 10 o'clock "All rise" was intoned by the clerk. Fred Biggs, the presiding magistrate, entered and took his place on the dais. The clerk then declared the court to be in session and enjoined God to save the Queen and the spectators to be seated.

With that, the spectators sat back to await the spectacle: the electrifying first look, for most of them, at the neighbor few of them knew. Cook entered closely escorted by two RCMP constables. He was wearing the clothes in which he had been arrested: a blue sports jacket, brown slacks, a charcoal-and-pink shirt - colors which some readers will remember as having swept the late Fifties like the Black Death - and a pair of brown loafers. He was haggard, lifeless and remote. The murder charge was read. Dave MacNaughton reserved plea on behalf of the client he had seen for the first time the day before when Cook had retained him to defend him on a charge of false pretenses - a charge now forgotten in the press of larger matters.

On that Sunday morning, when Cook faced or thought he faced only the false pretenses charge, he had arranged for a call to be made to Rob Sloan, a Stettler lawyer and MacNaughton's associate. Sloan was not available for a false pretenses defense, and MacNaughton inherited Cook, a routine small-time crook and as such nothing more to MacNaughton than an annoying interruption of a day off. MacNaughton nevertheless dutifully went to the Detachment, listened as Cook told him his father would be back from BC in a few days when everything would be straightened out, received a $40 retainer and made an application to a bail magistrate who set bail at $3000. Cook asked MacNaughton to ask a family friend to post it. He did so but was turned down. That afternoon MacNaughton learned from the RCMP that an additional charge - murder - was being laid against his false pretenses client[1].

[1] *In being dragged away from whatever Sunday morning diversion he was engaged in to make a routine bail application, MacNaughton was on the verge of being introduced to the case of his career at the criminal bar. Most of the next 504 days were to be devoted by him to the fight to save Cook's life. Everything else in the typical practise of a small-town lawyer became of secondary importance as he and Main and then he and Dunne toiled substantially without remuneration in an increasingly desperate struggle against an implacable judicial juggernaut. MacNaughton is now a Provincial Court judge.*

70

After the reservation of plea, the Crown prosecutor, 'Scotty' Macdonald, called Dr Donald MacKay to the stand to give medical evidence bearing on the question of whether Cook should be remanded for psychiatric examination to determine whether he was mentally able to appreciate what was happening to him, to instruct counsel and to stand trial. Over a year later, in September, 1960, the RCMP's K Division in Edmonton, would respond to a request from the Commissioner of the RCMP in Ottawa for information concerning the head injury Cook had suffered in the Durocher incident. The Department of the Solicitor General was engaged in a review of the death sentence and wished to know whether the injury might have affected Cook's brain. K Division's reply informed the Commissioner that "When Cook appeared...in Stettler on 29/6/59, medical evidence was given by Dr Donald McKay *[sic]*...that on examination by him Cook appeared to be listless and withdrawn. During [the remand] hearing Cook broke down during the reading of the charge. This evidence together with the knowledge as to the enormity of [the] crime in which entire family of the accused were *[sic]* murdered was reason for remand to allow for examination by psychiatrist." The report concluded by informing Ottawa that the head injury was not mentioned by MacKay during Cook's appearance before Biggs.

MacKay's evidence, coupled with the knowledge which Biggs already had, and which by this time, not yet 24 hours after the discovery of the crime, he shared with most of Canada, was enough to permit Biggs to reach his decision. Cook was remanded for 30 days to the Provincial Mental Hospital at Ponoka (PMH) for examination by staff psychiatrists who would report to the court. And there, 11 days later, Cook raised the curtain on a second drama whose dimensions were commensurate with "the enormity of the crime" which had resulted in him being there.

***

Cook's distress in Biggs' court was the second time since his arrest that he lost emotional control. The previous afternoon, when he was informed of the death of his father by Tom Roach, he cried out, "No. Not my father, not my father" and then broke down wracked by uncontrollable sobbing - it cannot be described otherwise. For either an hour or an hour-and-a-half (accounts vary), he was unable to speak. It never happened again. He maintained firm control over any display of emotion to the end of his life.

To Roach, the Sunday afternoon breakdown did not appear faked - an opinion he volunteered to a psychiatrist at Ponoka. Roach was to say at trial that he felt that in his emotional state, Cook had been incapable of understanding the standard police caution, and Roach had waited for apparent recovery before reading it again. Following the second reading, Roach thought better of it and deferred until the following morning again reading it and asking Cook whether he wished to give a voluntary statement.[1]

***

Cook was taken from Biggs' court back to the Detachment office where he was questioned. Roach then escorted him to Ponoka where he was relieved of his belongings including $92 for which he was given a receipt. Roach then met with Dr Bradley and provided him with sufficient information on Cook to permit Bradley to prepare an admission report - a four-page, closely typed document. In it, Bradley recorded that Roach had recounted to him as much information on Cook's childhood as the police had garnered - in less than 24 hours - which covered Josephine's death, Ray's remarriage, the advent of Ray's second family and Cook's reaction to it which the police were already speculating might be "a sign of the source of the trouble." Roach told Bradley that Cook was regarded by the police as "docile on the surface [but perhaps] capable of coming to blows." In Roach's opinion, Cook "could become violent", but he acknowledged that "his relationship with other people is described as outwardly good."

Roach reviewed for Bradley as much of the evidence relating to the crime as the police then had - a surprising amount considering the time

---

[1] *See Chapter 9. Roach was never able to reconcile Cook's seemingly genuine reaction to the disclosure of his father's death with his guilt about which Roach was never in doubt. He informed the psychiatrist that "the accused probably knows he has done something [and] that he became very indignant and on one occasion shouted at police not to dare say he ever did it to his father." Roach seemed to be saying that while Cook had killed his father, he did not know he had. If that was true, it imported some sort of psychiatric aspect - automatism, temporary insanity, amnesia or whatever - but that was not Roach's concern. He was a policeman doing his job; developing esoteric defenses was not part of it. The possibility of a plea of temporary insanity was canvassed by the defense lawyers, but Cook would not hear of it since it would have amounted to an admission of having killed his father.*

elapsed since the opening of the greasepit - but admitted that "the case is not by any means as yet 'worked up.' " Cook was not suicidal "so far as close observation has revealed", nor had he admitted guilt. Roach had had no experience of Cook prior to the present investigation, but even in its short duration - about 42 hours by the time Roach talked to Bradley - Cook had impressed Roach as being "too good a prisoner." This, Roach felt, "might lead to carelessness on the part of his custodians." In light of events not all that far in the future, Roach's observation was to become clothed with a certain prescient irony.

The 'Admission Summary' recorded that Cook was "believed to be violent, impulsive, especially homicidal", not because any such tendencies had been identified by the experts at the hospital - they had yet to see him - but because of what Roach had told Bradley and because of who Cook was: the prime and indeed the only suspect in a murder of unparalleled magnitude. Roach's modest disclaimer notwithstanding, there was not too much of a case remaining to be worked up. The RCMP knew who they had; it was now a matter of routine legwork to tie down proof sufficient to satisfy the court.

The PMH authorities accepted the police assessment of Cook as "especially homicidal" at par. Maximum security confinement was called for if ever it had been in the hospital's long history of dealing with homicidal maniacs - or whatever the current euphemism is - and Cook got the most security the hospital had to offer: a double-locked single room on the east side[1] of the ground floor of M6 - the admitting ward.

The eight-by-nine room opened on to a corridor on which were located three other such rooms and, at the south end, a large open ward where patients less homicidal than Cook were permitted to mingle. Cook was allowed no access to them; for the whole of his time in the PMH he was kept in strict seclusion.

A window looked east from Cook's room across grounds offering an abundance of concealment in trees and shrubbery to anyone of a mind to escape from the forensic ward. Running diagonally across the window a foot or so from it, a fire escape descended from the second floor[2]. The room was bare of furnishings. Cook was allowed a mattress, but it wasn't felt necessary to limit him to a 'strong blanket'- a blanket made of canvas duck which could not be ripped into strips by someone with a

[1] *But see p. 96*

[2] *See Plate 22*

suicidal bent. Cook was not thought to be suicidal, and he was given ordinary blankets and a pillow. He settled in evidently without much concern or interest in his circumstances, and was immediately placed under close surveillance by the ward staff whose duty was to log all patients kept in seclusion at half-hour intervals - one-half the frequency called for by hospital regulations but impossible to maintain because of a staff shortage. He was deemed to justify one special rule: he was not allowed to visit the washroom across the hall (nor to close its door while using it), nor to exercise in the screened veranda[1], without being accompanied by two senior staff members.

He was found on his first afternoon to be "sullen and uncommunicative" and that evening his first supper was seen to be "well taken". He slept well during his first night and thereafter, but with his pillow invariably clutched to his face, probably (one of the staff members surmised) to muffle the "screeching of a second-floor patient rather than in an attempt to block out hallucinations" - evidently the usual reason. During his second day his E.E.G. was found to be normal and his chest x-rays negative. His appetite remained good throughout.

As the first few days went by he began to open up a little and to chat in a friendly enough manner with staff members during his 15 minute mid-afternoon exercise periods. He talked primarily about cars - among them the briefly cherished Impala - and on one occasion about major-league baseball, but never about his family. He was capable of minor ingratitude: an attendant brought him an ice cream cone late one evening and he awoke with a surly "Do you have to wake me just for this?" - readers with the experience of being brought a glass of ice water at 5:30 am by hospital staff will know the feeling. In general however he impressed the staff with being sociable, in a guarded way, and - the word again - "likable." Unexpectedly there began to stir in some of his warders the first questions as to his guilt - which elsewhere was a conclusion long since foregone - and in this they were first among an ever increasing number for whom this was the surprised reaction to Cook. Who had still another surprise in store; for the moment, he slept well, ate well, read what was brought to him when he asked for reading material (he wrote on a magazine cover "I am not guilty"), responded well to the medical and ward staffs, and looked around for a means of escape.

He was seen on July 6 by D. J. Crause, a psychologist, who established that Cook's verbal IQ was "average", his performance IQ "dull-normal"

---

[1] *See Plate 22*

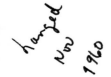
hanged
Nov 1960

and his full-scale IQ "average." The first of three psychiatrists to examine him was Dr T.C.Michie who talked to him for 20 minutes during Cook's first afternoon. Michie was accompanied by Hugh Johnson, a staffer, who, out of concern for Michie's safety, offered to precede him into Cook's room. Michie declined the offer and saw Cook alone. The interview may have been motivated by curiosity as much as anything. It went without incident and Michie left on vacation shortly after without having written a report.

***

The first of three in-depth interviews took place that evening, conducted by Dr J. M. Byers, the acting assistant medical superintendent. The second, by Dr F. J. Edwards, took place the following day, and the last, again conducted by Edwards, occurred on July 9. The Byers interview and the first of the two Edwards interviews seem to have had a 'get acquainted' aspect; the resulting reports do not go beyond recording what Cook told the two psychiatrists of his childhood and family and as little as possible about his criminal history about which, they both thought, he was unusually tight-lipped. The gist of both reports was a repeat of what he had already told the RCMP during the false pretenses investigation and in the course of the statement he gave to the police following his remand hearing.

Dr Byers' report following his routine first interview did not illuminate the question concerning Cook's fitness to stand trial, nor was it meant to. The interview was intended to inform Byers how best to proceed when he got down to cases, but for now he merely observed a man who was "quite pleasant [and] alert [who] answered questions freely." It seemed to Byers that Cook's emotional response was "perhaps inadequate in view of the tragedy having to do with his family." He had, Byers felt, "adopted a superficial attitude to the whole affair", an opinion shared by Dr Edwards who, in the second of his two reports, noted Cook's "statement to the effect that he felt upset by the whole situation and yet there was no clinical evidence of anxiety nor did there appear to be any depression." Similarly, the first-day Admission Summary had recorded that he was "concerned with present comfort [and] appears emotionally flat." [1] While rare, the attitude is not unknown. Dr Charles Hellon, then the Director of Mental Health Services for Alberta, told me that seeming indifference was something not often seen in patients in circumstances comparable to Cook's.

The second of the Edwards reports began to close with the question to be answered during the remand period: Was Cook fit to stand trial? In it, Edwards recorded that he had "been unable to find any evidence of psychosis nor did [Cook] appear to be mentally deficient, and there has been no abnormal behavior to date, nor has he expressed any ideas which could be considered bizarre. At all times during interviews he has been in good contact. There are no psychotic signs."

With which, with 21 of the allotted 30 days left to go, the psychiatrists were finished with Cook, although not necessarily by design. It may be that the three interviews were adequate enough in scope to permit them to form the opinion they in fact formed: that Cook was - in lay terms - sane, although he told Edwards, "If I'm not crazy now, I will be by the time the 30 days are up," suggesting he maintained a laconic sense of humor through a difficult time. But, finished with Cook or not, more interviews still to come or not, 21 days still to go or not, Cook was finished with the psychiatrists. Sometime between 11:25 pm, July 10 and 12:05 am, July 11, he "eloped."

The term, the hospital's, normally conjures an image beloved of cartoonists: a swain staggering down a ladder carrying a bridal-veiled maiden carrying a suitcase, but here there was a broken window, shards of bloodied glass in the window frame and somewhere in the night Cook fleeing without shoes (violently disturbed patients can use shoes as weapons and no chances were being taken with Cook even in the absence of clinical evidence of disturbance), clad in white flannelette pyjamas and socks. He may have been wearing one slipper; the evidence is unclear.

The window in Cook's room is shown in Plate 22, the one on the immediate right. It comprised, looking out, a heavy wire mesh screen in

[1] *The attitude was observed by at least two members of the ward staff, Hal Neufeld and Urban Holman. Neufeld remembered that Cook didn't appear all that concerned about his situation: "He had a lack of seriousness about the box he was in; he was sort of off-handed. He was more concerned about his neatness, his hair, being clean, that sort of thing." It struck Holman that "he had a present outlook - that he was not concerned with being charged with the crime. He did a lot of talking about cars. I remember him saying he wanted to go to the funeral. I thought this was a little bizarre in the circumstances. He seemed very nonchalant about his family being dead."*

a one-and-a-half inch angle-iron frame which itself was fitted into a steel frame set in the concrete wall. Twenty-four panes set in steel mullions in a steel frame made up the window proper which was 34" by 70". Each of the panes was 8" by 11", exactly the same length and a half-inch narrower than a piece of standard letterhead. After removing the screen, Cook smashed out one of the lowest panes (in which, unlike the upper panes, wire was enmeshed), and without dislodging or bending the steel mullions, made his way through the imposingly small opening.

At midnight Gary Anderson, a psychiatric nurse, came on shift, and at 12:05 am made what was meant to be the first of his half-hour checks on Cook. A green light set in the ceiling beside a standard light fixture (which had been turned out earlier by the staff) was permanently on permitting Anderson to see that "something had happened by the window." He told me what then happened: "I shone my flashlight in and saw that the grill was off and a pane of glass was missing. After I had reported what I had seen, I went back to the room. I had a check key with me and I did a very foolish thing as I look back on it. If you've ever looked into one of those rooms through the window in the door, you'll know that there are blind spots; you can't see into the corners near the door. I opened the door and stepped in. He could have been standing there in a corner waiting for me, but no, the bird had flown. He didn't even taken the time to pick all the glass out; there were jagged parts left." *June 28 or 1959 29*

The bird left behind him a facsimile of all hell breaking loose: Anderson's initial shock and disbelief and a hurried report to the night supervisor, general consternation, the first of an expanding network of frantic telephone calls to the medical staff, to the police, to hospital firemen and to off-duty groundskeepers and ward attendants, an order by Dr Byers that the fire alarm atop the powerhouse be sounded "in view of his particularly dangerous tendencies" and all of it leading to the start within minutes of the largest and most urgent manhunt in Alberta's history.

And unique; it cannot be imagined that it will or could ever be duplicated. This was no ordinary jail-break; this was *Robert Raymond Cook* - the name had overnight become ingrained in the public consciousness - who had mesmerized the province and who now enthralled a part of it larger than might be thought in terror. Out there somewhere, in the night, was Robert Raymond Cook. Only later would it be sheepishly recognized, by some, that what had consumed them was fear which owed as much to mass hysteria as it did to the apprehension of danger even from a Cook who was what he was believed to be.

The 45 miles between Ponoka and Stettler is wooded cattle country and rolling farmland, as beautiful in its way as anything Alberta offers elsewhere. It is a country of countless small hollows each holding a little landlocked lake (they cannot be called sloughs which are features of the open prairie) which cannot be drained because of the high relief of the countryside in which they nestle. They answer the unbridled dreams of Ducks Unlimited; each is the home of two or three families of mallards. There are larger lakes, Red Deer Lake and Buffalo Lake for example, each of which was to figure into the manhunt (and the latter more recently into the news as the home of a former premier of Alberta who fell in love with rural Alberta and sought a Stettler seat shortly after being unseated by his urban constituents). Buffalo is about 17 miles long and seven miles wide at its widest point. The country abounds in abandoned mineshafts and beaver dams. Surprisingly, for the heart of Alberta, there are long stretches of near-wilderness: sand hills and scrub pine good only for community pasture.

For Cook the possibilities for concealment were endless and, in that time of year in that country the prospects for survival were good. There were abandoned farmhouses as possible sources of clothing and footwear; farm gardens and native berries for sustenance. There were country service stations with cars parked in and near them for - for Cook - the routine theft of them. For someone flying out of the cuckoo's nest, Cook could not have chosen better than to disappear from its circumference into the 1500 square mile circle lying on the Ponoka-Stettler axis.

But had he? To avoid attenuating their finite forces at the outset, the police were forced to make what they hoped was an informed guess. They thought there was some reason for regarding Stettler as Cook's destination (which was to assume a destination as distinct from aimless flight), but none for, say, Calgary which lay outside the circle. There were, they thought, a number of people in Stettler who feared some sort of vengeance from Cook, and they predicated their decision to concentrate the search in that direction on the belief that Cook was on his way there to tie up some loose ends[1].

---

[1] *So far as I have been able to learn, no one in Stettler had anything to fear from Cook. For one thing, few knew him. One who did in a manner of speaking, from having viewed him recently for perhaps ten minutes from maybe ten feet was Fred Biggs, the remand magistrate. Biggs, the RCMP thought, was a prime target for assassination by Cook, and they assigned a two-man bodyguard from their already depleted ranks; it is barely an exaggeration to say that every RCMP officer between*

The guess was a good one as it happened, if for the wrong reason, and it meant that from the beginning the hunters and the hunted were in the same circle, albeit an impossibly large one. To find a needle in a haystack presupposes knowing where the haystack is. They at least had the haystack and, miraculously, it would be only a scant 22 hours before the first sighting of the needle.

***

Before eloping Cook knew that he could count on 30 minutes between staff checks, but not on the ten-minute bonus which resulted from the 11:30 check having been made at 11:25, and the midnight check not until 12:05. Forty minutes was enough; the flight from the hospital and from the grounds was unobserved. Cook melted almost without trace[1] into the warm summer night.

At 12:05 it took Gary Anderson only a few seconds to reach the night supervisor with the news which was to shatter the even tenor of Alberta's placid ways and galvanize it as no other event in its history save perhaps for the outbreak of a couple of world wars. The first call from the hospital was to the RCMP Detachment in Ponoka who immediately alerted the Subdivision in Red Deer, the Detachments in Stettler and Wetaskiwin, and K Division in Edmonton. Non-commissioned officers and constables not then on duty were telephoned - aroused peremptorily from bed in not a few cases - and ordered to report to their detachments to stand by for as long as it took to designate which roadblock they were to man. By 2 am there was not a highway within 40 miles of Ponoka which did not have a police car spotted on it at strategic points. It was a masterpiece of lightning-fast organization requiring the positioning of every car which could be summoned from every detachment within a hundred miles. This was merely the first step - the minimum response.

Stettler and Rio de Janeiro had been pressed into the manhunt. The crusty Biggs thought otherwise, and after a couple of days dismissed the detail. However, had he remembered it, Biggs had some reason to fear retribution. In 1952 he had fined Cook $20 for illegal possession of liquor, but it is doubtful the injustice of it all had festered in Cook in the intervening years. A press account of the incident refers to Biggs as a "cadi" - an engaging word which hasn't been seen since.

[1] *Almost but not quite completely without trace. There was a matter of a stolen car. See p. 81*

The effort to organize and deploy nothing less than a field force was already under way.

As many of the hospital staff as could be spared from their duties and all the firemen on duty were pressed into action on the hospital grounds on the slender chance - the more slender the better for these reluctant searchers - that the quarry might have remained on them. They began combing the grounds in pairs. They were unarmed - only later were staff members seconded to the RCMP and given arms - and their middle-of-the-night apprehension on peering cautiously into dark corners and under hedges is not easily imagined.

Looking back on it, they were searching for a killer so ruthless that he had crushed the skulls of small children like so many eggshells. It was prudent to suppose that he would stop at nothing less if one of them came between him and freedom. The staff members were versed in dealing with violent men but always in secure conditions. As close as any of the firemen had come to a situation such as this was to watch cop shows with the normal complement of five killings per half hour on the firehouse tv. Now they were pitchforked into real life masquerading as a cop show, and they entertained the not unreasonable apprehension of experiencing death other than vicariously.

The fact that a few of the ward staff had begun to wonder whether he was guilty was unknown to the rest of them, nor would it have mattered had it been. The escape swept away for the time being any emerging doubts as to Cook's guilt - indeed it confirmed it - and the picture by now half-formed in the minds of Albertans held sway in a fearful night. Its details were as yet vague but its broad outlines were not - cornered children cowering in terror, a house bathed in blood, a greasepit crammed with bodies - and here *they* were: men who measured excitement in terms of calming an unruly patient or hosing down the odd shed on the hospital grounds sent out to find the man who had imparted this new and scarcely imaginable dimension to murder.

They measured their success in getting through the night by the failure of their search, and with the arrival of daylight the rest was anticlimax. The search of the grounds was continued throughout the day, stopping only at 10 o'clock that night when word was received that Cook had been spotted 34 miles southeast of the hospital.

***

There are some perplexing questions about what took place during the first hour of Cook's freedom. The attempt to put it all together has proved inordinately difficult, but something roughly as follows happened. The hospital is located about a mile southeast of the town limits. Cook is supposed to have made his way from the hospital to the Riverside district in Ponoka's southeast quarter where he stole a 1951 Chevrolet purportedly belonging to a Mr Noyce Boddy, although other evidence indicates that someone else stole a car, perhaps Boddy's, and had it waiting for Cook near the hospital. The murkier the details, the thicker the plot. It might be thought that while it might have been difficult to say who stole the car, it should at least have been possible to say whose car it was since Cook wrecked it and abandoned it half way through the manhunt. Yet in one of those minor mysteries which dog the case, it cannot be said definitely, by this researcher, whose car it was. The police of course knew but never released the information.

Boddy had two cars, one of them a 1951 Chevrolet. On the night of the escape he was absent from home but returned at about 1:30 am. According to *The Edmonton Journal* he believed that that car was then in his yard. "I'm not sure though," he was quoted as saying, "it may have been gone but it seems to me I saw it when I arrived home." *The Journal* went on to report that an hour after Boddy's return home, the police phoned to inform him that his car had been recovered "overturned in a ditch near Nevis." The car in question - or at least a car - was in fact overturned in a ditch near Nevis 19 hours after Boddy's return home.

It seems probable that *The Journal* was in error; that the police did not phone Boddy within an hour of his return home. If one concedes that Boddy too was in error - that in spite of thinking that the Chevrolet was at home when he arrived, it wasn't - and if it is conceded that the car rolled near Nevis was his, then there is no mystery apart from who stole it. But then one is left to reckon with the observation of Gary Anderson, the man who had shone his flashlight into Cook's room and noticed with wild surmise that the screen had been wrested from its moorings.

We were discussing what had become the standard account - Boddy's car and Cook's theft of it - and the niggling discrepancies noted here. It wasn't good enough for Anderson: "There's something peculiar there. I don't know what it is, but I strongly suggest you talk to Boddy. He has a farm 12 miles southwest of town. The garage that Cook is supposed to have pushed the car out of is still there." If Cook pushed a car out of Boddy's garage on a farm 12 miles out of town, why was Boddy uncertain whether or not he saw it in his driveway in the Riverside district in Ponoka - unless of course Anderson meant that the Riverside garage was still in Riverside even though Boddy was now on his farm. The RCMP could have cleared all this up[1] - and obviated some faulty research - had they given some timely answers, but they elected not to do so, perhaps because they had enough on their plate in investigating the engineering of the escape.

***

In the Alberta of 1959 Sunday newspapers lay in a more secular future, and any news occurring on the Sabbath was necessarily left to radio and to television, then in its infancy. Thus when the Stettler story broke, the six-day-a-week broadsheets had to stand by fuming helplessly while their despised rivals made off with the biggest Alberta story of the year. Not that the print reporters weren't out in force and digging - getting quotes from police officers and townspeople, getting photographs, getting the stories ready for the Monday editions, getting it wrong in enough instances, but for the moment the presses sat silent and impotent, waiting for Monday.

The morning newspapers suffered the same unfairness with the story of the escape from Ponoka as had they and their afternoon brothers with the discovery of the murders. The morning papers had been put to bed an hour before Cook broke out, and had had to wait a full two days and nights (once again Sunday intervened) before they could cover a story which was by then, in its essentials, stale news.

The afternoon newspapers had a better time of it. Their first editions were on the street on the first full day after the elopement, and their front pages were once again given over to the now doubly newsworthy Cook. "Police Dragnet Thrown Out for Alberta Escapee" was *The Lethbridge Herald*'s headline of Saturday, July 11. Nothing would have elbowed the story off the page. It related as many of the particulars as *The Herald* then knew, and informed its readers that the manhunt had been well and truly launched almost from the moment of the escape, and was now being coordinated from a mobile command post set up at Nevis, a village 15 miles west of Stettler.

---

[1] *As perhaps could have Boddy, but I failed to find him on a single attempt to do so.*

At the height of the search the post controlled the movements of more than a hundred members of the RCMP[1], between 60 and 70 members of the Canadian Army Provost Corps who joined the search on the third day, a handful of PMH staff members armed and seconded to the RCMP as special constables, and men recruited from the police forces of nearby towns. The Provost Corps brought its equipment with it: a bus, panel trucks, 20 jeeps (one of them devoted to carrying nothing but ammunition for submachine guns) and armored cars. There were 30 or more police cars, and an RCMP boat on standby. Sten guns, telescopic rifles, .45 calibre automatic pistols, revolvers and walkie-talkies were issued. Army field telephones were deployed. The RCMP brought tracking dogs which joined the search with an astonishing if rather engaging lack of success which made of them Kanine Keystone Kops[2], and before the search was over the RCMP employed two of their own aircraft and enlisted the aid of three others owned by private citizens, two twin-engined aircraft from the RCAF base at Penhold, and a helicopter.

Call it "as many as 200" as the Canadian Press did. At the height of the search there were as many as 200 hundred men engaged in a grim search of bluffs, coulees, wooded valleys, fence lines, farm buildings, fields and a lake bottom which was dragged on the probable line Cook would have

June 1959

[1] *Personnel counts and descriptions of equipment cited here are from contemporary press accounts. Such accounts are given to dealing in "more than" rather than exact figures leaving one to wonder how the writers know there were more than the figures they employ, or why, if they know the exact figure, they don't use it? If they don't, then "about" would have done it, but it may be that "more than 200" sounds better. It is an example ("at least" is another) of the bafflegab in which journalists seek refuge when they don't know and don't want to admit it, and by which flak writers ("More than $100,000 in prizes!") whose idiom is meaningless hype hope to divert attention from the vapidity of their message. The result is that the guesses - which is all they are - in the press accounts of the manhunt are valueless.*

Had the figures been presented as estimates, they would have been called "conservative" - another instance of the same phenomenon - meaning that they know the actual number, otherwise they cannot know the 'estimate' is conservative, i.e. a number somewhat short of the actual number. Which is to say an estimate modestly identified as conservative is in fact not an estimate at all. A true estimate may be wildly wide of the mark either way and there is no way of knowing which until the exact number is established, at which point there is no longer any need for estimates. Suffice it here to say, because there is now no help for it, that there were a considerable number of police officers and army personnel in the field.

[2] *On one occasion a dog lost the trail after leaving it to check out some gophers, and on another the dogs were unable to pick up the trail from a strip Cook tore from his pyjamas to use as toilet tissue.*

taken had he tried to swim it. A provincial game officer was brought from Drumheller to supervise the dynamiting of five beaver dams on the chance that Cook might have drowned in a head pond. Every likely building in ten towns in the search area was searched as was every abandoned mineshaft and abandoned farm the searchers came upon. The effort was unprecedented in the sketchy annals of manhunting, and if it failed in the not inconsiderable sense of failing to corner the quarry, it succeeded in the less complimentary sense of forcing him to throw in the towel. At the end of the fourth day Cook gave himself up, defeated by the same factors as had hamstrung the searchers - fatigue, heat and mosquitoes - and by three they had not had to contend with: dead-end roads, hunger and a lack of clothing, particularly footwear.

Fatigue, heat and mosquitoes and the greatest of these was fatigue. They drove themselves without cease throughout the 90 hours Cook was at large. For Dave Beeching, the senior NCO on the ground, there could be no let up until the multiple killer was cornered and captured, killed if necessary since Cook's first priority would be to steal firearms and the police were acutely aware that they themselves were on the firing line anywhere and everywhere in what Keith Sutherland, then of the RCMP, later remembered as "that tough, tough country" in which the time and place for a shootout would be a matter of the unseen sniper's choosing.

Through it all, Beeching performed by drawing on the *savoir faire* of a senior NCO, but by the morning of the second day (he had not yet slept), as Tom Roach described it years later, "[Beeching] was travelling on nerves. He said distractedly to a couple of guys, 'You'd better go into Stettler for breakfast.' They looked at each other. 'Christ Staff! you've already tried to send us into Stettler twice this morning.' Beeching looked at them as if he hadn't heard them and turned back to the map table." He reminded Roach (who himself was approaching the limits of exhaustion) of Montgomery in his mobile staff headquarters during the desert campaign.

For all of them, 20-hour days were the norm. When they could, they would lie down beside or under their cars and attempt sleep. There they would last as long as it took for the mosquitoes to drive them into the cars where they sweltered in daytime temperatures which hovered in the high 90s throughout the search. Sleep was little enhanced by the necessity of running the engines constantly to supply the power required to maintain unbroken radio communication with the Stettler Detachment through which messages were relayed by land line to the mobile command post and back through Stettler to the field. But with the engines running, windows had to be left open. Bad as it was to be devoured by mosquitoes, it was worse to be dying of heat prostration while being devoured by mosquitoes and so, a moveable blood feast, they would try the ground again. After a couple of fitful hours of dozing, they would be aroused by the radio and would once more stagger, or drive, into the search, sweating, tired and dirty.

***

For the first 22 hours Cook vanished and then surfaced on the Lacombe-Stettler highway at a point near the command post. What he did and where he was during those hours is a matter for conjecture only, but it may be guessed that he drove to his first stopping point, concealed his car off whatever road he was on to await night and the chance to resume his progress towards Stettler. It is the best of a number of weak conjectures but there was no need to sit out the day; he could easily have driven to Stettler from Ponoka in the middle of the night in, at most, 90 minutes. Why stop? More to the point, why Stettler? Criminals sometimes return to the scenes of their crimes in response to some dark compulsion, but not, one would think, if a given scene would be known to be an armed camp in the heart of enemy territory.

Nevertheless, resume his progress he did, on the heavily travelled highway between Lacombe and Stettler. It might occur to some that any chance of making it undetected would lie in travelling the back roads in a manner calculated to attract minimal attention: not too fast, nothing more than a farmer on some errand or other to neighbors peering fearfully from behind drawn shades for whom every bellowing cow was proof that Cook was out there butchering the herd in broad daylight. While the chances of attracting no attention in a countryside in which farms had been turned into armed garrisons were few, insofar as there were any they might be seen as lying on the back roads. Not by Cook, perhaps employing the shrewd premise that since no one would think him foolhardy enough to use a main highway, where better than a main highway?

Buffalo Lake is drained by Tail Creek, which crosses the east-west highway on which Cook was now travelling, flowing in a broad, wooded coulee about two miles east of the highway's intersection with Highway

21, the north-south road between Bashaw and Three Hills. A police car was stationed at the top of the coulee on the west side, near the intersection and facing west. Seated in it, in a state of alertness which can only be guessed at, were constables Pete Thachik and Norman Inkster, the latter later to become Commissioner of the RCMP. Cook drove by, heading east towards Stettler. Thachik and Inkster awoke, figuratively at least, to the fact that this was their man. A number of shots were fired at the disappearing car, piercing its windshield, before Thachik and Inkster got theirs turned around to give chase. At the bottom of the coulee, Cook attempted a high-speed U-turn and rolled his car into the south ditch. By the time the police arrived, expecting to find him injured or dead, he had disappeared into the bush, drenched in purple gas from a couple of jerry-cans in the back seat. It is not known where the gas came from, but Cook was nothing if not resourceful.

Superintendent J.S.Cruikshank of K Division was quoted in *The Edmonton Journal* as saying the dogs (which were on the scene as soon as their handlers could get them there) tracked Cook for five miles from Tail Creek before losing the trail. If so, then they had held it to a point within sight of the village of Alix where Cook broke into a highway service station, drove out a 1957 Monarch, went into the office and switched on the pumps, gassed up and drove off into the darkness without being seen or heard except, according to a press account, by an unidentified woman "who observed the gassing up and thought it was the owner."

Vignettes which serve to vivify the time in the memories of those in the immediate area who lived through it abound - stories of keys left in vehicles so Cook could drive off and leave the family unmolested, stories of armed escorts to outdoor privies, stories of loaded shotguns beside countless beds (as far away as Edmonton), stories of farms abandoned and farms lit like the mid-day of noon with as many lights as could be jerry-wired into place. A handful of them will indicate the magnitude of the dismal - and, as we now know, largely self-induced - terror.

Mr Justice Sidney Legg, now deceased, was a lawyer in Stettler at the time. He was driving home from Lacombe and was stopped at a Tail Creek road block. He had been at the family cottage over the weekend and happened to have on the back seat a pair of pyjamas being taken home for laundering. Cook had been wearing pyjamas. Nothing was being taken for granted in those hair-trigger hours. Get out of the car. At first Legg had been inclined to take the whole thing lightly, but the sight of drawn guns impressed upon him that something about the situation called for wary gravity. Legg was able to persuade the police that he had not clothed Cook and sent him on his way while retaining his pyjamas for later laundering. He recalled that "for four days there seemed to be one of those black and white cars on top of every hill in the country."

Jim Stearns of the Lacombe Police was driving out of town one night. He spotted someone on the road with a flashlight and, thinking nothing of it, went to drive on by. He was stopped with four guns pointed at his head.

George Akers, an Edmonton lawyer, was told by his mother-in-law that she stacked books on the sill of her daughter's open bedroom window, somewhat reminiscent of the night the bed fell on Thurber's father. When Cook came through the open window he would topple the books, bringing the intrepid mother-in-law on the run. Her plan was to race in while her daughter was being murdered and grapple with the maniacal killer.

Floyd Halls, an Edmonton businessman, was stopped four times on the highway between Red Deer and Edmonton.

Dillon Hoskins remembers pigs and cows being dropped in their tracks "within sight of Stettler. People were shooting anything that moved, *even after he was re-captured*. The town was literally petrified." And Arnold Filipenko was out of town when Cook escaped: "I came back to Stettler on Monday morning and went to my sister's place. She was sure Cook was on his way to Stettler. The doors of the house were all barred; my brother-in-law had jammed them up with butcher knives. I knocked and told them who it was. I could hear knives being removed. The door opened and I stepped in. My brother-in-law was standing there with a knife poised in the air. How did he know Cook wouldn't say he was me? Anything to gain entry."

Farms were abandoned as their owners moved into town for the duration. Dave Beeching told me that the RCMP received "more than" one call from farmers asking for twice-daily armed police escorts to accompany them while they went home to feed the livestock - requests which were more or less politely refused by the harried and weary police.

***

In the first 26 hours after breaking out of a maximum security ward, Cook had made off in a stolen car which he himself may have stolen; had managed to conceal the car throughout the daylight hours of the first day; had successfully run a road block; had survived a fusillade; had rolled a car in a high-speed chase and had walked - run - away from it unhurt and drenched with gas; had been within scant feet of his pursuers and had eluded them and their tracking dogs; had travelled about six miles across an unknown country in the dark; had calmly broken into a service station in the middle of the night and stolen a car and enough gas to fill it; and had once again disappeared. He was a damned, elusive Pimpernel who, when he didn't have all that much to gladden him on his last day, wrote with delight of the merry chase when he had cocked a snoot at the mighty Establishment, a helpless, whimpering giant, and had tied it in knots. And so he had.

There were 64 hours to go. For the RCMP the unforgiving search went on against a background of rising political clamor familiar to every police force which fails to solve the murder and find the murderer within the 24-hour grace period the public graciously allows. The crackpots came out of the woodwork and they had to be dealt with; every sighting of Cook (in Edmonton, Grande Prairie, Lethbridge, Vancouver, Seattle and Prince George where he was seen descending from a bus) was checked out. Meanwhile, the Army Provost Corps arrived and was fed into the search. Nothing.

His movements in the 64 hours following his second disappearance to the time of capture are, like too much else, a matter of some conjecture. Based on a sighting thought at the time to be of more substance than any so far apart from Tail Creek (it wasn't), the command post was moved to Bashaw. The search area was now concentrated in the area between the north shore of Buffalo Lake to Bashaw - an area in which, fortuitously, Cook happened to now be. It is thought that when he left Alix he drove north-easterly to the north side of Buffalo Lake in an effort to get to Stettler by a route more indirect than the one which had ended in disaster at Tail Creek. Turning south towards Stettler and not being familiar with the east-west extent of the lake, he had attempted to turn its eastern end, but instead had driven down a series of roads which dead-ended him on the north shore costing him valuable time and gas. He abandoned the attempt (and apparently abandoned Stettler) and turned the car northwest, perhaps trying for Edmonton and sanctuary with friends which he assumed he would find. He might have, but it is doubtful. He had long since become too explosive for any kind of association.

On Monday, July 13, Mrs Richard Schulz of the Bashaw district informed her husband that she and a female companion had seen a car matching the broadcast description of the stolen Monarch on a highway east of Ponoka. They had watched it turn off onto a side road and, following it in the Schulz car (she was reasonably sure who it was; her foolhardiness invites admiration), they watched it turn off the side road and proceed across a field, past an abandoned barn, along an unused wagon trail and into a bluff of poplars in a little-used pasture belonging to one Bob Rutledge.

Discretion now tempered their valor and they turned and drove home. Richard Schulz phoned the police and the focus of the search was instantly switched to the new area. The car was quickly located, covered with branches (suggesting that Cook was not yet finished with it) and with enough gas for a further 300 miles. A three-sided cordon was formed: two north-south lines of men extending to the south shore of Red Deer Lake which formed the third side. Men were spotted around the shore of the lake and dragging operations begun across its narrowest part. Surprisingly, the box was left open on the fourth side which more or less took in Bashaw. Whether or not Cook was ever cordoned off is not known, but for *The Albertan* of Calgary it was a given: he was boxed in with only one escape route, towards the south. "With the troops and RCMP guarding the two sides of the suspected area and a lake on the third side, there is only one escape route - toward the town of Bashaw" the newspaper noted in its issue of July 14. If the police read it, they ignored it for in the following issue *The Albertan* could not conceal its hurt at police ingratitude: "This proved true Tuesday, although the police did not follow [*The Albertan's*] lead." It *had* proved true; Cook was southbound on foot and the three-sided box closed in on nothing.

At 4 pm on Tuesday, July 14 on the Norman Dufva farm two miles south of Bashaw (and about ten miles south of the area around which the searchers were tightening the net), Cook deliberately stepped out of a pig barn so that he could be seen by Mrs Dufva. She called her husband, and while he held a shotgun on the door of the barn (Cook had stepped back inside to avoid being shot whether inadvertently or otherwise), she phoned the RCMP. Within minutes a car swung into the yard, men and dogs emerged on the run, overshot the doorway inside which Cook was slumped, and disappeared in a bluff which ran up to the barnyard. A second car arrived. Cook decided enough was enough. Mack Sennet might have appreciated it, but he did not. He stepped out of the barn. It was all over.

July 14
1959
caught

He was ill-clothed: women's plastic overshoes, pants he'd picked up somewhere, no shirt, a jacket and, beneath the pants, the pyjama bottoms in which he'd escaped. He was hungry, lacerated by underbrush and unable to talk from weariness. He was taken to the town lockup and fed while a senior police officer went to buy him loafers, slacks and a t-shirt. While Cook was still inside being debriefed as it were, a crowd conservatively estimated as exactly one-half of Bashaw's more than 900 townspeople gathered outside hoping for a look at the illustrious captive. They were briefly fulfilled. He was led out in handcuffs surrounded by a phalanx of plainclothes and uniformed officers. He looked slight beside them, tired and resigned with nothing in him of defiance.[1] He was placed in a police car and driven to Edmonton. Not until the car was in K Division's underground garage was he allowed to leave it. The next morning he was taken to Fort Saskatchewan Provincial Gaol. It was his 22nd birthday. He may have reflected that three years earlier in a letter to his father he had predicted that unless he turned his life around, he would end up "kicking the bucket in a dirty provincial jail."

***

While Cook was still at large, K Division telexed its Red Deer Subdivision: "DAG instructs that when Cook is apprehended is to be escorted to Fort Saskatchewan Gaol. Cook is not to be returned to PMH." Deputy Attorney General's directive or no[2], it is highly unlikely anyone had any intention of returning Cook to the PMH, then technically a jail under provincial statute, but one found wanting as the police measure such things. Cook was clearly the concern not of psychiatric nurses and hospitals, but of policemen and guards and iron bars which could not be removed intact from their setting and set quietly on the floor.

It is not likely that the PMH wanted him back. For one thing, further psychiatric examination was not required. The minutes of a staff conference of July 23 attended by Drs Edwards and Byers recorded that "During [Cook's] period of hospitalization, he showed no psychotic

---

[1] *See Plate 31*

[2] *The fact that the Biggs remand order, requiring that Cook be confined in the PMH, still had 20 days to run at the date of the K Division telex, was trampled underfoot in the urgency of getting Cook behind more secure bars.*

signs. For the most part his attitude was one of sullenness. He was not anxious to dwell on previous anti-social conduct. He was of normal intelligence" The minutes concluded with the diagnosis "Not psychotic." Evidently such conferences were normally also attended by the patient himself for a sort of wind-up interview since here the minutes show Cook was interviewed "in absentia" which, in Cook's case, was to put it both mildly and confusingly.

However the conference seems to have been held as a matter of form since six days earlier in his official report to the court Byers had written that "Cook was considered fit to stand trial." He had prefaced his opinion by informing Magistrate G.W.Graves (who was to conduct the preliminary inquiry) that Cook had eloped on July 11, and had been "discharged from elopement the same day." The same-day discharge suggests that with its hands about to become full with the investigation of the escape, the PMH wished to have them washed of Cook.

***

The investigation descended on the hospital with the wrath of Dr J.Donovan Ross, the Minister of Health in E. C. Manning's Social Credit government. Ross issued a stern, stentorian 'no stone unturned' statement which included the curious assertion that, in a preliminary way, he had "found the hospital's precautions adequate," but "the fact that [Cook] escaped must be studied" leaving puzzled readers to ponder Ross's understanding of adequacy. Whatever precautions which did not prevent escape might have been - pretty good, all things considered; earnest and well-intentioned; not bad under the circumstances - adequate did not seem to be among them.

One of the questions to be answered was provided by an editorial writer: "What sort of watch is kept at a mental hospital where at least some of the patients should not be at large because they are a danger to the public and themselves, when a man can escape as easily and undetected as Cook did?" He was asking two questions: what sort of watch is kept where some of the patients should not be at large? and what sort of watch was kept which allowed Cook to escape? Only the second question was of concern to Ross; this was not the time to be asking whether selected patients should be granted passes so they could catch a movie in town.

The writer was right to question the adequacy of the watch and in fact, as we have seen, the prescribed frequency of cell checks had been halved because of a manpower shortage although there is of course much more to forensic ward security than cell checks. What is less clear is that his assumption that the escape was accomplished easily and without detection was grounded in fact. To explain it is necessary to frame three questions:

(1) Was the escape unassisted?
(2) If not, was there outside assistance and, if so, from whom?
(3) If this was an inside job, who was in on it?

The last question implied either a member of the staff or a patient as the inside man. If a staff member, then whatever else it was, an escape facilitated by him could not be said to have gone undetected.

The framed heavy mesh screen partly shown in Plates 24 and 25 was the key to the escape. With it removed the way was clear to one of the 8" by 11" panes. The left side of the screen frame was recessed in a channel iron set into the concrete, and the screen could be removed only by manipulation of the mechanism shown on the right side of the screen in Plate 25. Turning the square shaft counterclockwise with the wrench shown in Plate 24 drew back the deadbolt seen in Plate 25 and simultaneously withdrew two rods (faintly shown in Plate 25) which extended to the top and bottom of the screen and through its frame into holes drilled into the steel bars set in the concrete wall. There was provision for locking the mechanism; the keyhole is seen below and to the left of the dowel in Plate 25. Thus, in a properly secured cell, escape required a wrench - any adjustable wrench and perhaps even pliers would have served - and a key.

The sparse evidence bearing on each of the above questions will not be analyzed here where to do so would be to do nothing more than arrive at some probabilities. Rather, a series of ancillary questions will be set out demonstrating the scope of the problem. Whatever the answers, they have nothing to do with the main enquiry of this book. As much as may be said is that if, as seems probable, he was helped to escape, and more particularly if by someone charged with preventing escape, it says something in character with what we have already learned about Cook. The ancillary questions follow. The reader is invited to reach her own conclusions:

(a) When Cook was locked into his cell, were the deadbolt and rods in their closed position? If so, then the *locking* of them by means of the required key was immaterial since, in the absence of the right wrench, it would have required "superhuman strength" (as the Report on Elopement termed it) to turn the dowel and withdraw the deadbolt and rods.

(b) If the deadbolt and rods were in their closed position, were they also locked? If so, then a key fitting the old-fashioned keyhole was required before the dowel could be turned releasing the deadbolt and rods. An adequate wrench could have come from the outside through a broken window and through the screen. It is doubtful that the required key would have come from the outside. If a key was found afterwards, lying on the floor of the cell say, that fact was not disclosed.

(c) If the deadbolt and rods were in their closed position when Cook took up occupancy, who supplied the wrench indispensable to withdrawing them? Once again we do not know what was found afterwards. If no wrench was left behind (it is improbable he would take it with him), that necessarily indicates that the deadbolt and rods were not in their closed position when Cook was in residence, suggesting that the adequacy of the "precautions" was open to serious question.

(d) With the deadbolt and rods withdrawn, was it possible for one man to remove the screen? They were purposely made to fit tightly in the surrounding frame to prevent their removal by a single patient.

(e) Assuming outside assistance, how probable was it that such assistance could have come from someone unfamiliar with the hospital in general and M6 in particular? A strained scenario may be developed to account for the actions of a stranger to the hospital: learning where in M6 Cook was located; a clandestine first visit to the window to be informed by Cook through the louvered window (Plate 23) of the implements required - if any - and the timing of cell checks; the acquisition of the implements - the wrench would present no problem but the key would; a clandestine second visit to break the window (it could not be broken from inside without a makeshift hammer), and to pass the implements in through the screen. The key is the key[1]: how could Cook have known that it was necessary without knowing whether the mechanism was locked, which could not be determined by visual

---

[1] *Hugh Johnson, a staff member in M6 at the time, thinks that a key was found broken off in the locking device after elopement. If so, then it meant either that Cook had broken it off (but leaving the problem of where it came from), or that it was broken off prior to Cook being placed in the room. Either way, it was a hell of a way to run a railroad.*

examination? If a key was essential, they were presumably kept in a secure location. The outsider merely had to learn the location and contrive to get to it.

It will be agreed that outside assistance is improbable, but if it is also agreed that Cook could not have done it himself, then it leaves as a conclusion one that the hospital administration could not have welcomed.

***

With Cook again in custody, Albertans confidently sat back to await the revelation of the circumstances of the escape. There seemed to be reason for the confidence. Dr Ross had promised that "all aspects of this case will be studied", and although he did not say so, the widespread supposition was that when the study was concluded and all the questions were answered, the resulting information would be shared with them.

Not unreasonably they felt they had the right to know. They could assume that the RCMP's best investigators had been assigned, and that no matter where the investigation led, the results would be published. If Cook was assisted, then someone (who would be named) had committed the crime of aiding and abetting an escape from lawful custody. He would be charged. Assisted or not, negligence could be laid at the hospital's doorstep and the appropriate heads would roll. The citizenry's patience deserves commendation since it is still waiting for meaningful disclosure. It was, it is true, thrown a few scraps.

The RCMP set to with a will. Measurements and photographs were taken and fingerprints lifted. Doctors and staff were interviewed as was Cook who later told Dave MacNaughton that so desperate were the police to hear something - as it appeared to him - he told them what he thought they wanted to hear: he had been helped from the outside by two men, one of them Jimmy Myhaluk who, however, happened to be back in jail at the material time. There is no record of the RCMP having gone back to Cook to see whether he wished to issue a correction.

A comical element entered the investigation when the police attempted to duplicate the escape. Constable George Marshall Sproule who was similar to Cook in weight and build was asked to go through the same window. He managed to liberate his head and one arm but could go no further and had to be forcibly assisted back into the room. Ron Cave happened to be walking by with another staff member on his way back from lunch: "I'm going by and I see this one arm and a head sticking out. They weren't going anywhere as far as I could see. I stopped and made a smart-ass remark to the guy with me. I said, 'Well, there goes another one.' I didn't know that Byers happened to be in the room and that he could hear me. I felt about four inches high."

The Sproule experiment is interesting both because of its probable purpose and because of the conclusion which may have been drawn from the failure to feed the feckless officer through the window. If the purpose was to prove the impossibility of a man of Cook's physical stature having gone through it, the RCMP were left with an inescapable conclusion: not only had he received inside assistance but the escape route was an inside route. In that case the removal of the screen, the breaking of the glass and the blood left on the shards of glass in the mullions were nothing more than red herrings. It seems improbable; more likely is that they were motivated by a natural incredulity and, having satisfied themselves that Cook had accomplished the impossible[1], Sproule's experience to the contrary, they turned their attention to other matters.

In their report to the Attorney General the RCMP stated that there had been outside assistance. Two men had broken the glass and had passed in a wrench. They were "fairly certain" who they were but were unable to locate them. The Attorney General, Premier E. C. Manning, adopted the report and issued at least parts of it, but it seemed somehow incomplete. There was no mention of a key or, were it the case, that no key had been required because someone had overlooked ensuring that the screen mechanism was locked. There was no mention of the wrench having been found or, were it the case, that the wrench which was found was not one designed for the screen mechanism. The question of whether the screen could have been removed from the window opening by one man (an outside accomplice could have helped little here since the window impeded access to the screen) was not addressed. The "two

---

[1] *In the opinion of one staff member, the shoulders were impossible, the hips worse. He theorized that Cook had lubricated his hips either with hoarded butter or soap stolen from the washroom. He would have been able to reach the fire escape in order to pull his shoulders through, employing one arm, and then his hips using both arms. An outside accomplice would have assisted by pulling on parts of Cook's anatomy but would have risked dismembering him. If the reader folds a half-inch off the width of a piece of letterhead, she will see that the opening was impossibly small.*

men" were not identified nor was there an explanation of the RCMP's inability to find them.

At least one newspaper was not happy with the report. *The Calgary Herald's* editorial of August 4 castigated the report as "leaving much to be desired." The editorial reviewed what was known of the escape apart from the report and ended by castigating the police: "The inability of the police to detect who might have helped him is not a creditable chapter in the police record and the half-explanation does not make it any better." Intended as a hay-maker, the conclusion was wide of the mark. The police were fairly certain who the accomplices were; they merely couldn't find them.

When I questioned a former senior officer of the RCMP about the escape, he replied, "Is this confidential? There was no outside assistance. They moved him from one room to another and forgot to check the screen to see whether it was locked. You know those guys. The first thing they do when they're thrown into a cell is check the bars. But of course the hospital authorities couldn't disclose that that's what happened."

It was an interesting explanation and it added a twist, but failed to answer many questions. One staff member remembered that Cook had been moved from one room to another, but could volunteer nothing more to throw light on the vexing questions of screens, mechanisms, wrenches and keys which remained whether there was one room or two. Moreover, the senior officer's confidence ("There was no outside assistance") did not square with what I was told by someone who was encouraged by the police to confess complicity: police pressure was so intense that he and his wife left for Vancouver where they remained until the heat subsided. He knew of one other to whom the same pressure was applied. Perhaps. The source had to be taken into account.

***

On March 15, 1960, a few days before the appeal court announced its decision to grant Cook a new trial, Dr J.P.S.Cathcart arrived at Fort Saskatchewan to interview Cook. The practise of the Department of Justice in Ottawa was to have condemned men psychiatrically evaluated as part of a commutation review, but whether to receive an opinion as to guilt or innocence or as to whether they were becoming unhinged is unclear.

Cathcart knew of the escape from the PMH - who didn't? - but he chose to question Cook as to why he hadn't fled Stettler after the crime: "I asked the prisoner why he didn't escape - clear out. He didn't seem to grasp my meaning, but finally saw my point and replied, 'Because I didn't feel guilty.' It seemed peculiar to me that he stayed in the vicinity after the murder and acting as if nothing had happened." If Cook's 'feeling' left something to be desired as a ringing denial of guilt, it nevertheless contributed something to an understanding of why Cook appeared to be trying to reach Stettler after the PMH escape which Cook now introduced into the Cathcart interview: "Prisoner asked me if I knew why he had escaped from Ponoka. 'Because I wanted to go to the funeral. I offered to pay the expenses. I wrote to my lawyer about it, but nobody would let me go. The police knew I wanted to get to Stettler, so I said if they're not going to let me go, I'll....'"

Cook mentioned his putative purpose for breaking out to two or three others, but was prohibited from doing so when it might have mattered. In the first trial, in an attempt to counter the prevailing opinion (he had escaped only in order to escape and hadn't quite made it), Main asked Cook to relate to the jury what he was later to tell Cathcart. Cook was prevented from doing so by Mr Justice Greschuk, seemingly to protect Main from a tactical error which Greschuk ostensibly thought Main had stumbled into. Bad enough, Greschuk said in effect, that Cook had escaped, but worse that the jurors should be reminded of it on the off chance that they had all forgotten it.

But plausible or not, it *was* Cook's story, and he should have been allowed to have its veracity tested. It was scarcely a matter of the mercifully forgotten terror which had gripped Alberta all coming flooding back if Main was not saved from his well-meaning error. Cook's explanation such as it was was relevant to the fundamental question of the guilty mind, yet Greschuk ruled against it as irrelevant and as being inimical to Cook's interest. With friends like Greschuk, who needed defense counsel?

The Calgary Herald of March 11, 1960 reported that during argument before the Appellate Division on whether Greschuk had erred in keeping Cook's explanation out, the Chief Justice observed that "he went too far in advising [Main] how to run his case", and in particular "in passing judgment on the admissibility" of the escape evidence proposed by Main to be adduced from Cook. In running his case Main was not at his best in arguing his right to examine Cook about the escape. He started strongly enough by arguing that Cook's explanation was "just as relevant...as any other matters concerning his conduct following the deaths of his family." "Knowledge of that escape," he said, "was given great publicity, was widespread throughout the province and indeed throughout the Dominion of Canada, and it seemed at the time to create an assumption on the part of the accused [sic] of trying to escape punishment for this offense, and for that reason I felt in fairness to the accused it should be cleared up."

Had Main stayed with this position it would not have prevailed. No matter what the argument, Greschuk made it clear he would see any mention of the escape as potentially harmful to Cook. None would be allowed, but at least, persisting in the attempt, Main would have gone down with all bedraggled flags flying. Instead he unaccountably backed off saying that the reason he wished to adduce the evidence was because he was afraid it would only come out in cross-examination, and with a faint "I am not going to press for it" he capitulated.

What Cook would have said had Main been allowed to draw out the purpose of the escape can only be guessed at. He had told Cathcart that he was trying to get to the funeral, just as in a letter to MacNaughton he had asked MacNaughton to turn heaven and earth to get him there. The funeral was held in Hanna on July 2. On that date MacNaughton received the letter part of which survives: "The doctor here tells me there not going to allow me to go to the funeral. I've just got to be there, please for Christ sakes arrange it. I've got about $90 they can have that for expenses. If you could only understand how much it means to me. There the only people in the world I have that care if I live or die. So please try and fix it so I can go.

"I truly hope you belive me, for nobody else thinks I am inncent. You probly dont know what it feels like to be completely alone, since there gone.

"That crying[1] wasn't because I feel sorry for myself because life was just getting good for all of us. Dad and I would have had a garage, he'd of been able to keep his own hours & not work so hard. Why? why did it happen. What did the kids ever do to anyone tell me that? I want to see

---

[1] *Referring to Sunday afternoon in the Stettler Detachment when he was first informed of the death of his father. MacNaughton was present.*

you as soon as you can make it if you'll come down here. Please try to get me to the funeral. Thanks. Bob Cook"

Readers will form their own opinions as to whether this letter was a genuine *cri de couer* or part of a hare-brained escape scheme. The difficulty with funeral attendance as a plausible reason lies in timing. The escape took place eight-and-a-half days after the funeral, twelve-and-a-half days after the discovery of the bodies, fifteen days after the murders. The date of the letter is unknown, but it was written prior to the day of the funeral since MacNaughton received it on that day. It is reasonable therefore to think that, even without Cook knowing the date for which the funeral was scheduled, he might think that if MacNaughton acted expeditiously, he could arrange it. But he cannot have thought more than - literally - two weeks after the crime that there was still a funeral to come which he was going to attend come hell, high water, screens, keys or the RCMP.

He told Staff Sergeant Beeching that he escaped because he wanted to visit the grave, becoming, as he went along, implausibler and implausibler. It may be that by then he appreciated the problem with the funeral timing and tossed off for Beeching's benefit something more washable. But then one thinks again of the MacNaughton letter, his telling Urban Holman he wanted to attend the funeral; the Cathcart interview and the last thing he ever wrote in his life, an overview, in which he again offered up the funeral. Like Stalin, he was an enigma wrapped in a riddle inside a mystery.

'Tis now the very witching time of night
When churchyards yawn, and hell itself breathes out
Contagion to this world; now I could drink hot blood
And do such bitter business as the day
  Would quake to look on.

HAMLET, *Act III, Scene ii*

CHAPTER 6

THE SCENE - STETTLER

The prairie's surrender of its dominion to the aspen parkland is marked by an indistinct line running northeast-southwest across central Alberta catching in its straggling progress the town of Stettler, lying 50 miles east of a point roughly mid-way between Calgary and Edmonton. To approach the town from the east or south is to detect it first as a faint presence on the horizon rimming the treeless prairie, and from the north or west to discover it among the poplar bluffs of the parkland. It is a prosperous town which wears its prosperity without ostentation, attractive in a conventional way, as pleasant as the surrounding countryside. Its inhabitants, about 5000 in 1959, were the strength of Social Credit in its heyday, when rural and small-town Alberta stood alone against the big cities, Calgary and Edmonton.

An Economic Development Board brochure proclaims a vision for Stettler: "Get a piece of the action. Take a look at Stettler!" and goes on to list the standard complement of amenities offered as inducement to industry to settle there and build Gary, Indiana in Alberta's green and pleasant land. There are, the brochure tells us, two railroads, two highways, swimming pools, natural resources, many-bedded hospitals, and "excellent music, arts and crafts programs available", as if they were kept on ice or could be brought in from out of town to meet an unexpected demand. The excellent programs are attested by the brochure's depiction of the masks of tragedy and comedy, side-by-side with pictures of a Hereford bull, a drilling rig, and a sportsman, gun aloft in the act of 'harvesting' something, perhaps meadow larks, perhaps whooping cranes, - it doesn't say.

The brochure identifies Stettler as the "Heart of Alberta" - some harmless chamber of commerce hype that doesn't mean much except perhaps in an extended and unintended sense. For Stettler has a reputation having nothing to do with a retail trading volume beyond the dreams of an economic development board. It is now outliving it, but it came as close in the past as anything Alberta has to offer to being a heart of darkness. The Board would fain have it otherwise, but rightly or wrongly Stettler and its image as a town periodically given to mass murder were once inseparable. There are three cases: Clark, Cook and Welty. Stettler is stuck with them which seems unfair since only Cook took place within the town limits.

The first opportunity *The Calgary Herald* had to cover the murder of the Cook family was 24 hours after the discovery of their bodies. While the news was news no longer, the *Herald's* readership was avid for details and, in its noon edition of Monday, June 29, 1959, it rose to an electrifying occasion with all it was able to gather by press time. The greater part of the front page was given over to the story: headline and lead story, and five photographs - three of children, one of the Cook house and one of an RCMP officer striding past the open greasepit and peering into it.

The Herald also ran a front-page story headed "Slayings in 1956 Recalled", and in it recalled to readers that three years before, the Clark case had fastened on a shocked province. For the paper's purposes, Clark had occurred close enough to Stettler to rate belonging to it even though, as it happened, the Clark murders had occurred about 20 miles out of town. Clark was a Social Credit MLA with a history of mental illness who, one Sunday morning in August, took down his .22 rifle and carefully killed his wife, three children and a sailor who had the wretched misfortune to be a weekend visitor to the Clark farm. He then waded into a nearby slough and committed suicide[1].

To identify the Clark murders with Stettler seems to be stretching it. Stettler happens to be in what was Clark's riding - a tenuous connection upon which to hang a reputation - but Joseph Van Blarcom, formerly a corporal attached to the Criminal Investigation Department of the RCMP in Red Deer was able to make it. He had been involved in both the Cook and Clark cases, and looking back on his years in the Force, seemed to share the general opinion of the Stettler area as some sort of incubus of mass murder. He had no explanation for it (as for example had an anonymous Edmonton woman quoted in *The Edmonton Journal* as being sure that "there is something in the air or the soil or the water down there"), but there it was: "While I was in Red Deer, there was one year in which there were 21 multiple deaths in that area." The area he spoke of happened to be the whole of central Alberta - his bailiwick as a plainclothes investigator - but it included Stettler. Not a few people would agree, particularly when they add to Cook and Clark the Welty case.

Like Clark, Welty had a history of mental illness which took a religious turn. Egged on by God - frequently the impetus to do murder - Welty crept up to a farm kitchen window one evening, and shot the farm couple. No matter that the farm was out of Stettler and that the murder barely made a multiple rating. Two and two made four. Stettler again. Helter Stettler.

***

This somewhat unfair reputation was fixed for the foreseeable future with the Cook murders. The scene of them was unprepossessing: a small house which sat dowdily two blocks west of Main Street at the town's

---

[1] *The Clark case was not without some black humor. Constable Al Morrison, then of the Stettler RCMP, remembers interrogating the neighbor who had discovered the murder-suicide. "Stroud, Pringle and me were together on the Clark case. Some farmer gave a statement to us. First of all, he said, he went into the back porch and discovered the body of the sailor. Then he went into the kitchen where the body of Mrs Clark lay, and then into the front room where the bodies of the three children had been neatly laid side-by-side, each of them drilled through the forehead with a single shot. 'At that point,' he told us, 'I knew something was wrong.'"*

northern limits. The house faced east on an unfenced corner lot at the intersection of Railroad Avenue - an east-west truck route flanked on the north by the CPR right-of-way - and 52nd Street. In 1959 both streets were unpaved and there were no sidewalks. The house was a square four-room bungalow built, at a guess, in 1910. The wooden shingles were unpainted and curling, the drop siding white and peeling, the trim green and fading - not one of Stettler's show homes, but not without a certain down-at-the-heels charm which could have been enhanced had it been occupied by someone with a gift of making the best of a bad job, or by someone not burdened with raising a family of five small children. It was bought for $5300 cash in 1953 by Daisy Cook whose name alone appeared on the title.

As an afterthought to the original construction, someone prior to the Cooks had added what used to be called a sunporch - a gable-ended structure through which the interior was reached from the front. Seven windows extended across the length of the porch facing on to 52nd Street, and three were set into the north wall looking on to the truck route. A scraggly tapestry of virginia creeper covered most of the seven windows, and no view of any portion of the interior was afforded from any position on the street. Entrance to the porch was through a door in its south end reached by two steps.

On the south side of the house the livingroom looked out on an overgrown lilac hedge and a lawn - a rough greensward of quackgrass which withstood the abrasive passage of the Cook children and their friends. Completing the landscaping, a large poplar stood at the 52nd Street curb, providing a canopy for the unpaved path which led through two wooden posts standing as a gate at the property line. The lot was unfenced.

What had been the exterior door of the house prior to the addition of the porch now opened from the living room into it. A jerry-built partition divided the north third of the porch from the remainder, making of it a small room which had been used by Cook from time to time as his bedroom. Since Cook was frequently called away from home by the compelling demands of the law, Daisy had pressed it into use for storage. It contained a clutter of unused furniture and cardboard boxes mostly containing children's winter clothing.

The door leading from the porch into the living room had a full-length window set into it, and the south end of the living room expanded into a bay window. These two graceful features fought a valiant but losing battle to redeem the rest of the room which was furnished with what can best be described as make-do taste, and overall, in spite of a comfortably lived -in look, it was neat and clean. When the police arrived they found not so much as a vase overturned, but there was blood splattered on a veneer chest, on the television screen, on the floor beside the front door, on the floor beside one of the easy chairs, on the folding door to the front bedroom, and seven feet, four inches high on the south wall.

The kitchen, which occupied the southwest quarter of the house, was surprisingly spacious and airy. It too was orderly and clean. Not much of evidential interest was found in it beyond a beer bottle which stood on a north wall counter and a number of unwashed coffee cups stacked beside the sink on the east wall. No bloodstains were found in the kitchen.

Three doorways opened into the kitchen: through the west wall from the garage; through the north wall from the back bedroom; and through the north end of the east wall from the living room. To walk from the door from the front porch to the kitchen required walking past the triple-wide doorway which led off the living room to the front bedroom. If the bedroom doors were open, there was an unrestricted view into the bedroom from the livingroom, particularly if walking towards the front door from the kitchen.

***

Attached to the house on its west side, also as an afterthought, was a lean-to garage: a single-car structure pedestrian access to which (apart from the door from the kitchen) was through a door in the southeast corner. Vehicle access was by way of the large doorway opening on the north wall. The interior of the garage was littered with the junk of the family of a man who may have been a good mechanic but who had something to learn of shop management. Identifiable in police photographs are four mounted and two unmounted tires, three car wheels, a 5-gallon can, a boy's bicycle, a disemboweled television set, four rubber boots, a worn straw broom, a dishpan, a lawnmower and what might have been a wooden bed-frame. Stacked haphazardly in various places is a motley mess of cardboard boxes, gallon cans, bleach bottles and 'other goods too numerous to mention' - as auctioneers' ads have it. There were also some guns hanging on the west wall and some shotgun shells on a bench which, in light of what had happened, were not without a measure of interest. The garage served a double function as a garage and as the end of the line for the overflow junk of a large family. For the Cook family to throw anything out was, it appeared, for them to throw it in the garage.

The rough concrete floor of the garage was oil-stained, unswept and covered over much of its area with flattened cardboard cartons. Set in the floor was what was termed throughout both trials a greasepit, about two-and-a- half feet wide by four feet long and five feet deep. It was covered, when it was covered, with loose planks set flush in a recess in the floor. When the garage was first examined by the police, the planks were in place and concealed by flattened cardboard; nothing suggested a greasepit beneath it. The RCMP suspected when they first entered it that they were on a murder trail bloodier than any in their experience, but at first they did not know they were within a few feet of the end of a short trail. Given what they had then seen in the rest of the house, their first inspection of the garage could not be said to be perfunctory, but it was hurried and urgent; they were not stopping at this point to look for evidence. Daisy Cook was a good housekeeper, but her writ stopped at the kitchen door beyond which was her husband's cluttered domain. There was a surfeit of evidence in it, but it would require deliberate and unhurried sifting to fit it into a rational framework. The sifting would come later as would a framework.

***

A clockwise tour of the house starting at the front door and through the livingroom to the kitchen and to the garage brought one back through the kitchen and into the back bedroom. Here the three boys - Gerald, Christopher and Patrick - slept. The furnishings were spare and utilitarian: a double cot in the southeast corner, as single cot in the corner diagonally opposite, and two dressers standing along the walls. There was little of interest here to the investigators apart from blood where blood is normally not found: on three walls and on two mattresses. A strip of wallpaper was removed and sent to the Crime Detection Laboratory in Regina which reported that the attempt made to wash it had succeeded only in driving traces of blood into the grime.

Between the back and front bedrooms was a walk-through closet common to both. On a shelf in the closet the police found the black oxfords which, five days earlier, had been issued to Cook in the penitentiary. Stains on them had the appearance of dried blood. There was damp mud in the insteps.

The front bedroom was called throughout the trials the master bedroom. The name, a convenience, was more reminiscent of a real estate salesman's advertising copy than descriptive of the drab reality of the room in which Ray and Daisy Cook and their two daughters slept. Almost half the width and two-thirds of the length of the nine-by-nine foot room was taken up by a double bed against the east wall. Most of the rest of the floorspace was occupied by a double-deck army bunk standing against the west wall, a four-drawer dresser between the two beds and a low dresser in the southeast corner.

On first looking into the master bedroom, the police were rather quicker off the mark than had been "some farmer" in reaching his wild surmise that something was wrong at the body-strewn Clark farm. Bodies would have been almost superfluous to the evidence of murder found in the master bedroom. The scene was one of carnage - a bloody quarry crying on havoc. While they never admitted as much (there was a curious reticence on the part of the RCMP which we shall look at later), there is a pronounced possibility that long before they began their search of the house, the police suspected that disaster had befallen the Cook family. If so, their first few seconds in the house did nothing to confirm such suspicion, if any, since the porch was innocent of evidence[1] and in the few steps across the living room to the kitchen they did not happen to notice the blood splattered on the tv and elsewhere. There was little reason then to examine a wall beside which no human traffic could move (because of furniture) to see whether there happened to be any blood near the ceiling, as there in fact was.

RCMP officers testify in a trial as if they were schooled in taciturnity. Their tight-lipped demeanor suggests that if swords formed part of their dress uniforms, they would fall on them before they would admit to ever having been affected by anything they have seen, and they have seen it all. But none of the investigators moving cautiously through the Cook house on a warm summer morning *had* seen it all, not on this scale. Yet such was the measured guardedness of their expression in giving evidence, that for all they left an impression that what they had discovered was other than all in the day's work, they could have been forensic accountants grinding their leaden way through evidence of a bank manager suspected of skimming the odd day's take.

---

[1] *Apart from a newspaper which, like the coffee cups on the kitchen counter, was wrongly perceived as having no evidentiary significance. See Chapter 21.*

But if they were policemen they were also human and it seems improbable that they would not have recoiled at the gore which confronted them in the master bedroom. Worse was to come, but this was bad enough. They had visited the house the night before, and we will see that while they had not expected to find confirmation of Cook's jejune explanation for the family's absence, neither had anything they'd seen prepared them for the discovery the following morning of that family's annihilation in a night of unexampled violence.

The master bedroom was awash in the evidence of it. Elsewhere in the house the perpetrator (Cook's term as he struggled in his notes to give legalistic expression to his argument) had painstakingly attempted to remove blood from floors, from furniture, from the very wallpaper. But in the master bedroom it was clear that panic had seized him. The attempt at concealment continued there, but it now showed signs of a man emerging from a semi-coma into the recognition of the enormity of his act and of his peril.

The evidence of panic was everywhere. Pieces of the shotgun, fractured at least in part elsewhere in the house, were gathered up and thrown on the bed and a welter of clothing thrown over them in a crude effort at concealment. A bloodstained blue suit and an equally bloodstained shirt and a tie were stuffed under the mattress. Drawers and the closet were emptied and their contents thrown on the bed where they partially covered a sickening feculence of blood, brain matter, particles of flesh, shards of bone and the bodily excreta which discharge involuntarily on violent death. Thirty-six hours later the mattress was still damp to the touch of one of the less fastidious investigators who brought himself to poke an inquiring finger into it.

***

The full basement was partitioned with unfinished plywood into an open center area and three rooms: a combination laundryroom-bathroom, a vegetable storage room[1] and a small bedroom which, a few days before the murders the bedroom had been vacated by Leonard Gurney, a self-

---

[1] *One of two storage rooms which played roles - one insignificant, one major - in the Cook story. See Chapter 26. This one was labeled a root cellar by the police draftsman who diagramed the house and who appears not to have been far removed from antecedents on a prairie farmstead.*

employed oilfield trucker who had occupied the room for two-and-a-half years. The room had suited both his and the Cook's convenience since his hours were irregular and at night he could reach or leave his room without disturbing the sleeping family. His access was through the small door in the south-east corner of the garage and thence through the kitchen to the stairwell which reached the basement from behind a cabinet set out from the kitchen's north wall.

Gurney was called as a Crown witness at the preliminary inquiry and at both trials. His evidence had no particular relevance to the issues, but was not without interest because of what had been his recent nearness to the crime scene. In physical terms there had of course been a nearness to the murdered family as well, but it seems not to have ripened into the easygoing familiarity one might have thought would have developed between a truck driver, a mechanic and the mechanic's family. For example, he had trouble recalling the names of the children, at the preliminary inquiry at least. This is perhaps neither here nor there; one either warms to children and endows them with identity, or they are merely underfoot in which case they go nameless. By the first trial however, his memory - which Main in the preliminary inquiry called "pretty defective" on the matter of the children's names - had improved and he was able to recite them without hesitation.

What was more perplexing, given the length of his tenancy and his evidence that he was at least close enough to the adult Cooks to spend the odd evening with them watching television, was that he was not able to bring himself to use their given names. Whatever the reason - out of deference to the memory of the departed perhaps - Gurney referred to them throughout as "Mr and Mrs Cook", as "the deceased", as "the people who owned the place", as "the residents", as "the people who lived upstairs", but never once as Ray and Daisy which, those being their names, was how they were universally referred to both in court and in real life. Gurney's personality appeared as remote as he himself understandably wished to make clear he had been from the events which had engulfed his former residence.

His evidence touched on his having left Stettler to take up new employment in Edmonton eight days prior to Cook's return to Stettler from Prince Albert. Moreover, Gurney himself had returned to Stettler and to the Cook house on June 22, the day before Cook's release from the penitentiary. He was not asked why he returned, but whatever the reason it was not to pick up his belongings - primarily some clothing - which he had left behind on June 17, there "not being room in the cab of the truck for them." He intended to return a second time to pick up his belongings, having left them "on permission of the landlady there" but meanwhile the death of the landlady there intervened. He nevertheless took a few things with him either on June 17 or June 22: he took his shotgun shells.

As well as being somewhat distant in his interpersonal relationships, Gurney didn't appear to connect all that intimately with his physical surroundings. For example, he was not aware that there was a greasepit in the garage floor. The fact caught Cook's attention, not surprisingly since Gurney had walked across a corner of the garage (from the southeast door to the kitchen landing) more or less daily for a couple of years. In a marginal note Cook made in the preliminary inquiry transcript he expressed his skepticism: "His eyes must be pretty bad. We, my Dad and I used it when we were working on the 52 Chev I was to get. I am pretty shure he couldn't help but know it was there." Furthermore, Gurney himself had used the garage to work on his own car on one occasion. In the preliminary inquiry, it had been to "fix a spring or something", but in the first trial his defective memory continued to improve since "I worked on my carburator in my own car."

Cook's skepticism proved to be ill-founded however, and although Main shared it as early as the preliminary inquiry when his courtroom notes reflect puzzlement at Gurney's never having detected hollowness resonating underfoot[1], much less his never having seen it when it stood open (which was to assume it did on occasion), and although he questioned Gurney at length in the preliminary inquiry about his lack of knowledge of the pit's existence, he decided nothing was to be gained by exploring the denial further, and he dropped it apart from a couple of routine questions in the first trial.

Dunne too appeared to think that nothing much of value was to be obtained from Gurney, and that belaboring the fact that Gurney knew nothing of the pit (a single question put by Anderson had established in

---

[1] *Gurney would not have had to walk across the closed-in pit to reach the landing from the southeast door. See Chapter 23 and Plate 12. In distancing himself from the greasepit, he went further than he needed to go:*

"If you were told that there was a pit located in the floor of the garage in the Cook residence, could you say that that was correct or not?"

"I never saw a pit in the Cook residence."

"In the floor of the garage in the Cook residence?"

"I never saw one there either."

the second trial that Gurney was not "aware of the fact that there was a ~~truck driver~~
greasepit in the floor of the garage") was pointless. What mattered was
who *did* know of it (knew, that is, that it was there as a place to conceal
the bodies), and since Gurney was not one of them, as Dunne would
know from the first-trial transcripts, he allowed Gurney to leave the
stand without the searching questioning the subject might have seemed
to call for, if only for the light it might have thrown on the identity of
whomever *might* have known of it.

In other words, did the physical factors which prevented Gurney's
knowledge of it (planks invariably in place and cardboard covering
them) apply in favor of everyone else? On the face of it they would as
far as Gurney would know (if he didn't know of the pit, he couldn't know
if others might have); nevertheless there was scope for the cross-
examination which might have provided a clue to the identity of
someone who did. Someone - for the defense lawyers - apart from Cook
who, no one needed reminding, knew of it.

But in sum, Gurney was seen as having little to contribute, and he bowed
out of the *Cook* trials having contributed it. That he was there at all was
solely because of his association with the Cooks - a landlord and tenant
relationship with some casual social overtones - which had happened to
terminate about a week before the murders. We too take our leave of
him for the time being. Since he was a hunter owning both guns and
ammunition, we will have reason to return to him briefly in later chapters
in considering the problems posed by the murder weapon and the
ammunition used in it.

***

After June 28, 1959 it was no longer possible to look at the Cook house
without seeing it. Where before nothing about it was likely to have
registered on a first glance, and nothing merited a second, it now became
permanently imprinted on the minds of the people of Stettler. Those
who weren't drawn to it during the afternoon and evening of the day
when the news spread throughout Stettler like wildfire, to coin a cliché,
sooner or later found themselves coming to it to stand in the street or sit
in their cars speculating as to who had died in which rooms. The house
was the epicenter of an earthquake which had shaken Stettler to its
foundations.

Paradoxically, the imprint was the more indelible because the house was relentlessly ordinary and nondescript. No one expected Gothic turrets or belfries, but had the house been isolated on the outskirts of town, had its size been more commensurate with the magnitude of what had happened in it, had it been set apart in *any* way from a dozen other houses on that street and a hundred in Stettler, it would have been easier for the town to accept it as the scene of events bloody beyond the town's ability to admit them to its image. But it wasn't. Nothing distinguished it before the murders, and afterwards, to outward appearances, it had changed not an iota. There was not so much as a broken window; it had contained maniacal violence well. It sat there afterwards, as dumpy and benign in appearance as before, but it was precisely on that account that it was the more fearful - the banality of evil suggested by the banality of its setting.

Long after Cook's death, primeval fear, which the continued presence of the house did nothing to allay, gripped Stettler. The fear outlasted the house in the form in which Stettler had come to know it. It stood empty for a time and then, surprisingly, was not razed but moved a few blocks west, set on a new foundation and so extensively remodeled that no single feature of it, nor its outline, is now recognizable as once having been the modest home of Daisy Cook's menage. It had echoed the music of children's laughter, recoiled from the shrieking discordance of murder, stood boarded and silent - a compelling attraction from which townspeople and visitors alike recoiled in their turn, fascinated, contemplative, as silent as the object of their contemplation - and was now, what had seen the loss of so much of it, given new life.

The property on which it stood was sold by the Public Trustee to an investment company which built a walkup apartment on the site. Visitors are still driven by to have the site pointed out to them: "The house stood there. The garage...." The lower level of suites in the apartment is partially below ground level so that, standing in the north-easterly suite, an act of morbid imagination will remind the visitor that the bright, modern kitchenette occupies the same space that was once taken up by a greasepit which yawned in a garage floor, breathing out the contagion of most bitter business.

"Bonds to the whims of murder."

Isaac Rosenberg,
Break of Day in the Trenches

CHAPTER 7

THE SEARCH - SATURDAY

The sun which rose on Sunday, June 28, 1959 bringing to Stettler the promise of a summer day as lovely and temperate as only Alberta in the known world can offer, set on a town forever changed as if by the loss of innocence. For the eight RCMP officers completing their preparations at the Detachment at 11 am for the first full-scale visit to the Cook house, the day brought the promise of uncovering murder although that was a fact the RCMP held close to the chest throughout for some reason which continues to puzzle. Since nothing had aroused Sergeant Tom Roach's suspicion during his hurried examinations of the interior of the house eleven hours earlier, the preparations would have appeared an elaborate charade designed to conceal the obvious from any innocent who might have wandered by the Detachment that morning. A greeting may be imagined: "Morning Tom. What's happening?" "Oh nothing. We're just bringing a routine eight-man overkill capacity to a false pretenses investigation."

They were tough men and grim men, all of them tempered in the crucible of murder investigation: Staff Sergeant David Henley Beeching, Acting Sergeant Thomas Francis Roach[1], Corporal Joseph Luther Van Blarcom, Corporal Robert Denis Novikoff, Constable George Marshall Sproule, Constable Al A. Morrison, Constable Peter Thachik and Constable Allan Eugene Braden who remained throughout in the Detachment guarding Cook. All of them had seen death many times in many violent forms. As far as experience could, theirs had prepared them for anything they might encounter. But to a point. Nothing in the experience of any of them could have prepared them for the opening of the greasepit and confirmation of what they then knew they would find: the bodies of small children; for most cops the death of children is the worst thing they're called upon to deal with. No amount of experience makes the smell of death bearable and no description can convey the experience of it. When they lifted the cardboard and the first of the planks enclosing the pit, the stomach-churning smell came roiling from it and they drew back, breathing as shallowly as possible, steeling themselves for what was now required of them.

Murder speaks with most miraculous organ in Stettler as elsewhere, and before murder was confirmed by the discovery of the contents of the greasepit, the spectators had begun arriving, streaming around the barriers hastily thrown up on the nearby intersections to stop cars from approaching the house. Allowed to do so the spectators would have pressed in on the garage on foot. To prevent them from seeing into it however distant their vantage points, the garage doors were kept closed making of the garage a stifling charnel house in which, without gas masks, the police and two funeral home attendants worked two hours before the last of the bodies was bagged and they could emerge into the cleansing sunlight and uncorrupted air. One of the police officers was unable to stay the course and staggered from the garage, retching. He was excused from having to return.

Some of them were lucky enough not to have to assist in the garage, staying in the house proper to take measurements and photographs. The fingerprint man went around with his tiny duster and a jar of black powder. The 'ident' men tagged and initialed and bundled up what was of interest to them. When all of them had seen and done as much as they could absorb in one afternoon, two of them were assigned to remain in the house to guard against the likelihood of attempted entry by the

---

[1] *Roach, the NCO in charge of the Stettler detachment, became a full sergeant before Cook's second trial. He will be referred to as Sergeant throughout the balance of this narrative.*

souvenir hunters who would inevitably home in. A patrol car relieved them and checked the house periodically throughout the night. The next morning padlocks were installed and the house was boarded up. The last scene of that day's act was over.

***

The scene had opened with the arrival of the police at about 11 am, but the house had been visited by them twice before: shortly before and shortly after midnight 11 hours earlier, both times by Sergeant Roach accompanied by others. Before *them* the last visitor had been Cook himself who, he admitted at trial (denial would have been both pointless and futile), had come home at about 7 pm on Saturday evening. He was in the house for an hour, and in that time walked through both the livingroom and the garage at least twice. He noticed nothing, he said, not, say, the blood on the television set and 22 other locations in the livingroom and two bedrooms, and not that the master bedroom looked as if an anti-personnel bomb had exploded in it. Nor had he noticed anything out of the ordinary in the garage. At that time, rigor mortis had already passed. Putrefaction, described by the pathologist as advanced when he examined the bodies seven hours after their removal, had already set in. Whatever credulity the courtroom held in Cook's favor was stretched to the breaking point by his assertion that he had detected nothing out of the ordinary.

If there was any doubt, it was to be found in two facts, one of them doubtful: cardboard (and the planks) covered the greasepit and may have contained the odor; and Tom Roach was in the house and the garage shortly before midnight (about three hours after Cook) and he too failed to detect anything. He was there because Cook's story of the family having gone to BC didn't ring true. The search for the family - and perhaps even then for bodies - had started, and the question was could the Crown have it both ways? If, as Roach said, he detected nothing, could Cook be said to be lying if he too said he detected nothing? Evidently; but at most Roach merely misled the court which was small fry compared to the size of the fish Cook was seen to be frying.

***

115

Following his release from the penitentiary, Cook went home to Stettler for the first time in the evening of Thursday, June 25, and for the second in the evening of Saturday, June 27. The second trip was by a roundabout route which, as we have seen, started in Edmonton with the acquisition of the Impala, proceeded to Camrose, took in Whitecourt and Camrose again and ended in Stettler at the invitation of the Camrose police. Cook said it would have ended in Stettler in any event since he was expected to be there to take a phone call from his father, then in BC, early in the coming week.

The Camrose interlude, roughly 7 pm Friday to 5 pm Saturday (including the trip to Whitecourt) was generally viewed as something of a sideshow to the main action. Its chief importance was seen as having established Cook's movements for a 22-hour period commencing about 18 hours after the murders. His movements during the period (proved by Crown evidence) established that Cook had not been near Stettler in that 22 hours. This seems to have been accepted on all hands as of little relevance since the murders had taken place before the period and his highly suspicious actions in Stettler (in particular his hour-long visit to the house) after it.

Nevertheless there are some curious questions, four of them, that arise out of the Camrose interlude. They are asked here not because they are seen as bearing on the question of Cook's guilt - with one exception they don't[1] - but because the facts giving rise to the questions are seen as illuminating police methods, and police methods, in Stettler if not in Camrose, are one of the subjects of inquiry in this book. On occasion the police appear to see themselves as being beset by two hostile forces, the criminals and the rest of us. Criminals one can understand, but the rest of us are frequently at a loss to understand police reluctance to disclose what really happened in a given situation - the breakout from the PMH for example.

And so with Camrose; my best efforts have failed to put it together. If it is asked, reasonably, so what? given that whatever happened in Camrose had little to do with the murders in Stettler, I can only reply that it seems to me that there ought not to have been any unanswered questions about anything related to the Cook murders, however peripheral the

---

[1] *I do not wish to exasperate readers by continually holding up some facet of evidence and then referring them to a later part of the book, but an overview of the case makes it unavoidable. That is the case here where the exception referred to concerns the question of suitcases in the trunk of the Impala which was searched by the Camrose police. The question will be dealt with fully in Chapter 22.*

relationship appears to be. Light on a dark center sometimes comes unexpectedly from the periphery.

The first question concerns the reason for Cook's car being stopped by the Camrose police when he and his three teenage companions returned from Whitecourt on Saturday afternoon. Ostensibly Cook was stopped for a liquor check (Bell in fact searched the trunk and did not find any) supposedly because someone at the wedding dance at the Avenroy dancehall had phoned the police to lay a complaint of Cook having provided his companions with beer.

It seems straightforward since he had done precisely that. That no one at the dance knew Cook, ordinarily a bar to a specific complaint ("You'd better get out here; Robert Raymond Cook is giving beer to 15-year-old Lorraine Beasley!"), could be explained by resorting to the easily-described Impala ("A flashy white convertible with red upholstery is on its way into town. You'd better stop it. The driver was seen giving beer to the 15-year-old Lorraine Beasley!") But the problem here was one of timing. If someone phoned the police from the dancehall, why didn't Jack Bell, when he joined Cook and the other three for coffee at Junction Service later that same night, have a word with Cook then rather than waiting about 13 hours before getting around to stopping the car for a liquor check?

But the problem here was that no one at the wedding dance saw Cook, known to them or otherwise, supplying beer to the teenagers since Cook had taken the precaution of caching the beer in a ditch about two miles distant from the dance. Beasley was not called as a witness at either trial, but Feth and Teeple were. Neither was asked anything about a beer cache, nor for that matter anything about why they were stopped by the Camrose police. But the three were unanimous in telling me, independently of one another, of the existence of the cache and of the fact that such drinking as they did took place at the cache site and not at the dancehall. Which is to say it appears highly improbable that anyone at the dance complained to the police about minors being debauched because no one had any reason to do so.

Yet they were stopped. Why? To search the car for liquor Jack Bell told both the court and me. Charlie Starcheski told me (but not the court; he was not called as a witness) that the stop was made to search the car for liquor. Nor was Duff Franklin called to give evidence, but was there when Cook was stopped. The stop, he told me, was made to search the car for liquor. He went a step further: the complainant was Lorraine Beasley's mother. "The mother definitely phoned" were the words

Franklin used in the interview. It seemed conclusive: three police officers as one in the unanimity of their recollection. Liquor it was.

But the problem here was that Lorraine Beasley's mother did not phone the police to complain about Cook's corrupting her daughter or for any other reason. Her first and only contact with the police happened after a friend, Lois Paulson, phoned her to tell her she'd "better come down because your daughter is in trouble." Mrs Beasley was as adamant as Franklin. As was her daughter, but on a different tack. I asked Lorraine Beasley why the car was stopped: "Apparently someone had reported the ruckus at the Avenroy and that's why they stopped us." Later in the interview she came back to it: "I have a clear recollection that the reason they stopped us was because of the ruckus at the Avenroy." And the ruckus? "At the dance [Cook] did get into some kind of a fight. He made somebody mad, some man. It was just more or less an argument I think. I can't remember what it was about - maybe there was a little shoving and pushing around."

None of it - beer no one saw being consumed; a shoving match and some words about which no one was likely to have called the police - seems adequately to explain why three police officers thought it necessary to be positioned on the street waiting for Cook to drive into town, and the first of the subplot's four questions is who, if anyone, complained to the Camrose police and about what, if anything? Put another way, why were they waiting for Cook when he pulled into town from Whitecourt?

The second of the four questions: what was Bell doing at Junction Service at 4 am, Saturday, June 27? He had been on duty the previous evening when he cautioned Cook about the U-turn; was still on duty - or at least in uniform and driving a police car, if out of his jurisdiction - at 4 am Saturday when he pulled into Junction Service; and was still on duty at 5 pm that afternoon when he, Franklin and Starcheski made the liquor search. He was, if nothing else, tireless.

Starcheski had not known that Bell had been at Junction Service at that hour, and when I showed him the trial transcripts covering the episode, he expressed surprise: "There is something not quite right about this. Why would Bell be out at Junction Service? We didn't have jurisdiction. Why would he come back on shift unless it was a short change? But we wouldn't have had a short change on Saturday; it would be a Sunday for the short change. He must have worked until 8 am and then come back on shift on Saturday afternoon [in time for the liquor check.] But why a short change on Saturday?"

Beasley, Teeple and Feth (one half-expected them to sail off in a wooden shoe) all had a pronounced feeling that when the Impala pulled into town, the police had been out in force on the sidewalk for some time, waiting for them. At the first trial, Main asked Bell why Cook had been stopped. Its effect in the *Cook* trials ranged from minimal to non-existent, but in the first-trial transcripts, Bell's reply brings the reader to a full stop: "We had received a phone call from the RCMP that he was proceeding into town, so we went out on the street and stopped him."

The possible significance of the answer is easy to miss and Main did; there was no follow-up questioning to explore the surprising vista opened up by Bell's throwaway reply. Dunne, who may be taken to have pored over the first-trial transcripts in preparation for the second, either missed Bell's having told the court that the RCMP was watching Cook at a time when they had no known interest in him, or deemed it sufficiently unimportant that it could be safely ignored. He did not ask Bell any questions as to why the Impala had been stopped, and in particular he did not ask him the third of the present questions: why was the RCMP keeping tabs on Cook a full 19 hours before the RCMP knew they had "massive murder" (Roach's description) on their hands in Stettler?

When the car stopped in front of the police station, its occupants got out and Beasley broke into tears, never before having been accosted by the police and certain that she faced life imprisonment for whatever it was they had her on. Cook put an arm around her shoulder and attempted to comfort her, telling her that although he didn't yet know what the problem was, he would take the heat for it if he could. When she returned home to face heat Cook could not help her with - the fierce form of it emanating from a distraught and irate mother - she told her mother, "That's the best guy I was ever out with." He made an impression which, 30 years later, shone through the interview.

With the trunk of the Impala searched with negative results, the police told Cook's passengers they could leave and asked him to come into the police station. He was questioned briefly - about what is not known. He informed them of his intention to return to Stettler and was told that someone would be down later to serve him with a summons on some unnamed offense. And thus the fourth question: why was Cook not charged with whatever they had him for rather than postponing doing so to some indefinite future date requiring that someone make a 160 mile round trip to serve a summons which could have been served on the spot?

Add that Franklin had been in the RCMP in Stettler, knew Cook and knew therefore that the man he was interrogating was not Ray Cook, and the subplot thickens. Franklin told me that he instructed Bell to check out the Impala, knowing that however Cook had come by it, it smelled, but he was at a loss to explain why he himself did not detain Cook long enough to permit the necessary telephone calls to be made.

Only to a paranoiac mind which sees in every police action a dark conspiracy to thwart the truth ever being known, or which, in the instant case, thinks that the police were on to the murders and on to Cook long before he ever got back to Stettler the second time, does any of the Camrose interlude make any sense. Of course. They were keeping him under surveillance and giving him enough rope to hang himself but, for their own obscure reasons, chose not to divulge that information to a world with more than a passing interest in knowing. So went the laboriously contrived theory with nothing but some questionable reasoning and suspicion to support it.

Recently I canvassed the whole of the Camrose interlude with a friend who, with five years experience as a detective in his 13 years with the Edmonton City Police, was versed in the workings of the police mind and viewed them with ironic detachment. Everything I threw at him about the Camrose interlude he fielded with unflappable aplomb. Whatever the police do, he was saying, only another policeman can understand. You have to have been there.

In his persuasive opinion everything came down to two factors: a known criminal, newly released and a car which, however Cook had acquired it, had not been purchased with the proceeds of the sale of pop bottles. The rawest rookie would not need to be told twice to look twice; the combination of the two factors was a red flag, and everything - the liquor, the warnings, all of it - which happened after Bell's first sighting of the Impala could be explained in terms of a stolen car investigation. Cook was being given enough rope true enough, but for the routine offense of fleecing someone out of the Impala. Given enough time, he would have hanged himself on that offense had not the less routine offense of murder intervened. And yet? as Lytton Strachey used to say. And yet?

***

120

He arrived in Stettler for the last time ever at about 7 pm Saturday, but was in no hurry to go directly home. He drove up and down Main Street one or two times, in his own eyes at least and probably in the eyes of others the cynosure of all admiring attention. As Giffard Main was to put it more than once by way of reinforcing the obvious, the Impala was indeed "a gaudy and eye-catching vehicle." Gaudy may not have earned him the gratitude of General Motors, but eye-catching it certainly was: a brand-new glistening white convertible, top down, red Naugahyde upholstery shining, chrome gleaming, paper rosettes streaming from the aerial, radio playing and at the wheel a young, handsome, well-proportioned man seemingly with nothing more on his mind (there's the rub; there may have *been* nothing more on his mind; he had successfully compartmentalized the unthinkable and put it out of mind) than whether he'd be lucky enough to spot a woman worthy of him and his car.

The cruise proved fruitless and he turned for home. For his actions in the house for the next hour we have only his account and (his evidence relating to two suitcases and a small metal box apart[1]) there is no reason to question any of what he said he did. He may have done more than he was prepared to say he'd done - Mr Justice Greschuk was to suggest the dark possibility[2] - but it appears certain he did at least this much: He parked the car at the front of the house and went in by the front door. He crossed the livingroom to the kitchen, passing the triple-wide doorway to the master bedroom. He went through the kitchen to the basement where he washed up in the house's only bathroom. In what had been Gurney's bedroom he spotted Gurney's sports jacket and a car coat. He took them with him to the kitchen where he took a bottle of beer from the refrigerator. While drinking it, he spotted the suitcases on the floor near the portable sewing machine on the south wall and the metal box on the kitchen table. Because, he said, he thought his parents had forgotten them when they left for BC, he decided to take them with him since he was going to be going to BC - a story which might well have caused any minds remaining open in the jury box to close with an audible click. He backed the Impala up to the garage (where it was seen by a neighbor) and opened the sliding door. He carried the suitcases and box through the garage to the car and put them in the trunk. He closed the sliding door, walked back through the garage, through the house (passing the triple-wide doorway a third time) and out the front door, carrying Gurney's clothes. He drove back to Main Street.

***

[1] *Referred to above. See Chapter 22.*

[2] *See Page 143.*

Meanwhile, over the past 24 hours, a storm had been brewing at Hood Motors in Edmonton which was to gather strength and fury before breaking around Cook's head. The previous afternoon, with the car almost ready for delivery, the salesman, Leonard Amoroso, left the lot to phone Hood's insurers to see whether they would issue a binder to carry the car over the weekend, Cook having promised to return Monday morning to show Hood he had transferred the insurance on the trade-in station wagon to the Impala. Cook had not yet signed Hood's Application for Financing. Nor had he signed the conditional sales contract which Hood would assign to GMAC to permit it to be paid the purchase price. Amoroso returned to find Cook, and the new car, gone.

Amoroso was nothing if not zealous in pursuit of his employer's interest, not to mention his own. He set off in that pursuit, going first to the Myhaluk residence (how he knew of them or their address is not clear[1]), but the Myhaluks could not help him. Cook had given Amoroso his Stettler address and phone number. Amoroso phoned a few times that evening and again the following day but no one answered. He then left Edmonton for two central Alberta resort communities, Gull Lake and Sylvan Lake. There is no known reason for him thinking that Cook might be at either place, but some for thinking Cook might have gone home. However Amoroso did not go to Stettler. He was reluctant to be interviewed, but did disclose in a telephone conversation that he felt Cook's leaving Hood Motors without having signed all the documents was nothing more than oversight, and he fully expected Cook to return on Monday morning with proof of insurance, thus raising the question of why he felt it necessary to track down Cook. I did not ask him.

Meanwhile, Amoroso's sales manager, "Curly" Marvin, decided to take matters into his own hands. As a GM man he phoned the only GM man in Stettler he knew: George McTaggart. McTaggart knew Cook and - what else? - liked him even though two years earlier Cook had stolen a car from him[2]. Cook was employed by McTaggart at the time as was Ray who had been instrumental in McTaggart hiring his son who, Ray hoped, would be encouraged in the rehabilitation process by steady employment. The hope was short lived. Cook had reason to think the police were closing in on him in connection with a Bowden Treasury

---

[1] *Myhaluk had been at Hood with Cook earlier in he afternoon, but it is doubtful that, say, Myhaluk gave his name as a credit reference.*

[2] *In his two or so weeks at McTaggart Motors he stole more than one car although, in his mind, the others were merely borrowed. He would take a car in the night, head out for a break-in and return the car by morning.*

Branch break-in. Deciding on flight, he stole a McTaggart Motors car and fled for Edmonton and later Vegreville. Four break-ins later he was caught and sentenced to his last-ever penitentiary term. *last Pen term*

McTaggart knew of Cook's most recent release - he had seen him when Cook was wandering around Stettler on Thursday afternoon - and he quickly realized that the man Marvin knew, at second-hand, as Ray Cook was unquestionably his son Bob. He told Marvin as much. Marvin then phoned Roach. Marvin was not called at either trial, but I was told by Roach that Marvin said nothing much more than that Ray Cook hadn't signed some finance documents and that he, Marvin, was uneasy. Roach may have been keeping some of it back since it is unlikely Marvin would not have told Roach what McTaggart had told him: Bob Cook, a man with an impressive history of car theft, appeared to McTaggart to have changed his *modus operandi* from hot-wiring to false pretenses to meet the challenge of getting out of a new car showroom with a new car. He had, so to speak, hoodwinked Hood.

Roach's response to the Marvin call was unusual if he merely thought he had to run down Ray Cook to get him to go back and sign some documents, and it was unusual even if, for a reason not to be found in the Marvin call as Roach remembered it, Roach was already thinking false pretenses. The usual police reaction to a routine false pretenses complaint, if there appears to be the prima facie possibility of criminality, is to assign the file to one of the more junior members who then shuffles it to the bottom of a pile of ongoing investigations to be looked at when time permits. If it appears to be a civil matter only, the complainant will be shuffled out the door towards his lawyer.

Roach was at home watching television when Marvin called. He immediately phoned the Detachment office and instructed Constable Allan Eugene Braden to "pick up" Cook (Braden's first-trial evidence) or, his second-trial evidence, to "find" him. There may be here a trivial distinction without much of a difference between Braden's two versions, but both versions - the former more emphatically than the latter - suggest Roach knew Cook was either on his way to or already in Stettler. He cannot have been told as much by Marvin who, for all he knew and like the hapless Amoroso, might well have thought of Cook as heading for, say, Spitzbergen rather than Stettler.

Driving south on Main Street, Braden spotted Cook heading north. He signaled and Cook stopped. He asked Cook to accompany him to the Detachment but Cook did better: he drove there ahead of Braden (who had to execute a U-turn) and was waiting when Braden pulled up.

Braden took a hurried look in the Impala's trunk and then asked Cook to accompany him inside. A half hour had elapsed since Marvin's call to Roach.

Roach decided he would not leave the early investigation to Braden. Braden was qualified to handle false pretenses, and it may have been nothing more on Roach's part than why not give the boys a hand? Still, although Roach was not a man given to such conceits himself, there seems almost to have been a sixth sense at work in his decision. He arrived at the Detachment office (which was next door to Roach's residence) in advance of Braden and Cook.

In the few minutes he had before their arrival, Roach scanned the police bulletin containing photographs of recently released criminals. Cook was pictured - the first likeness of Cook Roach had seen. All the Cooks were strangers to Roach who, in the 11 months since he had taken over the Detachment, had not had occasion to meet or hear of Ray and Daisy Cook although he learned later from his wife that Gerry Cook, "red-headed like his mother", had been brought home one day after school by Roach's son Dennis for cookies and milk. If it could be called even that much, it was the only brush Roach had had with a member of the Cook family. He was about to get to know the surviving member of it more than he might have wished.

Roach's interrogation of Cook began immediately. Cook told for the first time substantially the story he stayed with until his death, but he larded it with falsehoods. He informed Roach he had driven his family to Edmonton in the station wagon where they were to catch a train for the West Coast, changing this later in the evening to his having left them in Stettler on Thursday night after plans had been agreed upon for their departure - he wasn't sure when. They would phone him on the following Monday or Tuesday[1] - he wasn't sure when - to make the arrangements for him to pick them up in BC. The trip back from BC was to be in the convertible - not the car for transporting a family of eight the station wagon would have been it might have been thought, but there it was. Cook was to experience great difficulty attempting to explain away the obvious, and indeed he never managed to do so.

Roach removed Ray Cook's wallet from Cook. It contained the station wagon's registration certificate, Ray Cook's driver's license and the usual assortment of documents found in hip-pocket wallets. How did Cook explain it? His father had given it to him to facilitate trading in the

[1] *He later changed this to Tuesday or Wednesday. See Appendix A, Q. 49.*

station wagon; he needed proof of ownership. And the driver's license? Cook had lost his and since his father had gone to BC by train, he'd have no need of it until his return. He ended by telling Roach his father would clear everything up when he returned - how, in Cook's mind, he would be getting home was now uncertain since his ride had just evaporated - which may have been nothing more than an audacious but not very promising gambit to win release and forestall police examination of the house.

Roach left the room to make a number of telephone calls: three to George McTaggart; to neighbors to ask whether they'd seen any recent activity around the Cook house; and to an employee of Modern Machine, Ray's employer. Without the calls Roach knew that he had enough to charge Cook with false pretenses. After them he felt strongly that there was more, much more, afoot. He now knew Ray Cook had not shown up for work on Friday, and from what he had learned from the neighbors, he did not expect he would find him at home. He did not believe anything Cook had told him, most ominously that the family had gone to BC. At 10 pm he charged Cook with false pretenses and placed him under arrest. It was time to have a look at the house.

***

The false pretenses charge was a convenience to permit Roach to hold Cook while he started his search for the missing family. He had 36 hours before he had to bring Cook before a magistrate on a charge he intended to pursue, or free him. The house would be the starting point, but rather than having one of his officers accompany him, he did a puzzling thing. He phoned Joe Haug, a mechanic at Modern Machine, and explained the developing situation. Haug offered to go over to the house and report back to Roach, but Roach insisted on picking him up and taking him to the house with him. This visit established only that there was no one home, and remains a puzzle to Haug ("I'm damned if I know why Roach called me" he told me), as evidently it was to the Crown. Haug was called as a witness at the preliminary inquiry but at neither trial.

His visit with Haug was the first of two Roach made that night. He took Haug home, returned to the Detachment, phoned Staff Sergeant Beeching in Red Deer and returned to the house at about 12:30 am on

Sunday now accompanied by Constable Al Morrison. Throughout Roach's testimony at the preliminary inquiry and at both trials confusion concerning these two visits was rampant: which parts of the house did Roach go into on which visits, which doors were locked and which were not, even whether someone other than, or in addition to, Morrison accompanied Roach on the second visit.

None of this was cleared up by cross-examination (although Main took a stab at it in the first trial but succeeded in having nothing clarified) but it is not particularly important unless as illustration of how imperfect and unexacting the trial process is, and I do not propose to subject it to analysis, jumping from police witness to police witness and from transcript to transcript making debating points at the RCMP's expense. Suffice it perhaps to say that the second visit (which has been included in this chapter as part of Saturday's search although it occurred early on Sunday morning) was merely prologue to what Roach now had an idea he faced in the morning, although he had as yet no idea of its enormity. He was curiously reluctant to admit his suspicions were aroused on Saturday, particularly after the second tour through the house which was conducted by flashlight - "just a cursory examination of the house" he called it. He did happen to notice "a jumble of clothing" on the double bed in the master bedroom, but he could not say how wide the doors to the room were open.

The question was not unimportant. The doorway contained two doors: a single panel hung on the left side of the frame (looking into the bedroom) and a hinged double panel on the right side. Both swung into the bedroom. If the doors were partially open only as much as is shown on the police diagram of the ground floor[1], Cook could not have seen the condition of the bedroom without going into it.

But there is no evidence showing the exact position of the doors when the police arrived on Sunday morning. The single police photograph of the master bedroom doorway[2] shows the left-hand door open and out of sight, and the left-hand panel of the two-panel right-hand door concealed behind the right panel permitting a partial view of the - now stripped - bed. But the stripping indicates the photograph was taken late in the investigation and tells us nothing of the position of the doors when Cook and then Roach were in the house on Saturday. Nor was the evidence of the police investigators of the position of the doors when they arrived

[1] *Plate 32.*

[2] *Plate 8.*

helpful: "It was open. How wide it was open I don't know." "I know there was an opening from there to the bedroom from the livingroom." "It was partially open as I recollect." "It was a light panelling type of door and to my recollection it was ajar." "It was open allowing access to the room. It wasn't completely open." If the doors were wide open when Cook was there on Saturday, permitting a clear view of the bed as he crossed from the kitchen to the front door; if he closed them in his ineffective attempt at concealment why not close them completely? There were things to be done in the house besides drink beer if he was concerned to cover bloody tracks which could have been made by a herd of rampaging elephants for all their inconspicuousness.

Cook of course claimed he saw nothing amiss in the bedroom; he could not have admitted otherwise. But if there was any doubt, he seems not to have received the benefit of it. Roach however did see something amiss in the bedroom (suggesting he peered into it from the doorway if the right-hand doors concealed the bed): a jumble of clothing on the bed. Perhaps however amiss wasn't the precise word for it for although he had seen more than Cook would admit having seen, "there was nothing that particularly aroused [his] suspicion."

To be sure, there were significant differences between Cook's one-hour sojourn and Roach's flashlight examination. Cook was in the house about four times as long as Roach and thus more likely to have noticed anything out of the ordinary. Cook's visit was in daylight, Roach's after dark without the benefit of lights (which were working but which were not employed by the police), making observation for Cook easier than for Roach under his self-imposed handicap of the darkness of midnight. On the other hand Roach was there to confirm his mounting suspicions, where Cook, to believe him for the moment, had nothing more on his mind than a beer, a change of clothes, and a convertible.

CHAPTER 8

THE SEARCH - SUNDAY

On the face of it, Roach's decision to call his staff sergeant in Red Deer late Saturday night might be seen as the action of a policeman lacking a sure touch. So far as he was prepared to disclose everything in a courtroom, what Roach then had was false pretenses and nothing more. He had searched the house and there was nothing that particularly aroused his suspicion. But an acting sergeant of the RCMP does not normally phone his superior late at night to inform him that he has scooped a man he believes "made a misrepresentation of a matter of fact" knowing it to be false and "made with a fraudulent intent to induce [Amoroso] to act upon it" as the Criminal Code, which has the last word in such things, has it.

False pretenses was cut-and-dried; Roach had him, but suspicion snowballed from the moment Cook opened his mouth to explain the car and the family's absence - a story, Roach told me, he dismissed as untrue in the act of hearing it for the first time. He quickly learned that Ray Cook had not reported for work on Friday which was the more unusual since a particular customer had an appointment to have his car worked on by Ray that day. He now knew the family had not been seen by neighbors for the whole of Friday and Saturday. He had learned nothing in the visit to the house with Joe Haug - apart from what he may have detected in the garage; a matter of conjecture - but the rest was enough to justify phoning Beeching who told him, "Whatever you do, don't let him go." And it was enough to call for his second visit to the house that night.

After the call from Roach, Beeching began to assemble in Red Deer a team of investigators: Joseph Van Blarcom, a plainclothes detective, and Robert Novikoff and George Sproule, both members of the Identification Section and both skilled photographers and fingerprint analysts. Beeching, Novikoff and Sproule arrived in Stettler at 7 am. on Sunday morning. For four hours after their arrival, the 'team' (they may not have thought of themselves with that civic booster mindset), augmented by the arrival of Van Blarcom at 9:30, made what can only have been exacting preparations when, to the lay mind, it might have seemed a matter of nothing more than deciding to go over and have a look.

***

While the members of the team were making their preparations, Roach was otherwise engaged. He wanted to have a look at Cook's clothing and asked him to remove it. To Giffard Main it seemed unusual that a man held only on a charge of false pretenses should have his clothes examined, and at the preliminary inquiry he taxed Roach with it:

"Was it customary when a man is arrested on a charge of false pretenses such as this to strip him completely?"

"Not customary."

"Why did you do it in this case?"

"Well, it was done - he was lodged in the cell as he was. I don't want to mislead you. That was removed from him some time later."

It is not possible to say what Main thought he had at this point, but whatever it was, it was not the why of stripping a man charged with false pretenses. Main continued:

"Was that removed from him after he was charged with murder?"

"No sir, before."

"Before what?"

"It would be sometime before or after - I am not positive - on Sunday morning or Sunday afternoon."

From the certainty of Roach's "before" the murder charge, Main had now succeeded in descending into uncertainty, and all that could be said with confidence is that Cook had been stripped either on Sunday morning or on Sunday afternoon. Cook himself had a view of the matter. Opposite this exchange in the preliminary inquiry transcript is his annotation:

"Early Sun morning, before breakfast."

In spite of an unpromising start, they did better in the first trial. Anderson asked Roach:

"Did you come into possession of any other articles from the prisoner?"

"There was - I believe the next day we had some clothing taken from his person...."

The "next day" Roach referred to was Sunday, and when Anderson returned to the subject a few minutes later, Roach's belief had ripened into categorical certainty:

"Any other articles come into your possession Sergeant Roach [on Saturday]?"

"Not until the following day."

"And what happened the following day?"

"The clothing of the prisoner Robert Raymond Cook was removed."

When Main cross-examined him, Roach confirmed Sunday as the day of the clothing removal. But by the second trial, the uncertainty of the preliminary inquiry had returned in spades - or say rather that the certainty of the first trial had been replaced with a different certainty. Anderson asked Roach to identify a pair of shoes:

"These are a pair of brown oxfords[1] that were taken from Robert Cook on Saturday night, the night in question."

---

[1] *They were loafers - a small point.*

131

"Look at these trousers please."

"These are the pants that were also taken from the prisoner, Robert Cook."

"Saturday night?"

"Saturday night."

"At Stettler?"

"Stettler, Alberta."

"Same occasion?"

"Same occasion."

It should be pointed out that there was only one occasion, "early Sun morning, before breakfast", when any clothing - and in fact all of it - was taken from Cook. It was not the case, say, that his shoes and pants were taken on Saturday night and the balance of it on Sunday morning. Had it been a matter of Roach saying Sunday on one occasion and Saturday on another, this could be put down to mere inadvertence - a catch-all excuse at most trials when a witness is caught out in an inconsistency. But credulity would be strained and inadvertence taxed unfairly by ascribing to inadvertence "Sunday morning or Sunday afternoon" confidently becoming "Saturday night, the night in question. The night (or morning, or afternoon) in question it was, but not in the sense Roach was talking about.

***

At 11 am Sunday the team was ready to move. Sproule, Novikoff, Morrison, Van Blarcom and Thachik left for the house, two blocks distant from the Detachment. No one had yet entered the house when Sproule began taking the photographs which would be entered as trial exhibits, starting with a view of the front of the house and then moving to the north side. Standing beside the north side and shown in the photograph Sproule took of it was a 1951 Chevrolet half-ton, newly restored by Ray Cook. Sproule then joined the others inside.

In the master bedroom they of course saw first Roach's "jumble of clothing" of the night before which concealed most of the mattress. In its visible parts the mattress was smeared with the substances I have previously described, as was much of the clothing itself. They did not take the time, neither then nor later, to accurately identify the garments and other fabric items found on the mattress, and, for example, were able to say at trial only that the "thought" they might have included some shirts. The photographs are marginally more helpful; it is possible to make out a bath towel and a floral-patterned dress (and the transcripts refer, somewhat improbably, to a mailbag), but it is not possible to go beyond that in spite of there appearing to be as many as 15 different items of clothing and the like in the three photographs taken of the bed. "Jumble" was more or less an adequate description, although the cause of investigation would have been better served by identifying all the white shirts, say, than it was by singling out a mailbag[1]. On a bare portion of the mattress near the head of the bed lay the barrels of a double-barreled shotgun with the breech mechanism intact. From it, Sproule extracted two spent cartridges. The wooden forehand piece and one of the exterior hammers broken from the gun lay near the barrels. These were the only parts of the shotgun found in the bedroom.

Hard up against the head of the double bed in the overcrowded bedroom was a four-drawer dresser. The second drawer from the top was partially pulled out and a white shirt was hanging from it. When the corner of the mattress next to the dresser was lifted, the jacket of the blue suit issued to Cook in the penitentiary was found. "On examining the jacket," Sproule said at the preliminary inquiry, "Corporal Van Blarcom and myself found three twelve-gauge shotgun shells. These are live cartridges. Three were found in the right lower pocket and two were found in the left lower pocket." The shells were to be marked as exhibits at trial, at the first of which Sproule described how he alone "reached into the pocket *[sic]* and there were five shotgun shells contained therein." Early on in the analysis of the trial evidence it appeared there was going to be much of interest.

Under the lower corner of the outer edge of the mattress Van Blarcom found the suit pants. He removed them, took them to the livingroom and laid them out on the chesterfield where they were photographed, unlike the jacket which was first photographed where it was found. The jacket was found within a few minutes of the police first entering the bedroom, but the pants not until later that afternoon.

---

[1] *See Chapter 14.*

They were found by Van Blarcom who, around noon, left the house to interview Dillon Hoskins, a boyhood acquaintance of Cook's whom we have already met. Hoskins had by then informed the police that on the preceding Thursday afternoon he had seen Cook walking towards him on the western outskirts of Stettler. At the time Hoskins was in a car proceeding in the direction opposite to Cook's. Hoskins did not distinguish himself as a reliable witness. He claimed, for example, to have seen Cook driving the Impala at a time when that would not have been possible. He missed by two months the date of his chance encounter with Cook on the western outskirts, but that was the sort of mistake any witness could make. But he said he'd observed Cook getting out of a car on the western outskirts when in fact it was a panel truck, and this at a time when the acuity of his powers of observation was in direct question. What was Cook wearing? Hoskins was able to tell them. In the few seconds it had taken for him to drive by, he'd observed Cook to be wearing a blue suit, a red tie, a white shirt and black oxfords.

When Van Blarcom interviewed Hoskins on Sunday afternoon he may have marveled at his good fortune since at the house they had, if not by then a complete blue suit, then at least the jacket of one, a bloodstained white shirt and a red tie (all taken from under the mattress) and, from the walk-through closet, a pair of black oxfords. It appeared therefore, at this early stage, that Hoskins would be a witness against Cook of inestimable value, but it turned out his evidence would not be needed. Witnesses more reliable than Hoskins were available if necessary who could identify the suit, tie and shoes as Cook's, but even they were not called. Cook could not deny their ownership where once again denial would have been, if not quite as pointless as denying he had been in the house, then at least as futile. But he would not - or could not - say anything about the shirt. Nor could anyone else.

After tagging the gun parts and the blue jacket and handing them to Novikoff for delivery to the Crime Detection Laboratory in Regina, Sproule accompanied Van Blarcom into the back bedroom. We have seen that there were two beds: a single cot along the north wall - they were called Winnipeg couches and were designed to collapse in the middle of the night without warning - and, in the southeast corner, a 'queen-size' double bed. There were no bed clothes on either bed, the larger of which had a mattress heavily bloodstained at one end.

There were two mattresses on the cot, one of them bloodstained. The transcripts leave a confused picture as to which it was (the top mattress might have been turned over by the police and they may have reversed the order of the mattresses; one can't be sure), but in and of itself it is not a matter of particular importance. What is is finding inconsistency in police testimony concerning an investigation in which everything at the scene was potentially significant and remained so until the investigation was concluded. Only then would they know which pieces belonged in the complete picture and which did not. One of the basic elements at most murder scenes is blood, and where it is is as good a starting point as any in deciding how it got there. But when the time came to piece the crime together, where the blood in the back bedroom then was was not necessarily where it had been when the murder scene was still in its pristine, pre-investigation state. Consistency in police investigation would have been re-gained only had there been some hasty backtracking on the part of one or other of the police officers who examined the mattresses, but such consistency was not an essential requirement of Her Majesty's case against Cook.

The cumulative effect of what he had now seen was enough - and then some - to prompt Van Blarcom to phone Roach to suggest it was time he and Beeching came to the house. In the half-hour or so since the first contingent had left the Detachment, Roach had made the first of many phone calls the investigation would call for, among them a call to Curly Marvin in Edmonton to ask him to check the trade-in station wagon for signs of its having been used as an impromptu hearse. The RCMP were now certain that the search for the victims would be long and arduous in a countryside offering an illimitable number of places to hide them. After phoning Roach, Van Blarcom checked the box of the half-ton truck standing beside the north wall to see whether it might have been used to carry the bodies. Someone was sent to the yard to look for signs of fresh excavation.

With the arrival of Roach and Beeching between 11:30 and noon, the search moved into the garage. Roach lifted the cardboard concealing the planks and Van Blarcom began lifting out planks. The miasma of rotting bodies was immediately overpowering. Sixteen hours earlier, Tom Roach had never heard of Ray and Daisy Cook and their five children. He was now about to encounter what remained of them, and might have wished his professional duty had not brought him to it.

When the last of the five ten-inch planks was removed, Sproule took his first photograph looking down into the greasepit. It shows two upright tires at the south end, two wheel rims and a car tire, all horizontal, and a set of tire chains. Daisy's body, which was uppermost, was almost

135

completely concealed (one leg was exposed) by an initial layer of debris under the tires and chains. From a space scarcely larger than a large home freezer the police now removed the seven bodies, the tires, rims and chains and all the detritus listed fully in Chapter 21.

In the ceiling a ring had been set to which Ray had attached a chain hoist used in car repair. The hoist was employed to lift out the two adult bodies, and the man who had volunteered to go into the pit to affix ropes to them, now lifted the bodies of the children to the gloved hands waiting above. The bodies were placed in body bags and carried to an ambulance to be transported to a funeral home where all the dry ice which could be rounded up ($8.10 worth) from as far afield as Red Deer was waiting. Putrefaction had to be arrested as much as possible until the pathologist could get to Stettler from Edmonton. With the lifting of "a male child" at 2:12 pm, the men in the garage could turn to the tasks for which their training had equipped them.

Sproule's had equipped him for both photography and, with Novikoff, for lifting and analyzing fingerprints. They attempted to lift prints from the shattered gun stock, pieces of which were found with a blanket-wrapped body. They tried without success to raise prints from the grimy cardboard which had covered the greasepit. There were smeared prints on the gun barrels, but here too their efforts to raise identifiable prints were unsuccessful. A thorough examination was made of the entire house, including the basement. Door jambs, window sills and furniture were dusted, but all that was found, Sproule testified, were two identifiable prints in the entire house: one of Daisy's taken from the refrigerator, and one of "a female child, body number 3" found on a toy in the front porch.

The meagre results of the search for fingerprints leads to one of two conclusions: either the search was not as thorough as Sproule said it was, or someone had been almost inhumanly thorough in obliterating almost all the fingerprints in a house continuously occupied by seven people and, from time to time, by an eighth, the basement roomer, Gurney. Whether or not it was, the Crown should have been embarrassed by the problem posed by the absence of fingerprints, but it managed to skate around it in a haze of ambiguity which served its purposes. Clearly stated (as the Crown chose not to state it) the Crown's implied position was this: the killer, Cook, had carefully removed all the fingerprints in order to get rid of his own, that being the customary reason for removing from the scene of a crime all trace of one's having been at it. (The alternative explanation for the shortage of prints, and one not voiced by the Crown, was that the RCMP had not done its job, but to say as much would have been to open up other parts of the investigation for scrutiny, a consummation devoutly to be avoided.)

The problem for the Crown however, had it closed with it, was that Cook had freely admitted having been at the scene of the crime, both on Thursday evening and again on Saturday evening - indeed to claim as much was central to his defense. Faced with an awkward truism, the prosecutor would necessarily have had to contend that while it was true Cook had been in the house both before and after the crime, and while it was true Cook admitted having been in the house both before and after the crime, it was also true Cook had attempted to remove his fingerprints so it could not be proved against him that he had been in the house both before and after the crime. Prima facie it put Cook on the level of Mortimer Snerd in terms of cunning. And yet someone - Cook? - removed the fingerprints; there seemed to be no gainsaying that. Wisely, the Crown chose to maintain a discreet silence.

Somewhat similarly with the argument that the reason for his returning to the house on Saturday evening was to complete the efforts at concealment - a purpose suggested obliquely both by Mr Justice Greschuk and by Wally Anderson. Anderson was prepared to credit Cook with cunning above and beyond the ordinary[1]. A measure of it was to be seen in his parking the Impala in the driveway where it was certain to - and did - attract attention, while he was inside assiduously removing the evidence of his ever having been there. But it was a near thing; smudged fingerprints were found on the beer bottle from which he had drunk.

The defense made nothing of the strange absence of fingerprints and in each trial the prosecution may be taken to have been relieved to move to more fruitful matters. But the poverty of Sproule's results was not the

---

[1] *Anderson told the writer that Cook was "a very cool customer, very cunning." When cross-examining Cook, he had the feeling "he was always two or three jumps ahead of the questioning; I could not rattle or shake him. He would say repeatedly, 'Would you mind repeating that question?'and I had the strong impression he was buying time in this fashion in order to prepare and shape his answer." Anderson's recollection is interesting. In two trials he put to Cook a total of about seventeen hundred questions. He was asked by Cook to repeat himself eight times: three times because the questions did not make any sense; once probably because he did not understand the word 'disassociation' which Anderson changed when he reworded the question; twice because the questions were open to a genuine lack of understanding on Cook's part as to what Anderson was getting at; and twice on trivial matters where Cook might very well not have heard the questions.*

end of the matter. An RCMP report found in the capital case file in the National Archives was able to expand on them: "The doors and windows were checked and no jimmy marks or signs of force were apparent. *Ten* [emphasis added] fingerprints were found suitable for identification and were compared against the fingerprints of seven deceased persons found in the garage adjoining the house. Five fingerprints identified as those of one deceased adult female, body number 1. One impression identified as that of a female child, body number 3. Fingerprints compared at the scene against Robert Raymond Cook with negative results."

Admittedly, an RCMP report of uncertain origin sitting in Ottawa is not sworn evidence in a courtroom. That acknowledged, one of the questions it poses may be stated provisionally: if there were four unidentified fingerprints left over, whose were they? Another question is why did the report not find its modest way into evidence?

And a final question, this time Cook's. A note written by him after the second conviction was an attempt to draft the argument to be made on appeal: "It is inconsistent with the Crowns theory [of guilt] the fact the suite was found under the mattress. As evedence is that finger prints were [erased?] or wiped up carfully from all places in the house. Is it reasonable to belive I would hide all signs of the crime and wipe all of the finger prints up and then leave my own suite under such an obvious place as the blood stained mattress?" It seems a reasonable question, but evidently so also was the jurors' belief in what, to Cook, seemed so "unreasonible."

***

To see Cook as guilty is either to see him as a consummate actor who carried off the part of innocence with superb aplomb, or as a man for whom the murders had never happened, so successfully was he able to relegate them to some dark corner of the subconscious where they no longer existed because they never happened. Whichever he was, if he was guilty, all his actions were consistent with innocence, starting with the whole of the Camrose interlude, and continuing through to his response to Braden when he was picked up on Main Street.

He was in stride when he phoned Rob Sloan to ask him to act for him on the false pretense charge, and when he asked MacNaughton to have bail set and to try to arrange to have it posted. Jim Hoskins, Cook told MacNaughton, was a good bet to post bail.

On Thursday evening Jim and Leona Hoskins were the guests of Ray and Daisy Cook. During the visit Ray offered to help Jim move some furniture to Red Deer on Saturday, and Daisy and Leona made the plans for holding their annual family picnic on Sunday. When Ray failed to show up at the Hoskins' at the appointed time on Saturday morning, Hoskins went to the Cook house to look for him. When he later tried to reach him by telephone, without much success, he put it down to Ray probably having gone to Hanna to visit his brother. For her part, Leona Hoskins told me that "We were waiting at home on Sunday morning with the picnic baskets ready waiting for them to call when [MacNaughton] phoned us and asked whether we'd bail Bobby out. Jim turned him down: 'I'll see Ray first.' Jim told him we don't know where Ray is, and we began thinking for the first time what with the furniture and that, that something must be wrong."

There was no one else Cook could turn to, but bail became academic on the afternoon of the same day, Sunday, when Roach laid the charge of murder. Nevertheless Cook continued to place some stock in bail having been set. On September 11, 1959 he wrote Main: "If I'm found not guilty do you think I'll be charged with exsaping custody and the resulting car theft and B&E. If I am do you think bail can be set. Will the $3000 bail still be in effect on the charge of false pretences. I'd kind of like to spend this exmas on the street if you think this is at all possible would you please let me know. Id try and get bail ready just in case. Last of all would there be sufficient funds for you to defend me on these charges? I know I am being a bother but if you'll kindly answer those questions for me I'll dummy up until trial. Respectfully, Robert R. Cook."[1]

The charges he hoped to get the chance to face, B&E, car theft and escaping lawful custody, for him would have been as comforting as a security blanket so familiar were they, particularly in his present predicament. But like exmas on the street they were to be denied him.

We will see in Chapter 20 that he thought better of dummying up until trial, and that when he broke his vows of silence, it was in connection with yet one more B&E, one which, at the date of the letter, Main knew nothing about.

---

[1] *The funds he referred to were a small legacy he expected to receive from the estate of an uncle on his mother's side. His entitlement proved to be $212, but the other legatees agreed to contribute from their shares such that Cook received $250.*

Sunday, June 29 was Constable Pete Thachik's day off, but that morning he was phoned by Roach and dragooned into duty along with a civilian known to Roach who had been shanghaied from the street. He was in the garage when the pit was opened. He assisted in the removal of the tires and rims, saw the first of the bodies and was then instructed by Roach to return to the detachment to "guard Cook" - an odd wording considering Cook at the time was securely locked up and being guarded by Braden along with the hastily recruited civilian. Roach may have been concerned about the possibility of escape such that he thought it prudent to increase the guard, but it seems more probable that Thachik was charged with the responsibility of getting from Cook whatever he could while Cook was still off guard. This in any case is what happened.

Thachik came into the cellblock and greeted Cook in a friendly manner, a greeting Cook returned in the same spirit. For the next half-hour they chatted through the bars with Cook evidently doing most of the talking which was as it should have been, Thachik's role (if he was there to pump Cook rather than merely guard him) being that of an interested and friendly listener - a good cop without the bad cop routine.

Nothing Cook said to Thachik implicated him in murder, although Anderson was to use it in cross-examination in a manner detrimental to Cook.[1] A month after the cellblock conversation, Thachik wrote a report, a copy of which survives. Part of the text of the report follows:

"Robert Raymond COOK stated that the Police have nothing on him, as he made a legitimate trade with his father's car and couldn't figure out why we were keeping him locked up. Stated that if his father didn't go to New Westminster, B. C., he would have him bailled [sic] out right now. Went on to say that his father and mother and children all went to New Westminster, B. C., on Thursday, June 25th, 1959, to buy a Service Station. The Service Station was all that he ever dreamed of, and that his father and him were going to be partners. He also stated that he gave his father $4100.00 in cash to purchase the garage with. COOK stated that his father gave him the station wagon so he could trade it off on a Chevrolet Impala convertible. The only reason he wanted to buy the convertible in question was to spite people in Stettler, Alberta, and another reason was no one especially the Police would suspect anyone driving a new car like a Chev convertible of pulling any jobs. Stated that before he was sent up for the job at Bowden, another person, not mentioning any names, hid some money 12 telephone poles from the corner, at the last street (south) and buried some 3 feet down, and some

---

[1] *See p. 159 ff*

was hidden in a tobacco tin, and covered with plastic so as the rain would not soil [the] money. He also stated that there was an unknown amount of silver; this silver was thrown away somewhere in the ditch. On Wednesday, June 24th, 1959, he took a peek at his money. He stated that his greatest ambition in life was to score $50,000.00 and then give the game up, and start a service station up. Went on to say that he knew all types of safes (CANS) and that he knew how to blow them all. Stated that he made one mistake and he didn't like the same on his record the time he chopped the bottom out of a safe, stated that this was a real amature *[sic]* job and he didn't like the same on his record.

"Also went on to say that he really made a bad mistake when he pulled off the job in Hanna, the time he took a drink out of a bottle of liquor, put the same back on the shelf, and forgot to wipe the prints off. Stated that he would never make a stupid mistake like that again as long as he lived.

"COOK went on to say that he had a pretty good job set up when he worked at McTAGGART Motors parking lot, pull a job or two (he called them scores), bring the car back, sneak into the house and go back to bed, and no one the wiser until he got caught with McTAGGART'S car at at Vegreville, Alta. Further stated that since Bowden job, he has worked alone, didn't want anyone else involved if he got caught."

This document could be dissected, analyzed, cross-analyzed and re-analyzed late into the night, but only by running the risk of becoming mired in a bog of inconsistencies, unanswered questions, Cook's untruths and the occasional insight. The risk is not accepted here. To cop out, suffice it to say that it has about it the air of a chat between equals, the shop talk of two men of the law - albeit of different branches of it - the one a motormouth (which was out of character for Cook), the other a kindly and sympathetic listener, worthy of hearing confidences such as these. There can be read into Cook an almost pathetic hope that he was impressing his auditor - an admired adversary - or would impress him if he pressed on far enough, telling more than he intended to, holding back very little until at some point Cook could not help but become Thachik's admired adversary. It was an astonishing performance from a man who presumably knew it was just a matter of a short time before he was charged with the murder of the man in New Westminster he prattled on about. But the ceremony of innocence was about to be drowned, partly in Cook's own tears.

The document appears to be, say, ninety percent Cook without question. The question about the remainder is was it Thachik's invention, remembering that Thachik wrote the report (whether from notes or not is not known) a full month after the interview. At the first trial, Thachik was required on a *voir dire*[1] to recall as much of the conversation with Cook as he could recall without reference to the report. His recollection of the conversation accurately corroborated the report. In giving his *voir dire* evidence, Thachik went through the business of the 12 telephone poles and the two reasons proffered by Cook for buying the Impala, and had just finished with the Hanna break-in when Cook erupted in his only outburst in two trials and the preliminary inquiry: "It's all a damn lie! You know it is!"

It seems Cook might have been slow to anger. Thachik had moved well past the poles when the outburst occurred, yet it was the subject of these selfsame poles which Beeching recalled distressed Cook during the Monday morning interrogation after remand court. Beeching told me that during the interrogation, he made up the business of the telephone poles on the spur of the moment since he was skeptical of Cook's story of having dug up the money, not to take "a peek" at it, but to take home to his father: " 'Oh yeah? Twelve telephone poles from where?' I was just being funny. I threw that in. I remember getting him upset." Beeching's recollection is borne out by Cook's statement where, when Beeching is recorded as saying "Twelve telephone poles from where?", Cook is shown in a parenthetical aside on the typewritten record of the interrogation as being "Very indignant and angry."[2].

To believe Thachik therefore is to believe that before the murder charge Cook himself was nattering on about 12 telephone poles when, when Beeching baited him with them, he blew up at the first-time mention of something which had caused him no distress the day before when he expansively disclosed them to Thachik, and which caused him to blow up again at trial.

Moreover, while it is probable Cook told Thachik of the existence of the cache of money - he unwisely bragged about it in the penitentiary, and Thachik was a more deserving confidante than a bunch of cutthroat cons - it is highly improbable that he gave anything away as to its location.

That is, that he mentioned telephone poles or anything else as a marker. Even when he was forced by circumstances to disclose the cache's

[1] *A courtroom hearing in the absence of the jury to determine the admissibility of evidence.*

[2] *Appendix A, Q.69.*

142

existence, he was reluctant to say anything more about its location than those circumstances made unavoidable. "What's the use to say anymore on that?" [1]

Would it were as simple as, say, Thachik having heard of Beeching's sardonic sally after the fact and its inadvertently finding its way into a report written a month later than the conversation it recorded. But nothing much in the *Cook* trials was very simple. At the second trial, Beeching told Dunne the only thing he could "definitely recall" being told by Thachik about the Thachik-Cook conversation was "about money being buried twelve telephone poles from somewhere at Bowden" which, he told Dunne, he, Beeching, then used in his interrogation of Cook, so that now the court had something concocted by Beeching (as he informed me) at the Monday morning interrogation finding its way as original conversation into a report written by Thachik a month after the fact, but nevertheless being regurgitated by Beeching as having come in the first instance from Thachik. Whether or not it was all a damn lie, it certainly was a puzzler.

***

When the police were winding up their Sunday search of the house, they noted all the desperate attempts made by the killer to cover his tracks: the washing of faded wallpaper, furniture and floors, the hiding of the shotgun and suit. It proved impossible; bloodstains were found in 23 locations in the bedrooms and in the livingroom - evidence doubtlessly of some of the children having fled before being cornered. In the plastic garbage pail on the back landing were found a number of soggy, bloodstained towels which Mr Justice Greschuk seized on and emphasized by way of an interesting juxtaposing of facts not on the face of them necessarily interdependent:

"Why was the car [backed up to the garage]? Do you accept the explanation given by the accused? Does the explanation raise a doubt in your minds as to that? No one was in the car or the vicinity of the car. Where was the accused? You will recall the damp cloths or mats found in the garbage can on Sunday. Does this mean anything to you?"

Greschuk cannot have forgotten that the reason no one was in the car or in its immediate vicinity was because the person most likely to have

[1] *Appendix A, Qs 70 and 71.*

been seen there had he not been elsewhere was - by the "explanation given by the accused"; His Lordship had not forgotten after all - elsewhere. He was in the house. The real question, one supposed, was was he in the house wringing out bloody towels or having a beer? It took a stretching of the judicial imagination to see the location of the Impala as having much to say about it one way or another.

Then there is the statement which was put in by the Crown and in which appears *[sic]* questions put by Staff Sergeant Beeching and the answers given by the accused. In my opinion, the jury should have the benefit of this statement read to them in full.

Mr Justice Peter Greschuk, *Charge to the first-trial jury*

***

Staff Sergeant Beeching, how close to a verbatim report is the information you have set down in this document?

In this document I set down everything that was said by myself or the prisoner or Sergeant Roach who was also present.

Word for word?

Word for word.

It is in fact an exact recording of the oral conversation?

Written at the very time it was said.

I think that clarifies the matter, My Lord.

J. Wallace Anderson, QC.
 Examination-in-chief, voir dire, *first trial,*
 Staff Sergeant Beeching

CHAPTER 9

THE STATEMENT

Exactly what Roach said to Cook when he first broached the subject of murder on Sunday afternoon is not known. But Dave MacNaughton was there and remembers it as being about as abrupt as "Your father's dead; you're under arrest for murder."

What is known is that in the 19 hours between then and the next morning when he was returned to the Detachment office after remand court, Cook uttered a total of seven words other than a couple of distracted yes's and no's to his lawyer. He cried out, "No! not my father, not my father" and then broke down, unable to speak. He was lodged in his cell, not now to chatter idly through the bars, but to withdraw into a dark night, equaled, if that, only by one which awaited him beyond the offing on a horizon as dark as Erebus, as black as Death. Whether the night was a sleepless nightmare because, in shock, he struggled to come to terms with the death of his father, or because, now cornered, he began to contemplate the dread prospect which faced him, is a matter of surmise tied to a question long since answered by his trials and conviction.

Clearly for police purposes something more was required than shock and tears, preferably a full-blown confession or, failing that, answers to pointed questions stripping him of credibility. Beeching decided therefore he would try and get a statement from Cook before he was taken to the PMH. To that end, while Cook was still in remand court, Beeching typed out six questions he wished to ask Cook. When Cook was brought back from court, unaccompanied by MacNaughton, they were waiting for him.

The first of the typed questions was asked by Beeching and Cook replied - a denial of guilt. Beeching then departed from his typed list to ask an unplanned question: "Do you wish to say anything else?" to which Cook replied no. Evidently detecting some underlying equivocation in the reply, Beeching read the second of the typed questions, and again Cook replied, affirming that his family was supposed to have gone to BC.

But now, rather than continuing with the list and the third of the prepared questions, Beeching decided that in light of Cook's answer to the second of them, he would abandon questions three to six and extemporize from that point. He asked Cook a further 75 questions[1]. Roach, who had recorded the answers to the two prepared questions as well as the extemporaneous question and answer, recorded the remaining questions and answers, and the 78 Q and A document became known as Cook's statement. It will referred to as such here, although it was not a statement in the normal sense of an accused being asked whether he wished to make one (as Cook *was* asked) and then, if the police are lucky, blurting out a confession. Nevertheless it comprised everything Cook said to the police following the murder charge, and it forms the subject of this chapter.

---

[1] *There are six distinct versions of the statement in the writer's possession. In three of them there are 78 question and answer pairs, and in the other three 79.*

A way of dealing with the statement would be to set it out[1] and comment
on various answers as they bear on related areas of the evidence, and on
the statement as a whole as an indicator of Cook's state of mind at a
juncture when his emotional equilibrium was shattered, at least to
outward appearances, but to do only that would be to miss its larger
importance which lay not in what was in it (important as that is) but in
how it was handled and mishandled by the courts. For readers whose
interest in the workings of the law in some of its more obscure reaches
is less than all-consuming, reading the following analysis of the
statement's fate at the hands of the courts may prove a formidable slog
through barren territory, but the story would be incomplete without a
moderately detailed examination of the part played by this central
document. To get through it, one can do no better than adopt the grave
advice of the King of Hearts and begin at the beginning.

***

When the caution required to be read to a person charged with an offense
was read to Cook by Roach on Monday morning, it was the third time he
had done so[2]. Cook's shocked outburst "No! not my father, not my
father!" was followed by a stunned silence during which Roach read the
caution for the first time. Cook broke down and Roach, seeing that
Cook was lost to him, set the matter aside. An hour or so later Roach
thought Cook was sufficiently recovered for him to try for a statement,
and MacNaughton asked Roach to read the caution again since, as he
informed Main in a letter a month later, he felt "the first time the caution

---

[1] *The statement is reproduced as Appendix A.*

[2] *The RCMP version of the caution reads: "WARNING TO ACCUSED PERSON:
you need not say anything. You have nothing to hope from any promise or favor and
nothing to fear from any threat whether or not you say anything. Anything you do
say may be used as evidence at your trial." The Criminal Code provides for a
similar warning to be given at the conclusion of a preliminary inquiry adding,
among others, the words "whatever you do say will be taken down in writing and
may be given in evidence at your trial." As the Code reads, the warning must be
read to the accused before he is given the opportunity to call his own witnesses
(which, as it happens, rarely happens in a preliminary inquiry), before, that is to
say, the court knows it has heard all the evidence upon which the decision as to
whether to commit the accused to stand trial is based. That there will be a trial,
whether or not the Crown has made out a prima facie case, the Code appears to take
as a foregone conclusion.*

was read to [Cook] he would have no understanding" - an opinion Roach had formed at the caution's first reading. He read it again, but could not be certain Cook had sufficiently recovered to understand it. With an eye on the admissibility of whatever Cook might say, Roach decided to give it up for the night.

On Monday morning MacNaughton did not accompany Cook back to the Detachment from court indicating he was not aware of Beeching's intention to grill Cook. The police had done MacNaughton the courtesy on Sunday of informing him of the impending murder charge giving MacNaughton the chance to be there, but on Monday morning Cook was on his own. Only later did MacNaughton learn of the interrogation. Much later; in his letter to Main of July 27, 1959 he wrote, "I do not know if he has made any statements that are incriminating to the R.C.M.P. but I doubt it" which is to say that a month after taking it, the RCMP had not made a copy of the statement available to MacNaughton nor had Cook informed MacNaughton that he had made one. Nor had MacNaughton asked him whether he'd made one, and this though he had an appointment with Cook immediately following the interrogation which was presumably kept.

In giving evidence at the first trial of the circumstances surrounding the taking of the statement, Beeching said nothing about Roach's two Sunday afternoon attempts, leaving the impression that only on Monday morning had the police decided to try to get Cook to talk. The standard practice when taking a statement, as reflected in the Code's wording of the caution, is to take down in writing whatever is said. While the Code does not require anything an accused has said at a preliminary inquiry to be read back to him and signed by him before it can be used at his trial, provided it has been recorded by a court-appointed stenographer, the law usually requires it of statements made to the police. It is however not necessarily fatal to the statement's admissibility if, for some sufficient reason, the practice is not followed.[1] In Cook's case, the statement was not read back to him nor did he sign it.

With Cook seated, comfortably the police were careful to say, and without handcuffs, in front of a desk behind which Beeching sat with Roach off to one side, Roach read the caution a third time. Cook indicated he understood it; he was no novitiate in going one-on-one with police forces. A tape recorder was turned on and the interrogation began. What caused Beeching to depart from the six pre-prepared

---

[1] *For a discussion, see A. E. Popple, Annotation, "Police questioning prisoners", C.R. Vol. 12, 248.*

questions in favor of winging it is not known, and thus none of the final four questions would be known had Greschuk not inadvertently read one of them into the trial transcript. Greschuk had decided the jury should have the entire statement read to them, and he proceeded to do so in his charge to the jury[1]. In doing so he read question 3 before catching himself and explaining that Beeching had not asked it of Cook. The reporter appears to have been confused at to what Greschuk was explaining since he garbled the punctuation badly, making a hash of both Beeching's voice and Greschuk's. It appears in the transcript exactly as follows: "Q On Sunday, June 28th, 1959, the Police examined the home of Ray Cook in the town of Stettler and there found the bodies of seven persons who had been killed by violence. They were your father, step-mother and" it says "step-brothers"; I imagine that should read "half-brothers and sisters. Have you anything to say to this?"

It is not difficult to sort out the inverted commas to make sense of what Greschuk said and Beeching typed, but it is of no particular importance. What is of interest is why, when in his previous answer Cook had told Beeching, 'That's right. That's where they were supposed to be when I left them last. That's where they were supposed to go. When I left I gave them some money. I gave them all the money I had except for $100 and they were supposed to leave the next morning'[2], Beeching could not then ask Cook if he had anything to say about the fact of seven persons having been killed "by violence."

---

[1] *One of the epigraphs to this chapter will be seen to contain a curious ambiguity. Greschuk probably intended to say that the jury should have the benefit of having the statement read to them, rather than that they should have the benefit of the statement read to them - which is not the same thing*

[2] *Comparison of the full text of this answer as it appear in the six versions of the statement is instructive:*

1. "That's right. That's where they were supposed to be when I left them last night, where they were supposed to go. When I left I gave them some money. I gave them all the money I had then except for $100 and they were supposed to leave the next morning."

2. "That's right, that's right - that's where they were supposed to be when I left them last night. That's where they were supposed to go. When I left them I gave them some money. I gave them all the money I had except for $100 and they were supposed to leave the next morning."

3. "That's right. That's where they were supposed to be when I left them last. I gave them all the money I had except for $100 and they were supposed to leave the next morning."

To use the statement against Cook, Anderson first had to have it admitted, that is he had to run it through the obstacle course thrown up by the rules before the jury would be allowed to read it or have it read to them. The rules required that if it had a confessional aspect, before it would be admitted before the jury it had to be shown to have been made voluntarily by Cook - a matter for vetting by the judge in the jury's absence. With the jury gone, Anderson launched his first-trial argument.

He started by saying it was "an exculpatory statement and a self-serving statement and not against the interest of the prisoner, and as such...not subject to the ordinary rules and principles surrounding the admissions of a confession or an inculpatory statement...." Inasmuch as Cook's first answer had been, "Just didn't do it - that's all", and inasmuch as he had stayed with denial throughout Beeching's interrogation, the statement indeed was, as Anderson said, exculpatory. It was an avowal of innocence and as such at the opposite end of the spectrum from a confession. Therefore, Anderson argued, there was no need to inquire into the circumstances of its being taken. It did not matter whether Cook had given it voluntarily. Only confessions had to be voluntary for them to be allowed into evidence.

But it may be guessed that Anderson was not anxious to have the statement before the jury because it showed innocence; quite the contrary. "Any time," Frank Dunne told the court in the second trial when Anderson once again tried to have the statement admitted, " the Crown are *[sic]* putting in a statement, they are not putting it in because it is exculpatory."

4. "That's right, that's right. That's where they were supposed to go. When I left I gave them some money. I gave them all the money I had then except for $100 and they were supposed to leave the next morning."

5. "That's right. That's where they were supposed to be when I left them last. That's where they were supposed to go. When I left I gave them some money. I gave them all the money I had then except for $100 and they were supposed to leave the next morning."

6. "That is right, that was where they were supposed to be when I left them last. Where they were supposed to go. When I left them, I gave them some money. I gave them all the money I had except $100 and they were supposed to leave the next morning."

It is seen that the six versions are substantially similar but no two are identical. The question is which version, if any, is an accurate record of what Cook said?

150

When Anderson had finished his first-trial argument, Greschuk turned to Main who said, "So far as the defense is concerned, we do not intend to object to the entering of the statement.... I am quite content that it was taken properly by the police without force or promises or anything like that, and in addition to that, as my friend pointed out, I think it is exculpatory." With that Greschuk asked that the jurors be brought back. Beeching (who had taken the stand for the *voir dire* but whom it had not been necessary to question in view of Main's lack of objection) was handed a copy of the statement. Beeching identified certain handwriting as his and related the circumstances of the interrogation. Anderson then asked to have it marked as an exhibit.

Main was immediately on his feet. "My Lord, I don't think that [marking it as an exhibit] is quite proper. I understand the statement made by the prisoner was an oral statement. It was not a written and signed statement. What the staff sergeant has and which he is going to refer to in giving his evidence from now on is merely his notes of the statement made by the prisoner and I don't think it is admissible as a document. The staff sergeant can read from it or refer to it in giving his evidence as to what oral statements were made by the prisoner, but I don't think the document itself is admissible as evidence. It is merely a memorandum, his written memorandum to refresh his memory."

Anderson expressed surprise, but Main's objection was well-founded where his earlier lack had not been. To attempt to retrieve his position, Anderson turned to Beeching who was still on the stand and the exchange which forms an epigraph to this chapter took place. On hearing it ("Word for word?" "Word for word.") Main reversed his field: "Well, I have no serious objection My Lord. I was just concerned with being correct, that's all. If my friend would really like to put it in, I have no serious objection and I will withdraw it." Main's concern with judicial correctness was commendable, and had he stood his ground he would have won the day. But he didn't. The statement was marked and the jury was now ready to hear what Cook had said to the police.

Beeching began by again relating (but for the jury for the first time) the circumstances on that now distant Monday morning when Cook had been brought from the magistrate's court where, a few minutes before, he had once again been in tears when the charge was read. Once again Beeching explained the matter of the six questions. By this time someone, probably Anderson, had handed up a copy of the statement to Mr Justice Greschuk who, unless he had read the preliminary inquiry transcripts, was seeing it for the first time.

151

Beeching read the first question: "You have been arrested on a charge of murder and you appeared before Magistrate Biggs at 10:15 am and at that time the charge was formally read to you, and you were remanded for 30 days to Ponoka Mental Hospital. Have you anything to say in answer to that charge?" Mr Justice Greschuk stopped him. "*That* charge?" and Beeching replied "*That* charge." Greschuk persisted: "*That* or *the*?" and Beeching replied "*That*" and then went on without further interruption to read the entire statement.

What was not recognized was that the version Greschuk was reading from (and Main for that matter) said "*the* charge" - a trifling difference of no importance in and of itself. But what was also not recognized was that between the versions of the statement being used by Greschuk and Beeching, to name only two, the following discrepancies appear. There were 12 words in the Greschuk version not found in the Beeching version. There were 22 words in the Beeching version not found in the Greschuk. There were 25 words in the Greschuk version found in slightly altered form in the Beeching. There were five phrases in the Greschuk version changed to a single word in the Beeching. And there were two phrases in the Greschuk version existing in lonely splendor *vis a vis* the Beeching.

In all, 71 discrepancies between the version the witness was reading from as a faithful word-for-word reproduction of what Cook had said and the version of it being read by the trial judge. Of the 71, Greschuk picked up on only one, although he cannot have failed to notice most, and probably all, of the other 70. Greschuk was known as a judge with a nice eye for detail, but for whatever reason he chose to let them go.

Main did marginally better when he rose to cross-examine Beeching. He read back to Beeching the second of the typed questions and then part of what Beeching had given as Cook's answer to it, prefacing it by saying to Beeching "...and then you read out this answer, I believe, unless I misheard you. The answer was 'That's right. That's where they were supposed to be when I left them that night.' " Beeching replied "That's correct." Main then said, referring to the yellow newsprint copy of the statement he had, "Well now, that is not is what it says here." Main's copy said "That's right, that's right. That's where they were supposed to go." Beeching said, "Whatever is right" and then admitted having misread his copy. Which is to say he admitted reading "that's where they were supposed to go" as "that's where they were supposed to be when I left them last night, and omitting from the first sentence an entire "That's right."

So far as is known, Beeching wasn't dyslexic or in need of a course in remedial reading or reading glasses. He had not misread his copy and he knew it, but no one with the possible exceptions of Beeching and Roach knew that there were more vaguely different versions of the statement around than could be readily explained, and when Beeching stood down they still didn't.

If one took all six versions and compared each with all the others, the number of differences would grow exponentially. but that would be an exercise akin to calculating the number of possible positions on a chess board. Nothing more need be said than that Beeching's version (which differed from his second-trial version) was neither more nor less damaging to Cook than the Greschuk version. Still, if Cook's statement was important enough to read into evidence, it was important to get it right. "Whatever is right" as Staff Sergeant Beeching said.

***

Having withdrawn his objection to the statement's admission, Main would have been in an embarrassing position had he nevertheless raised its admission as a ground of appeal. He chose not to, not (one would like to think) to avoid embarrassment - "But you withdrew your objection Mr Main" one can hear the court of appeal saying - but because he failed to recognize a valid ground of appeal just as he had erred in withdrawing his objection. Main was too good a lawyer and Cook now mattered to him too much for him to have allowed professional pride to stand in the way of doing for Cook whatever could be done. Had that called for him to stand and suffer the slings and arrows of an outraged court of appeal, he would have done so.

However as sometimes happens the court raised the point for him. After dealing with the ground upon which the appeal was allowed[1], the Chief Justice of the Appellate Division (and as such the Chief Justice of Alberta) turned to the admission of the statement by Mr Justice Greschuk of the Trial Division: "There is however another question of grave importance in the present case. It is whether or not [the statement] consisting of the answers to questions the appellant was asked by

---

[1] *See page 22.*

Sergeant *[sic]* Beeching should have been admitted. These questions were prepared and the answers written down by the sergeant[1]. They were not signed nor re-read to the appellant and were submitted to the court and admitted as evidence for the Crown. Counsel for the defense at first objected, but subsequently withdrew his objection to the admission of the document.

"Having reached the conclusion I have [on the 'Feth' ground], I refrain from saying anything with respect to this document beyond that I do not think it was admissible as a voluntary statement by the appellant. Its effect on the subsequent course of the trial was so great as in my opinion also to make a new trial necessary if it was improperly admitted. What I have just said has no bearing upon the proper use that might have been made of it at trial."[2]

The proper use to which the Chief Justice referred is a matter for lawyers, but is probably that the statement could have been used by Beeching under the rubric of 'notes made at the time' meaning notes made by the witness to which he may refer in giving evidence of the incidents described or words recorded in the notes. If so, then Beeching would have been entitled to have Cook's statement in hand as he struggled, without reading it, to remember the 78 - or 79 - questions and answers. But distinguishing between a witness genuinely refreshing his memory by glancing at a statement he is required to substantially remember without reading it, and one able to recite a statement only because he has just finished glancing down at it surreptitiously, calls for a power of discernment beyond the range of most of us.

***

Having read the Chief Justice's judgment on appeal, Anderson was not about to waste the court's time at the second trial by attempting to have the statement marked as an exhibit. Rather, he proposed having Beeching recall as much of what Cook said as he could, and possibly, Anderson informed Mr Justice Riley, Beeching "would require to look

---

[1] *We have seen (p.146) that they were written down by Roach.*

[2] Regina v. Cook, *127 C.C.C. 287 at 292.*

at his own notes for the refreshing of his memory." What Beeching would recall of the interrogation, Anderson now called in a *voir dire* argument an oral statement, and again he argued it was exculpatory. Therefore it was not necessary to canvas the surrounding circumstances in the absence of the jury and Beeching's oral evidence should be received without further ado. Further, Beeching should be allowed to refer to the written statement should his memory fail him at any time in the course of reciting as many of the 78 question and answer pairs as he could - six pages of them when reduced to the typewritten document Anderson hoped to have Beeching allowed to hold in his hand.

Whether or not this was what the Chief Justice had in mind was moot, but Dunne would have been safe in assuming that whatever Anderson had in mind, it augured ill for Cook, and Dunne should have fought to keep the statement out in either form: whether Beeching reading the document (although, after the judgment of the court of appeal, there was not much chance of *that* being allowed but in the *Cook* trials one never knew), or Beeching remembering what he could of what was said, referring to the written statement from time to time to provide a fillip to his memory. Instead, what Dunne said was, "I may say that I am not objecting too strongly to its admission. On the other hand I am not agreeing or consenting to its admission." Pusillanimity may have its place as a trial tactic, hard as it is to imagine where it may be.

Sufficient unto the day is the evil thereof, but the statement's day in court was not yet over. Riley heard the arguments; adjourned so he could read the court of appeal's judgment; excluded the jury so he could hear Beeching read the statement on a *voir dire*; heard Roach examined and cross-examined on the taking of the statement; heard Thachik examined and cross-examined for reasons which are not readily apparent - "I had better hear the whole story before I rule" - and found that while Cook's answers were "plainly exculpatory and [therefore] prima facie admissible", nevertheless the manner of Beeching and Roach taking the statement was unsatisfactory - Riley did not say why - and he decided to keep out what he called "the information", not as a matter of its inadmissibility under the rules of evidence, not because of anything the Chief Justice had said about it, but "on the basis of discretion."[1]

---

[1] *Confusion about the statement wasn't confined to the trial courtrooms. Mr. Justice Bruce Smith of the Court of Appeal, in electing to deny the application for a new trial, said, "There was no substantial wrong or miscarriage of justice by reason of the entering of the document as an exhibit* because its entire contents were orally related by Staff Sergeant Beeching." *[emphasis added] The precise point Main had taken on the appeal was that the entire contents had been anything but orally related by Staff Sergeant Beeching.*

In his report to the federal Solicitor General submitted at the time Ottawa was reviewing the second death sentence, Riley was able to add a couple of reasons for keeping the statement out that he had not voiced in his courtroom: "...the evidential value of [the statement] was slight, the prejudice to the accused could be great", where in court he had said only "in view of the final questions put by counsel...for the prisoner to Sergeant *[sic]* Beeching, the manner in which the information was obtained was highly unsatisfactory." The final and indeed the only questions put to Beeching by Dunne were three in number and illuminated the evidential value and prejudicial potential of the statement not at all:

"Tell me, were you in uniform Staff?"

"Yes I was, and so was Sergeant Roach."

"And the room where the statement was taken was where?"

"It was in what would be known as the Detachment office, the police office in the Post Office in the town of Stettler."

"I see, and relatively how long did it take you to elicit that evidence?"

"Probably three quarters of an hour. Mr MacNaughton had an appointment at 11:30 and we were trying to see that Mr MacNaughton had his appointment with the accused."

"Thank you."

How Beeching and Roach being in uniform and questioning Cook in the comfort of Roach's office could be seen by Riley as highly unsatisfactory is a matter of guesswork to which, while one was at it, could be added the guess that perhaps they all should have slipped into something more comfortable and gone to a coffee shop. Or that Dunne's time could have been spent to better purpose than getting chummy with Staff by listening carefully to what the police witnesses were saying, as the following will perhaps make clear.

Giving evidence in the *voir dire* at the second trial, Beeching described Roach's having given the caution and being satisfied that Cook understood it. Then Beeching said, "Sergeant Roach then said to him, 'You have been arrested on a charge of murder, you have appeared before Magistrate Biggs at 10:15 am and at that time the charge was formally read to you and you were remanded for 30 days to Ponoka Mental Hospital. Have you anything to say in answer to that charge?'"

On the same *voir dire*, Roach too related his giving the caution and Cook's apparent understanding of it. But at this point his account began to diverge from Beeching's for, when Anderson asked him what happened next, Roach replied, "Well, then *Staff Sergeant Beeching* [italics added] began talking to him [and] started off by saying "You are aware Robert Cook you appeared in magistrate's court this morning at 10 o'clock - or shortly thereabouts *[sic]* - 10:15 am where the formal charge of murder was read, and you [were] remanded for 30 days to the Ponoka Mental Hospital."

Two versions of one question asked by two men at one time stretches understanding. Roach's evidence occurs 12 pages later in the transcript than Beeching's - a matter of perhaps five minutes. It is probable Roach was in the courtroom when Beeching gave his evidence, since Roach was allowed to sit at the counsel table and was not excluded by reason of the fact that at some point he himself would be called as a witness. He said nothing. It is probable also that Beeching heard Roach's evidence since, now having given his, Beeching was no longer excluded. If so, he heard Roach give evidence which flatly contradicted his own of five minutes earlier, but he said nothing. Anderson heard both his witnesses but he too said nothing. Staff may have known his man; Dunne said nothing. Nor did Riley. Nor did Cook who had as much at stake as any of them but remained silent, perhaps remembering his first-trial experience when he had protested that Thachik's 12 telephone pole reference was all a damn lie and was told by Greschuk to "Just keep quiet."

***

Early in Anderson's cross-examination of Cook in the first trial the following exchange took place:

"And you told the jury and the court that this tobacco tin was buried three miles from Bowden?"

"Yes."

"Did you ever on any other occasion indicate a rather different distance?"

"Oh, I don't think so."

"Something in the vicinity of 12 telephone poles?"

"There was no mileage said. I never said 12 telephone posts."

"From the limits of the town of Bowden?"

"No."

"You didn't say such a thing?"

"I don't remember saying such a thing. I said lots of things that were untrue and mixed up."

"I see. You said lots of things that were untrue and mixed up?"

"Yes sir, I did."

"Why did you say the untrue things?"

"Well, it's kind of a - it's hard to understand because it's just about a rule with people that do these things that when you get picked up on something, you just don't tell the truth."

The "other occasion" Anderson referred to was the Monday morning interrogation, but Anderson did not bother to remind the jury that, on *that* occasion, the business of the 12 telephone poles had come, not from Cook, but from Beeching irrespective of whether or not he got it from Cook via Thachik. Cook had said nothing about telephone poles and, it will be recalled, got "very indignant and angry" when Beeching did in the interrogation.

The only other reference to telephone poles was in the Thachik report which had been ruled inadmissible thus preventing Anderson from employing *it* in his present tactic. What the jurors heard in this segment of cross-examination was a man who had lied to someone, probably the police since only they had a proclivity for picking people up. What Anderson hoped to impart was that anyone who would lie to the police would lie to anyone about anything. Cook himself had pointed out at another point that most people stopped in a 30 mph zone will deny they were doing 60 - will, that is to say, lie to the police.

Of course, Cook was saying, when people in his line of work got picked up, they lied. To tell the truth to the enemy was to court being jailed, the risks of which were enough as is. But Cook was proud of the fact that whenever he had seen that the game was up for the moment, when he had not been able to lie his way out of it and once again found himself before a court, he had never lied by saying he was not guilty of whatever he was charged with. For him it *was* a game - not one which all of us play, although not all that many of us are entitled to step up and cast the first stone. Lying to the police is not proscribed in the normal case. But nor was it that Anderson should undermine Cook's credibility by making use of the fact he had done so. The purpose of his wanting the statement admitted, no matter how exculpatory, was now clear. He would use it to shred the last vestige of that credibility.

The tactic was not merely to show he had lied to the police which was bad enough, but that what he had told the police was inconsistent with what he had said in court under oath in reply to the same question as those put to him by Beeching. Not that that made his trial evidence true; far from it. It too was suspect. If he had said black to the police and white in court, and black was false, that didn't make white true. If anything, it too was false. This of course is an exaggeration, but only just so such were the cards stacked against Cook.

The Canada Evidence Act required of Anderson that if he wished to employ the tactic, he had to call Cook's attention to the particular questions and answers in the Beeching interrogation which were inconsistent with what he had said in court either in examination by his own counsel or in cross-examination by Anderson. As a senior prosecutor, Anderson can be taken to have been familiar with the Act, but he chose to ignore it. Eight times he nailed Cook on answers in the statement inconsistent with what he had said in court, and eight times he omitted calling Cook's attention "to those parts of the statement that [were] to be used for the purpose of contradicting him." Had he stayed within the bounds of the Act, he could have done with equally devastating effect what he did by going outside them where he stayed until Mr Justice Greschuk twigged to what was happening and stopped him.

When he finally intervened, Greschuk got it right: "Mr Anderson, you should say 'Now I am reading from the statement, Exhibit so and so. Now were you asked this question by Staff Sergeant Beeching and did you give this answer?' I think that is the way it should be done." The point was well, if tardily, taken since Anderson had already transgressed eight times.

But then the trial judge just as quickly went wrong: "Perhaps Mr Anderson you better not take the line you are taking in your cross-examination because if the other statement you are referring to may be ruled inadmissible, then you shouldn't cross-examine on that." The other statement, the Beeching statement, had long since been ruled admissible by Greschuk.

Anderson replied, "But sir, I am referring to the evidence the witness gave and the statement that was entered in evidence." Quite so, except Anderson had never referred to the statement he was referring to; that was the point.

But the damage was done and the effect *was* devastating. It is near-palpable in the pages of the transcript as Cook floundered and stumbled, forced to admit the last thing a man on trial for his life wishes to admit: in the past at least he lied as a matter of course; as, in his case, an occupational necessity. Equally forceful in the transcripts is the anguish of his attempt to explain that at the time of the interrogation he was "mixed up." Fifteen minutes before Beeching started on him on Monday morning - which was his job - Cook had been so distraught in court, according to what Dave MacNaughton told me, there was a serious question in MacNaughton's mind that this seasoned court performer could appreciate where he was or what was happening. Nevertheless, he had recovered sufficiently by the time he was taken back to the Detachment to be able to tell his inquisitor more or less what seemed to him would serve a dangerous occasion, some of it true, some of it not. It returned to crucify him.

***

Approaching the end of the questioning, Beeching said, "Someone killed him." Cook replied. In the version of the statement used by Roach in a

July 7 report, there appears in parentheses Roach's observation of Cook's demeanor at that point. The observation does not appear in the two versions of the statement employed by Beeching in the trials and therefore was not read into evidence. The jury however did hear Cook's reply: "I know that. You think it was me - you all do. I can tell you right now if I can ever get my hands on that guy there will be something going on too. He never did anything in his life. A man with a softer heart you never saw. If you went and asked him for anything, you'd get it."

What the first-trial jurors did not hear read was Roach's parenthetical observation accompanying Beeching's statement "Someone killed him" and Cook's reply because it did not appear in either of the Beeching versions: ("very emotional - right arm shaking and on the verge of tears.")[1]

---

[1] *Beeching did not read in Roach's three parenthetical asides which recorded Cook's emotional state at various stages of the interrogation (Appendix A: Qs 69, 75 and 78.) It may be that they did not appear in the copy Beeching employed (or copies, since his version of the statement varied from trial to trial), although it is probable they did since Roach's observations at Qs 20 and 59 were paraphrased by Beeching. He may not have had any choice but to do so since Cook's attitude at Q 20 was, in a sense, part of the answer, and his gesture at Q 59 was the answer.*

CHAPTER 10

THE SON, THE STEPSON, THE SIBLING

With the benefit of hindsight the Monday morning interrogation can be seen to have ranged aimlessly and ineffectively over the whole of Cook's story without any of the searching questioning which would have illuminated the more difficult problems - the matter of the suitcases to choose the most obvious example where Beeching's inquiry was worthless. The investigation was not yet two days old, yet to RCMP intents and purposes it was concluded even before the man charged with the crime had been questioned about it. Over the whole of Sunday it had been intensive; certain of Beeching's question show much legwork was already behind them. While there was more to be done to tie up loose ends, the statement and everything coming after it was anticlimactic. There is a sense to the statement of it not much mattering what Cook said. There was ample evidence in hand which of course would require some fine-tuning, and there was no great need for any self-serving statement from Cook which, with luck, might incriminate him. A bonus if it did, but far from fatal to the police case if it didn't.

As the interrogation wound down, Beeching's final questions starting with the hard-edged "Someone killed him" brought the questioning full-circle with the death of Cook's father again in the forefront, leaving Cook overwrought and on the verge of tears, and leaving students of the case with the unwelcome prospect of having to grasp the nettle. Were the tears genuine, or was he counterfeiting emotion with the verbal trappings of woe?

And, if he was not, if his grief was as genuine as it appeared to be to those who observed it not excluding Roach, could it have gone hand in hand with guilt no less genuine? At that time the problem was Beeching's and Roach's. What they had seen and what they believed required of them that they leave unresolved a schizophrenic clash of grief and guilt such that their acknowledgment of the *bona fides* of the former would not get in the way of their proof of the latter. The problem is now one for advocates of Cook's guilt and, with a sense of relief, is left with them.

That said, it may be asserted by way of moving on that nothing, including his own impending death, affected Cook so profoundly as did the death of his father. Yet for nine years he had made his father's life a living hell, something peculiarly within the capability of sons whose fathers can no longer reach out and touch and greet them. It started with him leaving home at 13 never again to be a permanent part of it. Ray was left with the humiliating and heartbreaking necessity of explaining to friends and neighbors and shopmates the absence of his jailed 14-year old son. He had driven his father to the utter defeat of having to place him in a foster home and then, when the foster parents moved to BC, in another from which he fled in a stolen car in an unsuccessful bid for the States. He had exposed his father's children to the schoolyard taunts of other children, and his father's wife to the behind-the-hand contumely of those who did not like her and, which was worse, the pity of those who did. He had made of his father's life nine years of despairing hope that Cook would make for himself a place in his father's new family that not he and not Daisy were able to make for him.

He wanted two things from life, offering nothing in return: the car he had dreamed of, but that was secondary. He wanted a father-son partnership in a business of their own - a revival of the halcyon days in Hanna when it was him and his father against the world. For lack of trying, he could think of no other way to do it than to pool the paltry proceeds of petty theft with his father's savings, and he set out to get them, always looking for the main chance. In the meantime he continued to earn the wages of sin on a modest scale - a hundred and fifty for this B&E, three hundred and change for that, never dreaming as he rapped with Thachik about scoring fifty thousand that he had about 18 months to go before he would be paid the wages of sin on a hitherto unimagined scale.

His love for his father was beyond mere reputation; it was a hard-core fact at the center of the case. But 'twere better he'd forgotten him, which was not possible, than to return to Stettler again and again after each jail or penitentiary term, using Stettler as a temporary base, leaving it pursued or under arrest and leaving behind for Ray and Daisy fresh embarrassment, fresh shame for them to deal with in the unforgiving crucible of a small town whose main street was named Main Street - life mimicking art. In a shallow way he was not unaware of what he was doing to them, not concerned to do anything about it, and not capable of it if he had been. There is, as Yeats said, a pity beyond all telling hid in the heart of love, and so with Cook's love for his father. If there was poetry in the pity, it was a lament which told of thoughtlessness and selfishness - the usual stuff of love requited on terms different than those on which it is offered.

***

Who can know? It is convenient to think that it was Ray Cook who sowed the dragon's teeth of his own destruction in the three years preceding his second marriage, but the evidence of it is, finally, inconclusive. One hoped to have inquiry made easier by finding someone intimate with the family both before and after the death of Josephine - a resident grandmother, say, preferably purse-lipped and disapproving, able to see young hellions in all their grubby glory. Who better than a wise grandmother to say how things were in those distant days, and whether or not Ray Cook had gone too far beyond the normal measure of indulgence which, while his mother lived, doubtlessly fell to Cook as an only child.

There was a grandmother, but she failed to meet the exacting standard. Ray's mother was the only one of Cook's grandparents who survived Ray, and she had never lived with him in his adult years. There were enough people close enough to Ray after Josephine's death to say how things appeared, and we have looked at the testimony of some of them. On balance things appeared entirely normal in the two-man family, but much beyond that it is not possible to go.

The shattering of Cook's boyhood idyll was rude beyond any understanding he could have had of it. With Ray's marriage to Daisy things came apart. The center no longer held and a new one formed around the crabby Miss Gasper who overnight and without warning to Cook usurped her new stepson's rightful place at the core of his father's

165

affection. That it was now divided affection rather than, as he perceived it, exclusive in her favor was not enough for Cook even had he been persuaded that it was now shared by two people, and that he remained one of them. His father was to be shared with no one, and he began a bitter withdrawal into rebellion.

It is a neat and all-encompassing explanation, even lending itself to headline treatment - PLACE USURPED BY HATED STEPMOTHER. SPOILED SON TURNS TO CRIME - but it is not known whether it is true. There are certain demands one should be entitled to make of explanations, among them that they be true or, failing that, probable, but it is not really known whether even probability can be claimed for a Daisy-as-unwitting-villain theory. With her arrival Cook began to go wrong; that too is a given. Whether she was the innocent cause of it or merely hastened a development already on progress will remain forever unknown. It was probably a combination of those and six other factors - nothing is ever simple - and all one can do is record some sketchy evidence for what it may be worth.

When he was released from Lethbridge, he quickly disabused his parents of any idea that rehabilitation might have taken, and he was handed over to the child welfare authorities who placed him with his first foster parents, John and Edith Larson on their farm northwest of Edmonton. When the Larsons sold out and moved to BC, he was placed on "the Henry Stucke place", a few miles southeast of Edmonton. When I interviewed her, Mrs Stucke was elderly and her English heavily accented and difficult to follow, but her regard for Cook did not need translation; that sort of affection has a language of its own, somewhat disjointed though the relating of it was:

"Yes its true he stayed with us. He wanted to come back. He was really good. The other one spoiled him - another boy from jail that Pastor Hannemann had placed on the Sigmund Schulman farm near us. They stole the money and stole a car and left for the States. I bought him a suit and a white shirt for confirmation, but they stole the money and the car and he was never confirmed.

"He blamed his father altogether. He was fooling around with the teacher and she was pregnant[1]. He never made threats against his father, but didn't like his stepmother. He was twelve, thirteen. Said that Daisy was all for her children and he was nothing in her eyes. Never would

---

[1] *We have seen that Ray and Daisy were married July 7, 1949. Their first-born, Gerry, was born on February 19 1950.*

have laid a hand on his father, but maybe his brothers. I really liked him. Same as my own son. I gave him spending money, bought him clothes, dressed him up nice. Sundays in church with the rest of us same as my own children. He was so good. If he had been mean [the execution] wouldn't have been so hard to take. The kids liked him so much. He never lied to us about anything.

"He would sit there with us in the evenings. We'd talk. He'd cry all the time when talking about his father. 'We had such a good home. My father put a cushion on the seat and taught me how to drive. It was my father's fault my mother died. We had such a good home.'

"After his mother's death, he took his father's car and went to his mother's sister's place and his stepmother was mad. She phoned the police and they took him to jail and then she had a baby. Daisy invited him to come and see the baby but he didn't want to go. His father and stepmother came to see us. Brought him his bike. She said come and see the baby. He wouldn't go near it.

"I can't say one wrong word about him. If I told him to do something, he'd do it. We could hardly stand it that he should be hung. My son died four years ago; he was caught in a cultivator and bled to death before they could get him to the hospital. It wasn't as hard as when Bobby died."

She had said a couple of wrong words about him, but only because her honesty caused her to see him steadily and see him whole. It would be possible to take her account apart and separate what she might have learned from newspaper accounts and from third parties from her first-hand memories, but that is not important. What is perhaps is that Cook's death, she said, affected her more than her son's. It is a compelling statement, yet when Cook died she had not seen him or heard from him for about nine years, and it may be that she was caught up in the emotions of the publicity and the trials. Still....

***

That he disliked Daisy in the early years of their association seems beyond argument. Dave MacNaughton encountered the dislike in his background researches. He informed Main in a letter written about a month after the murders that "I have been advised that he was constantly with his father after his mother's death and there may have been some resentment after the re-marriage." Lila Larson, the daughter of the first foster parents, learned when he was with them that "he loved his dad but didn't like his stepmother."

For her part, Daisy told Mrs Joe O'Reilly that Bobby stole $100 from her trunk when she and Ray were first married, but "No, he likes me. We get along fine. He babysits for me and Ray. He's real good to the kids." Daisy told O'Reilly this in the spring of 1957 just as Cook was about to arrive home after his second penitentiary term. It may have been an augury of a relationship changing for the better. Or perhaps a presentiment of disaster which might be avoided if she could put as good a face as possible on the relationship between her and her galling stepson.

The reaching out was all one way: Daisy to her stepson. It may have been changing as he matured, but it took a long time for him to look upon her as "Mom" if indeed he ever did in any genuine sense. When he was admitted to Manitoba Penitentiary in December, 1953 (by which time Daisy had been a nominal mother for four-and-a-half years), he curtly informed the admitting officer that his father was alive but that he had no mother. Interestingly however there is a penitentiary form dating from this time on which newly-admitted inmates listed the names of the persons they wished to have recognized as approved correspondents: immediate blood relatives and so on. 'Father' was of course no problem: "Raymond Cook, Stettler, Alberta, Canada" in a penciled scrawl. The blank for 'Stepmother' was not filled in, but opposite 'Mother' the same hand had filled in "Daisy Gasper" and then erased it, but leaving it legible. Daisy did not know it, but maternal status had been briefly bestowed on her only to be snatched away. She had not however earned the right to the surname.

A week later he told the prison doctor his parents were both dead and he had no brothers and sisters. True, he as yet had no sisters, but nor had he license to deny existence to three half brothers. He was now an immature 16 - immaturity appears frequently in prison assessments -and he was not about to give up self-pity as a soother. Five days later he rang all the changes with the chaplain, telling him he had been "orphaned at 13" and had been "more or less on his own ever since" - an amalgam of truth and falsehood probably designed not so much to engage the chaplain's sympathy as to stoke the self-pity.

For the first seven months of the Manitoba term, his family lost contact with him, not knowing where he was. Contact was re-established with a letter from Ray - one of the few he ever wrote his son. It does not survive, but Cook's reply does: "You also asked me to come home which makes me feel wonderful and love you all the more after all the trouble I've given you." To this reader it is cloying and not quite the idiom of a 16-year-old; he may have been capable of feigning emotion after all. But take him at his word as he took his father at his. He accepted the invitation to come home, but with all the single-minded purpose of the whining schoolboy creeping schoolwards.

It took him 13 days to get from Stony to Stettler during which he first went to Winnipeg to see Alex Turk, the fight promoter who may, during this brief period, have sent him to Sioux City, Iowa to fight. Turk wanted to sign him to a pro contract, but having just escaped the seamy world of the prison system, he was not about to enter the seamy world of the pro fight game, and he moved on, attempting to repair his fortunes in western Ontario with a series of break-ins for which he was not caught. He then returned to Winnipeg intending, he was shortly to tell the Saskatchewan Penitentiary Classification Officer, to get a job "to make a stake to enable him to return home for Christmas. It was August and home was a not-impossible 700 miles away.

He failed to find a job and returned to his birthplace, Hanna, where he broke into the Central Garage scooping $1.50 for his trouble, and the government liquor store which yielded $17 from a cash drawer. He helped himself to a drink and replaced the bottle without removing his fingerprints, a mistake, he swore to Pete Thachik, through the bars in the RCMP lockup, he would never make again as long as he lived. He was as good as his word.

When he arrived home, finally, his father had waiting for him a 1940 Chevrolet bought for $425. When, later, he was back in Prince Albert, the Classification Officer made the following entry on his file: "The reception at home makes him realize how foolishly he acted and claims even though he was arrested [in Stettler for the two Hanna offenses] after only a few hours at home he had already been found a job by his parents. This apparently made favourable impression on subject who expresses strongly a desire to go straight in the future." The officer had heard it all before. So had Ray, and he was to hear it all again. In 1957, he again had a coming home gift waiting - another car - and once again he got his son a job. Perhaps the McTaggart Motors car lot wasn't the most propitious choice for someone who lived to steal cars, and once again his son failed him.

The remarks column of the Incoming Mail form started on Cook at the outset of his first Prince Albert term bears, opposite the recording of Daisy's letter to him of February, 10, 1957, the entry "Mother signs self 'Daisy'." In the attempt to understand Cook, there is always a temptation to read into a chance entry such as this what one is looking for, and thus the entry is fastened on as evidence of a changing relationship between the 35 year old woman and her 20 year old stepson. But changing in what way? Probably, in this instance, in the innocent direction of her deciding to put it on the basis of two adults related only by marriage, thus doing away with the strain of him having to regard her as "Mom".

Yet there may have been more, and it should be touched on. Jimmy Myhaluk, who was as close to Cook as anyone (he was allowed to read Cook's letters from home) considered the possibility: "I read the letter his father wrote him about their plans. Daisy wrote him too. He had an attraction or infatuation for her. Perhaps it was a sexual thing in the back of his mind, but with a respect for her." What Myhaluk was suggesting was the stuff of Greek tragedy: Phaedra and Oedipus warring in the bosom of a single state of affairs neither would have been comfortable recognizing.

Yet when the juvenile acne shown in the Stony mug shots had cleared, the Brylcreamed and overcombed hair of the typical teenager had gone the way of all flesh and his physique had filled out to its mature stature, Cook was a physically attractive man. Dave Beeching told me that sympathy began to swing towards Cook as early as the Red Deer trial when the courthouse groupies - some of them quite matronly - and the Clerk's Office staff caught their first glimpse of the mass murderer. If they were expecting fangs and knotted hair given the press he'd had, what they got was a young, good-looking man, cool, self-possessed, not playing to them or anyone else as a gallery. They also saw a man manacled to large RCMP constables, and he appeared to them vulnerable and defenseless - a sight to trigger mothering instincts and whatever dark urges go hand in hand with such instincts. No evidence suggests Daisy harbored such urges, but she would not have been less human had they slept in her subconscious mind, stirring from time to time to prompt her in unbidden ways.

She wrote her errant stepson fairly consistently through the first 18 months of his first Prince Albert term, but the letter-for-letter consistency of reply he maintained throughout his second term (when they wrote each other monthly) was absent. When she had written him in September, October and November of 1956 without a reply, she decided to write the warden to enlist his assistance. Her letter of January 15, 1957, written in the crystal-clear hand of a grade-school teacher exists yet in Cook's penitentiary records:

"Could you kindly let me know about Robert Cook? We haven't heard from him for some time and we are anxious to know how he is. He never said if there was anything we could send him. "We would be grateful for any information. Thank you for your trouble.

"Respectfully, Mrs Ray Cook."

The warden, T. W. Hall was a gracious man who took the trouble to talk to Cook and to reply to Daisy on January 25: "Replying to your letter of January 15, 1957, I had your boy in front of me today in the matter of his non-writing to you. He admits that he has not been writing home, but from what I can gather this lack of writing is not due to any thoughts on the part of Robert that he does not wish to have anything more to do with his family, but simply that he feels ashamed for bringing his family into disgrace.

"I impressed upon Robert the fact that no matter what he has done or where he was, his mother would always have the same thoughts for him, and asked him to consider that his mother would worry over him and for him to write as soon as possible.

"As far as your son's health is concerned, he looks very well and is working every day. His conduct is such that he is entitled to full privileges.

"Yours faithfully, T. W. Hall."

***

This letter and her constant letters to Cook over the years addressed to the penitentiary of the moment (the incoming mail records are filled with "Mrs Ray Cook") tell of a woman who had been given every reason to join issue with her husband over her refractory stepson, to issue a 'him or me' ultimatum, but who did not. They tell of a warm-hearted woman refusing to add to her husband's already unbearable burden when her inclination (of which there is some evidence) might very well have been

171

to write him off, to once and for all draw a line between him and her, her husband, and her attractive, happy and well-adjusted children who did not need an example such as Cook's to look up to. It seems certain they loved him - the boys at least; the two little girls would hardly know him - and just as certain that he doted on them, but it may be that he would have served them best by bowing out of their lives and the lives of their parents.

He could not do it, any more than he could turn back and lovingly shoulder his way into the open-armed circle. By his own sad lights he tried, and they tried, both Ray and Daisy offering him every encouragement, every inducement, Daisy in particular. But whatever the answer may have been to the desperate conundrum posed by Robert Raymond Cook, Daisy May Cook did not have it. She told Clara Behuniak just before he came home for the last time that he was starting to get quite attached to her; that he was finally starting to call her "Mom."

"She told me he was good in helping with the dishes for example and in looking after the kids. But she also told me there was something wrong with him - that he needed help; that he needed motherly love." Cook saw it differently. In one of his last letters he wrote: "If Dad had knocked hell out of me, I wouldn't be in the trouble I'm in today." From the verge of tears to the verge of insight in one cruel lesson.

But his father had not knocked hell out of him and if Cook blamed him for it (but with wry fondness), at bottom he did not and could not blame him for much else. To say anything negative about his father would be to be "as wrong as you can ever get. He was too friendly, too nice."

Motherly love? Perhaps. Just as Josephine had failed him by dying and Ray by not knocking hell out of him, Daisy had failed him by not giving him that which he would not allow her to give him although she never stopped trying (and was sorely tried in the effort) over many years and in myriad ways. For that she deserves to be remembered.

But it is a well known fact, it is almost an apodictic law of the universe, that given a moderate amount of time, all men grow up sooner or later. They invariably become strong, resolute, self-reliant, mature, considerate, able to stand on their own feet without - or at least with minimal - mothering, and it seems permissible to say that Cook seems to have been coming along. Not much to be sure, but some, and hers was the credit. She might have succeeded had her death not intervened.

He owed her much and he was not entirely incapable of acknowledging it. She had been better to him than he deserved. She was the mother of his brothers and sisters, and he was well disposed towards her on that account. She sought to maintain and strengthen his ties with home, and though he at once rejected them and clung to them, they were always there should he ever come at last to appreciate and use them as the priceless possessions they could and should have been. She did not fail him.

Nothing and no one failed him unless it was his genes, the gods, the Fates which decreed that he go irremediably wrong. But, as the late lamentable Al Jolson used to say, he hadn't seen nothing yet. The system was about to fail him in a failure to end all failures.

Guilt is present in the very hesitation,
even though the deed not be committed.

CICERO - *De Officiis*

He who hesitates...

CHAPTER 11

THE STRAGGLER AND THE SHOPPING BAG

We have reached a dividing point in the study of the *Cook* trials. What
has gone before has been intended as background to an analysis of the
evidence, much of which has been touched on in passing but will be
returned to in this and the following 11 chapters for a closer look. To
most of those directly involved - the judges, the jurors, the prosecutors,
the police - the evidence added up without noticeable difficulty to proof
of guilt beyond a reasonable doubt. That it did is a fact which cannot be
glossed over. But for some it did not. In the opinion of Cook's lawyers
- Dave MacNaughton, Giffard Main and Frank Dunne - it fell far short.
The opinion happens to be shared by the writer, and what follows is
unavoidably informed - colored is another word for it - by that point of
view.

For none of the defense lawyers who for small reward gave unstintingly of their time and not a little of their spirit was their conviction of the inadequacy of the evidence merely a formulaic approach to the job. Lawyers are not paid to believe that anyone who has the price, guilty and innocent alike, is innocent. Defense lawyers do not allow their own opinions as to the guilt or innocence of the man they're hired to defend get in the way of doing the job. But of course they most often do have them; they believe what they believe and perhaps as often as not their opinion will be at odds with a convicting jury's. So here. For each of Main, MacNaughton and Dunne the opinion that Cook was improperly convicted was strongly held, but two of them at least went further. Improper conviction does not imply innocence, but for two of them - and probably the third - Cook was innocent. Their opinions were leavened to be sure by the regard each of them had come to have for Cook, but they were not dictated or distorted by it. It is hoped to show their convictions were not misplaced.

In a study of a murder trial such as Cook's, nothing is easier, nothing more conducive to a sense of superiority than to sit back in academic tranquility and point out where the defense lawyers (and the prosecuting attorneys for that matter) missed the point here and what so obviously should have been done there. Nothing is easier in directing a defense from an armchair than devising the defense strategies which ought to have been employed, framing brilliant ripostes, hoisting police witnesses with the petard of their selective memories. It is the stuff of a Walter Mitty fantasy.

Yet that conceded, it has been felt that the efforts of Main and Dunne - Dunne in particular - are deserving of some criticism while trying to remember the circumstances in which those efforts were made. Anyone who has known the sweaty fear, vicarious and direct, felt in operating in that arena, anyone who has experienced the unimaginable pressure which comes with knowing that what Main and Dunne would see, rightly or wrongly, as the price of their failure was the forfeiture of Cook's life, will be inclined to make more allowances than someone concerned to score debating points. Still, it has seemed to me that it could have been done better in some ways, and I have thought it necessary to say so in the interests of objectivity.

***

A straggler, in the view of Webster's Twentieth Century Dictionary, is among other things one who departs from the direct or proper course, one who rambles without any settled direction, a wandering, shiftless fellow. The lexicographer could have had in mind the Cook who returned to Stettler at noon on Thursday after an absence of 25 months and then in the next nine hours never managed to make it home. The nine hours had to be met head on by the defense - on the face of it they didn't contribute much to the loving son-joyous reunion picture the defense hoped to leave with the jury. Other witnesses, most of them called by the Crown, would be called to fill in some of the gaps, but only one man could paint the larger picture: Cook.

His explanation was straightforward and plausible enough if one was inclined to sympathy for Cook. He did not go directly home, he said, because he wanted to talk to his father alone before meeting the rest of the family. He did not say before meeting Daisy, but one can't help wondering why he didn't go home and chat with her, have lunch, have a coffee until Dad got off work. One can't help wondering what this said about his relationship with his stepmother.

He could not, he said, talk to his father before Ray left Modern Machine having regard to the opprobrium the convict son would bring into the workplace. When Ray left work between 5 and 6, Cook missed him, but another three or four hours went by before Cook (who said he was then on his way home) was found by Ray on Main Street at 9 o'clock. Thus the bare bones of his explaining the nine long hours which we will now attempt to flesh out.

***

His faltering progress towards home was reminiscent of the 13 days it took him to reach Stettler from Stony Mountain Penitentiary. It started at 7:30 am, Thursday, June 25, as the motel party in Edmonton wound down, when he asked Eddie Read if he would drive him to Stettler in Read's panel truck. Read had other plans, but he offered Cook the use of his truck and suggested Cook ask Walter Berezowski to accompany him so that Berezowski could bring Read's truck back to Edmonton. Cook had spent his time at the motel party drinking (although he did not get noticeably drunk), bragging (which was unusual) to the women there about his prowess as a boxer, showing anyone who would look at them tattered snapshots of his brothers and sisters (they were never 'half' brothers and sisters), and telling anyone who would listen that his father had a car waiting for him in Stettler. Someone had to bring Read's truck back, and Berezowski agreed to come along.

They arrived in Stettler about noon having, as Cook was later to say, become lost on the way[1]. They drove around town for an hour or so with Cook pointing out the points of interest including the Cook house. They drove past it without stopping[2].

***

At about 1 pm Berezowski drove to the western outskirts of Stettler, guided by Cook in order, Cook said, to get Berezowski pointed in the right direction on the highway to Edmonton via Lacombe. Berezowski

[1] *It is hard to imagine becoming genuinely lost in the 130 miles of essentially flat and well-inhabited countryside between Edmonton and Stettler. The two are joined by two paved highways, more or less equally direct. No time is saved by leaving either highway and traveling cross-country on the grid-system back roads. Cook's assertion that they got lost doesn't ring true. It seems to be the product of a not very imaginative mind attempting to account for the two-hour trip having taken four hours even though travel time was not in issue. He sometimes lied when he didn't need to but, here, did he? A companion and I left one of the highways and got lost in the precise sense of not having any idea whether our destination, Stettler, was southwest or southeast of the point at which we realized we didn't know.*

[2] *Giving evidence at the first trial of this stage of the odyssey, Berezowski was brought up short by Anderson who asked why they hadn't stopped at the house. "Because," Berezowski replied, "it seemed as though nobody was home since there were no lights on in the house." Anderson was taken aback: "It was around noon?" "Around the noon hour; I'm not sure. "Anderson was not alone in wondering whether lights amid the blaze of noon were signs of the occupancy of a house. Mr Justice Greschuk intervened:*

THE COURT: "You wouldn't expect lights at noon. You just be careful. You are under oath. "

"Yes sir. "

THE COURT: "You behave. "

One guesses the fact that Berezowski was a friend of Cook's outweighed the fact that he was a Crown witness, and had something to do with His Lordship's displeasure since it is hard to see how Berezowski's innocent- seeming observation was a violation of his oath, unless of course the lights were on. There may have been a

left after agreeing with Cook that he would meet him in Lacombe where he would wait for Cook to catch up with him in the car Cook's father "had waiting for him." This and the following evidence relating to the intended Lacombe rendezvous comes from an interview with Berezowski. It was not referred to in either trial.

Cook anticipated it would take half-an hour to get the car and catch up, with Berezowski - which may be seen as saying something about Cook's eagerness for reunion with his family; he would remain in Stettler only long enough to grab a car and get out of it. After meeting in Lacombe, they would drive in convoy to Edmonton where Berezowski would park Read's truck on the outskirts since he was leery about city driving. Cook would then drive him to the motel where he would deliver the keys to Read and inform him of the location of the truck.

After an hour in Lacombe, Berezowski gave up on Cook and left for Edmonton. Read was not called to give evidence, but told me he thought Berezowski had delivered the truck to him (not merely the keys), where Berezowski thought he remembered parking the truck as planned where it was seized by the police as part of the murder investigation before he could inform Read of its location. Since the investigation did not get underway for three days after Berezowski would have parked the truck, it seems unlikely Berezowski would not have told Read of its location

touch of fatuity in Berezowski's reply to Anderson, but the literal truth - if it was - is sometimes fatuous. At the outset of Berezowski's testimony he was asked whether he lived in Edmonton. Berezowski was nervous, as many witnesses are in the early going. Like a latter-day Mad Hatter he replied faintly:

"That's right."

THE COURT: "You will have to speak up much louder so that all those gentlemen, six of them, can hear you plainly."

"That's right."

THE COURT: "You are a big man now."

Berezowski was 26, a big enough man at that and presumably able to count all six jurors for himself had it occurred to him to do so. He cannot have appreciated being addressed like a child of tender years.

Later in the same trial, the judge suggested to a 17-year old witness, also having trouble making himself heard, that "he pretend [he was] on the football field now", presumably as if he were a quarterback shouting audibles above the roar of the frenzied crowd. The ensuing sensation had the witness taken Greschuk at his word can only be imagined.

when Read would have then recovered it. Read's recollection seems preferable.

As shaky as Berezowski may have been as to when Read got his truck back, he was certain that when he left Cook in Stettler, Cook left in the truck a brown paper shopping bag[1] containing the clothes Cook had worn into the penitentiary in May 1957 which, since the penitentiary had issued him with new clothing, he carried out with him in June 1959. Moreover, the bag also contained what Berezowski called "some hobby stuff". At the motel party Cook had showed Gail Trudel a toy pistol and its leather holster. He told her (she told me) that he had made the holster in the prison hobby program, and that the set was a gift for his brother Gerry, and it seems probable therefore that that "hobby stuff" at least was in the shopping bag.

Berezowski was adamant, and if his recollection was accurate, the bag and its hobby stuff including the toy pistol set was in the truck when Berezowski drove off. Yet two toy pistols were found in the grease pit; there is no way of knowing whether one of them was the one Cook had waved around at the hotel. If it was not, then Cook had allowed Berezowski to drive off bearing Cook's gift for his brother which, till then, he'd been lugging around for the better part of two days together with a more or less complete change of clothes. On the other hand, if it was, then it found a companion in the greasepit since Van Blarcom too saw "some kiddies' belts with toy guns." The whole thing was in danger of receding beyond resolution.

But not quite yet. On March 21, 1960 MacNaughton wrote Main to say he had received an inquiry from Roach as to the whereabouts of some sheet copper pictures - "effects of Bob's that were found in Eddy Reed's *[sic]* truck. He thought you might have given them to Bob as there was some discussion about the copper plate *[sic]* pictures that Bob said he desired."

If Cook left a shopping bag full of clothes and hobby stuff in Read's truck[2], it should have had in it the copper pictures - hobby stuff if anything ever was - Roach was looking for. But if that was the case,

---

[1] *It started out in Prince Albert as (as described by Cook) "a box of my stuff." How it got transformed into a shopping bag by the time it got to Eddie Read's truck is not known.*

[2] *The police were never asked in trial what, if anything, their search of Read's truck disclosed nor, for that matter, were they ever asked if they had searched Read's truck. Anderson, for one, was not anxious to have them disclose they'd found a shopping bag. The whole subject recedes in a fog of uncertainty.*

why had they been released to Main (by the police, who had seized Read's truck and its contents), and if they were why would Roach, above all people, not know of it? And why, if Roach thought Main might have given them to Cook (continuity of possession was taking some strange turns) would he not phone the Fort to find out whether they were in Cook's effects rather than addressing an inquiry to Main through MacNaughton?

***

In the first trial Berezowski was asked nothing about a shopping bag by either Main or Anderson, and at the second trial nothing by Anderson. Dunne however asked him whether Cook *was* carrying anything when they parted on the western edge of town, and Berezowski replied not that he knew of. Since Dunne had not interviewed Berezowski prior to trial (Berezowski told me), his question was a shot in the dark which luckily elicited the reply Dunne wanted: Cook wandered around Stettler for eight hours after leaving Berezowski carrying nothing.

For his part, and for reasons which will appear shortly, Anderson was concerned to show that Cook was carrying something - a shopping bag - which explains why he did not ask Berezowski (his witness) if Cook was since he presumably knew what Berezowski's answer would be. But he asked five more Crown witnesses who had seen the wandering, shiftless fellow ambling around Stettler whether *they* had seen Cook carrying anything, and each replied he had not. Anderson was not a man to give up easily.

At the second trial Cook was asked if he was carrying anything and he too replied he was not. He was asked nothing about it at the first trial, nor did he volunteer anything. Nevertheless, in his charge to the jury Greschuk said, "You will recall that [Cook] stated he got home some time after 9 o'clock [pm] and said he was carrying a shopping bag and that the amount of money was $4300." The $4300 had nothing whatever to do with the shopping bag and here was a *non sequitur*. Of immediate interest was the shopping bag and in particular Greschuk's flat assertion that Cook had said he was carrying it. Cook had said nothing about the shopping bag and nor, for that matter, had he said "that the amount of the money was $4300."

Whatever Greschuk's shortcomings as a judge, inaccuracy in absorbing evidence and in reviewing it for the jury at exhaustive length was not one of them. He enjoyed the reputation, when sitting without a jury, of making findings of fact in such a way as to preclude the possibility of successful appeal by the party not favored by what Greschuk had decided, beyond peradventure of doubt, the facts were. When he was through setting out all the facts he was called upon to decide - for example that black had been proved by the plaintiff leaving the defendant in trouble with white - they admitted of no second-guessing by an appeal court. While there might be good reason for the defendant - and even the court of appeal - thinking white was the case, black it was in a Greschuk judgment. Period.

In a jury trial the judge does not decide what has been proved as fact and what has not, but by the time he has finished reviewing the evidence in a complex case, the jurors will be inclined to accept what he says was said as having been said. Thus when Greschuk said Cook said he was carrying a shopping bag, it would be too much to expect of the average juror that he remember that Cook had not. Or that it was Beeching who said Cook said he was carrying it. Or that Cook had said nothing to Beeching (in the Monday morning interrogation) about a shopping bag, and in fact expressly denied carrying anything (apart from a couple of suitcases which he was not carrying)[1].

***

After Beeching had finished reading in Cook's statement in the first trial, Main rose to cross-examine him:

"Now, he told you during the course of giving the statement that he had been driven home from Edmonton to Stettler by one Eddie Read?"

"Yes he did."

"He did, but later on in the day he changed that and told you that he had been driven home by Walter Berezowski in Eddie Read's truck, is that not correct?"

"During the evening he told me he had been driven by Walter

[1] *See Chapter 22 and see Appendix A, Q. 36.*

Berezowski in Eddie Read's truck."

"In Eddie Read's truck, yes. He corrected that and I believe he made another correction about that time. He said he had got to his home about 8 o'clock on Thursday or about an hour after that or two hours after that, and later on during the day he changed that to sometime after 9 o'clock?"

"That evening, yes, in conversation with him he said it was sometime after 9 o'clock."

"That he arrived at his home?"

"Yes, and he also referred to the money as $4300."

"Yes, he changed the figure of $4100 to $4300?"

"That's correct. He also said he was carrying a shopping bag."

"At what time?"

"During the evening when I had a conversation, he said he was carrying a shopping bag when he was at Stettler."

"At any particular time while at Stettler?"

"During the afternoon of Thursday."

Which was all well and good except there was no evidence indicating Beeching saw Cook on Monday evening. On Monday evening Cook was ensconced - if not that securely - at the PMH, and there was not (as the old English judges were fond of saying and by way of emphasizing the point) an iota or a scintilla, much less a jot or a tittle of evidence that Beeching was ever at the PMH.

It is true Cook changed Read to Berezowski, but that appears to have been done during - or at the conclusion - of the Monday morning interrogation. The statement will be seen to say "N.B. Later changed this to being Walter William BEREZOWSKI who drove him in Eddie REID'S *[sic]* truck"[1] and, one supposes, "later" could have been that evening at the PMH. But if Beeching interviewed him at Ponoka, he never recorded what Cook told him there nor did he disclose in court that he had been there. He may have been, but it is inconceivable that

[1] *See Appendix A, Q. 26.*

Beeching would travel to Ponoka, take another statement from Cook (or have the Monday morning statement clarified) and there be no record of the trip or of what Cook said.

Similarly with the $4100 to $4300 change; Cook did not make one. It will be seen [1] Beeching put the question to Cook in terms of "where [he] was keeping that $4100" - the amount Cook had imparted to Roach on Saturday evening when he was being questioned about the Impala. Roach, not Cook, was Beeching's source of the amount, and Cook never departed from $4100 as the sum given to Ray. As it happens, Cook did change from $100 to $200 as the amount held back when he handed the $4100 to his father and thus, impliedly, was changing $4200 to $4300, but Beeching was not talking about that.

What was he talking about? It is safe to conclude from all the foregoing that Beeching was not at Ponoka on Monday evening in spite of his having said to Main three times in cross-examination that the Reid to Berezowski change, the time of arrival change and the money amount change had occurred during a conversation with Cook on Monday evening. But he also said that Cook said he was carrying a shopping bag, and, to hear Beeching, Cook said this too on Monday evening[2]. Main failed completely to pick up on Beeching's having told him three times in cross-examination of having had a conversation with Cook which he had not had. It seems unfortunate since Main could have pilloried Beeching, but he didn't and now Beeching had a conversation which didn't occur into which he could slip a shopping bag when there had been no mention of it in the Monday morning interrogation. Anderson now had his shopping bag. It was to get even better for Anderson when the trial judge himself parroted Beeching.

We will see in Chapter 16 that Anderson had a problem: how explain the arrival of the double-barreled shotgun - the murder weapon - at the Cook house since it did not appear to belong to any of the occupants. Clearly Cook must have brought it there, but Cook had been observed wandering aimlessly around Stettler on Thursday afternoon by a dozen or so people, none of whom had seen him carrying a double-barreled shotgun. There had to be an explanation, and the shopping bag rather improbably offered one. Cook had concealed the gun in the bag. One might have thought that there would have been 36 or so inches peeking

[1] *Appendix A, Q. 68.*

[2] *First-trial transcripts, page 335: "During the evening when I had a conversation, he said he was carrying a shopping bag when he was at Stettler.*

demurely from the top, but no matter; it was the best Anderson could do and he started in on his witnesses. After the fifth of them he gave it up as what might have been anticipated as a bad job, and the whole forlorn subject of shopping bags doubling as scabbards was consigned to limbo. There was no mention of shopping bags in the second trial.

***

As long as he was with Berezowski, Cook had a reason of sorts for not stopping at the house. Even had Cook wanted to see Daisy in advance of his father coming home from work, Berezowski in those years was not the sort of man one took home to meet the folks, but Cook was not using Berezowski as an excuse for avoiding Daisy. For his own reasons (which were never divulged; he was never asked about them) Cook wanted to see Ray first, and after Berezowski's departure he had about four hours to kill before Ray was free. He began to walk back towards the center of town - it was at this time he was spotted by Dillon Hoskins - and for the next four hours he wandered around Stettler, looking over boyhood haunts (there cannot have been all that many when his time in Stettler was set against his prison time), talking with no one, "just reminiscing with the town" he said in a rather graceful phrase describing his peregrinations on a warm summer afternoon.

Main questioned him about this period:

"Why didn't you go home first?"

"I wanted to see Dad first. I had some things I wanted to talk over with him."

"You wanted to greet him before the rest of them?"

"That's right."

"Now what were you doing walking up and down the main street of Stettler and so on in Stettler?"

"Nothing in particular. I was just...I don't know, it was fun to walk around and look things over like. I had been gone quite awhile and I was

just walking around looking. It was the first time I was free to do what
I wanted pretty near. I was at the skating rink and all the places I had
been pretty well when I was smaller, when I was going to school there.
By the courthouse there used to be a kind of swimming pool we used to
go to all the time, and I was just kind of walking around. You know. It
is hard to explain. I hadn't been there for a long time and...."

"What did you do when you pretty well killed the afternoon?"

"I wanted to catch my Dad like when he came off work, but somehow I
missed him because when I went down to the garage I noticed before his
car was parked towards the side of the garage."

"Had you seen it before?"

"Yes I had."

"I see. You had seen his car parked...?"

"At Filipenko's or Modern Machine."

How Cook could have seen his father's car - the year-old station wagon
- "before", when he had been away from home for two years, is not
known.

He then recounted going to a cafe for supper after which the laggard
straggler finally started for home.

***

Walking home he met his nine-year old brother Gerry:

"He was riding a bike [Cook told Main] - come by on a bicycle and I
guess he seen me first and called my name and put the bike down and he
came running over and kind of wrestled around there for awhile."

"Will you explain yourself a little bit for the benefit of the court and the
jury:?

"He put the bike down and came running over and he kind of made a jump at me, you know, as kids do, and I kind of grabbed him and messed up his hair and things like that."

"Was he glad to see you?"

"Yes, very glad to see me."

"I see. It was a friendly little wrestle?"

"I guess it was a way to express your emotions, I don't know."

"I see. Would it be fair to say he crawled all over you?"

"Yes, pretty well."

"All right. Now did you tell him anything or did he tell you anything?"

"I told him that I would be home in ten, fifteen minutes, and I told him not to say anything to Mom and Dad; that I wanted to surprise them."

It rings true enough; it is consistent with what is known of Cook's feelings for Gerry. But as with many things Cook said it raised some questions.

For example, if he wanted to surprise Ray and Daisy, why not go home with Gerry and surprise them? It would not have been a surprise as it happens since they already knew from two sources that Cook was in town, but he did not know they knew, and the only surprise would have been Cook's on discovering the absence of theirs.

There are some other questions: did Cook know that there were visitors, Jim and Leona Hoskins, before he met Gerry? Was the meeting with Gerry as joyous as Cook said it was? There is some non-trial evidence indicating otherwise, but in most areas of the *Cook* evidence, a point is reached where a halt must be called to attempting to answer all the questions, or even to set them out, in favor of moving the story forward. We have reached it in the vexing matter of the nine hours, and leave them by saying that after the meeting with Gerry, Cook went back down town in order to undo at a cafe washroom the damage done by "this nine-year old boy" as Anderson described him when he sought to destroy Cook's account of his glad meeting with his brother. He was standing on Main Street when his father drove up. Left to his own devices it is possible he might never have reached home.

In retrospect, the defense could not have done much more than it did to explain away the nine hours: give Cook his head and hope for the best. Crown evidence was not damaging. There were eight or ten people who saw him that afternoon. His demeanor was innocent, but a man taking his time to meditate murder can be expected to look innocent. The reunion with his father was observed to be friendly and warm. They drove off to have a beer in the Royal Hotel, and when they left the hotel Ray was never again seen alive by any of his fellow townspeople.

At home there was no fatted calf, but the atmosphere was one of welcome - if only he would ever get there. Leona Hoskins was a visitor to the house that night and she discussed the imminent homecoming with Ray and Daisy. There was, she told me, no latent hostility or anything other than pleased anticipation of his arrival. Hoskins was at a loss to understand why no one in the three courtrooms in which she appeared asked her what she knew of the atmosphere in the Cook household: a mixture of excitement and disappointment that he hadn't shown up yet. The Hoskins left and Ray went to look for his son. He found him and brought him home and the rest, as they say, is history.

CHAPTER 12

THE SWAG, THE STATION WAGON AND THE SERVICE STATION

Three things consumed the thoughts of Cook's waking hours: money, generally stolen; cars, invariably stolen; and the abiding dream of George and Lennie which he shared with his father: a little place of their own not, to be sure, on which to raise rabbits (although who in their heart of hearts does not wish to raise rabbits?), but on which to operate a father-son service station. These three - money, a particular car and the partnership - are the pivots around which the three parts of his story to be examined in this chapter revolve.

We will examine first the burial and recovery of money stolen by him and given to his father; second Ray's gift to him of an almost new station wagon; third the long-cherished plan to buy a service station. It should be remembered at the outset that he and no one else said that he had given stolen money to his father, he and no one else said Ray had given him the family car, he and no one else said they had long planned to buy a service station (although there is evidence that Ray at least had such plans), and we are embarked on an inquiry as to whether he might have been telling the truth about each of the three.

We begin by retracing a couple of steps over familiar ground: Cook and Myhaluk arrived in Edmonton on the overnight bus from Saskatoon at about 7 am, Wednesday, June 24. Cook left Myhaluk and the taxi they had taken from the downtown bus depot and checked into the Commercial Hotel where he washed up. He left the hotel, ate breakfast and then made the first of three visits he was to make to Hood Motors where he saw for the first time the dream car: the Impala convertible. He discussed it briefly with a Hood salesman, telling him in passing that he was a mechanic "in business with [his] father"; and that he would be back on Friday, impliedly with a car to be traded in on the Impala.

He left Hood and walked south on 104 Street, at that time the extension into the city of the Calgary-Edmonton Highway. Short of the city limits, he stopped in at the first promising used-car lot - which was not to distinguish it since all used-car lots held promise for Cook. There he hot-wired a car and drove to Bowden, about 110 miles south of Edmonton. Somewhere near Bowden, he unearthed a buried tobacco tin containing the proceeds of a series of B&Es. He returned to Edmonton and replaced the car on the lot from which he'd stolen it. He was now carrying $4300 recovered from the tobacco tin, and he left for Stettler the following morning still carrying it. This, and everything which follows up to the time of his arrival in Edmonton on Friday morning, was his story. There was no corroboration except in minor details.

When, at long last, his father found him on Main Street, they went to the Royal Hotel for a beer. There they discussed their long-held plans to buy a service station, and decided the time had come to do it. A search for a suitable business would be conducted in BC by Ray to whom Cook gave $4100 as his contribution towards its purchase price, keeping back $200 as walking around money. For his part, Ray gave Cook the keys to the year-old station wagon - the car Cook had boasted about at the motel party and which he had told the new-car salesman was waiting for him in Stettler and which he would wish to trade in on whichever new car he decided to buy. Cook then left home for Edmonton leaving his family making plans for the departure for BC. On Friday afternoon, he completed the deal for the Impala.

In outline this is the story Cook related to Roach on Saturday evening when Roach questioned him about the Impala but he omitted any mention of Bowden and the money. Again omitting Bowden (except in another context) but not the money, he told it to Pete Thachik as they rapped through the bars on Sunday afternoon. Still with no disclosure of where the money had been hidden, he recounted the whole of the story to Beeching in his distracted answers during the Monday morning interrogation and then, at last revealing the money cache's approximate locale, he told it to his lawyers, to the court at both trials, to the psychiatrist sent from Ottawa, and he set it down in Murder by Infernce - his last-day testament. It may not have been true, but there was no denying its constancy.

While others would be divulged to his lawyers as the Crown's case was revealed at the preliminary inquiry and the exigencies of the defense position became apparent, the key elements of the story were in place by the time the police had finished with Cook and handed him over to the psychiatrists at the PMH: the reciprocal gifts - $4100 and the station wagon; the service station to be acquired in fulfillment of the dream - a dream freighted with Ray's hope that its realization would prove to be the salvation of his son[1], and the acquisition of the Impala.

***

Turning over the money to his father was the linchpin of this part of the story. Without the jurors' belief that he had done so, the credibility of the gift of the station wagon and the service station plan collapsed. It was essential to the defense therefore that the existence of the Bowden cache be firmly - very firmly - established; there could not be *any* question of the fact of its existence. Conversely, if the Crown was able to discredit Cook's assertion that he had driven to Bowden, the $4300 evaporated and with it the whole of Cook's account of the homecoming, the discussion of plans and the decision that the family would go to BC to scout the possibilities.

---

[1] *While Cook saw his future as encompassing the father-son partnership, he had no intention of allowing it to interfere with the resumption of his chief vocation: breaking and entering and car theft. As he saw it, they need not be mutually exclusive; they could flourish side-by-side. Pump jockey by day and jolly swagman by night - the best of all possible worlds. In the latter role, the convertible would render him invisible to the police as effectively as if he were being driven away from his latest break-in in a chauffeured limousine, so naive were they in Cook's view of them. The Classification Officer's "immature" was the word for it.*

The money was never described as swag at either trial, although all three senior lawyers used the equally archaic 'loot'. Swag was adopted here only to preserve the otherwise uncontrived (the tie apart) sibilance of the Table of Contents.

Anderson therefore had to undermine the Bowden episode, and Main (and, in his turn, Dunne) by electing to put Cook on the stand, elected to prove that Cook had stolen a car and had driven to Bowden. The rest might then fall into place. The issue was thus joined when Main began to explore the subject of the cache in his direct examination of Cook:

"What did you ultimately do that day?"

"I wired up a car on the South Side and took it to Bowden."

"When you say 'wired up a car on the South Side' what do you mean - you stole it didn't you."

"Yes."

"You took some car by shortcircuiting the ignition and what did you do?"

"I drove it to Bowden."

"You drove it to Bowden, and what did you do there?"

"I went and got the money I had left there in April '57"

Although Main went on to cover the return of the car to Edmonton, and the sources of some of the money in the tobacco tin, that was it for the Bowden trip on direct examination: Cook's say-so. And not very persuasive say-so at that on a matter of fundamental importance. There was nothing else - no independent evidence directly or even indirectly corroborating Cook. While Main could not, say, produce the lot manager able to say a particular car had gone missing from his lot on the material day since Cook said his theft of it was undetected, he could have produced him to say that a car of that description was in his inventory, although he hadn't happened to notice its temporary absence. But neither the make of the car nor the location of the lot were ever tied down before the jurors. They could have been. Not much perhaps but, in the premises, better than Main's vague "some car" which left the jurors with the latitude to conclude some car could be taken to mean no car.

Main's examination of Cook was as much as he did with the Bowden trip *per se* (although, as we will see, he approached the problem of proving the cache's existence from a different angle), and for the rest he contented himself with asking various police officers whether any of

192

them happened to notice $4100 lying around the house. None of them had, as Main of course knew.

But they were barren questions addressed to the police officers since the fact the money had not been found in the house said very little - more to the point it said nothing - about whether it had been there in the first place. Yet Main's purpose was to show that the money's absence was evidence from which could be inferred a stranger murdering for what was, after all, a sizable amount. But for this gambit to succeed, the jurors had to be convinced the money was in the house prior to the arrival of a stranger bent on stealing money he knew he would find there. The emphasis *had* to be here, nor could its importance be overestimated. Once convince the jurors that that much of Cook's story was true, that he had brought the money home and given it to his light-fingered father - we have already seen how Cook's lawyers failed him here - and they could not help but wonder, reluctantly perhaps, what had happened to it. They might not then be prepared to take the leap of faith Main hoped for, but to wonder about any part of the Crown's case was, with luck, to drive the thin edge of the wedge of reasonable doubt into it. What then to do? What to do was to show he'd driven to Bowden, and it might then be inferred he hadn't driven there to pick up a hamburger.

Main's effort shows he did not accord this critical part of his client's story the central place it demanded. There were too many questions left unasked most of which Cook could easily have answered if in fact he was telling the truth about Bowden. For example, Main's questioning might have run: What make of car was it?[1] What year? Was it locked? Two-door? How did you get into it? How do you hot-wire a car? Where did you get whatever you used to hot-wire it?

Where on the Calgary Trail was the lot located? What was the name of the lot? Where was the office located in relation to the car? Was it possible to drive off the lot without passing the office? Was anyone else on the lot?

Did you happen to notice the mileage? How long did it take you to drive to Bowden? Did you gas up? Where? How much? What was your average highway speed? Any unusual incident on the highway which you could know about only if you had seen it? Where exactly was the cache located? What did you use to dig it up? Where did you go and what did you do after you had restored the car to the lot?

[1] *He told MacNaughton it was a 1955 Ford, information MacNaughton related to Main in a letter of July 27, 1959.*

And so on - whatever it took to cover every foot and every minute of the return trip to Bowden. Main had to go to the lot to see it for himself and to talk to the manager. The trip had to be made real in a dozen details, each of them revealed in its own Q and A set, each exhaustively rehearsed beforehand - entirely legitimate and indeed indispensable trial practice. If it took an hour, if it took a *day* to leave no stone unturned between Edmonton and Bowden and the trial judge beside himself with ill-concealed impatience, it demanded nothing less.

But Cook was given only a cursory opportunity to flesh out his story, and the irony was that this master car thief was not believed when it became necessary to argue, with his life on the line, that he had stolen a car. In other circumstances it would have been a sticky wicket for Main, but not here where he had to show Cook as the most accomplished car thief who ever lived, painting an unflattering picture for the six honest burghers not one of whom, probably, had ever stolen a car in his life. The harder Main tried to clothe his client with credibility, the more sympathy he lost for him. Yet he necessarily believed Cook was telling the truth - he could not put him on the stand if he knew Cook was set to lie - and all he had to do was make what was so transparently a tissue of falsehoods appear as the truth it nevertheless was.

***

Since Cook had said he'd stolen a car to drive to the site of his stolen money, as part of showing Cook to be guilty of murder, Anderson had to show him to be innocent of car theft - the sacrifice of a pawn to set up the capture of the queen:

"Now then, you had this stolen car and you went to Bowden and you got $4300 and you drove all the way up the Calgary highway in a stolen car?"

"Yes."

"And you took it back to the lot from where you had taken it?"

"Yes."

"And you put it back as close as where you had taken it from?"

"That's right."

"And all the time you had $4300 in your pocket?"

"That's right."

"Rather dangerous wasn't it?"

"I didn't think so or I wouldn't have been doing it."

"A stolen car and forty-three hundred dollars worth of stolen money and it didn't occur to you it was dangerous?"

"I didn't think the car would be reported as stolen."

"You could have left the car a couple of blocks away and have been much better off, would you not?"

"It is much better to leave it where I took it from and then it isn't reported stolen and the guy doesn't miss it. Nobody is hurt and nobody knows different."

"Well, supposing they had been waiting for you when you arrived back and you had all this money in your pockets?"

"I would have noticed that before I got there I think."

"You had all the eventualities covered?"

"No. If there had been a policemen there I would have noticed him. There was no activity when I brought the car back."

"And all the way up the highway it could have been reported stolen and they would have been looking for you?"

"I had my own car stolen once and I know about what happens when a car is reported stolen."

"Oh I see. There is a possibility they could have been looking for you?"

"It is possible, but not very probable."

"At least looking for the car?"

"Usually when a car is reported as stolen, they look around the city itself...."

"Yes. When I ask a question, all I want is [for] you to agree or disagree, that's all."

MR MAIN: Now I think the witness is entitled to do more than that in cross-examination. He is not bound to agree or disagree with my friend."

MR ANDERSON: "I am not asking him to go into a long recital on each question."

THE COURT: " Perhaps the objection should be sustained."

Although couched in the phraseology of an American television courtroom (Canadian lawyers are not forever leaping to their feet shouting Objection! leaving little to be sustained or denied), the trial judge had awarded Cook a small victory, but an impartial observer sitting at ringside would have had to conclude that while Cook gave, he didn't give as good as he got over the length of the exchange. Anderson scored effectively. Cook's story was easy to disbelieve because Main had failed to supply the detail which might have made it believable.

***

With the trip to Bowden rendered highly doubtful by Anderson's skillful cross-examination[1], so too was the $4300, but there were two other approaches to the defense problem which did not rest so squarely on the shifting sands of Cook's veracity. The first stemmed from Cook's claim to have held back $200 when he turned over the proceeds of his life's work to Ray.

1 *If there was any doubt in the second trial about the point Anderson was making - that the whole Bowden episode was a fabrication - Mr Justice Riley drove it home in his address to the jury: "Then there is the evidence by the accused about picking up the cache of some $4300 near Bowden. He told of taking a car from a used-car lot in broad daylight on Wednesday morning. He told of restoring the car to the approximate same location - again in the hours of daylight. You will ask yourselves: would one experienced in the criminal arts do these things in broad daylight?" Since Cook had graduated in criminal arts heavy with honors, the answer of course was no.*

When Cook was released from Saskatchewan Penitentiary he had $31.81 comprising what he had managed to save from his prison earnings - $20.67 - and $10.84 held for him in an inmates' trust fund. Of the latter amount, $10 had been sent to him by Daisy just before his release. His bus fare to Edmonton was prepaid by the Penitentiary Service so that the $31.81 was untouched when he and Myhaluk began the beer parlor round in Saskatoon. When he arrived at the PMH seven days later, he was given a receipt for $92. Starting with about $30, he had ended up with three times that amount, and he had spent freely during the seven days. The question was how much? If it could be shown to have been about $140 then, adding that amount to the $90 still in his possession at the PMH meant that to balance the equation, there had to be added to the release money exactly $200. Set out in figures the equation looks like this: $30 + $200 = $90 + $140. Two hundred dollars was of course the amount held back from his father, and it was this amount the defense wished to demonstrate since, in a not very conclusive way, the $4100 gift was supported by showing that Cook had to have acquired $200 from somewhere. The risk the defense ran of course is that the trail of the $200 would lead to the murdered man's wallet rather than to a hole in the ground near Bowden, but it had to be taken.

We will see shortly that Main recognized the trail's existence and followed it, but ineffectively being hamstrung by not having done his homework. Dunne might have recognized a trail as broad as the Old Chisholm Trail, but he missed this one and careered off in a direction which recommended itself to him alone, as we shall see, reminding one of the dogs on the manhunt when they frolicked off after the gophers.

To me it seemed once prove the holdback (at the same time ruling out the wallet), and the entire story centering around the Bowden cache could be forcefully argued as falling into place: a tobacco tin buried at some rural crossroads; a car stolen as casually as the rest of us would hail a taxi; the hurried trip to dig up the money dreamt of (and bragged about) during all the interminable months inside; the gift of $4100 to a man able without discernible difficulty to turn a blind eye to the fact the money had probably not been earned from his son's paper route given his son had never had one; the nearly new station wagon as the *quid pro quo* for the $4100; the plan to buy the service station at long last at the point of realization. Merely prove the holdback.

By carefully - and occasionally creatively - combing the transcripts, it proved possible to prepare a list of all his expenditures covering all his purchases for coffee, meals, beer, cigarettes and the like; money paid to

Hood Motors; money paid to Dave MacNaughton and so on. As often as not precise amounts were referred to in evidence, but where they were not and a given situation impliedly called for the outlay of money, its amount was estimated as objectively as possible. While nothing was said about his buying gas for the Camrose-Whitecourt return trip for example, since it was his car, so to speak, and his trip, it was a valid assumption that the costs of the trip were his. A figure was calculated and added to the list.

The analysis of the money spent by him must begin with the acknowledgment that while it was hoped to show he'd spent about $140, the disconcerting total was about $180 too much: $320. Such a total would not do for someone concerned to prove the $200 holdback and exclude the wallet since it could be read as importing both. The 35-item list was returned to to see whether its total could be written down to more acceptable proportions. It will be appreciated that in the absence of hard evidence, the list's preparation was arbitrary to some extent, and paring it called for the same creativity as had gone into its preparation. For example, it was assumed that Cook paid for the trip to Stettler in Eddie Read's truck and the return of the truck to Edmonton. The trip was at Cook's behest with Berezowski along merely as a favor to Cook. Still, if Cook paid for the gas for the outbound leg only, the awkward $180 excess was reduced by, say, $10, and if (which is unlikely but not impossible) Berezowski paid for the entire trip, the reduction overall was a welcome 11%.

In the end however the $180 could not be honestly pared away in its entirety, and it had to be recognized that nothing much was being proved beyond the fact that he'd spent a considerable amount of money, but there was no conclusive indication of its source apart from the release funds. Nevertheless, two things stood out. Imprecise as the figures were, they showed without question that he'd spent most or all of the release funds before the alleged departure for Bowden, and about $80 following his return to Edmonton but *prior* to his departure for Stettler in Eddie Read's truck.

Prior, that is, before coming anywhere near his victim's wallet. Anderson took a half-hearted stab at promoting the wallet as the source of money over and above the release money, but he was not much concerned to say anything to the point about the total Cook might have spent, being content merely to pooh-pooh the existence of the cache which stood or fell with the Bowden trip. There was not much danger of anyone buying the Bowden trip so that, to the Crown, the existence of the cache wasn't a matter of vital concern. Yet the $80 was anything but immaterial. Wherever it came from, demonstrably it had not come from Ray Cook's wallet leaving the tobacco tin as the best bet.

Main was aware of the potential lying in Cook's expenditures as corroborative of the holdback, and he was in a position to tie them down while its component parts were still fresh in Cook's memory. But Main was unaware - or had forgotten - that Cook had arrived at the PMH with $92 in his pocket. It was never mentioned in court but was in Cook's letter to MacNaughton asking MacNaughton to arrange to get him to the funeral, and it was confirmed by PMH records. But if MacNaughton mentioned it to Main, Main had forgotten it when the time came to close with the problem at the conclusion of the first trial. Main, in a word, never sat down with Cook to ask him how much he had spent, where and on what. He failed completely to make the argument that the pre-Stettler expenditures themselves and alone indicated a source of money the Crown would have been at a complete loss to account for had it recognized that there was an argument to be made by the defense which posed a grave threat to its case. Such arguments write themselves: "We have showed you, gentlemen of the jury, that before he got any closer to Stettler than 130 miles he spent in excess of $110, and that all he had when he was released from the penitentiary was $30. Now where did this money come from if not...?"

Main's argument against the wallet being the source of all the money Cook spent other than the release money took the form of Ray Cook not being the kind of man to have "that kind of money" in his wallet a week before payday. But what kind of money? Main did not know. He had to work towards a precise figure - the total spent - by using precise figures which were his for the tracking down of them, but he failed to appreciate that at that stage of the proceedings there was no other route to proving the existence of the cache. The time for exploring the third route referred to above (which we will shortly reach) had long since passed.

Thus in summing up his case, Main started on the problem of the cache by admitting he didn't know what it was now too late for him to find out:

"Now we don't know exactly how much he spent, but it is open to you, gentlemen, to infer, starting off with the $90 he gave to [Hood Motors] and he finished up on Saturday night in the police station in Stettler with roughly the same as he had when he started out from Prince Albert Penitentiary [sic] on the Tuesday morning within a few dollars - $31 and

$34[1]. I put it to you, gentlemen, that it is logical to conclude that he spent in the neighborhood of roughly $200 which he says he kept back from the forty-three hundred *[sic]* that he gave to his father and mother.[2] That is corroborative of the accused's story that he gave them forty-three hundred and kept back two-hundred for himself. Where else would he have got the money? He wasn't working."

***

While Main was at least on the right track but with only a vague idea as to how best to follow it, Dunne's approach to the same problem was, to put it at its kindest, a positive force for mischief. The following two extracts from his address to the jury comprise the *whole* of his dealing with the problem of the trip to Bowden, the cache's existence, the gift to Ray and the holdback. He had just finished dealing with the matter of the shotgun shells and, without a word of introduction, launched into the question of all the money Cook had spent:

"Then we have evidence from various witnesses that on the trip from Camrose to Whitecourt, the accused was not short of money, and there is further evidence that his father did not get paid until after the first of the month, and I think it is fair for you to consider whether, on the salary of a garage mechanic, the father would likely be flush with money on the 25th before he got paid, and also the fact that he had five children to keep.

[1] *$34 was correct if one wished to go by Roach's testimony, as Main did. When Roach charged Cook with false pretenses, he asked him to empty his pockets and gave him, he said, a receipt for "approximately $34." The next morning Cook gave NacNaughton a $40 retainer, and on Monday afternoon he arrived at the PMH with $92. In less than 48 hours his money had quadrupled.*

[2] *Cook said that when he returned from Bowden, to protect himself in case he fell among thieves, he divided the $4300, all of it in bills of unspecified denominations, and put half in each rear pants pocket where the bulges were concealed by the hem of his suit jacket. Anderson scoffed both at the idea that the bulges would be undetectable, and at the idea that Cook would walk into the den of thieves at the motel party carrying that much money. To anyone at the party, the bulges would spell money and Cook would then be relieved of it.*

A sort of a battle of the bulges was joined. Main had MacNaughton stuff his rear pants pockets with bills roughly equivalent in thickness to what it was assumed Cook's would have been, turn his back to the jury and lift his barrister's gown in a sort of sedate suggestion of a kick line, demonstrating that that kind of money could be carried in that fashion, jacket hem or no jacket hem, and no one the wiser. It is thought the jurors were not much persuaded.

200

"The next point I would like to deal with is the evidence from Cook and from the Crown witness Berezowski that it was common knowledge in Prince Albert Penitentiary *[sic]* that the accused had a considerable sum of money cached, *and I suggest to you that in this case it is not so important as to whether the accused did actually have the money as the fact that the other inmates in the Penitentiary believed that he did*; and you will recall that there were something like 40 or 60 of them released in a two-day period, and that there were at least 40 of them - or roughly that number - in the same dormitory with Cook.   There is your possibility for a motive for somebody else. Consider that, along with the absence of a motive as so far suggested by the Crown on Cook's part." [emphasis added]

What little good Dunne did in his "salary of a garage mechanic" argument, he undid, and then some, by his casual dismissal of the cache (the keystone of the defense without which Cook's entire story collapsed) in favor of some off-the-top-of-his-head theory about Cook as a kind of Ali Baba with "roughly" 40 thieves padding furtively along in his wake waiting for him to tip his hand. Dunne's lack of understanding of what was required of him, of the case he had to make, was shocking. With an airy wave of the hand he had ascribed irrelevance to Cook's entire defense (with the exception of the alibi which was spared for the moment only because it stood alone), and had supplanted it with penitentiary scuttlebutt. There, if the jurors happened to be favorably disposed towards Cook, there, if they happened to be looking for the "possibility of a motive for someone else", was the peg upon which they could hang acquittal. But it was everything on one palsied throw of the dice. To argue that it is not particularly important whether one's client told the truth and to concede he probably didn't is not a strategy widely employed in the criminal courts.

Anderson may not have believed his ears or he may not have appreciated what Dunne had handed him. In either case, when he rose to answer the defense argument he felt he had to say something about the cache. But conveying meaning was not always his strongest suit:

"I recall for your consideration the defense's suggestion that the accused went to Bowden and obtained this money. Again in the light of the story concerning the stolen car, the stolen money and the fact that it was hidden in the ground, and the circumstances relating thereto. The time restrictions which was *[sic]* suggested by the Crown witnesses, placed upon the accused's evidence in this regard, the questions *[sic]* of did he have $4300? If he did, did he give it to his family? If the contention which the Crown urges before you is correct, it would certainly explain the fact and the reason of *[sic]* there being no large sum of money found in the house."

The transcripts are a matter of public record should it be thought that I have reproduced them with less than strict accuracy in respect of either Dunne or Anderson, and readers are referred to them. They will not need to be reminded that the prize to be rescued from this wasteland of the forensic art lying in shambles was a man's life.

***

The thrust of Anderson's cross-examination of Cook on the Bowden trip was to undermine a key part of Cook's story, and it was successful: there may have been a Treasure Island, but Cook never went there and Cook never brought any treasure with him to Stettler. He was well ahead of the game, but inadvertence was part of Anderson's makeup, and for a brief moment it turned out that there was a Treasure Island, there was treasure, and our hero had dug it up and carried it back to share with his father. Luckily the moment flashed by without anyone recognizing it, and tranquility settled again over the Cook landscape. To explain, it is necessary to go back to Giffard Main.

In his Notice of Appeal, Main raised as one of the grounds of appeal that "The verdict was perverse and contrary to the evidence in that it failed to give the Appellant the benefit of reasonable doubt, particularly with respect to...the fact that the Appellant returned to Stettler at about 7:00 o'clock on the evening of Saturday, 27th June, 1959, after having purchased and driving *[sic]* a 1959 Chevrolet Impala convertible, white in color, top down, with red upholstery and flying a penant *[sic]* of white rosettes from the car aerial, a most gaudy and eye catching figure in a small town."

It was Main's last kick at the gaudy and eye-catching cat, except here it seems to have been Cook and not the Impala who earned the cognomen - unless a car can be seen as a figure. It was a valid ground of appeal although not a particularly strong one. It could be argued certainly that there should have been some doubt raised as to whether these were the actions of a man who 40 or so hours earlier had wiped out his family, at least enough doubt to give pause long enough to consider some other doubtful aspects of the Crown's case, whether or not any doubt engendered by the Impala spectacle itself had any staying power. Main's point has never been satisfactorily answered, or answered at all except to say they *were* the actions of such a man. Difficult to believe, but there they were. The effrontery of the man was a caution, just a caution.

Following the filing of a notice of appeal, the contending lawyers are required to prepare and file a 'factum' - a document containing an outline of the argument they intend to pursue. The appellant's factum will expand on the grounds of appeal and the respondent's will answer the appellant's arguments one by one. Anderson as respondent therefore filed a factum which in due course dealt with Main's 18th ground of appeal (quoted above) as follows:

"The suggestion [made by Main with respect to the Impala] it is submitted by the Respondent would appear to assist the Appellant but little in view of his acknowledged familiarity with the manner of operation of persons and practices, both legal and commercial [,] and his acknowledged temerity in the instance of the theft of the car from a lot in Edmonton, to drive to Bowden, and the return with forty-three hundred ($4300) dollars of stolen money in a stolen car on one of Alberta's main highways and the subsequent return of the stolen vehicle to the position from which it had been removed."

Fair enough - although fair may not be the happiest word for it: anyone with the temerity not only to steal a car and drive it to Bowden but to acknowledge the theft merely to save his life, anyone who acknowledges familiarity with the manner of operation of persons and practises both legal *and* commercial, would have the temerity to drive back to the scene of his crime in a car with white rosettes, than which temerity doesn't get more temerous.

But the point to note here is that Anderson had explained the Impala, had answered Main's argument, by acknowledging (since we are dealing for the moment in acknowledgment) the truth of Cook's entire story of the car theft and the trip to Bowden. Had conceded, that is, that Cook had told something normally foreign to him, the truth, in a critically important part of his story. Anderson however had not made the concession before the jury where it might have mattered, but rather had buried it in a 44 page document which may or may not have been read in its entirety by the court of appeal. None of the learned justices on appeal commented on the gaffe.

***

The question seems to come down to this: had there been a hole in the ground - filled in to be sure - containing a tobacco tin containing "forty-three hundred dollars of stolen money" or more to the point of Cook's story, were there signs of there once having been a hole and, lying somewhere nearby, a rusty tobacco tin? Since the cache was the starting point of Cook's entire defense, evidence of its former existence would have been of incalculable benefit to it. It was self-evident that one of the defense lawyers, accompanied by someone of unquestionable probity to give sworn evidence of what was found, had to go to the cache site, guided by a Cook sketch, to bring back (as they would have brought back if Cook was telling the truth) evidence of there having been a cache: an empty hole, signs of disturbed ground, ideally the tobacco tin itself.[1]

A tobacco can in defense hands suggests a scenario. After being identified it would be marked as an exhibit and set on the exhibit table by the Clerk. MacNaughton would then move it strategically to ensure its prominence among the 80 or so exhibits arrayed against Cook, preferably juxtaposed with the blue suit. The one would shriek bloody murder, the other would suggest that true, the suit looked bad, but maybe it wasn't quite as cut-and-dried as not having to go any further for the killer's identity than the blue suit - admittedly a suit worn by a killer if ever one was. Given the tobacco can's intrinsic importance (discomfiture at the Crown's table would have been palpable), it could not have been as easily dismissed as MacNaughton's melancholy can-can which was intended to prove indirectly the existence of a can which might better have been on the exhibit table speaking modestly for itself.

But no one from the defense side went to Bowden. Prima facie it was immaterial to the police whether the cache was there or not just so they

---

[1] *There was a sketch found in Main's papers, but he died before I was able to ask him about it. It is thought to be Cook's. It is an intriguing document; there are enough physical features of the countryside in the Bowden area it purports to describe - a "burned down schoolhouse" and so on - shown on it to put it beyond question that whoever made the sketch had been in that country. There is reason to think Cook re-buried the tobacco tin (always with the proviso that there was a tobacco tin) with some rainy day money still in it, and if so it is an invitation to treasure seekers armed with a metal detector and with the sketch to look for it. They might have better luck than I did. The sketch pinpoints a crossroads as being near the site of the cache. Of interest is the fact that there are no telephone lines running down either road.*

There is reputedly also a hoard of negotiable (and doubtlessly soggy) securities buried by Cook "somewhere east of the tracks at Lacombe", but that is another story.

could say they had made a conscientious search. Like so many Joe Fridays, they were after just the facts ma'am, and it was a matter of indifference to them what they found. Had they found signs of a cache it might very well have caused momentary dismay and regrouping in the ranks, but there was no chance of that (they owned, after all, to a certain bias as to the direction they hoped their investigations would lead them) since, knowing Cook to be guilty, they could be confident they would find nothing. Indeed, finding nothing would have been the clincher their case was scarcely in need of, and it might be thought they would have conducted a diligent search for that reason alone. But perhaps they did not wish to run the risk of stumbling over a crumbling tobacco tin. Nevertheless, they took what appears to have been a desultory look for it.

There is a note in the capital case file in the National Archives, whose writer is not identified, in which Cook is said to have "stated in evidence on his trial or elsewhere that he thought he could drive to the scene where he had hidden the money. The R. C. M. Police tried to locate it themselves according to the information I have been given, but so far as I have been able to determine, it was never proposed to the accused that he should lead them to the scene. Neither have I seen any indication that the accused positively asked the R. C. M. Police to let him lead them to the scene."

The note's writer's information squared with that given me by Dave Beeching who told me the police had discussed among themselves how Cook could possibly have acquired the amount of money he claimed to have buried: "There was no way he could do this. He was a small-time crook. I recall we went to Bowden; we walked along a telephone line. He must have told us where it was, but we didn't find it. We didn't ask for verification of the location of the cache from Cook."

Beeching wasn't giving me any more than was dictated by ingrained but wary courtesy (we established early in the first of two interviews that we harbored different views about the *Cook* trials), yet guarded as he was, he gave away more than he could have intended. For it is reasonable to ask what is said of police work where a detail sets off in search of a hole in the ground (or, better, positive proof that there never was a hole in the ground where it was alleged to be) without Cook himself [1] or, failing Cook, without a sketch provided by Cook leading them unerringly to an exact location?

---

[1] *A judge's order could readily have been obtained permitting Cook to be taken under close escort to the putative cache site. Why Cook or his lawyers did not demand that it be done remains an abiding mystery.*

However, give them that they felt themselves sufficiently informed with what Cook "must have told [them]". But then it must be asked why, when they came up empty-handed, they did not go back to Cook to ask where they had gone wrong or, if not that, then why he had lied to them? It is not easy to think of Cook sending them off on a wild-goose chase, knowing their failure to find the cache where he said it was would seal his fate. Not that Cook was averse to sending the police off on wild-goose chases; one remembers Jimmy Myhaluk in jail somewhere masterminding - and assisting in - the escape from the PMH.

But at least they went, and that was something. While the methodology appears not to have been everything it might have been, they nevertheless had the result they wanted: they found nothing. Given which it occasions some surprise to learn that Anderson never questioned the RCMP in either trial about the cache search. The effect of what they would have said - "Yes, Cook told us where it was. We went but it wasn't there" - may be imagined. Knowing looks would have been exchanged in the jury box. So much for the $4100 gift and the plans for a service station discussed over a beer. So much for carrying the glad news home to "Mom" and the excited anticipation of a trip to BC - a family holiday really, opening into a bright new future. So much for the willing handing over of the keys to the station wagon. So much for all of it. And so much for Cook.

***

There were five people called as witnesses at Cook's trials who gave evidence of having heard him say that his father had a car waiting for him in Stettler, and there were as many again who told me the same thing. On two previous occasions Ray had bought a car and had it waiting for Cook as a homecoming gift, but this time there seems to have been a significant difference in that there was no suggestion in trial that the 1958 Chevrolet station wagon had been acquired and set aside as a gift for Cook. Rather, so far as is known (there is no evidence of how or why Ray came by the station wagon other than that he traded McTaggart another car and a half-ton truck for it or on it), it was the family car but nevertheless "it was waiting" for Cook.

Carl Thalbing, the Hood Motors salesman Cook had seen early on Wednesday afternoon before he left for Bowden, was one of the four

Crown witnesses to whom Cook mentioned a car "sitting down in Stettler." He told Thalbing he intended to bring it to Edmonton to trade in on an Impala if agreement could be reached on a trade-in allowance.

In what appears to have been a display of tactical obtuseness, Anderson adopted the stance that there was something underhanded in Cook telling Thalbing that he intended to trade in a car which, Anderson stressed, Cook had yet to see, as if in some manner Hood Motors was being fleeced two days in advance of having had an opportunity to appraise the car Cook would be bringing in when the time came. Cook had done nothing less than attempt to induce Hood into buying a pig in a poke in Anderson's view, a broad enough one but one which failed to include in its sweep that old and successful car dealerships get to be old and successful by appraising pigs before the salesman (who always finds himself having to take this up with the manager), goes in to see the manager, bearing the insulting offer which the manager will find unacceptable, but he might look at it if the prospective purchaser will come up a couple of hundred bucks.

It may have been the case that Cook intended to murder his father and drive off in his car, but it is difficult to see how either his murderous intent, or murder itself, is demonstrated by Cook's never having seen the car he nevertheless talked about, to a gullible salesman, in terms of a trade-in. On the face of it there was nothing much wrong with it, but Anderson could not give Cook even that much:

"And you told [Thalbing] you would possibly be interested in dealing with him?"

"Yes sir, I believe I did."

"And I believe you told him that part of the deal would be trading in a '58 station wagon?"

"Could be, I...."

"Well, that is what he says."

"Well, if he said it, it must be so."

"Now, this would have to be a '58 station wagon which at the time you had never laid eyes on until some 30 hours later, Thursday night about 9 o'clock?"

"I didn't have to lay eyes on it to...."

"Just answer my question, is that right?"

"Yes sir."

"Is that right?"

"Yes sir."

"You were trading to him a car you had never seen, never driven and personally knew nothing about?"

"I knew lots about it sir."

"Oh, all right. You tell me you heard *[sic]* in a letter do you?"

"Yes sir."

"But you were still trading in a car which you had never laid eyes on, never been inside, is that right?"

"That is correct sir."

Since Anderson was properly given to making as much as he could out of discrepancies between Cook's evidence and that of Crown witnesses as to the times of certain events, in fairness Cook should have been allowed to point out that Anderson was about eight hours out in the length of time elapsed between Cook's talking to Thalbing and his first sight of the car. Or rather Dunne should have done it, should have pointed out that even prosecutors err on rare occasions, but he failed to do so.

The last time Ray drove the station wagon was when he went looking for his son and found him standing on Main Street at 9 pm, Thursday. Cook was on the sidewalk on the other side of the street. Ray parked the car and walked over to him. The reunion was witnessed by Arnold Filipenko who remembered Ray as appearing excited and the reunion as warm. They got in the car and drove off. In "Murder by Infernce" Cook related that they doubled back to the Royal Hotel for a beer. He did not particularly want to, Cook wrote, but fell in with his father's suggestion when Ray pointed out that this would be the first time since Cook had come of age that they could have a beer together in public.

They "orderd two glasses of beer," Cook wrote, "and talked over then for about half an hour, mostly on a plan to go into action on getting are own garage. I told Dad I had $4300 in my pocket[1] and as he said 'were in busness.' With that $4300 and what Dad had and would get when the house was sold we figured we had enough for a suitible garage. We were going to use the $4300 and the cash Dad had in the bank, aprox $3000 for a down payment. Plans were made that Dad would make a trip to British Columbia, Vancouver, and inquire at real estate agencies for garages up for sale. Wed decided then we should talk it over with Mom and left for home."

There is not much to be added. His trial testimony filled in some detail: the plan was discussed with Daisy over coffee; the money was handed over in the kitchen; when he left them they were making plans for their departure on either Friday or Saturday - Cook was not sure which; and he would return to the house to take a phone call on Monday or Tuesday (or Wednesday at one point) - he was not sure which - informing him where in BC they were to be picked up.

There was corroborating evidence, some adduced at trial, some not. The house was listed for sale at the time of Cook's homecoming. The listing was known to Jim and Leona Hoskins for example, who knew as well the reason for it: the Cooks intended to leave Stettler. Leona Hoskins told me that "If they could sell it, they planned to buy a business of their own some place where they liked it." Jim Hoskins added, "If they sold it, they were going to buy a garage or something or maybe even move to Calgary. Ray had been trying to pick up a little service station."

Ten additional interviews of friends and relatives of the Cooks established with reasonable certainty that a move and the purchase of a service station were actively being contemplated by Ray and Daisy at the time of Cook's return. Of the ten interviewees, only two were called to give evidence of the Cooks' seeming intentions.

Unfortunately, Dave Beeching was not asked to tell the court what he knew of those intentions which, he told me, was that the police had learned of them. The defense would have been assisted had more than two solid citizens of Stettler been called to the stand to say that yes, they knew Ray Cook planned to leave Stettler and buy a garage. Eight such

---

[1] *We have speculated that Cook spent about $80 post-Bowden and pre-Stettler. If the $80 was money recovered from the cache, then he had $4220 in his pocket and either gave Ray $4020 or held back $120. He was not concerned to ease the way of either his lawyers or his chroniclers.*

citizens were standing in the wings waiting for a cue. The defense would have been assisted immeasurably more had a solid Staff Sergeant of the Royal Canadian Mounted Police been called to say the same thing. It might have tended to throw favorable light on Cook's cock-and-bull concoction of a man-to-man confabulation in the Royal Hotel.

***

Ray Cook *had* the $3000 in the bank to which Cook referred in "Murder by Infernce", and in fact slightly more: $3663.84 - a surprising amount for a garage mechanic with a larger than average family to have saved. Even more surprising was Daisy's own small fortune: $3777.43 in the bank at the time of administration of her estate - March, 1962. The jurors were not told of either amount. In March, 1962 Daisy's house was appraised at $3500 - a depreciation which may have been attributable to its bloody history - but before depreciation, they were jointly worth about $12,000 in cash or liquefiable assets.

With or without Cook's $4100, there was thus a significant amount available for the purchase of a small service station. Such a purchase could easily have been handled in the usual manner: some cash, the balance by mortgage. This however was not the view of Mr Justice Riley who was given to telling the jurors the questions they would be asking themselves, presumably to spare them having to ask them themselves: "You will ask yourselves if the accused was going into business with his father in a brand-new garage business which required an outlay of money, whether or not it was likely that the father would authorize the expenditure of needed capital on a brand-new Impala convertible."

In his defense, it should be pointed out that Riley was as much in the dark as everyone else in the courtroom as to the net worth of the Cooks. That conceded, one or two questions arise from Riley's question. While giving the station wagon to Cook to be traded in can, in a sense, be seen as an "expenditure of needed capital" (but equally as liquidating it for a more negotiable form of it - $4100), the more usual sense of such an expenditure is the outlay of money. If Riley was not prepared to take Cook's word for it, he had heard the Hood Motors salesman who informed the court that the difference between the trade-in allowance and the cost of the Impala was to be financed at $100 a month. It cannot be that someone's being saddled with hundred dollar monthly payments was "the expenditure of needed capital" to which His Lordship referred. And if, returning to the station wagon, this was the squandering of the sorely needed capital, there was a letter of June 9, 1959, Ray Cook to his son, saying the station wagon was waiting for him. Wisely the letter did not refer to stolen money as a *quid pro quo*; some things are better left unsaid in letters going through prison censorship. But Riley was absolved here too since the letter never made it into evidence.

***

How did Cook know of "the cash Dad had in the bank, aprox $3000"? It's the sort of thing which would be mentioned in a beer parlor conversation about buying a garage, but Cook never said specifically that Ray said he had $3000 in the bank. And had he said under oath that Ray was the source of his knowledge of the money, he would not have been believed. He told Dunne in direct examination that it was a matter of general knowledge with him that Ray had a Royal Bank account; he had "cashed cheques in there" with him. But this was to say nothing about a specific balance, in particular $3000.

But among the family papers found in a metal box removed by Roach from the trunk of the Impala was a Royal Bank passbook. We will see in a later chapter that one of the questions for the defense lawyers, who were never in danger of running out of them, was the time of Cook's putting the metal box in the Impala. Cook said he took it with him when he left the house on Saturday, while the Crown contended he took it with him when he fled the house in the station wagon after the murders. If the Crown was right, then he had the box - and the passbook - with him when he made the deal for the Impala. Passing himself off as his father, he told Hood Motors that he had an account at the Royal in Stettler, but he did not produce the passbook as proof of it.

When Mr Justice Greschuk approached the question of whether Cook had the passbook with him at Hood Motors, he was more direct than Mr Justice Riley would be, choosing not to frame the questions the jurors would be asking themselves, in favor of asking them himself: "How did he know [at Hood Motors] that his father had a bank account in Stettler? Does this indicate that he was fully aware of the fact that the bank book from the Royal Bank was in his possession in the station wagon when he left Stettler for Edmonton?"

To this reader, Greschuk's question suggests that to him Cook could only have known of the account if the passbook was in his possession at Hood, although one must guard against reading Greschuk as invariably prejudicial to Cook. Still, he would have achieved the balance one looks for in a trial judge had he added a disjunctive roughly to the effect "or could he be expected to know as a matter of general family knowledge that his father banked at the Royal?" - Cook's version.

In Cook's not entirely objective view of things, Greschuk was an enemy fully as committed as Anderson himself and if anything more effective. In all the notes he made at the Fort as he struggled to find the keys to acquittal, nothing stands out with quite the force of his perception of Greschuk's bias, particularly in the matter of the bank account. He wrote of it as if Greschuk had impugned the depth of his feeling for his father. In a note to Main of December 18, 1959 (surviving only in typewritten form with Cook's spelling corrected), he wrote: "The judge did make a lot of guesses that can be proved untrue and don't even make sense. He said the only way I could, know which bank my Dad had money in was by looking at the bank book in the [metal box.] There is one bank and only one as far as I ever knew. My Dad dealt with the same bank ever since we moved to Stettler. We both cashed cheques there. You could check to see if there is any other bank there but the Royal. Also you could find out when the account was opened."

So far as is known, Dunne adopted neither of these reasonable suggestions in preparation for the second trial; if he did he didn't make use of them. He would have found that there were branches of the Nova Scotia and the Treasury Branch in addition to the Royal, and he could have subpoenaed bank records to show the date of the opening of the account. The point of his doing so would have been to show a longstanding account in a narrow choice of banks, making it the more likely Cook would have known of it.

Cook could not let it go. In his "Points to Appeal" written after the first conviction is found the following: "The trial judge inferd that because I could and did state wich bank my Dad delt with at Hood Motors Friday that I must of had the bank book. Isn't it reasonible if I'd of had that bank book I'd have produced it.. Isn't it reasonible that I could have knoledge of the bank [? this former family affairs]. I also contend that infernce is prejudice on the Judges part. There was nothing of value in the [metal box] or that I could have made use of in any way. The only thing that could have been of any use was the bank book in dealing for the car. Since I never used it while making the deal, isn't it logical I didn't have it?"

What he could not be expected to know was that Greschuk was not drawing inferences where for him to have done so would have been to usurp the function of the jury. What Greschuk was doing was supplying the Crown's omission since Anderson said nothing about the bank book in his closing argument. For a trial judge to do so is unexceptionable; he has as much of an interest as anyone in ensuring that all relevant questions are canvassed, and assuredly Cook's source of his knowledge of the bank account was relevant in the context of the metal box's removal from the house.

That Greschuk failed to balance the two possible sources of Cook's knowledge of the account - the passbook at Hood Motors or his general knowledge of family affairs - can be laid at Main's doorstep. He seems not to have appreciated the danger which lay in not establishing Cook's legitimate and routine knowledge of the account. He did not ask Cook any questions concerning it or the passbook, leaving it open to the jurors to infer that the metal box was with Cook at Hood - one more fatal inference as we shall see.

***

His lawyers would have been forgiven if, on occasion, they appeared driven to distraction. To hear Cook, at one point his parents were going to Vancouver; at another to New Westminster. At one point they were going first to Edmonton by bus and thence to the West Coast by train; at another to Calgary and thence to the West Coast on "that streamliner thing." At one point they were going to fly out; at another Ray had bought "a '59 Olds" for the trip. At one point they were planning to leave Friday; at another maybe Saturday. He was due back in Stettler to take a phone call on Monday, or was it Tuesday? Or was it Wednesday? The only fixed point in Cook's wandering universe was British Columbia; they were going to British Columbia. It was something to seize on as we will do in concluding this examination of the third part of

Cook's three-sided dream: the intended purchase of the service station. No sooner said than the questions start to mount. Had Ray and Daisy planned to relocate in BC where Jim Hoskins said Ray was thinking about Calgary? Were they thinking of BC - or anywhere else for that matter - in terms of escaping the wayward son, as Mae Reamsbottom thought[1]? Had they thought about BC at all prior to his return? Did anyone in BC anticipate their arrival? And so on. Any number of questions can be manufactured, but the exercise is pointless given the paucity of any evidence having much to do with British Columbia. As much as can be done here is suggest some answers to some of the questions based on the sparse evidence in hand.

Addressing the first-trial jury Anderson said, "Now, a good many of the accused's actions are explained or an attempt is made to explain them in light of this story of his family moving to BC. That story of the move has to be very carefully considered I suggest. First, it is put forward by the accused. It is put forward in the exclusion of the knowledge of any of the close friends or business associates of the family, and the only person, it is suggested, whose interest is served by that story is this accused's ."

That only Cook's interests were served by what Cook said in his fight to save his own life, in another context might have gone without saying, but Anderson was leaving nothing to chance, the chance, for example, of a juryman buying into Cook's genuinely believing that when he left his parents on Thursday night, they were alive enough and well enough to be making plans to go to BC, and, even more basically, they were alive and well whether or not they were making plans. But of course they were not making plans:

---

[1] *Mrs Reamsbottom of Bowden, Ray's half sister, told the RCMP that Ray and Daisy were making plans to leave Alberta, leaving Cook behind. Daisy, she told Corporal Van Blarcom, "was trying to make Ray understand that Bobby could not come near the house or the children because he had ruined their reputation wherever they went. Daisy had the fear that he was going to wind up killing someone." "Mrs Reamsbottom," Van Blarcom told me, "knew in her own mind that Daisy was afraid of him although Daisy never actually said so. Mrs Reamsbottom's theory is that Ray must have told Bobby he was on his own and this angered Bobby into doing what he did." Mrs Reamsbottom also knew in her own mind that she did not like her half brother's son. The last thing she said to Van Blarcom as he went out the door, he told me, was, "If there's anything else I can do to help hang that son of a bitch, let me know." Van Blarcom remembers "being turned right off." Mrs Reamsbottom perhaps can be seen can be seen as an exception to the rule that just about everyone who knew Cook liked him.*

"Close friends of the Cook family, business associates of the deceased," Anderson continued, "had no reason to believe the Cooks were leaving that shortly to go to BC or even in the not-too- distant future. Here was the deceased with commitments; he had to be at work on Friday on a particular job; he undertook to move some furniture on Saturday; a picnic was contemplated for Sunday; and in light of these facts and together with the milkman and the utilities and one thing and another, right out of nowhere the Cook family of five children and two adults picks up and goes to British Columbia? The picture of this move must be one of tremendous pace and a good deal of confusion."

A good deal of confusion was the word for it, both for the preparations which were not made for the move which didn't take place, and for the fallout from Anderson's analysis. Which went on: "The accused is not consistent on the time of departure but certainly indicative of the fact that it was most precipitous. Now why was there any necessity for a rush? I suggest that so far there is no good reason for this precipitative *[sic]* departure. The accused in evidence states that on his arrival home, he spent this whole one hour in the bosom of his family during which time all these plans had to be made, and resulting from his one-hour stay, the precipitative rush of the whole family to BC."

What might have been delicately pointed out both to Anderson and to Mr Justice Greschuk ("If a person were leaving for British Columbia, would he go without telling his employees *[sic]* and friends?") was that Friday morning would have represented the first practical opportunity Ray Cook would have had to tell his employer that he wouldn't be in to work that day and perhaps never again depending on what he found in BC, and to tell Jim Hoskins that help with the furniture would have to be postponed until he got back. It would have been the first practical opportunity for Daisy to phone Leona Hoskins to tell her the Sunday picnic was off for the time being. Friday morning was the first available day after the spur-of-the-moment decision of the night before to do anything. Such decisions get made otherwise we wouldn't have a phrase for it.

But on Friday morning all the Cooks were dead, which is not to say they would not have made all the necessary arrangements and telephone calls had they not been so indisposed. The point seems elementary, but both Anderson and Greschuk had trouble with it. There had indeed been a precipitous departure but for an undiscovered country even more alien than is BC to Canada proper. But that departure was not part of Cook's story and, as Anderson put it, it had not been "tailored [by Cook] to fit the emergencies of the prosecution case." Probably because it was not in the accused's interest to be rushing to the prosecution's side in emergencies.

From trial testimony and interviews it was clear that over the course of months and probably years Ray Cook had thought of leaving Stettler. He had scouted service station prospects in Eckville (of Keegstra infamy), Mirror, Hanna, Calgary, Drumheller, Camrose and Bentley - all in Alberta. But Alberta was Alberta. To show that nothing, in the month of his death, was further from Ray Cook's mind than British Columbia, Anderson produced three letters Cook had written home, one in 1956 and two in 1957, none of which (was there triumph in Anderson's voice?) mentioned BC. Yet George McTaggart told me what, given the chance, he'd have told the court: "they planned to go to BC and set up a small service station operation. Ray was probably waiting to go with [Cook], but Daisy wasn't. The thing about Cook having paid his debt to society, Daisy wouldn't have any part of it." Beeching's memory corroborated McTaggart's. McTaggart, who seems to have maintained a connection with the Cooks even though he'd fired Ray, told me, "There was no question but that Daisy didn't want him back. And there's no question but that Ray and Cook were planning the garage business." Like Reamsbottom, Beeching felt that confronted with Daisy's perhaps unexpected hostility and learning the family was about to disown and desert him, something in Cook 'snapped'.

That was one scenario and a plausible enough one at that since no one could be certain what roiled beneath the surface of Cook's relationship between himself and his parents. If Cook was guilty, it was a close as anyone would get to motive. Believing he was guilty, Beeching was troubled about the absence of evidence showing motive, and sought one with the help of his own understanding of human psychology. It had nothing to do with a criminal mind in Beeching's view; anyone might have done what Cook had done. Cook had come home hoping to be welcomed with love and acceptance, aglow with the plans for the service station with "Dad." He was met with a wall of rejection, totally unexpected, thrown up primarily but not exclusively by Daisy. But instead of turning away more in sorrow than in anger, orphaned for the second time in his life, a wellspring of his character of which there had been no prior inkling surfaced and he became homicidal.

It seemed to me that Beeching was comforted with this view which he protested only barely too much. The normal way of a murder mystery is to find motive first and deduce guilt from it, but it is otherwise in murder investigations where proof of guilt comes first and motive only later if at all. In the *Cook* case Beeching had proof of guilt - an abundance of it - but not a hint of motive. Its absence may have troubled him for as long as it took him to clothe an explanation with sufficient plausibilty to pass muster in his own mind - or so it seemed to me who was searching for motive for Beeching's ratiocination, as he was for Cook's otherwise inexplicable act. The interview became momentarily tense when the suggestion hung in the air between us that he might have seen a man to his death not fully convinced of his guilt. To be convinced he had to believe he knew why Cook had done it.

Whether with or without Daisy's blessing, and whether in BC or elsewhere, it was more than a matter of vague probability that Ray Cook had waited what might have seemed to him half a lifetime for his son to come around. The father-son service station was Ray's only hope for his son, and Cook to saw it roughly in those terms, not, as we have seen, that he had any serious intention (or the capability) of giving up his criminal career. But the little business of their own would be the solid base upon which to build the rest of his life. In a letter to Ray of December 2, 1957 (one of those Anderson used to show that a year-and-a-half before Cook's release, no one was talking BC), he wrote;

"Remember Dad, what we were talking about at Bills. Maybe you can see what I mean now, thats why I cant work for sombody else all my life, for what? When I told I would sooner work for you for nothing, than get the highest wages working for sombody else I really ment it. Why make sombody else rich, work for them year after year, because of security? You just haven't got it, unless you are you're own boss, they don't care about anything, you or anybody else, so long as they make themselfs rich. Maybe my way of thinking is all wrong I don't know, its just what I belive."

The letter was a cry from the heart of a penitentiary written in the shadow of Christmas. He hadn't spent a Christmas with his family in seven years.

That was one scenario and a plausible enough one at that. Believing that Cook was guilty, Beeching was troubled about the absence of a clear-cut motive, and sought one with the help of his own understanding of psychology. But scenarios can be fashioned to suit any predilection, and one rather more favorable to Cook starts with the Royal Hotel decision to bring the grand plan to fruition at long last. Hitherto, nothing more had been done than Ray taking half a dozen sorties in Alberta, but now the wherewithal was in hand, found money, to permit the dream's fulfillment.

We have looked at a Ray Cook not averse to stealing property on his own account, and therefore probably not given to making nice moral distinctions between that and accepting property stolen by someone else, particularly stolen property as attractive as money - Greschuk to the contrary. Daisy, the scenario continues, would go along with it, stolen money and all, but with a heavy heart. She would do so because her husband wanted her to for his son's sake. Their problems with him would be behind them if, just this once, she would turn a blind eye to the want of moral rectitude in both her husband and her stepson.

And on the morrow, to wind up a fanciful scenario? The necessary phone calls would be made: to Modern Machine, to Jim and Leona Hoskins. Nothing needed to be done concerning the milkman (who, Anderson implied, would take off without taking care of the milkman?) When he came on Friday morning, Daisy would order the day's needs and tell him not to bother coming for a few days; they were going to be away. The utilities? Unless they were in arrears (nothing suggests they were), is paying them in advance a condition of, say, leaving for the cottage for a few days? In Anderson's view it was, but it seems about as unusual as stripping the beds and hiding the bedclothes in preparation for a brief absence - Greschuk's understanding of the ways of housewives. The school year was completed, or the next thing to it; no problem there[1]. There would be a dozen other things to be taken care of on Friday morning: bus and train schedules to be checked; children's clothes to be selected; suitcases to be packed ready for the Saturday morning departure. All moderately hurried perhaps, even rushed, but scarcely precipitative. But then, one wonders, what is?

---

[1] *Gerry Cook's teacher, anxious to be ready to follow the last kid out the door on Tuesday, June 30 for her two-month vacation, had prepared her attendance register in advance, in ink, recording Gerry's attendance on Friday, June 26 and the following Monday and Tuesday. Shamefacedly she admitted to her principal that she might have jumped the gun.*

He that judges without informing himself to the
utmost that he is capable, cannot acquit himself
of judging amiss.

Locke, *Human Understanding*
Book II, Chapter xxi

CHAPTER 13

THE SUIT

Mr Justice Harold W. Riley's demeanor in the courtroom was made up of roughly equal parts of abruptness, brevity and geniality, all of them, as perceived by observers in his courtroom, filtered through an alcoholic haze through which he himself peered at the dramas playing in front of him. He had been a visibly successful corporate lawyer in Calgary, scion of an old family which spoke only to God, had served the requisite amount of time in the Liberal Party[1] - but behind the lines at Staff Headquarters; a Riley did not serve in the trenches - had been rewarded in the fullness of time with his appointment to the bench, and had succumbed to the occupational disease of alcoholism which ultimately cost him his job and his life.

In running a trial he prided himself on what he saw as his no-nonsense ability to cut through legal and evidentiary thickets to the commonsense heart of the matter, a valuable enough gift except on those occasions when he lost sight of the fact that some legal and factual issues defy simplification and became distorted by being forced willy-nilly into cure-all molds such as Riley's.

His gift for brevity was displayed spectacularly in his charge to the second-trial jury in *Regina v. Cook* in which he expounded the law, reviewed the evidence and set out the defenses in a dizzying half-hour.

---

[1] *As a Liberal candidate for a Commons seat, Riley put out a quarto brochure bearing a full-size replica of the cover of Life Magazine reading "LIFE of Riley". Inside were pictures of Riley as a child in a Buster Brown suit, Riley as a youth, Riley convocating. In due course he received a letter from Life's attorneys, and may as well have received one from the attorneys for the American network which owned the William Bendix radio sitcom of that name. The brochure was withdrawn and the election campaign failed.*

In concluding his charge, stressing that it was merely opinion on his part and in no way binding on the jurors who had "the paramount right to disagree", Riley observed that "the person who was wearing that blue suit and placed it under the mattress was the person who did the killing." Had God said to Moses that He'd given the matter a lot of thought and in His opinion these were the laws which Moses should carry down from Mount Sinai but what did Moses think about it? it would not have been too much different from Riley offering merely as opinion - take it or leave it - that the man who wore the blue suit was the man who had killed Ray Cook. As it happened the suit was Cook's - one of the unquestionable facts of the case. He had worn it - another of them.

And thus the infamous blue suit of which it can be said - as it said to Riley - that of all the evidence against Cook, a veritable Ossa upon Pelion of it, the suit pointed most pointedly to Cook's guilt. It can also be said that together with the greasepit, it seized more powerfully on the popular imagination than anything else in the case, but in a way the greasepit did not. More than anything else, not excluding Cook's being in possession of his father's wallet and car, the blue suit told early students of the case - by and large a transfixed populace - that where there was smoke like this there was a raging firestorm, and minds snapped shut and were to remain in that condition until the Crown began to make its full-blown case against Cook in the first trial.

The purpose of the trial process, if one is on the defense side, is to instil doubt, and if one is the Crown, to dispel all of it apart from that which only unreasonable men would harbor. Cook's first trial started with not all that much to be dispelled - a matter mostly of going through the formalities of proving the more or less self-evident. For example, although technically it wasn't in evidence against him in spite of it being everywhere in the courtroom except in evidence, could anyone seriously think that the escape from the PMH was not the act of a man standing in the shadow of the scaffold, knowing it was just a matter of time before it claimed him?

Yet ironically it was during the first trial that the seeds of doubt were sown for the first time in Alberta at large - an unexpected by-product of a trial which was expected merely to nail down the details of what was already beyond question - and it is not entirely fanciful to suggest that the evidence which convicted him in the forum in which men accused of inordinately heinous crimes are first tried - the public mind - was the same evidence which caused the public to step back reflectively to take a second look: the evidence of the blue suit. It *seemed* there was too much about it that met the eye. There had to be something else, something more.

But in the meantime the suit (together with the greasepit and the words 'Robert Raymond Cook' which took on some of the attributes of a mantra) defined Alberta's claim to immortality in the annals of Canadian crime. If it were possible to single out one factor outweighing all others in the scales of justice as they tipped against Cook, everything about the cheap, robin's-egg blue polyester suit with a silvery-pink thread woven through it - its condition, its location, its ownership, its owner's clumsily contrived accounting for it prefaced with a bodyguard of lies - would be seen to be it. Only if one could not see the suit lying on the exhibit table bloodstained and accusatory, only if one had not heard Cook on the suit, could one have vague and (to the prosecution) groundless doubts about what it said to those who could see it and who had heard Cook. The lightweight, summery suit hung like a millstone around the necks of the defense lawyers, and the effect of everything about it was as a coacervation of impediments put there by Fate to hamper the defense.

***

To pick out the flaws in Riley's observation it is necessary to start from the end - the hiding of the suit under the mattress - and work backwards. The only part of the observation which admitted of no argument was that the man who hid the suit was the man who did the killing. No one would contend that some innocent had wandered into the bedroom after the murders and, in one of those compulsions to tidy up which can sweep over a person at the strangest times, stuffed the suit under the mattress much as a harried housewife who spotted unexpected company coming up the front sidewalk might do after frantically smoothing the doilies.

Add to that the reasonable supposition that the man who had hidden the suit had also worn it just before he hid it, and the chain back to Cook is half forged. But it cannot be assumed that the suit was *necessarily* worn during the killings. If even the possibility of that hiatus is conceded - as it must be in the total absence of any evidence of the suit having been worn *during* the murders - it will be seen that a necessary and logical progression from Cook arriving at the house wearing the suit through to Cook hiding the suit under the mattress - *and not otherwise* - is not possible. Riley, that is to say, was not entitled to equate "the person who was wearing that suit and placed it under the mattress" (and was, therefore, the killer) to the person who wore the suit to the house. It had to be made clear to a panel of men not accustomed to dealing in overarching subtleties that the one was not necessarily the other. To fail to do so was to invite conviction.

If it seems that Riley stopped just short of a directed verdict, leaving the jurors merely to identify "the person who was wearing that suit and placed it under the mattress" as Cook to justify their existence as a jury, the feeling is borne out by a reading of Riley's report to the federal Solicitor General[1] - a single-page document in which Riley said what he thought should be said to assist the Diefenbaker cabinet in considering commutation. For Riley it was Cook. There was no doubt in his mind, he wrote, "that the jury for the second time came to the right conclusion." He ended his report with a curious observation which might be thought to be out of keeping with what is normally thought of as judicial restraint: "This," he wrote, "was one of the most ghoulish, bizarre and savage murders in the books." Savage certainly, but one looks in vain for ghoulish and bizarre elements, much less for the bearing such elements would have had on the question of guilt or innocence, and concludes that Riley threw in a couple of gratuitous adjectives to pad out an impoverished and worthless view of the case.

But to minds less passionate than Riley's there was some room for doubt, however perverse. Proof of any fact about the suit between the established points of its being worn home, by Cook, and its being found under the mattress depended entirely on inferences to be drawn from whatever other facts were known about it or from its surrounding circumstances in the bedroom. The key question was whether the suit had been worn during the killings. If so, then it was likely it was worn by Cook at that bloody juncture since it was highly improbable someone else would put it on before the murders in a manner somewhat reminiscent of dressing before coming down for dinner. The question was not considered by either Riley or Anderson. It was, for both, a nonstarter. For the defense lawyers however it was a matter of getting Cook out of the suit before the killings. Do that, and the 'during' of the matter didn't matter. True, there was the question of the bloodstaining of the suit still to be addressed, worn during the killings or not - a problem which Main and Dunne misaddressed by failing to recognize the most promising avenue of approach open to them[2].

***

1 *See p. 231*

2 *See p. 227 ff*

Cook's first reaction to the recognition that the suit spelled peril was his usual one: he lied about it. Locked up in the Stettler Detachment, on Sunday afternoon he began to overhear snatches of police conversations about the house, among them references to the suit, owner as yet unknown. He was then charged with murder, and by the time Beeching was ready to interrogate him on Monday morning, he had ready a story which he seemed to think would explain something about the suit, but which in fact explained nothing and would not have even had it been true. It served one unintended purpose: it told the police it would only be a matter of time before Cook was ensnared in a web of lies.

Without having any idea of the manner in which the suit could plausibly be accounted for but wanting to distance himself from it in some awkward way, Cook informed Beeching that prior to going home for the first time on Thursday night, he had gone to the Club Cafe where he changed out of the suit which he then took home and gave to his father. Beeching never asked him where he got the clothes he changed into (bringing to mind the shopping bag full of clothes reputedly still in Eddie Read's truck), a question for which Cook of course had no ready answer had it been asked[1]. The problem for the police at this point was proof of ownership. Whether he had carried it or worn it to the house did not matter.

There proved to be no such problem. On taking the stand at the first trial, Cook abandoned the Club Cafe story in favor of the admission that the suit was his and that he had worn it home. Perhaps because he could not conjure a change of clothing permitting him to get out of the suit at the Club Cafe, but more probably because he now saw there was nothing to be lost by telling the truth, he told it, at least to the point of arriving home wearing the suit. But he was not allowed to forget that he had lied to Beeching on Monday morning[2]. In and of itself the Club Cafe lie was harmless enough to Cook. It was intended to get him out of the suit at what he then thought was the critical time: the time of arrival at the house accompanied by his father. The critical time of course was the time of someone stripping it off and hurriedly stuffing it under the mattress before fleeing into the forgiving night.

On the stand he added a detail which he hadn't told Beeching at the Detachment: he was anxious to get rid of the suit because, being penitentiary made, he felt it branded him as an ex-convict, a feeling

---

[1] *See Appendix A, Qs 38-44*

[2] *See Appendix A, Qs 39 and 40*

which is described by those who have experienced it as what they imagined was felt by World War II POWs whose jackets had red bull's eyes between the shoulder blades. Like the bull's eyes, ex-cons feel, prison-made street clothing tends to attract unwelcome attention. Moreover, getting rid of the suit was all the easier because there was someone who wanted it: his father. As he told Beeching, his father "was going to Vancouver and had no proper clothes and the suit wasn't in bad shape and it fit him good about the same size as I am." The suit should have been in good shape; it was about three days old although it had been worn continuously throughout them.

The bald assertion that he had given the suit to his father was seen by the police and by Anderson for what it was: a moderately clever embellishment where none was needed. But how clever? It would have been simpler for him to have said only that on arriving home he changed out of the suit and left it. His insistence that he had given it to his father can be seen as an adventitious detail contributing nothing (and indeed detracting from an uncomplicated lie), but can also be seen as giving an infusion of verisimilitude if not veracity to a story badly in need of one. Cook didn't have the subtlety - the cunning as Anderson called it - to see how falsehood could be lent a measure of credibility by adding a detail so improbable as to be probably true. If anything, quite the contrary as witness the crude attempt to ring in the Club Cafe as a way of avoiding admitting he'd worn the suit home when it didn't matter whether he had or not, accomplishing only the adding of one more falsehood to the Crown's growing stockpile of them.

The suit presented the Crown with an enviable position: nothing need be proved. Ownership was not in issue and there was nothing that needed to be said - or could be said - about whether the suit had been given to Ray. Cook said it had, but what Cook said was not one of the Crown's overriding concerns. The defense position at least had the virtue of clarity: shore up Cook's story of the gift of the suit with as much ancillary evidence as it could muster and, when the time came, be ready with an explanation for the blood on it[1].

---

[1] *These were the only two questions for the defense; anything else was digression serving to obscure the points on which the defense had to concentrate its resources if it hoped to make any headway against the damning suit. Dunne nevertheless cross-examined police witnesses at length on the finding and condition of the suit - irrelevant matters (which is not to say the way in which the suit became bloodstained was irrelevant.) The jurors could see the condition of the suit for themselves, and nothing was to be gained by them learning one more patience-trying time that it had been found under the mattress. The police might have been thrown off stride by being asked why it took them a couple of hours after finding the jacket to find the*

The suit was heavily bloodstained[1]. Three possibilities accounting for the staining suggest themselves: first, in preparing for bed, Ray took the suit off and draped it over the footboard where it was caught in a spray of blood from the two shotgun blasts which had killed him and his wife; second that it was worn during the murders and was caught in that spray, becoming additionally stained when the bodies were carried to the garage; third it was put on by the killer after the murders to protect his own clothing from the bodies. As far as we know, only one body, Ray's, was wrapped in a blanket, and then only partially, but given the condition of both adult bodies a blanket would have offered scant protection from blood contaminating the clothing of whoever carried them.

The first possibility was Main's choice, developed by him in the first trial and echoed with minor difference by Dunne in the second. Main was concerned first of all to show that the suit wasn't worn during the murders, and did this, in his closing argument, by pointing out that "there [were] bloodstains even well into the crotch of this suit, and that area might very well have been protected from splattering if the suit was being worn by the perpetrator." Main did not explain how it might have been protected during perpetration when there presumably would have been full frontal exposure, yet receive staining "well into the crotch" if it was not being worn, although it is true that the back reaches of the crotch are protected to an extent while pants are being worn.

The 'foot of the bed' theory was the best he could do, and he reminded the jurors of the pathologist's evidence "that when a person is killed in the manner in which Ray Cook was killed, that *[sic]* it is reasonable to suppose that there would be a huge gush of blood which, if the clothing were thrown over the foot of the bed, would splatter." It would splatter of course wherever the clothing was located; it was not quite what Main

---

pants under the same mattress, but Dunne made nothing of this droll delinquency. "Sam," someone might have said, "they made the search for the pants too long."

[1] *In negativing smear, Dunne missed what, it can be argued, was most significant about the type of bloodstaining. Looking ahead to Main's analysis, it is not possible to see the crotch in the single photograph of the pants entered as evidence - Plate 19. It is concealed by the right leg partially concealing the left. However, the whole of the front of the pants - as much as can be seen - is stained, not all of it 'splatter'. What is most pronounced about the pants is that there is a large smear - no other description fits - at the left knee, a smaller one just above it towards the outer seam and another just below it towards the inner seam. They seem to vary in their intensity. It would not be possible to attribute them to blood gushing from the far end of the bed.*

intended to say which was that clothing at the end of the bed would have been splattered. But there was nothing in his argument to explain why the whole of the front of the suit, both pants and jacket, was bloodstained when, had the suit been draped over the footboard, those parts hanging towards the floor would have been masked from the "huge gush of blood."

For Dunne too the blood had splattered: "If you examine that suit," he told the jurors, "you will notice that particularly on the trousers a good part of the staining is obviously what you would call splatter rather than smear, and in that connection I would remind you of the evidence of Dr Davey, that in this type of wound there would no doubt be a very considerable splatter of blood. Do you consider it likely or probable that the suit was on the bed where Mr Cook senior had left it, or that the suit was worn by the perpetrator of this offense? It is just another angle to think about." Dunne did not attempt to explain why the suit would be smeared if worn during the killings (he said nothing about the carrying of the bodies) but only splattered if over the end of the bed (and therefore not being worn by Cook - the point he was concerned to make) but, as he said, it was an angle which bore thinking about.

There were two implications of the Main-Dunne theory which required of the suit that it be entirely passive - being worn by no one - both during and after the commission of the murders. The first was that the defense candidate for complicity wore his own clothes throughout, but it seems inherently unlikely when one considers the condition such clothing would have been in at the end of the night's bloody labors.

The second is that blood has to be seen as spurting from a distance of about four feet to the foot of the bed but shotgun wounds produce the effect seen in the bedroom: quantities of blood and so on splattered on the headboard and on the east wall beside what was thought by the RCMP to be Ray Cook's side of the bed, probably erroneously; the order in which the bodies were thrown in the pit indicates Daisy slept on the wall side of the bed. Moreover, had there been a momentary stream of blood extending from one of the adult victims to the foot of the bed, there should have been a single blanket or bedspread showing the vivid traces of such a stream. No such item was entered in evidence.

The second possibility accounting for the staining on the suit - that the suit was worn during the murders - was of course Anderson's. Nothing much needed to be said. Cook wore what was after all his suit, killed his family and got rid of what even Cook could see was incriminating evidence by hiding it under the mattress where, with luck, it would never be found.

The third possibility was, for anyone with a stubborn conviction of Cook's innocence, the most plausible. The suit had served to protect the killer's clothing which he removed while he concealed the bodies. The theory had one lonely adherent, Cook,[1] but that says nothing about its merit or lack of it. Its merit (for the defense) was that it far more adequately explained the type and extent of staining, particularly on the pants, and it was a reasonable hypothesis which proved nothing but which opened the door to the possibility of the stranger for which Main and Dunne contended.

If the Main-Dunne theory was correct, then only the blood of Ray and/or Daisy would have been found on the suit (and perhaps the blood of one or both of the little girls who slept in the master bedroom), whereas if Cook was right (or Anderson for that matter) then it is highly probable that blood from all the victims would have been found on it. The suit was not tested for blood types. Had it been, depending on the results the entire case might have been advanced one step nearer the truth.

In Mr Justice Greschuk's mind there was no question but that the suit had been worn by the killer during the killings, the only question being who was wearing it at that time? He was the killer. Greschuk put it to the jury this way: "If you are not satisfied beyond a reasonable doubt that the accused was wearing the suit, shirt, tie and belt which were found under the mattress...did someone other than the accused put these articles of clothing on and do the killing and put them under the mattress, or are you satisfied beyond a reasonable doubt on the circumstantial evidence that it was the accused who killed his father and then hid the suit, shirt, tie and belt under the mattress and the shoes on the clothes closet?" The choice between Cook as the wearer of the suit at the time of the murders and some stranger creeping into the bedroom and carefully changing into the suit (and the tie since that was imported by Greschuk's "these articles of clothing") in the presence of his intended victims has something of a Hobsonian quality to it. Still, the trial judge had fairly laid out the alternatives as he perceived them.

***

---

[1] *In an undated post-second trial note, Cook wrote, "Also is it logical the perpatrator of the crime would not want to get his own clothes any more stained than necessary. It is probable and logical that other clothes being handy he might change before moving the bodies into the pit where they were found. Then change back into his own clothes before leaving the scene."*

One Gail Ellavina Marie Smith was called as a defense witness at the second trial only. Examined by Dave MacNaughton, she told of being a visitor in the Myhaluk residence in south Edmonton when Cook came to the house on Wednesday evening. He had mistakenly dismissed his taxi short of the house and had to walk the last two or three blocks through a rainstorm. He was wearing the blue suit. Since it was damp, Smith offered to press it for him. He accepted the offer.

On Friday morning (although Smith thought it was Saturday), Smith was still at the Myhaluk's and Cook came again to the house. MacNaughton asked her nothing about Cook's Friday visit, and it is probable he did not know she was still a visitor at Myhaluk's and could therefore be expected to have seen Cook a second time. MacNaughton finished his examination, handed her over to Anderson and sat back in anticipation of some innocuous cross-examination covering the Wednesday evening ground he had already traversed. Anderson surprised him. Without warning and after a dozen or so questions which did nothing more than have confirmed what Smith had told MacNaughton, Anderson switched to a line of questioning whose consequences MacNaughton could not have foreseen:

"Now did you see Cook on any other occasion after [Wednesday]?"

"Yes, I believe it was Saturday morning he came over."

"Saturday morning?"

"M'hm."

"Are you sure about the day?"

"Well, I can't really say for sure, but I think it was."

"Was he driving a vehicle?"

"Yes."

"What kind?"

"It was a station wagon."

"A station wagon, and did you hear Cook mention anything about what had become of his blue suit in the meantime?"

"He said something about tearing it or something."

"How did that come up?"

"I don't know. I believe Mrs Myhaluk asked him what happened to his suit or something."

"Mrs Myhaluk asked him what happened to his suit, and what did he say?"

"I think he said he tore it."

"He said he tore it. That was his explanation for not having it, correct?"

"Correct."

Anderson knew Cook had been at the Myhaluk's on Friday but he did not know that Smith was still there and had been continuously since Wednesday. His asking her whether she had seen Cook a second time was a shot in the dark, as was his asking her about Cook's explanation for no longer wearing the suit. Had he known what she would tell him about the suit, he would of course have called her as a Crown witness to avoid the possibility of Dunne not calling her for the defense. The first shot in the dark was purely fortuitous, but the second was a skillful probing of the ground opened up by Smith's having seen Cook a second time when he was no longer wearing the suit she had pressed on Wednesday. The question was why not? Both Dunne and MacNaughton should have known what Smith would say about the suit and should not have called her under any circumstances.

Anderson now had evidence from a defense witness of incalculable value. It was a classic example of the pitfalls which await a lawyer who is not thoroughly prepared for the sabotage which awaits his case if he isn't. Smith's pre-Anderson evidence was not essential to the defense although not without its importance. She was called only to establish that Cook was wearing a clean white shirt on Wednesday evening - evidence which could have been sacrificed had it been known, as it should have been known, that the price of calling Smith to give it would be leaving with the jury Cook's fatal explanation for no longer wearing the suit.

Apart from his concluding remarks quoted at the beginning of this chapter, Mr Justice Riley had this to say about the suit: "Now the suit, about which I will have more to say later. You will remember the evidence of Miss Gail Smith who told of seeing Cook on Saturday morning, the 27th of June, and who told of overhearing a conversation where Cook explained that he was not wearing a suit because he tore it." To coin a phrase, that tore it. Riley did not think it worthwhile to point out that on Saturday morning, June 27, Cook was in Whitecourt looking for Eugene Cebryk. Not that there was any serious question but that Smith's memory had failed her, but Riley himself had tried without success to have her correct the day before allowing her to leave the witness stand, which is to say he well knew Smith had seen Cook a second time on Friday and not Saturday. Since he was reviewing the evidence for the edification of the jury, he might have pointed out the conflict between her evidence and that of Feth and Teeple, passengers on the trip to Whitecourt. Then, if the jury was prepared to find that Smith's Saturday was in fact Friday, well and good.

He might also have reminded the jurors of Smith's evidence given when MacNaughton, locking the Augean stable, sought to undo the ruinous damage done by Anderson's cross-examination of Smith. He re-examined her:

"Miss Smith, are you sure or could you be mistaken about the explanation about the blue suit that the accused had given you?"

"Well, I had just got up and was half asleep and I wouldn't want to say for sure."

The common sense which jurors bring to their duties might have suggested to them that Smith's vague recantation notwithstanding, the truth probably lay in what she told Anderson: she had heard Cook tell Mrs Myhaluk something or other about the suit being torn. Semicomatose or not, the words 'suit' and tore' had registered with Smith. Or had they? Upon reflection, she "[didn't] want to say for sure."

The question then was were the jurors any more entitled to accept her evidence that she had heard Cook tell Myhaluk the suit was torn than that she wasn't sure what she had heard Cook tell Myhaluk? The answer is yes, the jurors *were* so entitled. Jurors are there to believe whatever they believe; it is their *raison d'etre*. But could it be said to have been proved beyond a reasonable doubt that Smith had heard what she herself was not sure she had heard? Evidently. Not that the verdict in the second trial necessarily turned on the Smith evidence, but it cannot be doubted it had its impact. Cook had stuffed the bloody suit under the mattress and accounted for his no longer wearing it with an excuse on a par with not having his homework with him because his dog ate it. Mrs Myhaluk may have bought it but the jurors knew better. As did Mr Justice Riley. And when a justice of the Trial Division of the Supreme Court of Alberta - the very title discourages frivolous dissent - says that Smith said that Cook said he had discarded the suit because it was torn, and omits saying what Smith said to MacNaughton when, too late, MacNaughton tried to repair the damage, the jurors, to coin another phrase, are apt to follow suit.

The lawyers in the Solicitor General's Department in Ottawa were not happy with Riley's one-page report (which contained seven errors of fact) which added nothing to what they already knew beyond there being some ghoulish and bizarre aspects to the case which they can't have known about merely from reading the trial transcripts. The report, not to put too fine a point on it, was a travesty of judicial responsibility, and Riley was asked by the Department "to confirm that the Solicitor General should regard the report of Mr Justice Greschuk of December 17, 1959 as an appropriate commentary, mutatis mutandis, on the trial at which [Riley] had presided."[1]

Riley replied that he had not read the Greschuk report or the transcripts of the earlier trial, but that he had had a chance to discuss the case with both Greschuk and Anderson. There was no mention of Main or Dunne. The evidence at both trials, he wrote, "was essentially the same", but there nevertheless were some differences "which should be drawn to [the Solicitor General's] attention." After informing Ottawa of his three reasons for keeping out of evidence the statement Cook had given Beeching, two of which would have come as news to anyone in the courtroom at the time[2], Riley went on to advise that "There was called by the defense a witness named Gail Ellavina Marie Smith.... Her evidence was really of no value because in cross-examination she admitted seeing the accused ...on the Friday following the commission of the offence, and that the accused had told her *[sic]* that he had discarded the suit because he had torn it, whereas in his defence he

[1] *Undated "Memorandum for the Honorable Solicitor General", National Archives.*

[2] *"A statement given to Staff Sergeant Beeching of the R.C.M.P. was excluded for the reason that the method of obtaining the same I regarded as unsatisfactory; the evidential value of the same was slight; the prejudice to the accused could be great."
It will be recalled that the statement was entirely exculpatory, and therefore not prejudicial to Cook unless used as Anderson had used it in the first trial. Anderson had given Riley no intimation that this was how he intended to use it in Riley's courtroom.*

alleged he had given it to his father." Smith had left the stand still thinking Friday was Saturday, and it was not open to Riley to say she admitted seeing Cook on Friday. However it didn't matter in light of the interesting, if not widely known, legal proposition upon which Riley relied in dismissing Smith's evidence *ex poste facto*: evidence harmful to the accused is of no value if evidence favorable to the accused contradicts it. Mr Justice Riley must have temporarily lost sight of it when he charged the jury since he did not tell the jurors to disregard what Smith had told Anderson.

***

He gave the blue suit to his father, he said, and in exchange got some clothing, some of it his father's. Ray got the best of the swap; the only thing of Ray's Cook was wearing when he was arrested were a pair of brown slacks and a sports shirt. For the rest, he took another sports shirt which he was "pretty shure" he had bought in 1957. He exchanged his prison oxfords for a pair of loafers which were probably also his. He did not change his shorts or socks, and the blue-flecked sports jacket he was wearing when he was arrested on Saturday evening he had taken earlier that evening from the basement. It belonged to Gurney, but Cook said he thought it was his which, for him, was good enough to justify his taking it.

Evidence supporting the one-sided swap which is not self-serving (Cook's statement to Beeching and his trial testimony) is sparse: an undated letter from the penitentiary to "Mom and Dad" saying "Don't send that overcoat and overalls. They will fit you if you want them. In fact keep it all and send me another twenty. I think that pair of strides cost eighteen bucks or something like that." There was nothing more and one was forced to fall back on probabilities. They were the same height, but Cook outweighed Ray by about fifteen pounds so that in purely physical terms (leaving taste out of it for the moment) it was not beyond possibility's realm that they would wear each other's clothes. It is not unheard of for father and sons - mostly sons - to wear the other's clothes if they can get into them. Nor was it improbable that Ray would be glad to get an almost new suit that Cook was glad to get out of because of its - mostly imagined - prison character. The feeling is real enough in such men, but in this instance one is left wondering why Cook didn't change earlier? He had carried clothing from the penitentiary although it can't be known whether it was a complete ensemble. Probably not. Penitentiary records show he sent clothing home during his last term, and it may be that he didn't change until he got to Stettler because he didn't have sufficient clothing to change into.

Main used the undated letter referred to above, but not as the only evidence he had which in any way supported Cook's account of giving the suit to Ray. For Main, the letter was evidence only of the warmth of the relationship between Cook and his parents, and he missed the probative value, minor though it may have been, of Cook's invitation to his father to keep and wear his overcoat and overalls, and his "strides." As might be expected, Dunne said nothing about the gift of the suit to Ray. For the jurors, if the defense made nothing of the gift of the suit, why should they?

***

For Anderson, Cook's reason for hiding the suit under the mattress hardly required exegesis. Still, it couldn't hurt to say a couple of words about it: "My learned friend suggested that the accused would do himself no good by leaving that suit in those circumstances if in fact it was him. Well, why not? He couldn't wear it. He could hardly carry it. He could hardly take the responsibility of having that suit found in his possession. What else are you going to do with it? What is so dangerous in leaving it there? I suggest that again you have the mind of this murderer which must be at the peak of frantic frenzy, that you can conclude from the facts of the crime itself, and certainly not in a position to give much adequate consideration to factors of that kind."

One wishes to avoid being facetious, to avoid shooting fish in a barrel, but can avoid the temptation only by declining comment.

Cook himself was merely contemptuous of the suggestion he'd hidden the suit. In notes made after the second conviction, he tried to set out the points which he thought should be appealed, referring to himself in the third person perhaps hoping that Dunne would take his memorandum and use it whole: "The following evedence is both inconsistent with the accuseds guilt and consistent with his innocence: The evedence that finger prints were carfully wiped up and all obvious signs of violence covered and the suit being found in such an obious place and no attempts to destroy it or hide the owners idenity. The evedence that the accussed is well versed in crime and is not an idiot."

He sometimes got it right; he was not an idiot and his points were well-taken. Precisely because of the suit's being found in such an obvious place with no attempt made to destroy it nor to dissociate it from its owner were the seeds of doubt sown which ultimately swung a majority behind the conviction of Cook's innocence.

He could have made one of his points in more telling fashion. Why, if he was guilty, when he was having an idle beer in the house on Saturday evening prior to backing the Impala up to the garage to load suitcases, would he not think to retrieve the blue suit from wherever it then was and take it with him? He did not expect to be arrested and, instead of promenading up and down Main Street, it would have been a simple matter for him to drive out of Stettler and deep six in any one of five hundred potholes within five miles of Stettler the one thing which more than any other tied him to the crime: the blue suit.

MR JUSTICE PETER GRESCHUK:
>You are not suggesting that the evidence in
>this trial is dubious are you?

MR GIFFARD MAIN, QC:
>Oh yes, I am sir.

MR JUSTICE GRESCHUK:
>Ridiculous.

MR MAIN:
>I suggest it is quite dubious.

MR JUSTICE GRESCHUK:
>Ridiculous, that statement. Go ahead.

Exchange, first trial

CHAPTER 14

THE SHIRT AND THE SEVENTEEN RESULTS

Just as (as Robert Benchley once observed) the class comprising everyone may be divided into two classes - those who divide everyone into two classes and those who don't - so may that class made up of roughly half of everyone - men - be divided into men who, without working at it and without knowing or much caring why, are found attractive by women, and men who would be found attractive by women were it not for woman's perversity and purblindness.

Cook fell into the former class, was probably aware of it but wore the mantle easily. He was known to refuse to take advantage of women when advantage was offered up with eager hands, but he was not celibate. He was known also to loosen the reins on the normal sexual drive on occasion, but taking opportunity as it came rather than as the result of active pursuit driven by the conviction he was God's munificence made incarnate for the delectation of womankind. Not that opportunity presented itself all that often since he spent most of what were, for him, the deformative years cooped up in institutions where conjugal visits were a thing of the distant future. Such opportunities as there were had to work themselves into periods of liberty measured in weeks and even days.

But during them, on the street or at the wheel of the car of the moment, or in the purgatory between the street and prison when he was on his way into or out of a courtroom, women's heads turned to follow him, and not because of any figure he cut as a fashion plate. He did not cut such a figure. He was always neat, well-groomed and ordinarily concerned with the supposed effect of what he was wearing, but he had spent those years in which awareness of appearance develops in institutions not much given to encouraging the study of male fashion coordinates.

In his brief interludes of freedom - little more than breathing spaces for hatching the next ill-starred series of B&Es and car thefts - he never acquired either the taste or the know-how for dressing well. Whatever came to hand as it were, as witness the clothing being worn by him or in the trunk of the Impala at the time of his arrest: clothing - borrowed, stolen or taken in the mistaken belief it was his - from two wardrobes: his father's and Leonard Gurney's.

There was therefore a certain incongruity to be found in the fact that in a real sense clothes were the death of him. Police photographs apart, items of clothing formed by far the largest class of things displayed against him on the exhibit table where, because of the generally bloody condition of that part of it which belonged to Cook, it sat in mute indictment. But clothing formed as well a body of evidence outside the strict rules governing the admission of objects into evidence in a criminal trial, chief among them being that those objects be present in the courtroom where they can be seen and handled and pondered.

The police were not slow off the mark in their appreciation of the fact that clothing was going to figure large in the unfolding investigation. For example, the police diagram of the main floor plan made early in the investigation carefully depicted such things as the location of the children's runners as they were found in the house and before some meticulous gumshoe, for all the world like Snow White tidying up the hut in preparation for the return of the dwarfs from the diamond mine, lined up seven pairs of shoes smallest to largest left to right and, for no readily apparent reason, took their portrait. And of the 33 police photographs entered as prosecution exhibits, eight of them either featured clothing or showed it as incidental to the main subject of the photograph. Clothes which made up the better part of the Crown's case simultaneously unmade the man.

Twelve items of clothing were marked as Crown exhibits[1], among them two shirts including a nondescript pink-and-grey sports shirt which had belonged to Ray and was being worn by Cook when he was arrested. The only question about it was whether Cook had come by it innocently as part of the clothing swap, but the question was of little importance; the shirt was marked as an exhibit in both trials, set aside and forgotten. Its claim to a place in the courtroom was tenuous.

The second shirt - a blood-stained white dress shirt found under the mattress - was altogether more interesting than its companion. For one thing its appearance compelled a second look, but more compelling was the fact that after a police investigation which started on June 28, 1959 and was still going on almost to the day the second trial opened - June 20, 1960 - and after eighteen days of two trials, nothing more was known about it than was known in the first five seconds after Van Blarcom peeled back the mattress and spotted it beside the blue suit jacket. It sat in the courtroom as a taunting, almost malevolent presence, demanding explanation, defying it and in the end defeating, without exception, everyone who took a run at the insistent problem it posed.

So far as white shirts went, it was alone in the courtroom, but in a larger sense it was not alone since there were two other white shirts which never managed to make it to the exhibit table as Crown exhibits. Had the Crown (or, for that matter, the defense) recognized their significance, it would have been seen that their absence from the courtroom suited the Crown's purposes exactly since nothing of significance could be said about the white shirt which was in the courtroom without reference to the two shirts which were not. What was significant (for defense purposes) is that it not be tied to Cook, where tying it to him was easier in the absence of the other two shirts. But that is to get ahead of the story.

---

[1] *Eighty-four exhibits were marked by the Crown in the first trial, 77 in the second. In the first trial the defense entered Cook's correspondence record from Saskatchewan Penitentiary as its lone exhibit. In the second trial, the record was entered and a toolbox as added. See Chapter 20.*

Both Main and Dunne argued the imperative of Anderson accounting for the shirt. Both failed. Nevertheless Anderson too failed. Unable to say anything about the shirt beyond the undeniable fact that it was in the courtroom demanding that something *be* said about it, Anderson ignored the demand in the first trial and adopted the only expedient open to him. He swept it under the rug and found a compliant jury prepared to avert its eyes while he did so. In the second trial he took an ill-conceived stab at explaining the shirt - an effort which may have embarrassed even Anderson when it unfolded in the courtroom - and again ended by sweeping it out of sight where it remained conveniently out of mind. When the tumult and the shouting died and Cook along with it, no one had the least scintilla of an idea how a bloody white shirt made its inexplicable way to the underside of the mattress in Ray and Daisy Cook's bedroom.

***

In 1959, no matter what a man had worn into the penitentiary, it was the policy of the Penitentiary Service to issue him a complete change of clothing on release. He was required to wear it out of the penitentiary. The clothes worn when he came in he carried out. For those new clothes requiring tailoring - the suits - inmates were measured a couple of weeks in advance of release. The suits were then made up by an inmate in the tailor shop followed by one fitting to adjust sleeve and leg lengths. The pants of Cook's suit were, Cook wrote, "shortened by the same guy who made them [who was] also the one who got me the materail, wich he'd saved for his own discharge suite."

The fitting took place on Monday, June 22. The unnamed inmate who had generously stepped aside in Cook's favor, giving to him the material set aside against the day of his own release, could not have guessed that when Cook stepped through the main gate on the day following the fitting, wearing - and detesting - the new suit, it would have a service life of not quite three days before coming to its bloody end side by side with a bloody shirt under an even bloodier mattress.

At the time the deputy warden was one John Henry Weeks. Weeks was called as a Crown witness at the preliminary inquiry chiefly to give evidence relating to the correspondence record, although he also identified the belt (found in the loops of the suit pants) as having come from penitentiary stock. No chances were being taken of not being able to tie Cook to everything found under the mattress, and the prosecution did not then know that Cook would ultimately admit ownership of the suit, a red tie, the belt and the pair of black oxfords found in the walk-through closet.

Weeks therefore was not needed by the Crown at either trial (in advance of the first trial Main had signaled his intention not to dispute ownership), but in the preliminary inquiry Main spotted a use for him and he called him as his witness at the first trial. He first asked Weeks what he knew of the Durocher dormitory attack hoping to set up Durocher *in absentia* as someone who hated Cook so much that he would stop at nothing not excluding wiping out Cook's family to avenge himself on Cook. After Main had finished, Anderson cross-examined him to no particular effect and Weeks stood down. But then Main, as an afterthought, had Weeks re-called to cover some new ground:

"What clothing was issued to the accused upon his discharge from the penitentiary on the 23rd of June, 1959?"

"Every inmate discharged from the penitentiary gets an outfit right from the shoes right to the head. We give him shoes, underwear, socks and a suit, and in the winter we give him an overcoat but in the summer we don't give him any overcoat."

"What about the question of shirts?"

"Shirts, we issue shirts, yes."

"And what type of shirt is issued?"

"Well, it is a bought shirt. It is a white shirt."

"You say it is a bought shirt. It is not a manufactured shirt?"

"No. We used to give them manufactured shirts from prison. They wasn't contented with them and we changed that and we bought them."

After an indecisive attempt by Main to straighten out the difference between bought and manufactured (since 'manufactured' could be taken to mean manufactured outside the prison and brought into penitentiary stock), the resolution more or less was that the shirt issued Cook was bought, that is it might have come from outside the penitentiary. Or maybe not as later evidence would show. Weeks was also able to tell

Main that on June 9 Cook had received a parcel from "R. Cook" containing, Weeks said, "one shirt, one tie and one pair of socks which was put into his effects."

At the second trial, Weeks was again called as a defense witness. He was examined by MacNaughton primarily concerning the Durocher attack. When MacNaughton turned to clothing, Weeks told him what he had told Main except now the bought shirt was "prison made - just an ordinary shirt made up by the prisoners" who, it turned out, were female prisoners in Kingston Penitentiary who "made them a little better", but on cross-examination it turned out as well that Saskatchewan Penitentiary discharge shirts were still being made there. It was all getting a little confusing. By the time Weeks was finished no one had any clear idea where the shirt issued Cook was made: Saskatchewan Penitentiary, Kingston Penitentiary or somewhere out in the wide world. Nor, after MacNaughton, did the court know whether the shirt issued to Cook was white or patterned, but luckily for our purposes Main had had Weeks identify it in the first trial as white.

Weeks had not been asked to describe the shirt which came from home on June 9, but Cook was. He told Main it was brand new and still pinned up, and Dunne that "it still had a cardboard thing around the collar and plastic over it." Cook agreed with the Weeks evidence: he had worn the prison-issue shirt out of the penitentiary and carried the gift shirt. Only in direct examination in the first trial did he get it reversed, but no one noticed the slip.

After questioning Gail Smith about her offer to press the damp suit, MacNaughton asked her whether she'd pressed anything else:

"Yes, his shirt."

"What type of shirt was it Miss Smith?"

"It was a french cuff."

"And why do you particularly think it was a french cuff shirt?"

"Well, there was a pair of cufflinks and one was broken."

"Was this a soiled shirt Miss Smith?"

"No, I don't believe it was. It was quite clean and new."

"I beg your pardon?"

"It was quite clean and new."

"It was quite clean and new?"

"M'hm."

"Did you notice any other wearing apparel of the accused Miss Smith?"

"No, just a button missing off the shirt and a pair of stockings, but I couldn't tell you what color."

"Do you recall if the shirt, the color of the shirt or what type of shirt it was?"

"It was a white one."

For reasons which will shortly become apparent, Anderson was anxious to have Cook at Myhaluk's in anything but a clean shirt, white and new, and he therefore had to do what he could do to undermine Smith's straightforward evidence:

"And you pressed a shirt?"

"M'hm."

"Did you wash it before you pressed it?"

"No, I didn't have to."

"You just did a dry press did you?"

"M'hm."

"Is that an advisable use to put shirts to or is it hard on them?"

"Well, it was quite wet."

To suggest ironing a shirt is to use it is roughly equivalent to suggesting it be worn as a form of preventive maintenance, but Anderson had done what little he could to shake Smith and he turned to attack a more promising foe - Cook:

"Now, there was a matter came up today of shirts and I believe your evidence was that when you left Prince Albert you were wearing the prison-issue shirt; that later on in Edmonton you changed to the new white shirt your father had given you and it was [*sic*] french cuffs?"

"Yes sir, that is true."

"And I suggest to you that that was the first occasion on which you had ever mentioned french cuffs?"

"I know I mentioned it to my lawyer. I don't know if...."

"I am speaking now of [Cook's first-trial evidence when he hadn't mentioned french cuffs]."

"It could be."

"I suggest that until you mentioned that on this occasion you weren't quite sure of what sequence, or in what sequence, you wore this shirt?"

"That is true. I wasn't sure whether I had worn the penitentiary shirt out of there or the prison-issue shirt, but I have recalled that - I know now that I wore the prison-issue shirt out."

"And you just remembered in the last few days that it [*sic*, i.e. the prison-issue shirt] had french cuffs?"

"No sir. I sometime after or maybe it was even during the last - in December."

Cook was confused since the penitentiary shirt *was* the prison issue shirt, and it in any case was the only one prison regulations permitted him to wear out. Anderson may have thought he had him, may have thought that only now was Cook aware that there was a shirt with french cuffs (as, say, a result of having heard Smith's evidence which he was anxious to corroborate since she was a defense witness), but Anderson too was confused since, inadvertently perhaps although one looks to a prosecutor in a capital murder case for more than inadvertence, he started with the french cuffs on the gift shirt where they belonged, and ended with them on the prison-issue shirt where they didn't. Cook had changed out of the prison-issue shirt into the gift shirt before he got to Myhaluk's.

Neither Dunne nor MacNaughton picked up on Anderson's mistake, but by this time it didn't seem to matter much any more. What with bought and manufactured, a broken cufflink seeming to turn into a missing button in mid-testimony and french cuffs now on the wrong shirt, at this point in the second trial the whole subject of shirts was in danger of turning into something akin to a laff riot. But the defense could not allow it to become a laff riot. Nothing about shirts was trivial. The french cuffs had to be on the right shirt. Was it a missing button or a broken cufflink? If it was a broken cufflink (as a general rule cufflinks are lost rather than broken) was it still hanging in the french cuff? What was the condition of a given shirt at a given time? And, most vital of all, which shirts had Cook worn when?

To recapitulate: Cook left Prince Albert wearing the prison-issue shirt which may have been manufactured outside the penitentiary system, in which case it would have borne a manufacturer's label. Somewhere and sometime before arriving at Myhaluk's on Wednesday evening he changed from the prison-issue shirt to the shirt sent from home. This probably occurred at the Commercial Hotel since he had taken the room only that morning, but the question wasn't explored. Smith volunteered to iron his shirt. Her evidence was that the shirt she ironed was new, clean and white. There is no reason to disbelieve it. The stage is now set, and it is time to have a look at the bloody shirt which has been waiting in the wings sitting on the exhibit table.

***

"Did you," Anderson asked Corporal Joseph Van Blarcom at the first trial, "encounter a white shirt?"

"Yes, I did, from under the middle left edge of the mattress on the large bed in the master bedroom."

"Is this the same mattress under which the suit coat and jacket *[sic]* were?"

"That is correct. I removed a white shirt from there and laid it on top of the bed towards the foot."

Van Blarcom went on to tell of finding a red tie close to the shirt and Anderson, staying with the order of events of a memorable Sunday morning, turned to questioning Van Blarcom about the opening of the greasepit.

Van Blarcom's evidence of finding a shirt was uncomplicated: he found it, removed it and laid it on the bed towards the foot of the mattress. But there were two other men in the room with Van Blarcom, George Sproule and Robert Novikoff, and one of them[1] picked up the shirt from where Van Blarcom had laid it, looked at it and laid it down again, but now towards the center of the mattress. It was an act of extraordinary carelessness since the shirt was now lying in what Sproule described as a "pool of blood". When Sproule took the stand he elaborated: "I have a white dress shirt. This item was first viewed by me on top of the mattress. I wish to say that the red portion of material, pieces of material appearing like blood, be disregarded in this instance as we are only concerned with the splattering of red substance where the buttons - where the buttonholes appear. This red substance adhered to the shirt as it was replaced on the mattress and has no significance on the upper left portion of the shirt."

It was not criminal investigation's finest hour. There was some reason as we shall see for no one wanting to handle the shirt any longer than it took to get rid of it, but dropping what could conceivably prove to be evidence in a murder trial (a status not accorded all the remaining white shirts seen in the bedroom) into a pool of blood might very well have raised eyebrows among Sproule's superiors at K Division.

***

Two things distinguished the shirt; first, its condition. Main was anxious to fix in the jurors' minds that the shirt was torn and, which they could see for themselves, dirty. He cross-examined Sproule:

"It is apparent that there is some damage to this shirt. There is a portion of the shirt bearing the lower two buttons from the front which has been torn off the right side and it remains dangling by one button from the second lower hole. Do you notice that?"

---

[1] *The identity of the shirt's second handler was never established. Although unlikely, the way the transcripts read it could have been Van Blarcom himself who laid the shirt in Sproule's "pool of blood." An actual pool is somewhat improbable, unless the mattress had an impervious cover. These events in the bedroom took place about 60 hours after the murders suggesting the amount of gore on the mattress. "Pool" or not, there was enough of it still undried to bloodstain the shirt beyond what it was when Van Blarcom extracted it from beneath the mattress.*

"Yes."

"Now, was the shirt in that condition with that damage and with the button buttoned through the buttonhole in that manner at the time you first located it?"

"I did notice at the time there was one button through the buttonhole and I thought that strange because the buttons were all on the other side and this was the only button through the buttonhole."

"Did you notice the damage?"

"No, I didn't observe the tear on the right side of the shirt. If I did, I didn't pay any attention to it."

Main returned to the condition of the shirt when he cross-examined Van Blarcom:

"Now, the shirt is in pretty dirty condition is it not, ignoring the bloodstains?"

"Yes."

"The neck is stained?"

"Yes."

"Dirt-marked. The collar itself is dirty?"

"Quite."

"The cuffs are filthy?"

"Yes sir."

"Dirt grimed into them?"

"Yes sir."

"Both cuffs, correct?"

"Yes sir."

The word picture Main was painting was of a filthy, bloodstained shirt, a shirt which looked as if had done journeyman duty in a pigsty, a shirt to be handled, if it had to be handled, with surgical gloves. As Dunne put it, blood apart it could only have achieved its condition "by being worn several days at a stretch or alternatively by rolling in the gutter." Or, as he might have said, by being worn several days at a stretch, all of them rolling in the gutter. It was, that is to say, a dirty shirt. It was more than that: it was foul and disgusting.

The experts were summoned. Constable William Picton of the Hair and Fibre Section of the Crime Detection Laboratory in Regina was able to say the shirt had not been worn since being torn. The serologist, Peggy van der Stoel, also of the Laboratory, identified human blood "on the outside left half of the front and a little below that in the vicinity of the buttonholes." Main tried to get her to identify stains "on the inside and outside of the shirt up towards the collar on the laterals" and "on the underside of the back of the collar" as blood but, not having tested them, she was not prepared to do so.

Another RCMP witness agreed the tearing indicated the wearer had removed the shirt by first violently ripping it open after the top three buttons had been undone normally (or had come out of the holes of their own accord during the ripping action), and with the second button from the bottom holding in its buttonhole, the bottom 14 inches of the double-thick strip of fabric to which the buttons were sewn ripped away from the body of the shirt on the right-hand side. If the hypothesis was correct, the bottom button had not been buttoned otherwise it too would have remained buttoned through the hole in the 'buttonhole strip' on the left side.

In general terms, the chief question posed by the shirt was whose was it? For the prosecution the question was not quite so simple. Anderson either proved Cook's ownership or, failing that, brought the shirt home to Cook by showing Cook brought the shirt home, in which case ownership might prove to be immaterial. It necessarily had to be one or the other since it had been found side-by-side with the suit. No one other than the murderer had hidden a bloody shirt in the same place the murderer had hidden the suit. Cook had to be tied to the shirt, otherwise the Crown was nowhere.

It did not take long for it to become clear to Anderson that proving Cook's ownership was not a possibility open to him and he was thrown back on the alternative of showing Cook had brought the shirt home with him. If he could do that and, as it might have seemed to a disinterested observer, *only* if he could do that, did he stand a chance of succeeding. But there was still the matter of ownership. Immaterial or not if it could at least be proved that it arrived at the house with Cook, ownership was nevertheless the natural starting point for the Crown in its dilemma.

As long as Anderson still considered the possibility of proving the shirt was Cook's, he was faced with a different order of difficulty than that which would have been presented by, say, the blue suit had Cook denied it was his. Identification of the suit was a matter of routine: taking it to Prince Albert (as was in fact done prior to the preliminary inquiry) for identification by the tailor-instructor and the inmate who had set aside the "materail" for Cook.

But the shirt, a Van Heusen, had clearly come from neither Saskatchewan or Kingston Penitentiaries. It was both a bought and manufactured shirt (if one wasn't bound by the Weeks definition), which is to say it wasn't the shirt issued to Cook on release. Nor did it have french cuffs and was therefore not the gift shirt he'd carried with him out of the penitentiary. Add Cook's denial of ownership, little as it counted for, and the Crown's prospects were not promising. Anderson gave up proof of Cook's ownership as a bad job and switched to the alternative: showing that wherever Cook got it, it came home with him.

But still ownership could not be ignored, partly because it was the natural starting point in charting the shirt's trip to the house, and partly because the name of someone who had once - and perhaps still - owned it was written on the shirt in indelible ink. A juror turning the shirt over in his hands if he could bring himself to handle it, the press, a bemused public, all might insist on knowing whose name it was. The name was the second thing which distinguished it.

***

After Van Blarcom agreed with Main that both cuffs of the shirt had dirt "grimed" into them, Main, still on the shirt, asked him:

"And it bears on the neck band of the collar what is probably a laundry mark, the letters R-O-S-S?"

"Yes sir."

"Is that right?"

"That is correct. I noticed that at the time we moved it."

It showed signs of becoming interesting. The RCMP had found in a murder bedroom a shirt owned or formerly owned by one Ross who, judging from its appearance, sent his shirts out once every two or three years for laundering. They had found a shirt bearing a laundry mark imprinted by a machine described as being similar to a cheque writer: four inked letters were set and a handle pulled. They had found a shirt which contained a handsome clue to ownership, and now it was merely a matter of moving out in widening circles, starting with Stettler, checking laundries and drycleaners until they found the machine which had imprinted the mark. Do that, and they had Ross who might be able to throw some light on how his shirt[1] happened to end up in Ray and Daisy Cook's bedroom.

***

When I interviewed Giffard Main seven years after the events described here, he was visibly bitter about the quality of police efforts in searching for the owner of the Ross shirt, comparing them to those in an English case in which Scotland Yard had investigated the murder of a girl near a military base. Her body had been found with a greatcoat button clutched in her hand, and in the course of the investigation some 6000 greatcoats were checked before the one with the telltale shortage of a button was found.

Main's lingering embitterment may not have been entirely fair. It is perhaps easier to have the CO of a base order everyone to report carrying his greatcoat than it is to check all the laundries and drycleaners in, say, Alberta. On the other hand, the RCMP was engaged in a murder investigation without parallel in that province, and had they not got their man in Cook, it is doubtful they would have been allowed to close the file on just one more unsolved murder. Questions would have been

---

1 *It will be called the Ross shirt throughout the balance of the book.*

asked, and one of them might very well have been why hadn't they found Ross? Checking as many laundries as it took, however wide the circles in and even beyond Alberta, would have been seen as the response expected and required of the RCMP.

But they never did; they didn't come close to finding Ross. The reason they didn't suggested by a reading of the transcripts is that they didn't try very hard - Main's complaint. The cross-examination of one of the RCMP officers reveals the foundation of Main's bitterness. Corporal Van Blarcom was up and Main asked him:

"Now, what steps did you or the police authorities take to circulate the laundry marks amongst the laundries locally in Stettler and in western Canada amongst drycleaners and laundries to try and trace that shirt? Can you tell us what steps you took?"

"I myself checked the laundries in Stettler with no results. The laundries here in Red Deer were checked and the laundries in Edmonton were checked. Now, in the City of Edmonton I didn't do this myself, but I have reports on it, I mean...."

"Were there any results?"

"Yes, there were seventeen results, all with the name Ross on the collar, all different people."

"Was this shirt taken around to various drycleaning and laundry establishments?"

"No, photographs of the laundry mark were taken."

"Now, did you find a laundry mark which used this type of lettering?"

"Yes, there were several. As I recall - that mark is made by a machine and it can be - the search for it can be cut down to any laundries which use that type of machine."

"Did you see one of those machines?"

"I saw one at Stettler."

Main continued with a number of questions about the nature of such machines although with none about the particular machine found in

249

Stettler even though it was "that type of machine" - whatever that may have meant since Main had asked about "that type of lettering." At the very least it meant the search had been cut down to the extent of one laundry in Stettler, but not to the extent of whether that laundry was included in or, recalling Sam Goldwyn, included out. Nor to the extent of establishing whether there was more than one type of machine used to imprint indelible laundry marks, or whether the Stettler machine was the right type but, if so, not the one they were looking for. But Main had not finished:

"Now, was there any attempt made by the police authorities to compare the lettering on this laundry mark, the R-O-S-S as impressed by this type of laundry marking machine with the various machines that were checked in the various drycleaning establishments, such as the police authorities compare typewriters and cheque typing machines in other types of cases?"

"Not to my knowledge, no."

It was an astonishing answer. One cannot help wondering what Van Blarcom, the senior detective in the investigation, and the officers in Red Deer and Edmonton were doing if not, precisely, trying to find a machine which imprinted a R-O-S-S identical, say, in ten points of comparison with the R-O-S-S they had in hand, much as is done in a fingerprint analysis - blowups and all the rest. If they did not do so (and none of them including Van Blarcom did so far as Van Blarcom knew), then they had fanned out in their quest with no clear - or discernible - purpose in mind. Main was not slow to pick up on their failure:

"I suggest to you Corporal that it would be a logical line of investigation to take - that the typing, if we can call it that, as it appears on this shirt could be compared with different types of machines just as easily as could the typewriting on a cheque or any other document could be compared for mis-alignment of letters or irregularities in the letters and so on?"

"It is a possibility. I don't know how accurately those machines are made."

It *was* a possibility, but evidently one which had not occurred earlier to Van Blarcom. But Main knew, as Van Blarcom can be taken to have known, it was precisely distinguishing irregularities in the printing he should have been looking for. He himself had not looked very far; he checked Stettler and found a machine. Main asked him nothing about it, but it is safe to assume it was not *the* R-O-S-S machine otherwise Van Blarcom would have said something.

Someone, perhaps Van Blarcom himself, had checked Red Deer, but the results of the check were not disclosed. Edmonton was better. The laundries were checked, but for what? Photographs were taken around, but the investigators, while coming away with seventeen results, came away empty-handed in terms of a single hard fact bearing on the question of the whereabouts of the machine which had made the mark whose photograph they had in hand. Not even that that machine was *not* in Edmonton. They knew, one supposes, that the machine was not in Stettler (where, the Yellow Pages show, there were two laundry-drycleaners in 1959) but they did not know - so far as *we* know - that the machine was not in any of the places they had looked for it in the four-and-a-half months they had at their disposal before having to answer to Main.

While Main's cross-examination generally tended in the right direction, he had a tendency to pull his punches, for example letting Van Blarcom get away with more or less leaving the impression (with Greschuk for example) that every reasonable effort had been made to find Ross when the truth was the effort was a sorry semblance of what first-rate police investigation should be. It was in fact a pro forma stab at finding Ross which could not be avoided. There was, they could not forget, a shirt which said R-O-S-S - it might as well have been in flashing neon - but they left the impression almost of relief in not finding him where to have done so would have left an awkward tuck in the seamless garment of guilt being woven around Cook.

In Edmonton they came up with "seventeen results, all with the name Ross on the collar, all different people." If this means anything - a moot point - it means they found seventeen shirts all marked "Ross" which, in turn, meant each of seventeen laundries had a customer named Ross, all of whom happened to have shirts in for laundering at the selfsame time as the police showed up with their photographs. "They were," Van Blarcom said, "all different people." But, the question seems to be, different from whom? From each other? That might follow since any two people chosen at random can be taken to be two different people as a general rule. Different from the Ross they were looking for? But that would mean they knew who they were looking for and they didn't. Whoever he was, they had only his name and his shirt - not bad starting points, but only that. In the last earnest analysis of Van Blarcom's evidence, it is seen to mean nothing at all. A photograph or photographs had been sent to Edmonton Someone had trooped around to at least some of the laundries - there were 63 of them in 1959 - and had come away with seventeen results. But they had not come away with a lead on Ross. They had come away with nothing, leaving behind seventeen men in Edmonton named Ross each of whom would have been relieved to learn it was not his shirt which had come to rest under the mattress in the murder bedroom.

***

If Main was satisfied with whatever it was he thought Van Blarcom had told him, Mr Justice Greschuk was doubly so, and moreover was prepared to absolve the overworked policemen of any taint of not having done everything humanly possible to track down the machine and track down Ross: "The reports indicated that there were seventeen 'Ross' laundry marks in Edmonton. These marks are usually made by a machine like a chequewriter, but no check was made to see if the laundry mark on the shirt was similar in lettering to the laundry mark made by a machine in Edmonton. Would it be reasonable to expect the police to check the laundry mark with every lettering machine in the City of Edmonton?" To Main at least it might have seemed so since there were only 63 of them and remembering the 6000 greatcoats.

Cook too thought they might have done more than the next to nothing which, in Edmonton, Greschuk saw them as having done[1]. In a letter of February 14, 1960 to Mrs William Hansen [2], Cook wrote: "I was reading where they questioned 20,000 people in London in connection with a woman who was murderd in a Y.W.C.A. Here the judge Mr Greschuk implied that the jury couldn't expect the police to trace the shirt because they would have to check seventeen differnt laundries." Cook didn't get

[1] *"No check was made by the police to see if the laundry mark on the shirt was similar to the laundry mark made by [any] machine" - charge to the jury.*

[2] *Mrs William Hansen was a remarkable study. She was an elderly widow who lived by herself in an unelectrified shack on the prairie near Youngstown, Alberta. Her son Robert Clive had been killed in WW II. Because of the name and some New Age convictions, she wrote Cook shortly after the first conviction and a correspondence developed. His last letter, written on the day of his death, was to her, asking her not to trouble herself with what was about to happen to him, expressing his confidence that she would be reunited with her son and wishing her well.*

it quite right, any more than Greschuk had, but he was near enough that the point was made. The foundation of his bitterness was even more profound than Main's.

***

When the court of appeal granted Cook a new trial, it meant to Anderson his nemesis of the first trial, the Ross shirt, would return to haunt him. In that trial, as we will see[1], he finally dealt with it by pretending it was not important. He invited the jurors to ignore it - an invitation they seem to have accepted with some alacrity - as having nothing to do with the case. But he of course knew that that was far from the fact, and he knew it would be unwise to count on the Edmonton jurors in the forthcoming trial being as undemanding as their Red Deer cousins had been. He knew - still knew - that he had to fix Cook, not with ownership of the shirt which was patently not the case, but with possession of it when he came to the house at about 9:30 on Thursday evening. A possible means of doing so came to hand.

The police had not been idle after the first trial. They were fully as aware as Anderson what a near thing the Ross shirt had been in that trial, and so they retraced their steps, no doubt with some encouragement from Anderson, to see whether they'd missed any leads on Ross. It proved they had. Arriving at the Commercial Hotel - nothing indicates they'd been there before, and if they had not, then steps were not being retraced here - they discovered that one Donald Ervin Hughes Ross, a traveling draftsman-designer (as he described himself) from a place in Saskatchewan which political correctness had not yet infected, Squaw Rapids, had been a guest in the hotel, probably at the same time as Cook, June 24 and 25, 1959, As luck would have it, Ross wore a size 15-32 shirt and one of his preferred brands was Van Heusen. The Ross shirt was a 15-32 Van Heusen.

It was not so much a matter of it all being too good to be true as one of being too close - or at any rate close enough in the absence of anything else - not to be tried, and Ross was duly summonsed as a witness for the prosecution in the second trial. He was not a surprise witness - Dunne knew he was being called - but he was a surprised one.

[1] *See p. 261*

Anderson produced him as the probable source of the refractory Ross shirt which had yet to yield up a single secret. Rarely has the proffering of someone as a probability been so improbable.

A perplexed Ross took the stand and said that at any one time, he "normally had on hand ten or twelve dress shirts, sometimes more." Anderson asked him to explain "that relatively large number":

"Well, when you're traveling all the time, just like I am now, my laundry is in Carrot River and I am here in Edmonton and I have got one shirt, the one I have on. So I go downtown and buy a clean shirt. Toll them all together in one time and you have quite a number of shirts."

"Now are you in - at all times in complete touch with the number of shirts you have on hand or where they may be?"

"No sir."

"How do you account for that?"

"Well, I couldn't tell you how many I have in Saskatchewan on the farm and how many I have in Carrot River Drycleaners and how many there is in dormitory at camp."

"Would you be in a position to say whether or not you lost track of any while you were residing in Edmonton in the Commercial Hotel?"

"No, no sir."

"You mean it is possible?"

"It is possible; I could have lost them."

"What was your habit when you resided in the Commercial Hotel as to your room? Did anyone have access to that room other than yourself?"

"Not to my knowledge except the maids."

"Was it locked at all times that you were aware of?"

"Most of the time, but the lavatory was down the hall, and I would get telephone calls downstairs, there was no telephone in my room, and I would periodically, because it was a skeleton key lock, took time to lock

it or unlock it so I know there has been occasion I never bothered locking
it."

"[The Ross] shirt that I have shown to you here, do you recognize it
specifically?"

"No sir."

"Does it bear any similarity to shirts that you have owned?"

"That I own?"

"Have owned?"

"Oh, could be one I have owned."

"You can't say for sure?"

"No sir."

Anderson asked him nothing about the laundry mark - for example did
it look as if it might have been made by Carrot River Drycleaners? - so
that as close as he got Ross to the Ross shirt was an acknowledgment
that he could have owned it. It wasn't much. Anyone who ever owned
a 15-32 Van Heusen could have owned it, *mutatis mutandis* as lawyers
are wont to say, and Anderson had to turn him over to Dunne who cross-
examined him sparingly - ten questions:

"So far as you are aware Mr Ross, you have no knowledge of losing any
shirts last summer?"

"No sir."

"You mentioned that you were living at the Commercial Hotel and a
private home?"

"Yes sir."

"Were you living at both at the same time?"

"No, I moved out of the Commercial into the private home because my
employment was on 125th Avenue, the opposite side of the city, so I
moved over closer to the work."

"When was the move made, do you recall?"

"The exact date? No, I don't."

"Might you have moved in June?"

"I could have, yes."

"Mr Ross, would you ordinarily wear a shirt in your work long enough to get it as filthy as this one is?"

"No. Oh no. No."

"What would you wear them, one day or two?"

"One day or, if I got stuck, I would go back over them and pick out one that I could get two days out of."

"I see. And you just sent your laundry to wherever was the most convenient place at the time?"

"That is right sir."

"By the way, in your type of work, do you ordinarily get shirts dirty in the sense of staining them the way that one is stained?"

"No sir."

"Fairly clean type of work that you are doing, is that right?"

"That is right."

Dunne's cross-examination was effective, and he got from Ross exactly what he had to get: the possibility that Cook and Ross might not have been in the Commercial at the same time; and, immeasurably more important, that by no desperate stretch of the prosecutorial imagination did the Ross shirt belong to the fastidious Donald Ervin Hughes Ross. That was it for Ross. Anderson had produced him to prove that Bob, Bob, the mechanic's son, stole a shirt and away he run, but he failed.

Had Anderson seriously believed Ross was his man rather than merely someone to be thrown into the gaping breach in the Crown's case who, with luck or sympathetic jurors, might plug it, there was something he could have had done. Ross had said he dropped his shirts off in Carrot

River for cleaning. Although he also used other convenient places, he said, Carrot River was a promising point. While RCMP resources were doubtlessly stretched thin in working up the seventeen results in Edmonton, if they could have spared a man, and if Anderson seriously believed the Ross shirt was Ross's, then Carrot River Drycleaners might well have had the machine which had imprinted the shirt. But in sending a man to Carrot River, they ran the risk of discovering that Carrot River Drycleaners did not have the machine which had imprinted the shirt and they would have succeed in doing nothing more than reducing a large number of laundries by one - albeit a significant one. In any case no one went, suggesting the RCMP did not have a lot of confidence in Donald Ervin Hughes Ross as the answer to Anderson's dilemma.

***

To the end Anderson was of two minds about the Ross shirt - a dichotomy he never resolved. The first was that Cook had stolen the shirt in order to wear it, otherwise there was no purpose to his spiritless attempt to have Gail Smith recant her testimony that she had ironed a shirt for Cook on Wednesday evening. For the Crown to concede she had ironed one was to concede she knew exactly what she had ironed, namely a "quite clean and new" shirt. Namely anything but the Ross shirt which, Anderson contended, Cook stole in and wore from the Commercial Hotel, was wearing when he arrived at Myhaluk's, and was wearing still when he arrived home on Thursday evening.

Its presence in the bedroom was explained if Anderson could show the theft of it from Ross's room. But if one was inclined to accept the possibility of its being Ross's shirt, some awkward questions were raised. Why would Cook steal, for wear, a shirt one would hesitate to use as the lining for a dog basket? Why would he change into such a shirt out of a new one worn for the first time the day before - the prison-issue shirt? Or when he had another new shirt not yet removed from its manufacturer's protective wrapping - the gift shirt? Or when he could have stepped out of his hotel and bought another brand new shirt for $5 if he happened to have a shirt fetish?

The other half of Anderson's mind harbored a 'carry' hypothesis to be compared to the one just outlined which I shall call the wear hypothesis.

Both required the theft of the Ross shirt from Ross's room, but now not to be worn, but carried, and not merely carried but carried back to Stettler to be stuffed under the mattress as a means of throwing the police off the scent. Once more I would remind the reader that the transcripts are a matter of public record. The hypothesis doesn't require any comment, but comment offers a light moment in a grim narrative and the temptation is not to be resisted.

Thus, plotting on Wednesday morning the murder of his family on Thursday night (thus taking care of the element of premeditation), Cook cast about for a means of ensuring the police would be left floundering helplessly in the master bedroom. Of course! A stranger's shirt under the mattress! Why hadn't he thought of it? He stole down the hallway and found that someone had conveniently left his room to take a telephone call downstairs, leaving his door open. With the shirt under his arm, he left for the new-car dealership, to the used-car lot, to Bowden, back to Edmonton still carrying the shirt, to Myhaluk's, the Selkirk Hotel, the liquor vendors, the Pan American Motel, to Stettler in Eddie Read's truck and around the streets of Stettler for nine hours, still carrying the shirt.

It must be admitted that he could have been wearing it all this time (meaning there was only one hypothesis all along, but it was Anderson who postulated at one point - when he had given up on shaking Smith - that the Ross shirt was carried home by Cook), meaning that when he took off a clean white shirt to be pressed by Smith, he had the Ross shirt on underneath - a spectacle which might have been expected to elicit some comment from Smith when Anderson was asking her about the uses to which she put Cook's shirt.

***

Nothing meaningful about Cook *vis a vis à* the Ross shirt could be said without regard to the whereabouts of the gift shirt and the prison issue shirt, both of which were lying somewhere on Cook's trail. Cook said in direct examination at the first trial that he changed from the prison-issue shirt to the gift shirt "on the night before I left Edmonton" which is to say just before he went to Myhaluk's on Wednesday evening, and on cross-examination that he had left a white shirt - he wasn't sure which - at the

Commercial Hotel. There was no reason for him to lie (which was never to say he wasn't), and it cannot be doubted the prison-issue shirt would have been found at the Commercial had anyone thought to look. No one did.

That meant the gift shirt was somewhere in the Cook house. Where? There was a white shirt hanging from the open dresser drawer at the head of the double bed. There were two white shirts, if Sproule wasn't "mistaken" and as he told the first trial court, "hanging over the headboard." He *may* have been mistaken since by the second trial he couldn't "recall having seen any other white shirts except the one entered as an exhibit that was found on *[sic]* the bed in the front bedroom." There were, Van Blarcom told Main, "several dresses and shirts and various articles of clothing thrown haphazardly on the bed." Suffice it to say, as it necessarily must, that there were quite a few white shirts in the master bedroom, and if one of them showed signs of only a day's wear and had french cuffs and maybe a missing button or a broken cufflink, even the most skeptical might have been persuaded that Cook did not come home wearing - or carrying - the Ross shirt whose secret was never penetrated.

***

We will conclude the examination of the Ross shirt and Van Blarcom's results by setting out segments (except in the case of Dunne and Riley where their contributions will be set out in full) of the approaches of the senior lawyers in their final arguments and the trial judges in their charges, to various aspects of the problem of the shirt, suffixing each of them with a brief editorial comment.

GIFFARD MAIN: "I want to be a little bit critical of the investigation at this point. We have here Exhibit 43, the filthy white shirt bearing the laundry mark 'Ross'. You will recall that during the hearing of the evidence, Corporal Van Blarcom told me that checks were made at laundries and drycleaning establishments at Stettler and they couldn't trace this shirt; that checks were made at laundry and drycleaning plants in Red Deer and also in Edmonton and they could find no trace of this shirt or this laundry mark. They found seventeen cleaning establishments which had similar machines to the machine which had imprinted this laundry mark 'Ross' on this shirt, but Corporal Van Blarcom told us no effort was made to make any microscopic comparison of the individual letters R-O-S-S as they appear on this shirt against the similar letters on any of the other machines which could make a similar mark."

Everyone it seems - Cook, Greschuk, Main - had a different idea of what Van Blarcom had said, and each of them got wrong what they could only have got right by pointing out that what Van Blarcom had said was meaningless. Main may have harmed his client's case by singling out this part of the police investigation for particular criticism, since to name one was to run the risk of excluding all the others, leaving the jurors with the latitude of forgiving the police a single shortcoming. He concluded his argument on the shirt by submitting "with respect gentlemen that the police investigation was not vigorously enough pursued with regard to the ownership of this mysterious shirt." He did not attempt to dissociate Cook from the Ross shirt by stressing that he came home wearing the gift shirt which would have been found in the master bedroom had the police bestirred themselves to look for it.

FRANK DUNNE: "Now, may I turn next to the shirt. The evidence of the deputy warden from Prince Albert is that Cook was given what is called a prison-issue shirt, and that this shirt had not double cuffs but single cuffs. The evidence of Gail Smith is that she ironed Cook's shirt on the Wednesday evening, and she remembered it particularly because it had double cuffs, and she remembered the broken cufflink. That is what drew her attention to the double cuffs. There is no suggestion and no evidence that he changed his shirt on the night in question, and I would remind you that it is entirely up to the Crown to answer these questions, not the defense.

"Consider also if you will gentlemen the absolute grimy condition of that shirt. I do not know how you could get a shirt that dirty except by wearing it several days at a stretch or alternatively by rolling in the gutter, but aside from the bloodstains, the condition of that shirt is absolutely filthy, and it looks as if it had been worn, and well worn, for a considerable period of time.

"The best efforts of the RCMP have also failed to trace the origins of that shirt. You will recall they checked all the drycleaning establishments in Stettler, Red Deer and Edmonton and they came up with seventeen different ones which use the laundry mark 'Ross', or had used it, and in the result they had proved nothing as to the shirt. It, like the gun, is a complete stranger as far as this case is concerned."

That was Dunne's treatment of the problem in its entirety. His understanding of the issues was superficial and his argument an unsure touching on one or two trivial points which, with luck, might suffice. While it was true it was "up to the Crown to answer these questions", the question was what were the questions? Dunne cannot have known otherwise he would not, for example, have dismissed the new shirts in a handful of words, none of them showing even a rudimentary appreciation of what they would have said about the ultimate question: had Cook *ever* worn the Ross shirt either to Stettler or in the master bedroom?

To convince the jurors of the likelihood of the Ross shirt having arrived at the house either before or after Cook's Thursday visit was to be half way home in convincing the jurors there was no reason conceivable by reasonable men such as themselves for Cook to put the shirt on when he got there. Why? To preserve his own while he lugged the bodies to the neighbor room? Then why put the suit jacket back on before he did so?

These were the questions, a few among dozens, on which the Crown had to be called to account, but it could be only be called to account if the jurors had them firmly in mind when the time came for Anderson to sidestep answering questions for which he had no answers, no more than anyone else. But Dunne did not know them.

He had to mount an attack on the evidence of Ross, or rather (since Ross was blameless) on the Crown's thesis as an insult, he would tell them, to their intelligence - as indeed it was. He had to question Anderson's questioning of the Smith evidence. He had to question the evidence of Van Blarcom and particularly the evidence of Sproule who, on the strength of the first trial transcripts, was a dead duck had Dunne recognized it and had he not been concerned to curry favor with the RCMP by extolling their efforts as being their best. And perhaps, a sobering thought, they were, and perhaps this was Dunne's. In any case it did not get any better.

J. WALLACE ANDERSON (first trial): "Now at the outset the prosecution suggested that with the exception of the white shirt, evidence would be led to show that the clothing found in the house was that of the accused at the time of his arriving home. Now this white shirt could have come from any number of sources. It is not suggested that the murderer had to wear the white shirt. The white shirt was just another article, among many articles, that were present in the house."

There it was. The bloody shirt hidden beside the murderer's suit was just another humdrum article in a household full of them with no more relevance to the problem of murder than, say, the broken bicycle in the garage or the kitchen tablecloth. It worked. Audaciousness doesn't get any better than this, and it is difficult to withhold admiration.

J. WALLACE ANDERSON (second trial): "If the murderer was a stranger and he put the blue suit - Cook's blue suit - and the tie and the shirt under the mattress in order to cast suspicion on Cook, would it advance his interest, would it advance his attempt to cast suspicion on Cook to leave the white shirt there - which has been so difficult of identification - or does the presence of that shirt better serve the purposes of one wishing to cast suspicion on a stranger?"

The plant theory. It is possible to supply some of the blanks. Thus, having stolen Ross's shirt, slightly soiled though it was from Ross having pawed through a pile of them and chosen it for a second day's wearing, Cook carried it around Edmonton and Stettler for a couple of days, perhaps stuffed in a suit pocket. When the time came for him to doctor it for use as a plant to finger the all-unsuspecting mild-mannered designer-draftsman from Squaw Rapids, Saskatchewan, he tore it in such a way as to paint a picture of "frantic frenzy", bloodied it perhaps by laying it in a pool of blood, and then stuffed it under the mattress beside his own suit. This wasn't mere cunning; this was diabolism.

MR JUSTICE PETER GRESCHUK: "How did this shirt get under the mattress? Are you convinced beyond a reasonable doubt that the shirt and tie found under the mattress in bedroom number one are the same shirt and tie worn by the accused on June the 24th and 25th, 1959, and that the accused placed them there?"

Greschuk seems not to have been prepared to credit Cook's saying he had changed from the prison-issue shirt to the gift shirt some time before the Wednesday evening visit to the Myhaluk's. In Greschuk's view, he had worn one shirt only through the two days - the Ross shirt if he was guilty. If true, there was nothing in evidence suggesting where he might have got it, this being a time before the RCMP's felicitous discovery of Donald Ross. It was also to leave up in the air what had become of the two new white shirts, but no matter. If the jurors were convinced beyond a reasonable doubt that Cook had picked up the Ross in Edmonton from, say, the Salvation Army, that was pretty well the end of it.

MR JUSTICE HAROLD W. RILEY: "Under the mattress in the first bedroom was found a pair of blue trousers, bloodstained, a bloodstained white shirt, a bloodstained red tie and a blue suit coat matching the trousers."

This was Riley's lone reference to the Ross shirt - an instance, one supposes, of his gift for cutting through to the heart of the matter. But the gift is not without risk even in hands as sure as Riley's since there may have been one or two jurors hung up on questions about the shirt who could have used an assist from the trial judge in identifying the questions as being of no importance and as such safely ignored. But while it is one thing, and a good one, to throw out the bathwater, it is quite another to throw out, if not the baby, then everything which might help identify the baby: from the very bathtub itself through to the kitchen sink and Uncle Tom Cobley and all, leaving, shivering and forlorn, a foundling clamoring for attention and wondering wherefore born.

CHAPTER 15

THE SCARLET TIE

In the brave new world order in which every child not named Kianna
Brendon Larissa will be named, may God forgive us all, Kasara-Shaylee
Justin Alyssa, an old-fashioned name from another time, Daisy May, is
like something else from another time: a breath of clean air. Daisy May
Cook was, like her name, honest, unpretentious, likable, and she was
perhaps never more likable than when she sent a package to Cook just
before his last release. Month in and month out, for six years she had
been writing and sending packages to penitentiaries - of all places to a
mother and former grade-school teacher the most mortifying and alien.
Whatever else their recipient, her son the convict, meant to her, he meant
the certainty of more such years without foreseeable end. In the still of
the night she might forgivably have wished him dead, but to her credit,
to within a few days of her death - and, it is thought by one of her friends
in a position to know, to the exact day of it - she never stopped trying to
reach out to him and to understand the rage within, the demons which
drove him into himself and beyond her reach.

Without him in her life she had as much as she might reasonably have
asked of it: a husband colorless to the point of invisibility but a steady
provider and loving to her - their - children all of them more than
normally attractive; a modest home but hers and paid for; her own and
her family's good health. With him in it or, worse, drifting on its margins
never quite in or out, its even tenor was undercut by her helplessness in
the face of his intransigent aversion to truth; by having to cope with her

husband's low-key despair over his well-loved son; and by family disgrace renewed every two or so years with the predictability of clockwork.

Now, in June 1959, like the door being opened on a caged hyena showing no recognizable signs of rehabilitation, he was being released again, giving new impetus to the familiar cycle: release, slouching towards Stettler, promises of reform by day; kicking in doors and skylights by night; and then the dreaded RCMP car pulling up to the front sidewalk, visible from behind every front room curtain in Stettler - or so it would seem to her in her anguish.

But there was nothing else for it but to try once more to break the malignant pattern, to reaffirm the place being held for him in his father's house and in the family from which, in his willful blindness, he had estranged himself for all his adolescent years. And thus another package from home as if to the front lines. In an act poignant in retrospect she bought a white shirt and a scarlet tie[1], packaged them up with a pair of yellow monogrammed socks and sent them off. Their combined action was to prove no stronger than a flower 'gainst the rage which prompted him to blow half her head off - or so it is said - in one view doing nothing more than confirming her prediction - the culmination of the pattern she had sought bravely to alter.

Unlike the Ross shirt and the blue suit, the red - let us call it - tie found with them under the mattress by Van Blarcom held an inconspicuous place on the exhibit table. It could not be ignored entirely given its condition and location in the bedroom, but references to it were most often in the form of including it in recitals of the things that were found under the mattress, following which it was promptly forgotten, damning Cook in only a minor way. It seemed to speak for itself, but in a barely audible voice and with not much to say.

That it was dismissed on both sides of the aisle separating the counsel tables as being of little importance poses the temptation to do so again for the fact is it is a seriously troubling element to anyone concerned to make the posthumous case for Cook. In preparing the ground for someone to make that case, an argument has been advanced here accounting for the hiding of the suit and the Ross shirt: X, let us call him, came to the house wearing the shirt which was worn through the

---

[1] *When the tie was referred to at all, it was always as red, but since fine distinctions were not being made between red, crimson, magenta and the rest, a certain poetic license has been appropriated in terming it scarlet.*

murders. He stripped from his own clothing - except for the shirt which became bloodstained both during the murders and in the act of carrying the bodies to the garage - and wore the suit while he carried the bodies. He then hid the shirt because R-O-S-S might provide a clue to ownership and, as with the suit, as part of the general effort to conceal evidence of the crime. Washing wallpaper in the back bedroom and hiding clothing were driven by the same purpose, with the laundry mark providing an additional purpose with respect to the shirt.

But whatever its merit the same argument cannot be made to cover the tie. No one replaced his own tie with the red tie in order to protect the one removed, but before embarking on an argument which can be made to force the tie - a Procrustean fit - into the framework of Cook's innocence, I will first set out the facts relating to it before considering - and dismissing by way of narrowing the focus - some possible explanations for an incriminating piece of evidence. There were five facts, none of them in dispute.

First, the tie was a gift from Daisy sent to the penitentiary on June 9. If he wore it on release - it is not certain - it would have been worn in contravention of prison regulations unless they did not extend to minor accoutrements. Similarly with the socks she sent him which, whether or not he wore them out of the penitentiary, he was wearing on the night of the murders.

He did wear the tie in Saskatoon - the second fact although the second-trial jury did not learn of it. The tie is identifiable in a passport-type photograph taken in a bus depot booth. Whether or not he wore it from Saskatoon to Stettler (he was the sort of man to go open-necked), he was the agency of its arriving there - the third fact. He admitted ownership.

When we consider the problem of bloodstaining, it will be seen that whether he wore the tie home or, say, carried it stuffed in a pocket, was a significant question. Eleven of thirteen opportunities to determine whether it was worn or carried were lost since the importance of the distinction was not recognized. Twenty or so people saw him between Saskatoon and Stettler, twelve of whom were called as Crown witnesses and one by the defense. Of the thirteen, only two were asked to say anything about the tie.

Lea Myhaluk of Edmonton was the first. While she was examined and cross-examined six times in the course of the preliminary inquiry and the trials, only Main in the first trial thought to ask her whether Cook was wearing a tie when he came to her house on Wednesday evening. She could not remember, and Main let it go. It appears to have been a question asked for the sake of asking it since Main never mentioned the tie again throughout the remainder of the trial.

Dillon Hoskins was the second. We have seen that he observed Cook to be wearing a red tie when he passed him on the western outskirts of Stettler, and on the strength of what cannot have been protracted observation, he was able to identify the five-piece ensemble the police had assembled. It appears possible his power of observation was enhanced by his susceptibility to suggestion brought helpfully to bear by others.

The fourth fact was that three spots on the tie were identified as blood by the serologist. It was not "bloodstained" (Riley's description) in the usual sense. The suit and the Ross shirt were bloodstained; the tie was spattered.

And finally, the tie was found under the mattress by Van Blarcom. Such interest in it as there was derived primarily from its proximity to the shirt, but it was fleeting. Beside a plethora of photographs of bodies, beside a shattered shotgun, the tie was inconspicuous. It may nevertheless have been the most incriminating evidence of all since it is impossible to tie it to anyone other than Cook (in a manner other than its ownership which was not in issue), and there is no reason for anyone other than Cook to have hidden it under the mattress, not as a conscious and deliberate act.

***

Assuming it was worn during the murders and in their immediate aftermath, there are three possible ways to account for the three spots of blood, and one if it was not:

The first of the three is that a stranger came to the house wearing the Ross shirt and, spotting the tie where Ray (who had acquired it as part of the clothing swap) had laid it for the night, put it on for reasons best known to himself. The blood is explained, but the explanation seems improbable.

Second, Cook came to the house wearing the suit, the gift shirt and the tie, the latter becoming spattered with blood during the murders. One fact and one probability militate against this explanation: the jacket was sprayed, not spotted and the location of the spots on the tie indicate the jacket would have had to have been open. The tie therefore would have almost inevitably picked up more than a minuscule three spots. And the gift shirt which, on this hypothesis, he was wearing? It too would have been sprayed with blood, but the same myopia which blinded the police to the significance of the genus shirts rendered the gift shirt - and the blood which would have been on it had Cook worn it through the murders - invisible.

Third, had they reasoned it through it would have been clear to the jurors that the murderer either came to the house wearing the Ross shirt or, if it was Cook, put it on in the house. It was also clear that no one but the murderer had any reason for ripping it off and getting rid of it. But, remembering we are attempting to account for the blood on the tie then, if Cook is our man, after getting into the Ross shirt he put on the tie and the jacket, both just removed to permit him to don the Ross shirt? When all this might have happened doesn't bear overnice analysis. In a darkened house before the murders? After them in a bloody one? Absurd scenarios are made up of diverting elements so that one imagines Cook straightening the tie before Daisy's dresser mirror (a lighted bedroom is called for here) and then trying to shoot nonexistent cuffs on the Ross shirt before turning to shoot his victims sitting bolt upright in bed watching the sartorial exercise with fascinated interest.

***

A plausible explanation - nothing more can be claimed for it - for the blood on the tie lies in invoking the Main-Dunne theory accounting for the blood on the suit and applying it to the tie. Thus Cook came home with the tie, probably stuffed in a jacket pocket; it is difficult to think of him driving the Bowden round trip and living through the all-night motel party, or walking around Stettler for the whole of Thursday afternoon and evening wearing a tie. It was in the pocket when Ray tried on the suit which "fit him good." It will be argued in Chapter 18 that Ray had occasion to put some articles in the jacket pocket, and if he did what more natural than to remove the tie and carelessly throw it over the footboard to be hung up in the morning by an exasperated Daisy?

In that location the tie being hit with three drops of blood from the carnage at the far end of the bed can reasonably be inferred. Support for the theory lies in Cook not wearing the tie when he came home which is why it mattered to get from the myriad people between Saskatoon and Stettler whether he was wearing it when they saw him. Had some or all of 13 people said he was not wearing a tie when they saw him, that made it probable (although not conclusive) that he was not wearing it when he arrived at the house. (Conversely of course, had they seen a tie does not mean he did not remove it after being seen by the last of them, but probabilities enter into proof of guilt more often than it might be thought, and here the probability could only be inferred from the direct evidence the court denied itself.) Admittedly the theory is stretching it, but the way the *Cook* trials unfolded dictates going outside the courtroom evidence to test answers to questions not answered - or asked in the instant case - when the wherewithal was at hand to do so.

***

Forcing the tie into the framework of innocence gets appreciably more difficult when the second problem is confronted: the hiding of it. The problem is knotty for advocates of Cook's innocence. That it was hidden seems beyond question since ten times in the course of the three court proceedings Van Blarcom described without equivocation his discovery of it under the mattress. His evidence was accepted without demur by both Main and Dunne, as well they might. Probing cross-examination was not going to get from Van Blarcom anything other than that he found the tie where he said he found it. Insofar as Main and Dunne thought of it at all, for them as for Anderson it was merely as of a piece with the suit but scarcely worth noticing in and of itself. And so with both Greschuk and Riley who mentioned it only in passing in their charges. The tie never made it into Anderson's closing argument and the jurors, if they as much as saw the tie, saw it as (a) Cook's and (b) hidden, beyond which there didn't seem to be much need to go.

To get the tie to the footboard in order to have it *found* there, presented a formidable obstacle, if not an insuperable one: Van Blarcom's flat assertion that he found the tie under the mattress. The evidence of Sproule (who left the bedroom before the tie was found, returning shortly afterwards) and Van Blarcom was combed and re-combed and tables were made for side-by-side comparison of what Sproule said at the preliminary inquiry and what he said at each trial, and for comparing Sproule's evidence throughout with Van Blarcom's, to see whether it was possible that Van Blarcom was either mistaken or, for tactical purposes, bending the truth about an insignificant matter. To see, that is, whether the tie had been found draped over the footboard.

Nothing worked. While the evidence of Sproule was vaguely suspect - it could be read as protesting rather too much that when he came back into the bedroom the tie was then on the foot of the bed where Van Blarcom said he had laid it along with the Ross shirt - in the end it withstood dissection. By bringing paranoia to it, Sproule's evidence could be read as going further than was really necessary to ensure there was no mistake about the tie having been found, before he returned to the bedroom, somewhere other than on the mattress where he first saw it. He repeated this more often than he was asked, seeming to want there to be no misunderstanding about it. But paranoia is not the way of objectivity.

In the face of the impregnable evidence, how strong a case could be made for the tie being in plain view when the police first entered the bedroom? Such a case called for the police learning early on that the suit and the tie were Cook's and recognizing that the Ross shirt was going to be intractable unless it could be tied to Cook. It could be tied to Cook, maybe, if it appeared the shirt and tie belonged together in the sense of having been hidden together. If, that is to say, the tie was under the mattress side by side with the Ross shirt rather than draped over the footboard. The tie already had two of the attributes of the suit - it belonged to Cook and it had blood on it. If a harmless appearing third were added - its being found where the suit was found - what prejudice to Cook over and above that he already suffered at the hands of the suit?

It had finally to be admitted that it was not much of a case, and it implied police perjury - not a pleasant bog in which to become mired in what might have been a wrong-headed effort after all to absolve Cook. The tie said as much since, if it was hidden, no one but Cook had any reason to hide it, but to acknowledge as much comes close to subverting a major part of this book's entire argument.

One straw remained to be clutched at. X, in his panic-stricken effort at concealment, grabbed up the tie and stuffed it under the mattress. He can be imagined as staring around wildly, seeing nothing and snatching at anything, although it must be admitted that other things hidden - the

271

suit, the Ross shirt - were not things caught up in blind panic such as, say, the mail bag found on top of the bed probably was. Still, the mere fact of attempted concealment of that crime in that setting raised irrationality almost to a fine art, and it is perhaps not unreasonable to see the hiding of the tie in those terms. If so, then that is the end of the matter. X is our man and the police are blameless of bending evidence to shore up the Crown's case. They are blameless of everything but identifying X.

***

Ultimately there are no answers and it is time to close the book on the Ross shirt and the red tie. They arrived at the Cook home from different quadrants and, having arrived there, their significance became intertwined in a way which can only be guessed at. A putrescent shirt and a tie whose 1959 garishness is softened in retrospect by the touching gesture which launched it on its journey into the heart of a mystery. They cannot be considered in isolation one from the other, yet oddly one spelled a flaw in the Crown's case which would have destroyed it utterly had Cook been tried in another time and place, and the other must give pause to anyone sure that Cook didn't do it because, knowing him, they knew "he just couldn't have done it."

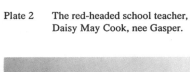

Plate 2   The red-headed school teacher, Daisy May Cook, nee Gasper.

Plate 1   The Hanna birthday party. Cook in back row, right.

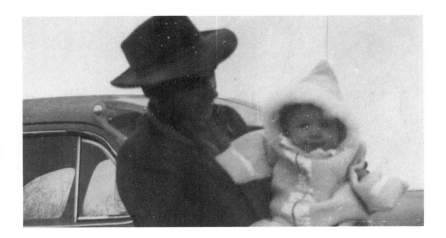

Plate 3   Raymond Albert Cook with his first-born son by his second marriage, Gerry.

Plate 4   From left, Patty, Chrissy, Gerry.

Plate 5   The Cook children one week before their murder. Standing from left, Chrissy, Patty, Gerry. Sitting from left, Linda, Kathy.

Plate 6   5018 - 52 Street, Stettler, Alberta.

Plate 7   The front porch and the
Saturday newspaper.

Plate 8   The livingroom looking north. Door to adults' bedroom in background.

Plate 9   The livingroom looking south. Entrance to kitchen on right.

Plate 10   Kitchen looking west. Door to garage right background. Note beer bottle on counter.

Plate 11   Kitchen looking south. Note cups on counter and fingerprint powder on cabinet doors.

Plate 12 The garage looking south from vehicle entrance. Kitchen entrance landing on extreme left.

Plate 13 The greasepit. The pit was closed in after the removal of the bodies and this RCMP photograph is posed.

Plate 14

Plate 15   The 'Winnipeg' couch in the boys' bedroom. Note bloodstaining on mattress.

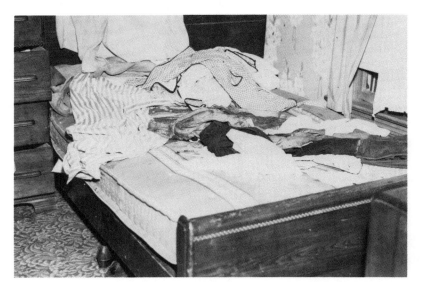

Plate 16   The 'master' bedroom in the condition first seen by the RCMP.

Plate 17   The double bed mattress with the "jumble" of clothing pulled back or removed to reveal shattered shotgun.

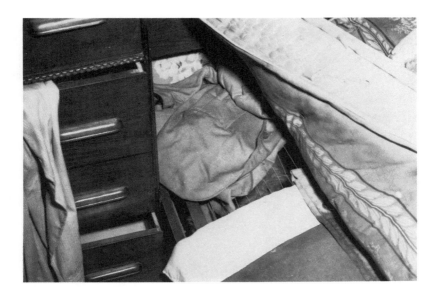

Plate 18 Corner of mattress on double bed lifted to reveal hiding place of blue suit jacket.

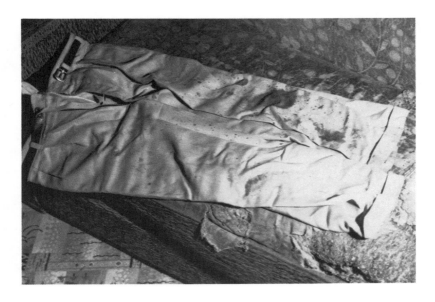

Plate 19   The blue suit pants. Removed from under 'master' bedroom mattress and photographed on livingroom chesterfield.

Plate 20　　The Impala convertible photographed behind RCMP Detachment, Stettler.

Plate 21　　The male admitting ward - "M6" - Provincial Mental Hospital, Ponoka. Cook confined far side of wing on left.

Plate 22
"M6" exercise
veranda.
Cook escaped
through
window at
right, lower
pane, second
from left.

Plate 23   The escape
window was identical
in size to the center
pane shown here, but
was of meshed glass
and set below the
louvred   window
shown.   Note fire
escape descending in
background.

Plate 24   Framed screen
barring access to escape
window.   Note sprung
section   through   which
mechanism-activating
wrench can be passed
through louvred window.

Plate 25   Screen release mechanism. Note deadbolt and rods inside frame at right extending up and down.

Plate 26   The Command Post at Bashaw. (Provincial Archives of Alberta Photograph Collection)

Plate 27   Part of manhunt contingent.   (Provincial Archives of Alberta Photograph Collection)

Plate 28   Tail Creek and the escape car rolled by Cook.   (Provincial Archives of alberta Photographic Collection)

Plate 29   In the Red Deer Lake cordon. (Provincial Archives of Alberta Photograph Collection)

Plate 30   Temporary police headquarters, Bashaw, conclusion of manhunt. (Provincial Archives of Alberta Photograph Collection)

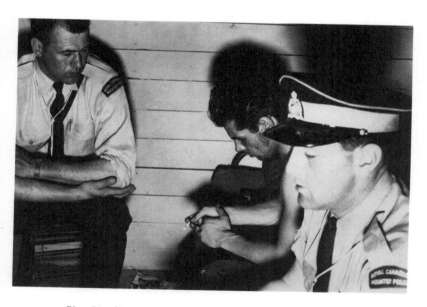

Plate 31   (Provincial Archives of Alberta Photograph Collection)

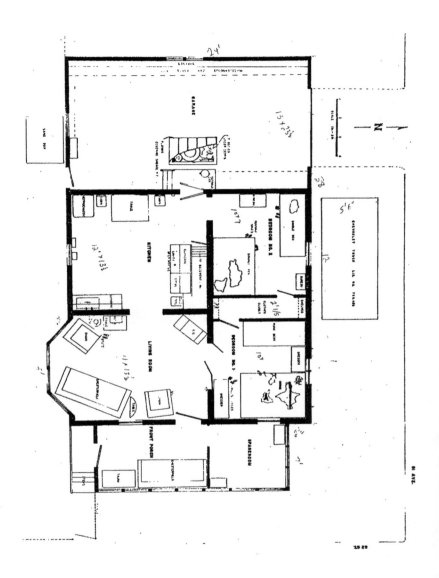

Plate 32   The RCMP Diagram of the main floor of the Cook residence.

To Mr. Gifford Main, Q.C.
ADDRESS 20?. QU'APPELLE BLP.
Edmonton, Alta,
FROM....Robert R. Cook....
BAG 10, Provincial Gaol,
Fort Saskatchewan, Alberta.

Prisoners allowed no parcels
except clothing and reading
matter. Any person known to
have been confined to a Penal
or Reformatory Institution
shall not be permitted to visit
a prisoner without permission
of the Warden.

Dear Sir;   ALIBI?

I have some information that I did not want to give out before on where and what I was doing on that (thursday night) I think that you should know before this. I'm sorry I didn't mention it before, but didn't think it was too important. Will explain when I see you.

When you have the free time please come down to see me.

Thank you

Robert Cook.

Plate 33 The letter that set in motion the torrent of screwdrivers. Main's notation in the left hand margin.

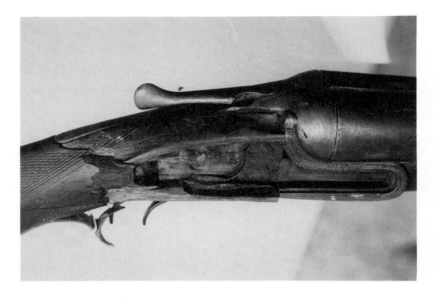

Plate 34   The roughly re-assembled Demon.

Plate 35   S. Giffard Main, QC

Plate 36   J. Wallace Anderson, QC

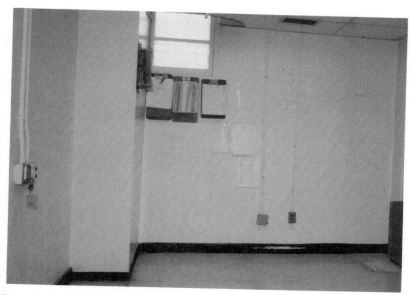

Plate 37   Cook's death cell; converted to office use after the abolition of the death penalty when 110 volt outlets were added.

Plate 38   The scene of the last walk - the pipe-filled corridor. Death cell doors standing open on left.

Plate 39   The author. Twenty-six men and one woman walked - or were carried - through this door on their way to the gallows.

Plate 40　The Storage Room showing trapdoor opening filled with plywood. Release lever was mounted in opening under the small square to immediate left of plywood.

Plate 41　The Autopsy Room showing Death Pit in background.

Plate 42

Plate 43 The hood. Mercerized cotton; cotton twill weave lined with a cheap suiting material not unlike the material of the blue suit.

CANADA

DEPARTMENT OF JUSTICE

1022

TO HIS EXCELLENCY

THE GOVERNOR GENERAL IN COUNCIL:

       The undersigned has the honour to
submit herewith report of the Honourable Mr. Justice
Harold W. Riley, in the case of ROBERT RAYMOND COOK,
convicted of murder at Sittings of the Supreme Court
of Alberta, held at the City of Edmonton, during the
month of June, 1960, and sentenced to be executed on
the eleventh day of October, 1960, -reprieved and
execution of sentence postponed, by Order of the
Court, to the fifteenth day of November, 1960, -
together with transcript of the evidence adduced at
the trial, and other documents relating to the case.

       Upon careful consideration of all which,
the undersigned respectfully recommends that the
death penalty be commuted to a term of life
imprisonment in the Saskatchewan Penitentiary.

                Respectfully submitted,

Plate 44

EXCLUSIVE CONNECTION WITH WESTERN UNION CABLE SERVICE
CORRESPONDANCE EXCLUSIVE
FORM 61228

CANADIAN NATIONAL
J. R. WHITE
GENERAL MANAGER · GÉRANT GÉNÉRAL
TORONTO
TELEGRAPHS

MOA413 YB146
Y DA222 RX 41=FD EDMONTON ALTA 14 133PMM=
T D MACDONALD ASSISTANT DEPUTY MINISTER
OF JUSTICE= OTTAWA ONT=

I WISH TO ACKNOWLEDGE RECEIPT OF TELEGRAM WHICH READS
AS FOLLOWS: "GOVERNOR GENERAL IN COUNCIL HAS DECIDED
NOT TO INTERFERE WITH DEATH SENTENCE PAST ON ROBERT
RAYMOND COOK WHO*S EXECUTION FIXED FIFTEENTH INSTANT
STOP PLEASE REPEAT FOREGOING MESSAGE BY TELEGRAM
IMMEDIATELY"=

W A SHORT SHERIFF..

Department of Justice,
RECEIVED
NOV 14 1960
CRIMINAL LAW SECTION

Plate 45

EXCLUSIVE CONNECTION WITH WESTERN UNION CABLE SERVICE
CANADIAN NATIONAL
J R WHITE GENERAL MANAGER
TORONTO
TELEGRAPHS
STANDARD TIME
1960 NOV 14 PM 2:20
FORM 61XX

MOA186
MO GB152 RX 21=OTTAWA ONT 14 351PM=.   ●04242
F R DUNNE ESQ, BARRISTER & SOLICITOR=
708 MCLEOD BLDG EDMONTON ALTA=

:GOVERNOR GENERAL IN COUNCIL WILL NOT INTERFERE WITH DEATH
SENTENCE PASSED UPON ROBERT RAYMOND COOK TRIED FOR MURDER
AT EDMONTON ALBERTA=
T D MACDONALD, ASSISTANT DEPUTY MINISTER OF
JUSTICE.

017

Plate 46

<u>DECLARATION OF SHERIFF AND OTHERS.</u>

1

THE PROVINCIAL GAOL,

FORT SASKATCHEWAN, ALBERTA.

We, the undersigned, hereby declare that Judgment by death was this day executed on ROBERT RAYMOND COOK in the Provincial Gaol at Fort Saskatchewan, in the Province of Alberta, in the Dominion of Canada, in our presence.

_____

Sheriff - Edmonton Judicial District.

_____

Warden - Provincial Gaol, Fort Saskatchewan

Dated this 15th day of
November in the year
Nineteen Hundred and
Sixty.

Plate 47

CERTIFICATE OF EXECUTION OF JUDGMENT OF DEATH.

THE PROVINCIAL GAOL,

FORT SASKATCHEWAN, ALBERTA.

I, A. G. SCARTH, Physician of the Provincial Gaol at Fort Saskatchewan, in the Province of Alberta, in the Dominion of Canada, hereby certify that I, this day, examined the body of ROBERT RAYMOND COOK, on whom the judgment of death was this day executed in the said Gaol, and that on such examination I found that the said ROBERT RAYMOND COOK was dead.

Physician.

Dated this 15th day of November in the year Nineteen Hundred and Sixty.

Plate 48   Note that like Mr Justice Peter Greschuk the physician refers to the death sentence as a "judgment".

Ubi exparari vera non possant, falsa
per metum augenter - When truth
cannot be clearly made out, what is false
is increased through fear.

Maxim

CHAPTER 16

THE SHOTGUN

For a man reputed to prefer sitting in the car to getting out of it and
slaughtering ducks when he went hunting with his friend Jim Hoskins,
Ray Cook had an unusually large arsenal of guns both real and notional
in his house. Two of them were not his. There may have been three that
were. One of them which the evidence suggested should have been
there may not have existed and the last of them, the instrument of his
death, may have been his as well but it will remain forever unknown.
The owner of the murder weapon - the double-barreled shotgun - was
never identified, and the manner of its arriving at the house was never
established.

The RCMP were able to give Anderson nothing on the shotgun other
than another insoluble - or at any rate unsolved - problem. To give
Anderson such a problem was for him to rise to the challenge in novel

ways and to offer solutions which would not have occurred to less daring men; the Ross shirt as just another homely article in a household full of them comes to mind.

And so with the shotgun. In the first trial Anderson argued the murder weapon probably belonged to Ray Cook who had acquired it in the two years since his eldest son had last been home - a way of explaining why Cook said he did not recognize it. In the next breath Anderson argued that it was probably a gun stolen by Cook two years previously which he had cached, recovered and brought home[1]. Anderson did not suggest where the cache might have been located or when Cook unearthed it, but there was no doubt he'd brought it home in time to murder his family. In other words, Anderson was floundering, and so we had a singular state of affairs in which the Crown had not the faintest idea how to account for the gun, and accordingly didn't, and the defense, which should have been able to capitalize on the disarray in the Crown's case, was unable to do so.

***

To a taste violated by the mere thought of television, turn-of-the-century mail order catalogues are a delight. In the teeming pages of Sears Roebuck's 1900 catalogue is a cornucopia of whimsical junk: corsets, cabriolets, kerosene and magic lanterns, stereopticons, optigraphs, electric belts (batteries presumably not included) and "genuine Stradivarius model violins sought after and admired by the world's greatest players" whose optative admiration of these priceless rarities could ripen into ownership if the world's greatest players were prepared to cough up two dollars and fifty cents.

There were shoes for women having feet resembling anteaters, and clothes at the absolute nadir of the whole history of feminine fashion.

---

1 *The two explanations occurring cheek by jowl without being expressed to be alternate possibilities was reminiscent of the trial of the Knave of Hearts with some of the jurors writing on their slates "The shotgun was Ray's" and the others "The shotgun was stolen by the accused." Either would have sufficed as an explanation, all enabling circumstances such as proof being assumed, but the incriminating force of one was not discernibly increased by hitching it in tandem with the other since they were mutually exclusive. In the second trial Anderson severed them, abandoned the first and went with a variation of the second which continues to defy credulity.*

There were guaranteed cures for cirrhosis, croup, colic, cough, cold in the head, cholera, chronic congestion, catarrh, constipation, cankers and crying babies. There were cures for biliousness, quinsy, sallow complexion, ague, scanty menses, salt rheum, scrofula, hemorrhoids, diarrhea, flatulency, belching, gonorrhea and gleet. There were, indeed, electuaries for everything but the dread slobbering fits.

There were also guns in the catalogue - 35 pages of guns in effusive testimony of the right of the American people to bear arms and with them shoot everything in sight including their fellow citizens, stray barns, the odd chicken and immobile cows, defending their right to do so on the immutable premise that guns don't kill cows, people kill cows. There was page upon page of pistols, revolvers, something called bicycle guns (for shooting bicycles? bicyclists?), rifles, derringers and shotguns. There were 53 shotguns pictured, differing in minor detail and in price starting at $6.00 and ranging through $7.50, $11.59 and $13.10 to $33.75 and beyond. In the cheerfully exuberant lying of the text accompanying each illustration there was a certain sameness. There was a truly miraculous choice of guns for each of which there were "no equals regardless of price" except for those which were merely "the equal of any gun you can buy elsewhere for double the money." The huckster's argot made for a delicious agony of choice coupled with the happy certainty that whatever the choice it could not be improved upon, every gun being better than all the others.

The type of double-barreled shotgun pictured was standard: breech loading, external hammers, inexpensive and utilitarian. Tens of thousands of them hung in the back porches of prairie farmsteads and houses of prairie towns throughout North America. It was from the pages of such a catalogue the gun used to kill the Cook family probably came; it is a good bet its started its journey to Stettler in a Canadian mail order house.

It was a 60-year old, 12 gauge, side-by-side double-barreled shotgun named, with a certain grim aptness presaging its demoniacal last use, a Demon in evidence of which a tiny imp was imprinted in one of the barrels. Also stamped on the barrels were the serial number, the proof house marks and the name of the manufacturer: The Midlands Gun Company of Birmingham, England. It was about 48 inches long. Its walnut stock and forehand piece were checkered. It bore the signs of its age and hard usage.

There were three pieces of the shotgun found on the double bed in the main bedroom: the barrels with the breech mechanism intact, the forehand piece and one hammer. The barrels were bent in two places suggesting that in being used as a club, some unyielding object - perhaps the upper and lower steel army cot in which the two little girls, Linda and Kathy, slept - had been hit with it with near unbelievable force. Three pieces of the splintered stock were found in the greasepit wrapped in a blanket used as a makeshift winding-sheet. In all, only these six pieces of the gun were found.

The police photograph of the roughly reassembled gun however show the stock to have been splintered into at least five pieces (three distinct pieces show in the photograph of the incomplete stock with two pronounced gaps in it) and the trigger guard was broken off. Add to the six pieces found, the trigger guard, the two missing segments of the wooden stock, one hammer and the two lock plates and it will be seen that in terms of numbers exactly half of the total number of pieces into which the gun fractured (so far as the total can be determined) were found.

Of most interest among the missing pieces were the two lock plates - metal plates about three inches by seven inches by which the breech mechanism is attached to the stock. In an exacting search of a murder scene they would be hard to miss suggesting the killer took them with him. They sometimes offer the means of identifying a gun; gun owners frequently have them engraved - scrollwork and the like, initials, sometimes full names, but without them there was no equivalent of, say, R-O-S-S to provide a clue to the gun's ownership. The initials "PS", not as large as they appear here, were scratched into a small fragment of the stock which happens to be in the writer's possession. If they were noticed, they were not mentioned in evidence nor was the fact that the lock plates were not found. The significance of the initials, if any, is not known.

The results of RCMP efforts to identify the owner or the source of the gun matched those obtained in the Ross shirt investigation. "Exhaustive inquiries," Van Blarcom said, produced negative results", and Roach confirmed the lack of results when asked by Main whether there had been a "very extensive and exhaustive inquiry in an endeavor to learn the source of the shotgun." They had drawn another blank.

As the first trial approached, Main became uneasy about having heard nothing from the RCMP about the shotgun - a matter of concern to him - and asked the police to run a picture of it in *The Stettler Independent* in the expectation or hope a reader might recognize it. The police obliged by having published a picture not of the Demon but of a gun similar in appearance which was not much of a problem because they were all similar in appearance. Nevertheless the caption described the Demon, reciting the serial number and manufacturer and asking "anyone who knows anything about such a gun...to contact the R.C.M.P at Stettler." "There were," Van Blarcom said, "numerous calls but no results."

***

Since one of Anderson's theses was that Cook had brought the Demon to the house, we will start with it. Since he did not have it with him when he was observed standing on Main Street at 9 pm Thursday (and nor, of course, at any time during the afternoon or early evening wandering around Stettler), he necessarily left the house sometime after the kitchen conference with Ray and Daisy and recovered it from wherever he'd hidden it at least two years earlier. As with the money at Bowden, he had cached it. Anderson summarized the evidence of the existence of such a cache for the first-trial jury: "you have heard the evidence of the accused himself - nightly forays off down the highways, breaking and entering, loot. Is it inconceivable to conclude that his own loot might have included this shotgun? He tells you that much of the loot he did acquire on those nightly forays was stashed away for periods of two years and no one ever found it. Could that not be true in the case of this shotgun?"

Now it was stole a gun and away he run. Cook, to hear Anderson, was a collector of antiques: a 60-year old shotgun and - for second-trial purposes - a shirt which, judging from its appearance, was about the same age. The fact that the only loot the jurors had heard of was money, indeed stashed for two years but Anderson was having no part of that, cars (difficult in the nature of things to stash) and a furtive pull from a bottle of whiskey (returned to the shelf) in the Hanna liquor store, did not of course preclude the possibility of his having stolen a battered old shotgun from some hardware store as Anderson suggested he had without specifying that this was necessarily a hardware store which dealt in second-hand shotguns. If the jurors found that plausible that was their prerogative.

But just as vague possibilities are not proof, improbability is not impossibility, and the possibility of a cached shotgun must be considered. If it was, it was in or near Stettler to allow Cook to leave the house leaving his parents preparing for bed, retrieve the gun and return to the house by midnight - the generally accepted time of the murders. The cache was still an essential element in Anderson's second-trial argument, but only by implication of what he said to the jury on the question of the source of the gun, the whole of which takes up seven lines of transcript:

"I can only agree with the suggestion of my learned friend that very extensive efforts have been unable to indicate or bring to light the owner of this gun, but I disagree with the suggestion that in order to arrive at the conclusion that it was employed by this accused, you must disbelieve all the witnesses who state that they saw him arrive in Stettler or that when he was in Stettler he was without a gun in his possession."

Which was to say the jurors could believe the Crown witnesses (there were six of them) who saw Cook and could be expected to have noticed it had he been carrying a four-foot shotgun, and said that he wasn't, but only if the jurors postulated (as Anderson himself did not expressly postulate) a cache from which Cook recovered the gun just before midnight. Since they could not very well not believe the Crown witnesses, a cache was imported by necessary implication, and Dunne's counterattack should have been on the existence of a cache starting with the fact that there was no evidence of one and none from which one could be inferred unless one wished to infer from the fact the RCMP had no idea where the gun came from, that therefore Cook brought it home. As it happens that is about what happened.

No gun being carried around Stettler and no cache (had Dunne mounted such an attack and succeeded) meant either the gun was brought to the house by someone other than Cook or it was owned by someone in the house and was already there when Cook arrived home from Prince Albert. If the defense could show it was not owned by anyone in the house - Ray Cook and Gurney were the two possible owners; it is assumed that Daisy was not a duck hunter - this left, as owner - and bringer - someone other than Cook. The attractiveness of him to the defense was that he wouldn't even have to be identified. Someone other than Cook was, by definition as it were, not Cook.

The starting point then for the defense was to show the gun was not owned by anyone living in the house, which incidentally meant that the defense was in the position of having to prove its case while the Crown stood idly by, but there was no help for that as things developed in the *Cook* trials. The approach required of the defense would have embodied the same principles as those underlying the theory of the best way to catch lions in the desert: take a sieve and sift out all the sand; what's left over should be pure lions. Here however the defense advocates would be attempting to get rid of the lions in favor of sand unadulterated by lions. The sieve required would separate the guns by holding back all those owned by Ray or Gurney; all the others would fall through. If the Demon ended up on the floor with all the other guns not owned by Ray or Gurney they would have their someone other than Cook.

***

The effort of the prosecutor on the other hand - and before him the police investigators - should have been to show first whether Ray Cook had owned any guns at all and, once having shown that he had, then to show one of the guns he owned was the Demon. Once accomplish that and the nonsense about midnight forays, highways, loot and caches could have been forgotten. The Demon would now be shown to have belonged in the house and at that point it would not have mattered that Cook claimed he'd never seen it. It would be entirely reasonable to infer that it had been acquired by Ray during Cook's most recent absence. But the RCMP's efforts to learn a number of things were dogged by ill-luck or lack of manpower, or whatever it was, and the attempt to learn whether Ray had owned any shotgun (not just the Demon) was no exception. "Was any investigation made by the police as to whether Ray Cook had actually owned a shotgun?" Roach was asked in cross-examination, and he replied, "Not that we could definitely determine" which can be taken to mean that they had not been able to learn whether Ray owned a shotgun, not that they had not been able to learn whether or not they had conducted an investigation.

Interviewing Ray's good friend Jim Hoskins would have proved helpful to the RCMP. Hoskins told me that "Ray had a shotgun, an old long-barreled, cock-eyed thing. He'd go out with me but he'd never get out of the car. I never saw him fire a gun. He wouldn't take the old long-barreled gun out - an old single shot 36 inch barrel. A kind of keepsake is what it was. I don't even know what became of it. I think it was

279

hanging in the stairs to the basement. It wasn't in the garage, I'm damn sure of that. I think it hung right in the stairway to the basement. I remember looking at it there. He went out twice with me shooting ducks and he sat in the car until I was finished."

Hoskins mentioned the shotgun in the second trial: "To my knowledge he had two guns that I know of: a .22 and an old single-barrel shotgun. He told the court he'd "probably seen them a hundred times." However, rather than the shotgun hanging in the stairwell, it now, Hoskins thought, hung with a .22 in the garage. His son Dillon told me there was "an old shotgun that Ray kept [in the house] - must have been over 50 years old. An old single-barrel I think. But he never shot a gopher. I think he used to beat them over the head with it." At the second trial he had not been able to remember whether Ray owned a shotgun so that in a sense the interview and his courtroom evidence canceled each other leaving his father's evidence of an old, single-barrel, single shot shotgun either in the garage as Hoskins told the court, or in the stairwell as he told me. The matter of where it hung was not unimportant, but the real question about guns in the Cook house other than the Demon was what were they and how many were there in what locations?

They were found in three locations: the bedroom where the Demon - most of it - was uncovered on the mattress; the garage where as few as one and as many as three were seen depending on which police witness was giving evidence in which trial; and the basement where there were two. In the gun investigation there was an echo of the Ross shirt investigation in which nothing meaningful could be said about the shirt without taking into account other shirts. And so here. Nothing could be known about the Demon - was it Ray's and if not whose was it and where did it come from? - without regard to all the other guns in the house. Except for a slipshod inventory made of them, no regard was had to the other guns and the investigation and the trials ended with nothing more known about the gun than its name, rank, one supposes, and serial number. It proved to be enough to meet the easygoing standards of the *Cook* trials.

***

Constable Sproule was the first to see the basement group. He told Main at the preliminary inquiry:

"When I examined the basement of this residence in Stettler on the 28th of June, 1959, immediately below the stairs and to the right of the chimney along the wall there were two firearms."

"Of what nature?"

"They were shotguns. The two shotguns were located on the wall opposite from the heater which is shown [on the RCMP diagram] in the washroom. The shotguns were against the wall, that is on the other side of the wall behind the heater."

Cross-examined by Main at the first trial, Sproule was more specific as to the type of shotguns seen by him in the basement:

"You told us you found two other shotguns, was it, or a shotgun and something else?"

"Two shotguns."

"Two shotguns. And what kind of shotguns were the two shotguns found
in the basement?

"I have no idea what make they were."

"I mean single-barrel or double-barrel?"

"Single-barrel. One appeared to be an older type. It was a very long gun, approximately four feet long, and they were covered with dust as I mentioned."

....

"Did you notice if there were any signs of disturbance of dust and so on that another gun had been removed from there?"

"No, I couldn't see. I shone a very bright light along the floor, along the wall where these guns were, and there were no signs of another gun having been placed there or having been removed."

At the second trial, Sproule's single-barrel certainty of the preliminary inquiry and first trial had given way to uncertainty. Dunne asked him whether the two guns in the basement were single- or double-barreled:

"One I definitely recall was a single-barrel shotgun and the other I could not say definitely. I did not put any significance on these guns as I mentioned they were behind a thin board next to the wall at the bottom of the stairway, and when I carefully removed these two guns it was apparent they hadn't been handled for some time, so I didn't take any further notice of these two guns."

It is advisable to pause here to summarize what was learned from Sproule over the course of the preliminary inquiry and two trials. What, in the preliminary inquiry were simply two shotguns became, as the result of a more searching cross-examination in the first trial, two shotguns, both single-barreled, one of them an inordinately long older type, and in the second trial two shotguns, only one of them definitely single-barreled and neither of them meriting mention as being unusually longer than the other. Perhaps of more significance was that where we learned in the first trial that Sproule merely shone his light on the guns, "not putting any significance on them", in the second it transpired that he had "carefully removed" them, but evidently not so carefully that he noticed whether they were both still single-barreled.

No one asked Sproule where he removed the guns to or why, and it may be that removal meant merely picking them up and setting them down again. But "removed" suggests more, and a clue is provided in an answer of Beeching's when he was being questioned about the garage guns and said he saw them and as well saw "another long-barreled gun, a single-barreled shotgun which was there in the house which I was told where it came from." Nobody but Sproule, either before or after Beeching, mentioned seeing a long, single-barreled shotgun in the house after the murders, and it can be taken that the one to which Beeching referred was one of the two guns Sproule had seen in the basement, the one which had earned the first-trial mention as being inordinately long, presumably when compared to its companion of unknown barrellage - to coin a word for the occasion. But where then was the companion gun? Why did Beeching not see both of "these two guns" which Sproule had removed?

Leonard Gurney, the former roomer, was able to throw some light on the subject of basement guns. He had moved out of the house about a week before Cook came home, and when Main asked him about which of his possessions were still in the house at the time of the murders he replied that among other things there were "a shotgun and a .22."

"A shotgun and a .22?"

"Yes sir."

"Now, where was the shotgun left?" [1]

"I left it underneath the stairway as you go down the basement with the understanding of the residents too, the people who owned the place where it was and it was behind half a partition. That was put there especially so that the kiddies wouldn't get it. That too was understandable with them."

"And what kind of shotgun was that?"

"Well, it's called a Long Tom. It is inscribed right in. It is a single-barrel 12 gauge shotgun."

Sproule had said nothing about seeing a .22 in the basement; the selfsame guns that Gurney was talking about were both shotguns in Sproule's thrice-stated testimony. But Gurney's evidence is to be preferred; a gun owner's loving heart can be taken to know its own guns.

At the first trial Main was aware that Sproule and Gurney could not both be right - there were either two shotguns or a shotgun and a .22 in the basement more or less out of reach of the kiddies - but rather than asking to have Sproule re-called for further cross-examination as the first salvo in an unremitting campaign to discredit police witnesses (it was part of a defense lawyer's job description), he chose instead to leave it until his address to the jury when, out of the blue, without leading up to it and without it leading anywhere, he referred to Sproule's mis-identification of the guns as an illustration of how anyone could make an honest mistake, even police officers who were, Main said, after all only human beings.

There was no point to Main's observation. Had he been saying in effect "If you can't believe Sproule here (and you can't), when can you believe him? Which police officer can you believe?", that would have been a point if not a particularly well taken one. But he wasn't and as much as one can say for it is that he was anticipating the time later in the closing argument when he would have to ask for absolution for one of his own witnesses[2]. But Main was wrong to allow the frailty of Sproule's memory to go unchallenged on the stand. To destroy Sproule, if he could, was

[1] *It will be noted that Main asked only about the shotgun, and Gurney answered to the point. At the preliminary inquiry he said that both were stored together in the basement.*

[2] *See Chapter 22.*

what he was there for. If the destruction of Sproule was the cost of saving Cook, Sproule was expendable. It was as if Main needed reminding that they were engaged in the search for the owner of a gun used to kill seven people in a house which had begun to show signs of there being seven guns for seven victims.

When questioned at the first trial as to whether he had used his shotgun recently, Gurney replied "this year" meaning, if Sproule's 'dust' observation accurately indicated the basement guns had not been moved for a long time prior to the murders, that Gurney had used his "Long Tom" sometime after the murders and before the first trial. But in the second trial, asked the same question, Gurney replied "not recently, but recently at that time that year".

It is a difficult answer. If "recently at that time" is taken to mean a short time before the murders, as it reasonably can be, then the basement guns would not have been, like the little toy dog, all covered with dust. He could have used his shotgun after the murders however since he was invited by the police to come and pick up his Long Tom and .22 indicating that Sproule wasn't alone in the RCMP in not "[putting] any significance on these guns." Yet they - or one of them - may have had some significance for, as Jim Hoskins told me, Ray too had an old Long Tom, "a long-barreled, cock-eyed thing", raising the intriguing possibility that there had been two Long Toms in the Cook household. But if that was the case, or in any case, where was Ray Cook's? Not, surely, behind the half partition in the basement? But then where was Gurney's, or was Gurney as mistaken as Sproule as to precisely what was in the basement? But he can't have been, he knew he owned a Long Tom; it was "inscribed right in."

***

The garage group of guns can be dealt with in short compass. They hung on the west wall at about eye level as one came through the door from the kitchen and on to the small landing.

Gurney said at all three judicial proceedings that he had no knowledge of any guns in the garage suggesting he must have had his eyes on the ceiling every time he walked through the garage since he was not aware either of the greasepit in the floor. At the preliminary inquiry and first trial, Sproule recalled seeing two .22s on the garage wall, but at the second trial he was down to one, perhaps remembering his first-trial experience when he remembered seeing twice as many shotguns in the basement as, after Gurney, there proved to be.[1] Beeching gave evidence of the garage guns at the preliminary inquiry only, and thought he remembered (he wasn't sure) seeing a single-barreled shotgun and two .22s on the wall. Van Blarcom gave evidence of garage guns at the first trial only and thought (he too wasn't sure) he remembered seeing two "rifles" on the garage wall and, as it happened, two shotguns in the basement just as Sproule thought he had.

Roach was asked about guns only at the second trial, and in particular specifically whether the police had investigated the matter of Ray's ownership of a shotgun. Roach cannot have understood the question. He replied:

"Well, you mean - there were guns in the garage."

"I know. Were they shotguns?"

"There were .22s."

It is probable Roach meant all the guns in the garage were .22s - meant to say *they* were .22s rather than *there* were .22s, rather, that is, than that there were some .22s and one or more shotguns, but Dunne did not pursue it, leaving hanging the question arising from Beeching's evidence at the preliminary inquiry: did he see a single-barreled shotgun on the garage wall which Sproule, looking at the same wall, did not see, and Gurney, looking wherever Gurney looked, did not see, and Van Blarcom did not see unless he mistook a shotgun for one of the two rifles he thought he saw?

(To digress for a moment: part of the very extensive and exhaustive police efforts - as Dunne called them - to trace the Demon was to lean on people susceptible to being leaned on. There were such people in Cook's

---

[1] *Sproule persisted with two shotguns in the second trial which was either to his credit or attestative of his obduracy - or he saw himself as being more or less bound by his sworn evidence at the preliminary inquiry and the first trial. But, as we have seen, he was no longer quite so certain that they were both single-barrelled, being now well aware that Gurney had identified one of the basement guns - one of his guns - as a .22.*

circle among them Eddie Read and Walter Berezowski. "When the cops got to me," Berezowski told me, "I was just starting a new job. That was all I needed. They were trying to pressure me into saying he had a shotgun on him."

When they got to Eddie Read, a new trial had already been ordered, and the police prepared for it by again attempting to establish that Cook had brought the gun to Stettler in Eddie Read's truck. Had they got from Read and Berezowski what they wanted, the six Crown witnesses who testified to having seen Cook carrying nothing when he left Berezowski would have found themselves bystanders at the *Cook* trials. Read was in jail at the time and thus, Read thought the RCMP thought, more than normally vulnerable to being leaned on. "I was in Spy Hill when the RCMP came down there. The warden said, 'The RCMP want to talk to you.' I told him I wouldn't talk to them. But it was a case of talk to them or wind up in the damper. I talked to them. A Constable Irvine of the RCMP in Edmonton tried to pressure me into admitting Cook had a shotgun. There was a threat of a beef [a further charge] against me and he tried to use it. A grade-A bastard. 'Are you sure you never saw a shotgun in there? If we could place a shotgun in the back of [Read's truck] we've got him.' Irvine was an ambitious man. He kept insisting 'Are you sure you never saw the shotgun?' He wouldn't let up; tried hard to intimidate me: 'You saw Cook with the shotgun didn't you?' "

***

The sixth and last person able to say something of the guns in Ray Cook's house was Jim Hoskins. Although called as a Crown witness at the preliminary inquiry and at the first trial, he was queried about guns at the second trial only. Anderson asked him if Ray Cook had any guns he knew of:

"To my knowledge he had two guns that I know of, a .22 and an old single-barrel shotgun."

"When was the last time you would have seen these?"

"Well, I just couldn't say. I think they always hung on the garage wall there. I think I have probably seen them a hundred times."

"You say there was a single-barrel shotgun you recall?"

"Yes, I think it was an old - I'm pretty sure."

Dunne got up, asked Hoskins 12 questions none of which had anything to do with Ray's shotgun and sat down, missing the opportunity to learn what Hoskins was about to say before he hesitated and settled for confirming merely that Ray's shotgun was "an old single-barrel." An old Long Tom? He told me it was. The basement guns and the garage guns could have been on the exhibit table where Hoskins could have had a look at all of them, but they were not. For the RCMP to decide against ascribing significance to potential evidence was to ensure that no one else got the chance to do so, remembering however that it was their job to decide what was significant and what was not otherwise the courtroom might have been cluttered with broken bicycles, used tires and shirts.

Since no significance was attached to any guns other than the Demon, there was ultimately no way of getting at the problem of its ownership; no way of sifting out the guns not owned by Ray Cook other than by conjecture with little to go on other than Hoskins' memory of the "old cock-eyed thing" being Ray's only shotgun. The underlying assumption in all the aimless courtroom rhetoric, all the intensive and exhaustive police investigation (one wonders what it consisted of since it stopped short of Jim Hoskins), was that if the Demon was not Ray's, then, if one was Wally Anderson, it was brought to the house by Cook or, if one was Giffard Main, it was brought by some shadowy stranger, probably a known criminal or, if one was Frank Dunne, it was anybody's guess, and none of them stopped long enough to sift through the four possibilities (there were no others): (1) it was brought by Cook - Anderson's cache theory; (2) it was brought by X - Main's stranger theory; (3) it was owned by Ray and in the house when Cook arrived, having been acquired by Ray during Cook's absence - Anderson's side-by-side with the cache theory explanation, but each of them offered as the way of it rather than as alternatives; (4) it was in the house but owned by someone other than Ray when Cook arrived.

***

We will conclude this sketch of a bleak landscape in the *Cook* trials by looking at the way in which the judges and lawyers dealt with the Demon problem in their closing addresses to the juries.

Main's theory was that since the Demon did not belong in the house (Anderson having failed to show it belonged to Ray Cook), it was brought there by a stranger, most probably an ex-convict - Main's candidate for complicity throughout.

Dunne's argument was that since the jurors could not disbelieve six Crown witnesses who were in agreement that Cook was not toting a four-foot shotgun around Stettler, they therefore had no choice but to believe Cook when he said he had not brought the gun home with him, and there Dunne left it. He noted in his closing argument that there was "a suggestion that [Ray] may have owned a single-barreled shotgun, but that does not matter because there is no suggestion that that shotgun had any bearing on this case." It had in any event no bearing on Dunne's understanding of the case.

As was Dunne, Anderson was a never-failing source of wonderment. In the first trial he felt he had to say something about the Sproule-Gurney conflict as to the types of guns in the basement, even though Main had made little it: "Reference has been made to the fact that there were discrepancies in the prosecution's case - a description of whether it was two shotguns or a shotgun and a .22, as to date of certain happenings. Those are discrepancies but are they in any way to be compared with the inconsistencies and, it is suggested, outright lying displayed by this accused in these instances that I have just referred to and more that were pointed out to you in evidence?"

Discrepancies in the evidence of Crown witnesses about something as unimportant as shotguns in a house where seven people were killed with a shotgun no one could identify were, to Anderson, as nothing compared to Cook having told his parents in a letter home in 1955 - one of the examples of outright lying Anderson used - that he was going to "straighten out" when so patently he had done anything but. Having exonerated Sproule on the novel ground that the greater lie cancels the lesser mistake (a mistake made three times under oath), Anderson moved on to his 'owned by Ray Cook but nevertheless brought home by Bob Cook' explication of the Demon problem:

"Now in considering [Main's argument], may we commence with the shotgun. It is true that investigation did not indicate its source. The accused said, 'Well, I know it wasn't mine and I don't think my father ever had one', but that must be considered in the light of the fact that he hadn't been home or closely associated with his father for two years."

If the jurors wished to consider what Cook had said in that light, there was no denying Cook had been away for two years and Ray could easily have bought the Demon in that time. Anderson was inviting the jurors to believe that that is exactly what happened, otherwise what he had just said was so much flapdoodle. The jurors scarcely got the chance to absorb it however for without pausing for breath Anderson went on to expound the nightly forays-loot-cache thesis quoted above.

The RCMP investigators could with profit have taken a leaf from Mr Justice Greschuk's book on exhaustiveness. In his five hour charge to the jury, he took up the subject of the Demon five times, and when he was finished there was not much the jurors didn't know about it apart from who owned it and how it got to the house. He dealt with the other guns briefly, stating as a fact that there were two shotguns in the basement thus resolving the Sproule-Gurney conflict in favor of Sproule even though they were Gurney's guns.

Riley was superficiality writ large. He mentioned the Demon three times, reproduced here in their entirety:

"Observed in the bed were parts of a shotgun."

"In the same pit were found parts of a shotgun which, when put with the other parts and specifically with the barrel *[sic]* found in the bedroom, were found to match and make a complete *[sic]* shotgun. The breech of the shotgun contained two expended shotgun casings. The stock of the gun was badly broken. The barrel was bent."

"The defense urges that the shotgun was a complete stranger to the Cook home."

He did not mention the other guns.

CHAPTER 17

THE SEVENTEEN SHOTGUN SHELLS

The requirements for membership in the brotherhood of duck hunters are modest and reasonable: a member is expected to own a gun and to shoot ducks with it. Many are called, most accepted, but when it came to Ray Cook futility thy name was duck hunter. For one thing, he couldn't be bothered to get out of the car long enough to track the ducks to their lairs, lolling around in it while the others were out there risking their lives. For another, if he had bothered, it would have been without much purpose since he did not own the means - a gun - to shoot the ducks when they were flushed out.

Or did he? Not as far as the RCMP was able to determine, and in a sense that became the official fact of the matter. They had exhaustively investigated the question of Ray's ownership of a shotgun, any shotgun, going as far in attempting to trace the Demon's provenance as addressing one inquiry to Scotland Yard, and another to its manufacturer, the Midlands Gun Company of Birmingham, England whose records, they learned, had been destroyed in a WW II bombing raid. Although the RCMP did not learn of it, Ray had once owned an old 'Long Tom'[1], but

---

[1] 'Long Tom' was a name generically employed by the hunting fraternity to describe a type of inexpensive, single-barrelled shotgun manufactured prior to and through the turn of the century before the development of the modern shotgun. Their barrels were in fact longer than today's average by a matter of some four to six inches. The extra length of the barrel was claimed to impart increased accuracy and power. Some of them went back to the era of muzzle loaders. I have been informed by a gun expert's gun expert that in addition to the name being employed generically, it was appropriated by Sears Roebuck for a particular model in its catalogue. The guns' frames were inscribed with the name, and Gurney therefore had accurately described his.

the consensus, as expressed by Dunne, was that Long Toms had no bearing on the case. They may not have had. Ray had used his only to beat gophers over the head with - a bit of hyperbole on the part of Dillon Hoskins but probably an accurate measure of Ray Cook the hunter: not much on ducks but deadly when it came to gophers. Not that it mattered in the larger picture; the death of gophers was not the RCMP's primary concern.

In all then, a hunter who may or may not have owned a gun who went on hunting expeditions but didn't hunt apart from flailing around after gophers - a confusing picture made moreso by the fact that shotgun shells were found in three locations in his house: the top drawer of the dresser beside the double bed in the main bedroom in which there were two; a workbench in the garage on which half-a-dozen or so were seen lying in the open; and the pockets of the blue suit jacket which contained five.

***

Sproule described the finding of the dresser shells:

"Two 12 gauge shotgun shells, Olympic No.5, were found in a small plastic container in the top drawer, the front part of the drawer, in the dresser beside the double bed - that is, the drawer in the dresser. They appeared to be fairly new. The surface was not scratched as you would expect an old shell [to be] that is kicking around in a plastic box and other sharp articles, and they appeared to be untouched."

"There were some other articles in the plastic dish were there?"

"Yes. I don't quite recall what they were, along the line of paper clips and hairpins and such like."

As well, Sproule was there when two spent cartridges (both Olympics) were removed from the breech of the Demon, and when the shells were found in the blue suit: "On examining the jacket, the light blue jacket, Corporal Van Blarcom and myself found three 12 gauge shotgun shells, No.5. These are live cartridges. Three were found in the right lower pocket and two were found in the left lower pocket. These are live cartridges, two of which are Olympic and three are Imperial cartridges."

The garage shells were seen as of a lesser order of importance than the others and were not mentioned at either the preliminary inquiry or first trial. They came to light only in the second when Anderson questioned Roach as to any shells he had found:

"If I can be more specific, did you find any shells on the premises?"

"On that Sunday I noticed some shells in the garage, loose shells."

"What type of shells were they?"

"There were several of the Imperial brand and several of the Olympic brand."

"What kind of container were they in?"

"They were loose on the shelf [sic] in the garage."

"Could you tell us whether they were of recent origin or had they been there some time?"

"They looked reasonably new."

"How many were there, do you recall?"

"I don't recall just how many there were."

Anderson then showed him the shells taken from the jacket and asked him whether the garage shells were similar. Roach replied, "There were some of this particular color - the blue-purplish shells. There were some of those out there, and a few of these too." He later gave Dunne an estimate of the number of shells seen in the garage: "I would say in the vicinity of six or eight."

To summarize: there were two shells in a drawer in the main bedroom, both Olympics; five shells in the jacket, three in the right pocket and two in the left, some of them Olympics and some Imperials; two spent Olympics in the breech of the Demon; and a mixture of six or eight Olympics and Imperials on a workbench in the garage. All were more or less new in appearance. The shells of that pre-plastic era were paper-hulled.

***

For Anderson, the problem was to tie Cook to the shells which he did by opening his argument with a form of logic: "Now, an odd fact I think is this: if a stranger came to that house bringing with him the shotgun, apparently he didn't come with any shells because the prosecution indicates that there were two expended Olympic shell cases in the breech." Whether a fact or not, it was at least odd since it is not apparent why a stranger couldn't have brought shells to the house, including the two used on Ray and Daisy, simply because two had been used on Ray and Daisy. The most flexible and forgiving form of syllogism can make nothing of Anderson's argument; the presence of shells in the Demon says very little about where they came from, who brought them, whether he was carrying a shotgun or whether he was a stranger.

Having laid the groundwork, Anderson pressed on: "There were further shell cases *[sic]* of a similar kind in a *[sic]* jacket of the accused's blue suit, and there were also similar shells in a bureau drawer of the Cook residence. Now, in the first place, why would there be shells in the bureau drawer if there wasn't a gun somewhere around in which these shells might be utilized? Secondly, if a stranger brings this gun into the house without any shells to fire there, he must be a person who had some personal knowledge of that house and its occupants to be able to acquire shells out of a bureau drawer in the master bedroom."

Inadvertently perhaps, Anderson was back at Ray owning the Demon ("Why would there be shells...if there wasn't a gun somewhere around in which these shells might be utilized?") having just offered the jurors the cache theory to account for the presence of the Demon. It is possible the cache was offered to explain Cook's ownership of the Demon, and Ray's ownership of the Demon to explain the shells, and if so it was a neat solution to a couple of tough problems provided one considered them discretely and didn't attempt to make a connection.

Anderson was not yet finished with demolishing the stranger: "Now I ask you to consider what significance these shells play in this case. You will recall that there were five shells in the pocket *[sic]* of the blue suit, there were two shells in the breech of the gun, there were two shells in the plastic tray in the bureau drawer, and we are told that there were six or eight shells in the garage on the work table *[sic]*. I ask you to consider those shells in this regard. If they were kept in the drawer of the bureau, which possibility is indicated by the fact that two of them were found there, then the person who utilized them had to know they were in the drawer, had to get to the drawer to find them, and had to get there without arousing the concern of the family. He had to get them out of the drawer.

"Now if they were not kept in the drawer but were kept on the garage work bench as the possibility appears to exist, a stranger had to come to the house, find his way out to the garage in the dark, find the shells there and take certain of them into the bedroom to utilize them. Now this leads to the conclusion that if this stranger came to do this deed, he must have oddly enough come without any shells at all, and had to rely upon the fact of finding some available in the residence so that he might use them. I believe it is significant to note also that there were two expended shells in the breech of the gun, there were five shells in the pocket [sic] of the blue suit. That is a total of seven shells, and that corresponds to the number of members in the family."

He had argued effectively against a stranger as perpetrator, and had done so by reasonably pointing out that it was unlikely a stranger would have stumbled around in a darkened bedroom occupied by four sleeping people on the off chance he might find the shells he had not had the foresight to bring with him. He was right: a prospective murderer who goes to the scene hoping to be able to perfect the instrument of murder when he get there would be well advised to keep his day job.

It was therefore entirely understandable that Anderson should insist on the dresser drawer as the source of the shells used by the murderer. Where a stranger could not know shells were kept in the drawer, Cook would and did and it was Cook therefore who crept into the dark bedroom in the presence of his sleeping family, extracted two shells from the drawer and loaded the shotgun. He then took out an additional five and put them in his pockets showing he'd done his arithmetic. He may then have turned and bludgeoned Ray with the butt[1] (meaning he momentarily pointed the loaded shotgun at himself - an unwise practice) before retreating to the end of the bed, turning and shooting his adult victims.

As with many of Anderson's arguments, it has a surface plausibility which holds up only as long as it takes to supply the deficiencies (the necessary implications of Ray having been bludgeoned for example; he may not have been, but the question deserved exploration) and to work

---

[1] *There was no evidence in court of Ray having been bludgeoned, and in fact when Dr Peter Davey, the pathologist, was asked at the preliminary inquiry if there were any head injuries "in the case of the adult male", he replied no. However when Roach delivered Cook to the PMH, he informed hospital authorities that Ray had suffered a right rear skull fracture, and Dr Donald MacKay, who examined the bodies, told me, "It's true that Ray had been battered in the skull." Whether he was bludgeoned or not is important only in terms of attempting to reconstruct what took place in the master bedroom.*

through to the corollaries necessarily following from Anderson's sparsely developed theories. Or as long as it takes to see whether it can co-exist with another of Anderson's arguments. Here it is found that it cannot. Since Ray had acquired the Demon during Cook's last imprisonment (as Anderson had argued to account for Cook's knowing nothing of it) it seems reasonable to assume he had acquired shells for it at the same time since it is unlikely he was buying shells for someone else's gun. If so, if Ray bought both the gun and the shells during Cook's most recent absence, then Cook could not have known there were shells in the drawer, or anywhere else for that matter. If he thought about it at all, he thought he was coming home to a shell-free environment.

A more likely source of the seven shells was the garage workbench, but Anderson preferred the drawer since, he thought, it was easy to paint Cook as having gone into the master bedroom knowing he would find what he was looking for. And so it was, superficially and given an atmosphere where whatever was needed to be believed about Cook, was believed with only enough questions asked to lend to appearances. The reader will not need to be reminded that both juries went down the line with Anderson, and if Anderson said Cook took seven shells from the drawer, Cook took seven shells from the drawer.

There was little need to go further. No nit-picking inquiries needed to be launched into the feasibility of loading a gun in a dark and cramped bedroom; into whether the victims would have been in deep or r.e.m. sleep at the time; into the possible bludgeoning of one of the victims with the butt end of a loaded shotgun; into whether a bedroom dresser was the place Ray Cook would store shotgun shells given his (not to mention Daisy's) solicitude for the well-being of the kids; into the distinct possibility that the shells did not belong to Ray Cook or, if they did, whether they'd been purchased (like the gun they would have been bought for) after his son's last arrest and imprisonment. Cook took seven shells from the drawer, loaded two in the gun and stuffed the other five in his suit jacket; what more was there to say?

***

Nothing perhaps, but it occurred to me (just as it will have occurred to some readers) to wonder whether Cook would have been so fatally forgetful as to leave five shells in his suit jacket after having spent precious minutes washing wallpaper and so on, and difficult to believe that on Saturday evening he could not have found time from having a beer to pop into the master bedroom and remove the suit, shells intact. Some difficulty too was encountered in believing that he put the shells in the jacket pockets in the manner Sproule described: three in the right, two in the left. What would Cook be apt to do finding himself in a dark room surreptitiously counting out from a drawer enough shells to kill his intended victims? An experiment was indicated.

An old Demon-like shotgun was obtained and the hammers removed to guard against the possibility of the events of the master bedroom being reproduced with too much realism. In my office there was a windowless room not appreciably different in size from the master bedroom. With the light switched off and its one door closed it was utterly dark. On the wall opposite the door was a counter with four drawers side-by-side immediately beneath the countertop.

As clients came into the office they were invited to participate in an experiment. With the light on, a drawer with nine shotgun shells in it was pointed out to them. They were supplied with a suit jacket (if they were not already wearing one), asked to put it on and go into the room carrying the gun. They were then asked to make their way to the drawer, open it without putting the gun down, and take out two shells and lay them on the countertop, this being intended to represent the loading of the gun. They were asked to then take out a further five shells and "put them in the jacket" - a wording carefully adhered to. The door was then closed behind them and in a few seconds each emerged. Of 34 participants, one put two shells in one pocket and three in the other. The other 33 put all five shells in one pocket, either the left or right depending on the arm under which the gun was being carried.

Statisticians may quail at the amateur's methodology and quibble with reading anything into the results, but they nevertheless appear indicative of something, and the reader is invited to draw whatever conclusion seems borne out by them. One such is that the shells were put in the pockets after the murders either as a place to get rid of them out of sight or, possibly, as a plant. If it is conceded the shells were put in the jacket after the murders as indicated by the pocket test, then there is less reason for thinking the shells originated in the drawer than for concluding they were secreted elsewhere in the house or were brought to it by a stranger. It was argued in Chapter 13 that a stranger stripped out of the blue suit after carrying the bodies to the greasepit. On getting back into his own clothes, he would find in them the surplus shells which, on this reasoning, were on his person when he first went into the bedroom.

Here however the plant hypothesis hits a blank wall. If the murderer supposed the suit was Ray's (a reasonable enough supposition if it was in the master bedroom), then nothing is gained by planting shells in his victim's suit except perhaps to momentarily befuddle the investigators. On the other hand, if he knew Cook and knew the suit was Cook's, then of course planting shells in the pockets would divert suspicion to a prime target. But who knew Cook and knew the suit was the suit he'd worn from the penitentiary? It may be that this was the most promising avenue for both Main and Dunne in their otherwise poorly developed attempt to implicate a stranger.

It would have left them however - as it leaves us - with the problem of accounting for the two shells in the drawer. Anderson had a drawer starting with nine shells and ending with a residue of two. The plant hypothesis has a drawer starting with no shells and accreting two, and will be seen as a struggle to explain what, at bottom, cannot be explained on such evidence as we have. The effort is worth it only if the sole alternative is to buy into the Crown's version of events which shares with the plant hypothesis an absolute impossibility of proof one way or the other but exceeds it in implausibility.

While the dresser drawer could be considered as a repository for shotgun shells, however unlikely, even less likely was the garage workbench, at least in any long-term sense. That being so, Cook could not remember it as one. In any case, for either a stranger or Cook, the garage was subject to the same objection as the bedroom: both were dark. True, the garage light could have been switched on by the murderer heading for the workbench either on the off chance of finding shells there or with foreknowledge of their presence, but the time comes when a halt has to be called to 'what ifs' and 'might haves' in favor of allowing common sense to have a run at it. When all the objections are weighed, the arguments analyzed, the possibilities mooted, common sense - the writer's version of it - indicates the shotgun shells did not come in the first instance from either the dresser drawer or the garage workbench.

Leaving the basement as a possible source of the shells for someone who knew the house, its probable contents and its occupants, particularly Gurney since Gurney owned a shotgun and the shells to go with it. But the basement can be ruled out. Gurney, on June 17, had moved to Edmonton to take up new employment, and either on that day or on June

22 when he returned to Stettler and "called in to see [the Cooks]", he removed his shells from the basement and took them with him to Edmonton. He was not asked on which of the two days it was nor why he took only his shells, leaving behind his guns, tape recorder, tapes, magazines, books and clothing. He volunteered the information that there was no room in the cab of his truck for the clothing at least which he left behind for the time being "with the understanding of the people who owned the place." It will be remembered that the people who owned the place were Ray and Daisy Cook.

***

The cluttered condition of Ray Cook's garage suggests that shop management was not his forte. A place for everything and something else in it seems to have been his guiding precept. Nevertheless, was he the kind of man who would throw shotgun shells in plain sight on a garage workbench or, for that matter in a dresser drawer? Jim Hoskins didn't think so when I recounted to him Anderson's argument that the seven shells came from the drawer: "Sounds like bullshit to me as far as I'm concerned. He was pretty careful with the kids and wouldn't leave shells lying around, I'm damn sure of that. If I ain't mistaken, they were sitting on a goddamned shelf down by the old Long Tom - that's what he called it." In other (less colorful) words, both locations were devoid of shotgun shells prior to the murders in Hoskins' view which seems a reasonable one. For kids, a shotgun shell lying in the open or in a drawer easy of access is a chance to hit it with a hammer to see what happens. After the murders, for someone moving back and forth between the bedroom and the garage too often to make for peace of mind, both locations invited divestiture of a lethally incriminating surplus.

Hoskins was one of two men with any first-hand knowledge of shotgun shells in the house. The other of course was Gurney whose knowledge extended only as far as his own shells and is included here only to complete the record:

"Incidentally, for your shotgun, what kind of shells did you use as a rule?"

"Canucks I believe."

"Did you ever use Imperial or Olympic?"

"No."

"Neither of those two?"

"No."

"And you had none in your possession?"

"No."

"Is there any possibility that you could have left any shotgun shells lying loose in the garage?"

"Not to my knowledge."

There was nothing more anyone could say about shotgun shells, and we leave them wondering whether *any* of them belonged anywhere in the house. If they did, it is easiest to assume they were Ray Cook's wherever he might have kept them. Gurney we have ruled out since his shells had long since left the house for Edmonton, although there is an outside possibility that he didn't take them all. To his knowledge, he said, he hadn't left any in the garage. He would know whether he'd *ever* kept shells in the garage, but he was not asked if he had, and his answer as it stands leaves him open to the supposition that he had on occasion, but the shells spotted by Roach were not his unless he'd merely forgotten he'd left them there. But it seems unlikely since the garage shells were Olympics and Imperials and he used Canucks. Or believed he did, which can be taken to amount to the same thing.

But *were* the 15 shotgun shells (or 17 depending on the number on the garage bench), all of them new in appearance, Ray Cook's? He wasn't the kind of man to leave shells lying around because of the kids, Jim Hoskins was damn sure of that. But was he the kind of man to have them around at all, safely stored or otherwise? Why lay in a supply of new shells when he held the joys of hunting in such light regard that he couldn't be bothered to get out of the car long enough to stalk and dispatch the odd duck? Why lay in a supply of new shells when, as far as we know, at the time of his death he no longer owned a shotgun? No serious argument can be made for his ownership of the Demon, and his old Long Tom had evidently long since disappeared.

But if they weren't Ray Cook's, nor Gurney's, that meant the murderer came to the house carrying as many as 17 shells. Anderson thought that if the murderer came carrying the gun, he didn't have any shells with him "because the prosecution indicates that there were two expended Olympic shell cases in the breech." He may have had it backwards. The murderer may have arrived staggering under a load of so many shotgun shells that he couldn't manage a shotgun, hoping against hope he'd find one when he got there. Rather than coming with a gun hoping he'd find shells of the right gauge, he came with shells hoping he'd find a gun. Could such a man even *get* a day job, much less hold one?

CHAPTER 18

THE SMALL BOX, BLACK AND WHITE

Humor has its place in most places, although murder trials, particularly those that were once held in the long shadow cast by the waiting gallows, don't immediately spring to mind as one of them. Mr Justice Harold W. Riley however couldn't resist the odd *mot*, and he allowed himself a couple in the second *Cook* trial. They would have been warmly received by an appreciative audience: lawyers, knowing which side their bread is buttered on, know which side of a judge rewards buttering. But Riley's light-hearted sallies cannot have much warmed the man in the prisoner's box. Bad as Greschuk had been, in Cook's view, Riley was proving even worse if that was possible, and once again Cook was losing the fight to avoid being put to death. He may have failed not only to get the joke, but to see that there was occasion for any.

Nor would Cook have appreciated the risible quality of the earnest testimony of Constable George Marshall Sproule. Sproule was a man who, to avoid calling a spade a spade, brought the art of circumspection to a new level of development. He was the RCMP's fingerprint man, the photographer, the measurer and drawer of crime scenes, and while it may be unfair to think so, the pages of the transcripts seem to reveal also a man devoid of humor, a bit of a martinet, a man who prided himself on self-control and mastery of his evidence, always with - and sometimes a step ahead of - the questioning. The questioners themselves he seems to have suffered none-too-gladly, occasionally usurping their function in what is perhaps too easily seen as an exasperated expectation, born of experience, that lawyers would manage to miss the obvious.

Thus he was given to deciding, and informing the court, what was significant about a particular piece of evidence - normally a matter for lawyers to argue and judges and juries to decide. From time to time in the preliminary inquiry he asked to have various items of evidence marked as exhibits - normally the exclusive function of the lawyer who produces them to the witness, and in whose case they are intended as proof of something or other. He tried to continue the practice in the first trial until caught up by Mr Justice Greschuk, who ran a tighter ship than had Magistrate Graves. Little nonplused, Sproule was throughout the *Cook* trials a confident man on top of a case in which one might have thought he saw himself as having a proprietary interest.

No serologist, Sproule was nevertheless the 'blood' man in the sense that he gave the bulk of the testimony establishing where in the house blood (and brain matter and shards of bone and gristle) had been found. But he was a curious amalgam of a man who rushed in where lawyers had not yet had a chance to tread, and a man who would not have said "blood" had he had a mouthful of it - since, in Sproule's mind, only a serologist was qualified to identify what everyone else would have dismissed as blood without a second thought. To him it was at most a red substance, occasionally a "blood-like" one, which happened to have been found in twenty-three distinct locations in the house; let others make the connection between it and one of the vital bodily fluids of the battered and shattered bodies in the greasepit should they be able to do so.

But nor was the substance anything as straightforward as red. Sproule's evidence became a kaleidoscope of near-colors such that (compiling from the three transcripts) reddish-brown made 36 appearances, reddish 41, brownish-red 9, and dark-reddish's 1 appearance was balanced by bright-reddish's like number. Forgetting himself, Sproule identified dried blood three times as brown before reverting to brownish. His red-pencil markings on certain exhibits were most often red, but even they sought refuge in the safety of reddish on 2 occasions.

It went on. Grease was "grease-like" or "greasy-like," and a homely piece of blood-spattered wallpaper was a "paper-like material." Daisy's shoes were "greyish in color," the suit jacket "bluish" and Ray's body "had turned greenish and bluish." The station wagon, which in the preliminary inquiry was "reddish and white," had, as Sproule gained confidence, become "rust and cream" by the second trial - which, at that, was to be preferred to rustish and creamish. His testimony led to some delightful exchanges:

MACDONALD: "You say 'reddish.' Do you really mean red?"

SPROULE: "It was a dull red."

MACDONALD: "Would that be brownish?"

SPROULE: "Reddish-brown."

***

For Sproule, the preliminary inquiry was to prove reminiscent of what happened to whoever it was who went down to the woods today: he was in for a big surprise. The situation developed as if tailor-made to call out the essential Sproule. He had been one of the primary investigators in the Cook house, and as such was able to describe to the court their moving from room to room and what they found in each. In direct examination he had finished giving his evidence of the finding of the suit jacket under the mattress, and the prosecutor had moved on to begin questioning him on the finding of the shells in the jacket pockets when Magistrate Graves, who was presiding, interrupted to ask Sproule to clear up a minor point. While the colloquy between Sproule and Graves was going on, Main got up from his place and went to the exhibit table to have a closer look at the suit jacket, which he was seeing for the first time. He idly pulled something from a pocket, and the following exchange then took place:

THE COURT [to Sproule]: "You spoke of the lower front of Exhibit 17...."

MR MAIN: "Is that part of the exhibit?"

CST. SPROULE: "I have no knowledge of that."

THE COURT: "Do you know anything about that?"

CST. SPROULE: "I do not recall those two items."

THE COURT: "This small box, black and white?"

CST. SPROULE: "That can be explained by other members sir."

THE COURT: "It can be explained by another witness. It was found in the pocket of Exhibit 17 [the jacket]."

THE CROWN: "Sir, my learned friend has discovered a small box in the pocket of Exhibit 17. Perhaps I should say for clarification that it does not form part of Exhibit 17."

At first the exchange is confusing as to how many articles Main had taken from the pocket, since before anything was identified there were references in the singular ("Is that part of the exhibit?" "I have no knowledge of that"), and then in the plural ("I do not recall these two items"), and then, in the first identification of anything, a reversion to the singular ("This small box, black and white?" and "That can be explained by other members"). So it appears that while there was more than one article, among them was a small box. There was: a circular white cardboard box, two inches in diameter and eleven-sixteenths of an inch deep, divided into two equal halves: a bottom section and a lid. Around the circumference of each half was a strip of shiny black, ribbon-like material. Although it did not have a proprietary medicine label, it could have been a box for non-prescription pills such as once cured the range of ailments from sluggish kidneys to tired blood, and it was referred to most often in testimony as a pillbox. Whatever its initial use, it was the sort of small box that would be given an extended life in a sewing basket as a receptacle for buttons, say, or in a dresser drawer for cuff links and the like.

Graves asked Sproule if he knew "anything of that," and Sproule replied that he did not recall what were now "these two items" although the magistrate persisted in the next question in the singular: "This small box, black and white?". Confusion is heightened momentarily when it is learned that there were in fact three items in the pocket: the pillbox, and in it a half-inch flat washer (identical in circumference to a quarter and suitable for plugging the jukeboxes of the era) and a GM ignition key.

On the face of it, it appears Main had removed - or thought he had removed - a single item: a closed pillbox. If so, then his reference in the singular is explained, as are the magistrate's and the first of Sproule's. But if so, someone, probably Sproule, then opened the box and discovered the key and washer (which the magistrate had not yet seen when he questioned Sproule about "this small box") and Sproule's "I do not recall these two items" reflects his opening the box and making the additional find. His inability to recall the key and washer was not surprising since they were initially in a closed box of which he had "no knowledge," which can be taken to mean he had never seen it before.

Main concluded the exchange by observing, "For the record, [the pillbox] contains what appears to be an automobile key and a steel washer." Sproule agreed, "Yes", and then, as if there were still a question in the air from a few minutes earlier when he had been interrupted by Graves - there wasn't - and as if anxious to get the box behind him and the proceedings back on track, he forged ahead without pause: "Two additional 12 gauge shotgun shells were found in a dish." The magistrate however was not quite as ready as Sproule to move on: "Excuse me one moment. Would you remove that box from Exhibit 17 and leave it here? It is not part of 17 and its contents. Hand it to the prosecutor please." It is too much to think that Graves' "leave it here" suggests that an enterprising Sproule was about to pocket the small box and spirit it away, although it will be seen that it would not have been surprising had he thought there was some reason to do so.

The inventory of the right pocket of Bob Cook's penitentiary-made suit was now as complete as it would ever get: three 12-gauge shotgun shells and a closed pillbox containing, somewhat incongruously, a washer and a key. None of this - Main's discovery of the pillbox, Sproule's disclaimer of any knowledge of it, Graves' still dealing with the box when Sproule was already dealing with its contents, Sproule's evident surprise on encountering the key and washer - would have been of any overriding importance but for some questions raised by later evidence. The momentary confusion of the opening exchange was supplanted by an abiding confusion surrounding the pillbox and its discovery, which lasted through the two trials. Nothing was made of the box (or the washer) during the first trial, and by the end of the second both had long since been forgotten. Their significance, if any, was denied recognition from the outset. The key was accorded some in the first trial, less in the second, trailing off to none in Anderson's closing argument and Riley's charge to the jury - two of the people who were paid to ask the questions raised by the key but who did not. Much less did they offer even exploratory answers.

***

After Sproule found the suit jacket under the mattress and photographed it, it had then been sent to Regina for forensic examination. It was returned to Stettler for the preliminary inquiry. When Main pulled the box from the pocket, the jacket had been in police possession for 58 days. For the first two or three of them, it had been in the closely guarded possession of investigators so meticulous that they had picked up shotgun pellets from the bedroom floor with tweezers and put them in small envelopes, which they carefully initialed before adding them to the growing mound of evidence. Yet Sproule, for one, had missed finding in the right pocket - from which he had extracted three shotgun shells - a small box roughly equal in volume to one of those shells. It will be recalled that Sproule had not attached any significance to the basement guns, which, as he saw it, entitled him to more or less ignore them. We cannot know what significance, if any, he might have attached to the pillbox and its contents had he gone deeper into the pocket and found them.

Sproule's self-possession in what might be thought to have been an unnerving turn of events was wholly in character; without missing a beat he averred that the pillbox could be "explained by other members" - despite his having "no knowledge of [it]," including, presumably, knowledge of whether other members had any knowledge of it. A reprieve came in the form of the noon-hour adjournment. During the adjournment, at Main's suggestion, the police took the key to the Cook residence, where they found that it fit the ignition of the refurbished half-ton truck now locked in the garage. On Sunday, June 28, the police had photographed the truck where it was parked on the north side of the house. Sometime before the preliminary inquiry, they had pushed it into the garage, unaware that they had in their possession the means of starting it.

Main may have thought the pillbox was his discovery, but it turned out over the noon-hour that the pillbox was old hat to the RCMP. There *was* a member who could explain it, just as Sproule had said there was. The police had known about it all along, but hadn't seen it as important enough to take it out of the pocket long enough to consider what, if anything, its contents might mean. It turned out that it was Corporal Robert D. Novikoff who had made the discovery. Except it also turned out that Novikoff had discovered not Main's box (which Sproule had said specifically could be explained by other members, and he said this before it was opened and its contents revealed), but the key and washer only.

Novikoff was the first Crown witness called after lunch:

"When I previously examined the blue suit . . . I did notice in one of the bottom pockets of the jacket a key and a washer similar to what I am

308

holding in my hand now. The articles were not removed from [the jacket] at any time by myself, and when the suit jacket was handed over to the Laboratory staff at Regina, the key and the washer were still present in the pocket. That was the only examination I made up to that time of this article."

"Article" and "articles" seem to have been interchangeable terms in that more easy-going time, and he probably meant to say he'd removed the articles from the jacket once, long enough to identify them before reinserting them in the pocket. What is of more interest here is the absence of any mention of the pillbox which, when finding the key and washer, Novikoff had not noticed - leaving one to wonder how the box had acquired the contents it had when Main removed it from the pocket. But let that go; it may be that someone in the Crime Detection Laboratory, noticing not only the key and washer, as had Novikoff, but the box as well, decided to pop the two smaller items into the box. It is, admittedly, to stretch for an explanation, but how else to account for the key and washer being loose in the jacket when it left Novikoff for Regina, but being concealed in a closed box when Main, with his awkward find, interrupted what until then had been Sproule's smooth progression through his evidence?

Continuing his direct examination, Scotty Macdonald asked Novikoff about "other investigations" concerning the pocket's contents. He replied that he, along with other police officers, had taken "this pillbox with the two articles" to the Cook residence, vaguely suggesting he was then seeing the box for the first time. He later confirmed this indirectly. In direct examination at the second trial, Novikoff told Anderson of having observed only the key and washer on Sunday, June 28. But, he said, "at a later date I did observe this pillbox containing the key and washer." The later date was necessarily the day during the preliminary inquiry when he was handed all three items so that he could test the key in the truck's ignition. Given that the key and washer were in the box when Main lifted it from the pocket (and dismissing as fanciful the possibility that they were placed there in Regina), two possibilities suggest themselves: either Novikoff was mistaken in thinking he had found only the key and washer on Sunday, June 28 (and was mistaken when he said he'd seen the pillbox for the first time "at a later date"), or he was mistaken in thinking he had found anything at all. No third possibility is readily apparent.

At the preliminary inquiry and in direct examination at the first trial, Main had heard Novikoff tell the Crown that he had found the key and washer only. But when, in trial, Main rose to cross-examine Novikoff, a clumsily-worded question suggests he had not taken in what he had heard:

"Now you produced and put in evidence . . . a General Motors ignition switch key and steel washer I believe, is that not so, in a little box somewhere . . . that you found in one of the side pockets of the jacket?"

"I did."

The ellipses are the reporter's. The question cannot be read as Main's asking Novikoff whether he had found the key and washer only, which now happened to be "in a little box somewhere" since just a few minutes before, in the direct examination of Novikoff, the box (together with its contents) had been marked as an exhibit. That is, without protest by Main (or by Novikoff for that matter), Novikoff had been credited with finding not only the key and washer, but also the pillbox containing them - when he had just finished confirming (and was to confirm at the second trial) what he had said at the preliminary inquiry he had found: a key; a washer.

If Main's question was hopeless, Novikoff's answer to a question put by Main a short time later invites despair: "I believe when I saw the pillbox containing the two articles, it was separated from the jacket when I was making the check at the Cook residence." That seems to mean, if it means anything, that the pillbox had made the trip with Novikoff to check out the ignition key, but the jacket hadn't - not that he was quite sure (he "believed"), and not that anyone had suggested that it might have. The answer was in response to Main's asking him whether he had found the pillbox in the same pocket as Main had found it at the preliminary inquiry, but Main seemed satisfied with the answer.

By the time of the second trial, Sproule (who had not been asked at the first trial to say anything about the discovery, consistent with his having no knowledge of the box and no recollection of its contents) had recovered the power of recall which had earlier deserted him. He now said that he was present with Van Blarcom at the time of the discovery of the key and washer [1]. Sproule did not say that Novikoff too was present - a curious omission - but by reading between the lines it can be said the omission was probably deliberate because of Sproule's imperfect understanding of the hearsay evidence rule; he did not want to

---

[1] *Van Blarcom said he didn't know who had found them.*

310

say he'd seen Novikoff find them. But he too said nothing of the pillbox, and from Novikoff at the preliminary inquiry and the first trial, through Sproule at the second, it was as if Main had lifted from the pocket a figment of an overactive imagination. The pillbox, which was in the courtroom, was now a non-item with none of the jurors any the wiser as to what it was all about. They were not alone.

If consternation had reigned in the ranks of the RCMP at the long-ago preliminary inquiry when Main, a perplexed Little Jack Horner, had stuck his hand in the pocket and pulled out what might be thought to have been a veritable plum of evidence - the murdered man's key in his murderer's suit - it had long since been replaced with casual indifference to consistency, much less to the probable truth of the matter: that the find was Main's in the first instance, and the police had seen none of the three items before the preliminary inquiry and had had to scramble frantically to stonewall that embarrassing fact.

***

When the time came in the second trial to put a prosecutorial spin on Novikoff's evidence of his finding the key and the washer, Anderson backed off entirely - as he had in the first trial. He had no idea why the key was in the pocket; he could conjecture nothing and accordingly said nothing - always a provident course. For their part, the defense lawyers didn't have much more, but at least they had someone to give it voice. They had Cook:

"Dad and I went out [from the house] by ourselves, just him and I, out to the car, and I remember before I left I still had the keys for the station wagon in my pocket, since like leaving the hotel, and he asked me for the keys back to get the key for the half-ton truck out of the key case. So I handed him the key case and he took that key out of it. He said at the time that he would need the half-ton truck to pick up his tools from this Modern Machine Shop where he was working."

It was plausible enough except for two things: first, Ray planned an absence of only a few days; only if he found a suitable garage business in BC would he return to Stettler and resign from Modern Machine. At that point he would pick up his tools. Second, the clothes Cook had worn home from the hotel where he and Ray had had a beer were not the clothes he was wearing when he took his leave from his father. The keys cannot have "still" been in his pocket, and to believe Cook here is to believe that when he changed out of the blue suit and gave it to his father, he took the key case from it and transferred it to the clothes he changed into.

He went on to say that when his father had extracted the truck key from the case, he didn't happen to notice what Ray had done with it. Main picked up on this in his address to the jury:

"I asked him, 'What did your father do with the key to the half-ton truck which he took off the keytainer?' and the prisoner said, 'I don't know; I didn't notice.' He could just as easily have said, 'I saw him put it in the side pocket of the [blue suit], but he didn't say that. He said, 'I didn't notice what he did with it.'

"I put it to you gentlemen of the jury that it is a reasonable inference to draw that this General Motors ignition key is the key to Ray Cook's half-ton Chevrolet truck parked beside his house, and that it is the key which Ray Cook, the prisoner's father, removed from the keytainer at the time the prisoner and his father parted company at about 10:30 or 10:35 on Thursday night. It is also within your province to draw the inference that Mr Cook placed the key in this pillbox and placed it in his pocket because, as reasonable men, as ordinary everyday people, it is within your province to realize and to know that keys such as this, which are placed loose in a side jacket pocket, are easily lost and easily work their way into the lining."

Main was reaching; it was not a strong performance. Apart from the questionable psychology of referring to Cook as "the prisoner" - he had a propensity throughout to do so - and to the jurors as "ordinary everyday people" - which they were, but who wants to be reminded that they are rather undistinguished members of the common herd? - and apart from the gaffe of inviting them to infer a fact already proved - that the key was the key to the truck, leaving it open to the jurors to find that the key had nothing to do with the truck, thus fatally weakening Cook's account of his father's having asked him for it - it made the case. The 'lost in the lining' detail added nothing except to show that Main was straining. The suit was three days old and the lining would hardly have been frayed to the extent that a key could have worked its way through it. It would have been enough to make the not unreasonable suggestion that Ray Cook, preparing for bed by removing the blue suit, spotted the pillbox in the dresser drawer, say, and decided to use it as a temporary case for the key to the truck he would need in the morning to attend to a thousand and one details in preparation for the trip to BC.

312

The washer? The jurors' guess was as good as Main's, and guess was all anyone could do. Think the worst of Cook if they would, but their picture of him wasn't darkened appreciably by the fact that a washer, of all prosaic things, ended up in the infernal pillbox. For a mechanic to have pocketed a flat washer was, if anything, more consistent with the reasoning of common-as-dirt, everyday folk such as the gentlemen of the jury than was the assumption that Cook, for no reason, removed an ignition key, which he retained, from a key case, which he also retained.

***

At the second trial, Anderson tried unsuccessfully to get Cook to admit that one of his earlier answers could be taken to mean that he had blundered into an admission that he was still wearing the blue suit when he was standing by the station wagon talking to his father. Anderson never attempted to explain why, if that were true, Cook would remove the truck's ignition key from the key case (on which was the key for the station wagon he was about to drive to Edmonton), and put it, together with the washer, in a pillbox in the suit's jacket. Thin as it was, there was an explanation for Ray Cook's having pocketed the box and the washer to go with Cook's account of the key. There was none for Cook's having done so (and some, which we have examined, for his not having done so, so far at least as the key is concerned) - unless one wished to ascribe it to a spur-of-the-moment whim, which was even thinner. In the *Cook* trials, when the evidence called for a difficult explanation from the Crown, there seems to have been a standing rule to ignore the necessity and the jurors would follow suit.

In spite of his well-deserved reputation for a terrier-like worrying of all the minutiæ of evidence, Mr Justice Greschuk too chose to ignore at least the pillbox and the washer (he did not mention them in his charge to the jury), although he fastened on the key:

"In the right lower pocket of one of the pockets *[sic]*, in addition to the five live shells, there was a key which fitted the half-ton truck. How did this key get there? Why would the pocket contain a key to fit the half-ton truck standing near the Cook residence? Do you accept the explanation given by the accused that his father took the key off the key ring and must have put it in that suit as he was wearing it? Would an unknown killer have bothered with this key?"

There were two minor inaccuracies in Greschuk's appreciation of the evidence. There were three shells in the pocket in which the key was found, not five; and the evidence was that Ray Cook carried a key case rather than a key ring. The difference is negligible enough, but one might as well get it right considering the context. Further, he can be read as suggesting the truck was still standing on the north side of the house when the key was tested rather than in the garage, but that is even more minor. Trifling errors and trifling ambiguity to be sure, but surprising from a man who was thought to prefer death to being found in error by a court of appeal.

Far more important from Main's point of view was yet another buffeting of Main's 'stranger' theory, as implicit in Greschuk's final question. Would an unknown killer have bothered with the key? The jurors were being offered a choice between two men - Cook and some will-o'-the-wisp stranger - neither of whom had any reason for removing the truck key from the key case. Yet Greschuk, rightly dismissing the stranger as a candidate for removing the key, left Cook in the running but did not suggest a reason for Cook's having done so. But someone removed the key from Ray Cook's key case and put it in what was - or had been - Bob Cook's blue suit, and the only explanation that stands up to scrutiny is Cook's. Suppose however for the sake of argument that Cook killed his father. He now had the key case containing the keys to two vehicles, either of which he could drive away. He chose the station wagon, but not before removing and pocketing the truck key, just before removing the suit. It falls just short of making any sense.

To absolve Cook however is not to finger a stranger. If an "unknown killer" had bothered, as Greschuk put it, with the truck key, it was to remove it from the key case and pocket it in the blue suit (donned for the purpose of transporting the bodies) before handing the key case to Cook who, a model of patience while his family was being slaughtered, was standing around somewhere waiting to drive off in the station wagon. To answer Greschuk's self-answering question: no, an unknown killer wouldn't have bothered with the key. If it is conceded that nor would Cook, one is brought up hard against Ray Cook, against Cook's account, and against the possibility of Cook's innocence - which wasn't in the forefront of Greschuk's analysis.

Nor was it in Mr Justice Riley's. The pillbox was in his courtroom, but since no one was asked who found it - like Everest it was just there - or even that it had been found in a place in some manner relevant to the issues in *Regina v. Cook*, it was not in evidence against Cook. Anderson had chosen to leave the pillbox out of his second-trial case - not surprisingly given the rocky road it had travelled through the preliminary inquiry and the first trial (not that Dunne was aware of it; had he been, he would have insisted that it be marked as an exhibit - even if that meant calling Main as a witness - and proceeded to hang the RCMP out to dry), and it joined the key and washer in judicial oblivion; neither the key nor the washer rated a mention in Riley's business-like charge. He had his answer in the blue suit, and who cared that someone - who cared who? - had put in one of its pockets to be found there by someone - who cared who? - a small box, black and white, with some junk in it - who cared what? - all of it beneath Riley's magisterial notice.

The time has come," the Walrus
said, to talk of many things;

Of shoes...."

Through the Looking Glass

CHAPTER 19

THE SCRAPINGS; THE SHEETS; THE SHOES; THE SHORTS

On a couple of occasions in the investigation of the Cook murders things had a tendency to go backwards just as they did in the world discovered by Alice behind the looking glass. We have looked at one of them: at some point between the two trials Sunday became Saturday as the day Cook was ordered to remove his clothing, and coincidentally the purpose of his being ordered to remove it - to permit a physical examination of Cook by Dr Donald MacKay - could be seen as an instance of the cart arriving ahead of the horse. An examination of that magnitude is normally reserved for murder investigations, where ostensibly all the RCMP had at the time was false pretenses. "First find murder and *then* strip the suspect" the training manual probably reads.

Neither Main nor Dunne chose to examine Roach as to the purpose of the strip-search. Main contented himself with questioning Cook, revealing in his first question a shaky grasp of the sequence of events:

"Cook, I understand something occurred at the Royal Canadian Mounted Police barracks *[sic]* at Stettler following your arrest. I am not just sure of the time, whether it was Saturday afternoon or evening or the following Sunday. Would you tell us about what it was?"

"They come down and took all my clothes away and the doctor come in and he took fingernail - like scrapings from underneath my fingernails and he examined me all over, like arms and legs and all."

"I see, and what was your condition at the time of the examination so far as clothing was concerned?"

"I didn't have any on."

Perplexity might best have described Cook's reaction to this apparent overkill, and he cannot have failed to wonder whether there wasn't much more in the wind than having to answer for - and waiting for his father to return from BC to answer for - some trivial untruths told at Hood Motors. In addition to being aroused before breakfast and told to hand over his clothes and to hold out his hands while a doctor carefully cleaned his fingernails, there were now snatches of conversation about a blue suit wafting down to the lockup. He may have been aware of the arrival of four new RCMP officers - a staff sergeant, two corporals and a constable - so that there were now at least eight on the scene urgently coming and going. There was an extra guard detailed around noon to watch him. Put them all together they didn't spell mother.

***

The lot of forensic scientists is not enviable in terms of the unpleasant substances they work with: blood, semen, hair, the contents of distended stomachs, and fingernail scrapings as they were called in the *Cook* trials, although on occasion Main called them 'parings' and Dunne, in occasionally calling them 'clippings', casually equated the nails themselves with the materials mined from beneath them. The scrapings obtained by MacKay were sent to Regina for analysis by the serologist Peggy van der Stoel who testified at both trials. In the first she told Main: "When clothes have been washed, especially in the case of cloth, we have to cut out a piece to extract [blood]. If the cloth has been washed the extract will be very weak and it is very hard to find it that way. It isn't like scrapings. Just a bit, a small amount of scrapings will give you a positive test."

Dunne asked her whether she'd received any "fingernail clippings." She corrected him, replying she had received a field envelope containing scrapings:

"Did you test those?"

"Yes sir, they were tested but there was no blood found in them."

"No blood in the fingernail scrapings?"

"No sir."

"Thank you kindly."

What Dunne made up in courtesy he'd previously lost in the missed opportunity to get from van der Stoel what Main got, although in crude form: that only a small amount (and in fact a minute amount) of scrapings is all that is required to permit detection of microscopic amounts of blood in them. For all the second-trial jurors knew when van der Stoel stepped down, blood was detectable only if present in quantity roughly equivalent to that dripping from the hands of an Aztec priest as he ripped the heart from a sacrificial virgin.

If Cook murdered his family, it is probable to a point just short of certainty that in the absence of gloves (none were found) he could not have avoided getting blood under his fingernails. He would have bloodied his hands at one or both of two times depending on whether he spent time only immediately after the murders in his attempts to conceal the crime, or continued them when he returned to the house on Saturday evening. In either or both cases he cleaned his nails so thoroughly that van der Stoel's sophisticated testing procedure failed to detect blood.

However, it will be seen that if he cleaned them just before leaving the house on Saturday evening, then sometime between that cleaning and MacKay taking scrapings on the following morning, his nails had to have acquired a new deposit of grime (otherwise MacKay would not have found scrapings to take), has to have acquired it, that is, in the act of driving the Impala a couple of blocks and during the night spent in the cells. It seems unlikely; the steering wheel of a new car is not a notorious source of grunge, and RCMP cells, while probably not models of surgical cleanliness, are nevertheless not a setting in which one would dirty one's hands by engaging in busy activity.

Which is to say he did not clean his nails on Saturday, eliminating

Saturday as the day he carried the bodies to the greasepit and wrung out soggy and bloodstained rags used to wipe down furniture and wallpaper and wipe up floors. The material obtained by MacKay was the material present under his fingernails prior to his arriving at the house on Saturday. But to eliminate Saturday evening as the time when Cook concluded the concealment efforts started on Friday morning, is to concede he was telling the truth about what he was *doing* in the house on Saturday. It is not to concede he was telling the truth about what he saw or didn't see, but it is to take one small step in that direction.

But to concede him Saturday, or part of it, is not to say he was telling the truth about not being in the house in the early hours of Friday, immediately after the murders, but that was another problem about which the scrapings said nothing since he had ample time to clean his nails to the extent necessary to command negative results from the van der Stoel tests.

Her evidence died having caused scarcely a ripple. Main made his closing argument strenuously enough - "I can assure you gentlemen of the jury that if any blood had been found from the scrapings under the accused's fingernails, evidence would have been adduced of it before you during the last few days" - but he did not stress (nor had he stressed it in cross-examination) - the critical core of van der Stoel's evidence: a trace amount of blood was all it took.

Dunne did, but to little effect. He devoted perhaps ten seconds of his closing argument to the van der Stoel evidence which held such promise for the defense. In Dunne's view, the results of her tests permitted the sweeping conclusion of Cook's innocence rather than being taken for what they were: a means of lending credibility only to his account of Saturday evening. Dunne asked too much of the serologist's evidence:

"You will also recall that his person was examined by a doctor on Sunday, June 28th I believe. It was examined for bloodstains, and that scrapings or clippings were taken from his fingernails. These were sent to the serologist in Regina, Miss Peggy van der Stoel. Absolutely no traces of blood whatsoever" and that, in Dunne's view, was that; no elaboration was necessary.

Which was to leave the jury with the latitude to infer that Cook had gotten rid of all traces, not that he had not picked up any - at least on Saturday. Neither Main nor Dunne seemed capable of taking hard evidence as a datum point - here the negative blood test - and reasoning back from it to an inescapable conclusion. In certain matters - the scrapings evidence is a case in point - Anderson was fighting paper tigers, and in both trials he countered the best efforts of the defense by ignoring both them and the evidence. He never mentioned van der Stoel or fingernails scrapings in his closing arguments, and nor did Riley for whom neither van der Stoel or her evidence existed. For his part, Greschuk let it go at repeating Main's argument, reminding the jurors it was Main's and not his. He did not attempt to expand on it by voicing any of the questions raised here.

***

Except for the bed in the main bedroom on which a folded blanket was found, and Gurney's bed which was made up, the beds in the house had been completely stripped and the bedclothes either used as a makeshift winding-sheet for Ray's body, or thrown loose in the greasepit. There was no evidence of bedclothes being found elsewhere in the house. The lawyers on both sides ignored them, but in Mr Justice Greschuk's mind the bedclothes assumed a significance peculiar to him alone. To him, the murderer stripped the beds to use the bedclothes not to transport bodies nor to add to the detritus in the greasepit in the concealment effort, but to create the spurious appearance of the family having left on vacation. In Greschuk's view, one of the last things a housewife does to leave a house in a condition she can live with while she is away from it is to strip the beds to their bare mattresses, fold the bedclothes and put them away.

It seems an unusual practice, but it may be that some few housewives do - something on a checklist to be done much like putting down, if not the cat, then food and water for it before locking the door behind her. Nevertheless a killer in Greschuk's view of him would reason as Greschuk did: when the police arrived on the scene they would be thrown off the trail - they would be duped into thinking there *was* no trail - by what the naked beds made obvious: no problem here; the folks have all left for a few days. Greschuk did not say it, but only Cook had a reason for fostering the appearance of the folks having left for a few days. In the act of stripping the beds his busy mind was already working out the parameters of the BC story.

For Greschuk it became an *ideé fixé* . He returned to the subject of

321

bedclothes eight times in his charge to the jury, three excerpts from which will serve to illustrate his singular insight into the minds of murderers familiar with the ways of families about to depart on vacations. In the third of them he will be seen to have introduced an untenable connection between the bedclothes and the station wagon:

"Why were the suitcases placed in the trunk of the Impala convertible? Have they any connection with the bedclothing which had been removed from the beds to give the impression that the Cooks had left their home?"

"Are you satisfied or are you willing to infer from the established facts that at the time of the killing it was the accused who washed the walls and removed the bedding clothes so that the house took on the appearance that the Cook family had left on a trip?"

"You will recall that when the police entered the house, the bedrooms were stripped of bedclothing which gave the appearance that the Cooks had left the house. *Did Mr and Mrs Cook place these articles of clothing in the station wagon or were they placed in the station wagon by the accused in order to give the appearance that the Cooks had left the residence?*" [emphasis added]

There were no bedclothes found in the station wagon and no evidence that any had ever been in the station wagon beyond some disputed evidence that a package of sheets, still in its manufacturer's cellophane wrapper, was in it at one point[1]. To say there were was an invitation to convict since if the jurors retired believing Greschuk, they had no choice but to believe Cook was in the house immediately after the murders, there being no other time he could have stripped the beds prior to leaving for Edmonton in the station wagon. To have gone along with Greschuk - as they did - the jurors were left with a murderer witless beyond the run of them: a man who took the time to strip five beds and carry the sheets and blankets to the station wagon while leaving behind his blue suit.

Mr Justice Greschuk in the third of the excerpts quoted above, said "these articles of clothing." While the juxtaposition makes clear he was referring to the bedclothes of the immediately preceding sentence, since clothes - wearing apparel - were found in the trunk of the Impala which had been transferred from the station wagon at Hood Motors, one wished to give the trial judge the benefit of the doubt and assume he had referred to those clothes. But that would have been to imply a practice no less curious than stripping the beds "to give the appearance of the

1 *See p. 361*

322

Cooks having left the residence": rifling the closets for the same reason.

***

In the southwest corner of the master bedroom a door opened into a walk through closet accessible from the back bedroom. The black oxfords issued to Cook by the Penitentiary Service were found on a shelf by Sproule who gave the following evidence at the preliminary inquiry:

"On the lower shelf of the south side of the closet there were *[sic]* a pair of black shoes and I have a pair of shoes which I removed from the closet. On examining the shoes I noticed they were covered with mud. The mud on the outside was dried and on digging the loose mud from the instep from the underside, I noted that the leather was still damp and the mud was damp also, and there were areas of brownish-red stains on the shoes. The pair of shoes were *[sic]* handed over to Corporal Novikoff and Corporal Novikoff took possession until handed back to me. He will give further evidence as to the possession of this exhibit."

"Did you find any stains on these shoes similar to bloodstains at all?"

"There were reddish-brown stains, dried, on the shoes. They were faint and you have to turn them to the light to observe them. There was a staining on it along the outside of the heel."

"You are pointing to the left shoe?"

"On the left shoe, along the outside, below the outside of the left ankle you might say."

"Above the heel?"

"Yes."

There was more of the same, but what it came down to was that Sproule had found a pair of shoes which appeared to be spattered with blood, although Sproule struggled manfully to avoid identifying the red-brown stains as what they clearly appeared to him to be: blood. Since the shoes were Cook's the defense could not ignore them, and Main asked Cook:

"Now, what shoes were you wearing when you arrived home with your father on this Thursday evening?"

"Those shoes there."

"What did you do with them?"

"Well, when I changed into the loafers, I just - the last I seen them they were just lying on the floor beside the chesterfield."

He hadn't gone as far as he did with the suit, he hadn't given the shoes to his father, and perhaps on that account was the more believable. They were left sitting on the livingroom floor, they became bloodstained and they ended up on a closet shelf. The first question, one supposed, was how to explain the bloodstains. But was that the first question? Was it blood? Sproule was no fool and he knew dried blood when he saw it which, on black leather, looks like what it is, and is in fact reddish-brown. But were it that simple, there would be no need for serologists.

Van der Stoel had had no difficulty in identifying blood as blood on the suit, the Ross shirt and the tie, but the shoes were a different proposition. Her preliminary inquiry testimony revealed the problem serology encounters when examining leather for bloodstains:

"Were you able to detect blood on the black oxfords?"

"No sir, I didn't find any."

"Is there anything unusual that arises when you try and detect blood on leather goods?"

"Well, it is sometimes hard to find on leather and it is especially hard to group blood on leather."

"Why is that?"

"Well, I think it is the leather that interferes, which make the factors which determine the blood group disappear."

She made a distinction which is important to bear in mind: it is sometimes difficult to find a substance on leather which appears to merit testing as blood[1]. once identified as blood it is difficult to group it. Yet the distinction was not made clear in either trial so that the jurors would have been entitled to think that the reason van der Stoel did not find blood on the oxfords was because blood on leather cannot be identified as blood. Greschuk himself failed to make the distinction: "Miss van der Stoel could not detect human blood on these shoes because it is difficult to group blood on leather since the leather makes the factors which determine blood group disappear. Is there any reasonable doubt in your minds that the spots or stains on the shoes were human blood?" Judges will sometimes question a witness. One wonders what van der Stoel's answer might have been had Greschuk put the same question to her.

***

Armchair lawyers are a breed not universally appreciated by their courtroom counterparts - a matter for regret since the practicing profession could profit from the incisiveness of their analysis and the brilliance of their insights. Let us digress for a moment to spin a Mittyan fantasy of one of them who has been handed the brief for Cook's defense as he considers how he will handle the problem of Cook's briefs - anything goes in a fantasy - which were taken from him by Sergeant Roach on Sunday morning - or was it Saturday night? the day in question whenever that was. We will permit him anything including the persona of Norman Birkett, KC, robed and bewigged, sitting at the counsel table with his respectful - worshipful almost - clerk with him. Birkett is silent, motionless, attentive and relaxed as the direct examination of the police witness proceeds. The press corps is poised, waiting for Birkett to take over from the plodding prosecutor, waiting for his next *mot*, wondering what subtle trap is even now being fine-tuned in the limitless reaches of the Birkett mind, what finishing touches being put on which petard which will blow the Crown's case at the moon.

As the examination of the police witness drones on, probably wide of the mark if Birkett knows his adversary, he gets up from his place and walks idly to the exhibit table, just as Giffard Main QC (the eras have merged) had done at the preliminary inquiry. But where Main (Main it was who

[1] *Cross-examination, first trial: "Well, I couldn't find any areas that I thought might be blood that I could test." Direct examination, second trial: "No sir, there was nothing that appeared to be blood."*

had handed the defense to Birkett: "Birkett, old man, I've done my best but this case calls for the very best....") had stuck his hand in the jacket pocket and pulled out a pillbox, Birkett leaves it undisturbed, examining it thoughtfully. Standing at the exhibit table examining each of the exhibits in turn, Birkett misses nothing of what the witness is saying for there is cerebral capacity here enough to parcel out adequate portions to half the criminal bar of England. This, remember, is a man who plays chess blindfolded and Bach chaconnes for unaccompanied violin on his battered old Gaurnerius, often simultaneously, by way of unwinding after a routine day of unbearable drama in Old Bailey.

Birkett picks up the black oxfords, looks at them briefly and sets them down. He lifts his head momentarily to catch what is playing on the witness's face - does it accord with what he is saying? - and turns back to the foul heap of bloody clothing. Something has occurred to him. He is pensive. He has looked at the blue suit pants a dozen times, but he picks them up and looks at them again with a quizzical and reflective eye, turning them this way and that. He notes anew that blood has soaked through in the fly area. He forces himself to pick up the Ross shirt and notes the blood on it, both inside and out for nothing escapes him. He sets it down, the faintest flicker of repugnance playing across his saturnine yet kindly, physiognomy. What he has seen of human depravity over the years has set there the lineaments not of anger but of sorrow. He turns and returns to his seat to think about what has just occurred to him, devoting one half his mind to the task. Another half is given over to absorbing the witness's testimony, yet a third to charting the forthcoming cross-examination.

He is ready. He hears the prosecutor say, "Thank you. Would you answer my learned friend please?" He rises and pauses for a few seconds, taking off his glasses and rubbing the bridge of his nose, thinking - or so it appears for he is not averse to playing for dramatic effect, but always within the bounds of impeccable taste. Birkett has learned the limits of courtroom decorum at the feet of masters, not from American television or, worse, the histrionics of the CBC which has learned them from American television. The press corps tenses; the jurors' pencils are poised expectantly over their slates. He puts on his glasses with a smooth, practiced motion, pauses again just long enough to sense the exact psychological moment when the witness's easy confidence has flip-flopped, stomach beginning to churn faintly. He lifts his head to the witness and, without so much as a step away from the counsel table, moves in softly and politely to set the witness up for the *coup de grâce* to be administered both to the witness and, in good time, to the Crown's case itself. "Sergeant Roach...," he says, ...

What Roach would have told him was that Cook's shorts, removed from him on Sunday morning, were not sent to Regina for examination since there was no blood on them even though blood has soaked through the fly area on the blue pants. "There were," Cook wrote, "stains found on the inside of the [Ross] shirt by Peggy van der Stoel. She also said they could detect infinite amounts of blood stains." He forgot to add she had also said blood was hard to detect on washed fabric, but his shorts had not been removed - much less washed - since he had put them on new at the penitentiary five days before Roach took them from him. Had there been even a finite amount of blood on them, it would have been sufficient to permit van der Stoel to perform her exotic tests.

At the second trial Dunne obtained from van der Stoel only that she had not received the shorts for testing, leaving himself in the position of not being able to explain to the jurors the significance of that unadorned fact since he had not obtained from Roach earlier that they were not sent to Regina because they were free of blood. He did not mention the shorts in his concluding argument. He did however point out to the jury that Cook's socks were not bloodstained, and asked, "Wouldn't you expect that, with the suit bloodstained as it is, particularly right down to the cuffs, that *[sic]* the socks would also be bloodstained had Cook been wearing them?" It was not a bad point and one worth getting right since, like the shorts, Cook wore the socks from Tuesday to Sunday.

CHAPTER 20

THE SUEDE CLEANERS, SONNY AND THE SCREWDRIVERS

By the beginning of October, 1959 Giffard Main was entitled to feel his preparations for the trial scheduled to begin on November 16 were well in hand. The preliminary inquiry transcript had been thoroughly studied and annotated and then taken to Fort Saskatchewan for Cook to read and add whatever notes he chose to make. The case had been discussed at length with Dave MacNaughton, with his partners Frank Dunne and George Forbes and, when his parliamentary duties permitted him to get back to Edmonton, with Terry Nugent, also a partner. Potential witnesses had been interviewed. He had traveled as often as necessary to the Fort to discuss this or that point with Cook and had made notes of his interviews in his large, open hand on unlined yellow bond. He had been assured by Cook - had insisted he be assured by Cook - that Cook had told him everything there was to tell.

He was an experienced criminal lawyer who knew what had to be done to prepare for trial. He had blocked out the time to do what remained to be done and would be ready. He looked forward to Cook's trial - who and where is the criminal defense lawyer who would not have? - although he sought the challenge, not the spotlight. There was nothing flamboyant about him; he is remembered by his colleagues as a soft-spoken man, quiet and confident, and these were the qualities he brought to his preparations for the *Cook* trial, continuing to run a busy practice as he did so. As he put the finishing touches on the defense applecart, it was upset without warning. He had a mild heart attack and he received a letter from Cook. The latter may have triggered the former.

The letter was dated October 5 and it read: "I have some information that I did not want to give out before on where and what I was doing on that thursday night. I think that you should know about this. I am sorry I didn't mention it before, but I didn't think it would be to important. Will explain when I see you. When you have the free time please come down to see me. Thank you, Robert Cook"

The information he had to give out - as if he was issuing a press release - was that he was in Edmonton on Friday morning (his "thursday night") at a time making it impossible for him to have been in Stettler at the time of the murders. He had, that is to say, an alibi. All things considered it was the sort of information a defense lawyer would prefer to have his client share with him, the sooner the better.

Procrastination in the legal profession is not unheard of, although not as common as it might appear to a litigant at a loss to understand why his case hasn't reached the courts after fourteen years. Still, apart from someone interviewing Cook about the contents of the letter, perhaps one of Main's partners, nothing was done for a month to begin to check out the information contained in it. Since Main was hospitalized, it fell to Dave MacNaughton to write a lawyer in Prince Albert on November 10 to ask him to determine whether one Albert Victor Wilson was in the penitentiary and, if so, to interview him to see whether he could verify the information now elicited from Cook following Main's receipt of his letter. That information, set out in MacNaughton's letter, was that Cook and Wilson together had broken into a drycleaners in Edmonton at about 2 am on Friday morning. The murders had been committed about midnight.

The Prince Albert lawyer responded with admirable swiftness to MacNaughton's letter of November 10. By November 13 he had interviewed Wilson in the penitentiary and had written MacNaughton to inform him Wilson had verified Cook's information in all of the few particulars MacNaughton had set out, apart from a half-hour discrepancy in the time they met. Cook therefore had an alibi and he had two witnesses to corroborate it, Wilson and one Jack Mitchell who, Cook said, he had met at an all-night cafe in Edmonton shortly before his chance meeting with Wilson.

***

An alibi calls for proof by the man relying on it that at the identical time the Crown says he was at A committing the crime with which he is charged, he was at B - or at least on his way to B which he reached at a time making it impossible for him to have been at A when the Crown says he was. The first thing to be determined therefore is the time whatever happened at A happened. In establishing the time of the murder of the Cook family, the only proximate time known with any degree of certainty was the hour of Arnold Filipenko seeing Cook meet his father on Main Street: 9 pm. From that hour until Cook showed up at South Park Motors in Edmonton on Friday morning, the time of any given event, with the exception of the time of death, came either from Cook or from his alibi witnesses. For the time of death the Crown relied in both trials on the evidence of the pathologist, Dr Peter Davey, supplementing it in the second trial however with the evidence of another witness which will be reached shortly.

Davey had come from Edmonton on Sunday evening to examine the bodies in Brennan's Funeral home. At the preliminary inquiry the best he was able to do in estimating the time of death was to place it within a span of 72 hours. From the condition of the bodies, it appeared to him death had occurred at the earliest at 7 pm Wednesday and at the latest at 7 pm Saturday. He could not be more precise; the science is as inexact as is the practice of it unenviable[1].

At the first trial however he reduced the span to 48 hours - 7 pm Thursday to 7 pm Saturday - and at the second a further 24 hours so that the earliest time at which death might have occurred in his second-trial opinion was 7 pm Friday, and for the second time the latest time of death remained at 7 pm Saturday. Given the whole days being lopped from successive estimates, resurrection was a possibility had it gone to a fourth estimate, but the problem arising from Davey's second-trial estimate was more immediate than that posed by the vagaries of the three estimates which, in any case, no one ever noticed. If Davey was right at the second trial in thinking death had probably not occurred before 7 pm Friday, Cook was home free. Every minute of his time for all the daylight hours of Friday through Davey's earliest time of death estimate - 7 pm Friday through to the latest - 7 pm Saturday - were accounted for by Crown witnesses. Since providing Cook with an out was not high on the list of the Crown's priorities, it could not be left at Davey.

[1] *"I remember the undertaker using a can of spray deodorant. He would spray it on me and himself while the autopsy was going on. Oddly enough, one of the most effective aids is Noxema in the nostrils and a surgical mask" - interview, Dr Peter W. Davey, January 24, 1979.*

Luckily - there does not seem to be any other word for it - one Mavis Dawes came forward in time for the second trial. For whatever reason, she had not made her evidence available for the preliminary inquiry or the first trial. That evidence was that at 12:10 am on Friday she was sitting at her kitchen table doing her hair when she heard two loud reports which she told the court she thought might be either gunshots or a truck backfiring. They appeared to her to have come from the far end of the block, but she could not be sure from which side of the street. The Cook house was on the opposite side of the street at the far end of her block. It occurred to Dawes to look at her clock when she heard the reports, and she remembered the time.

Dawes was not asked on the stand whether what she'd heard sounded to her more like gunshots than backfiring, but when I interviewed her there was no question: "I am familiar with firearms. I have used them up till recently and this was no truck backfiring. I was frightened when I heard it. I thought 'My God! someone has been shot.' I thought perhaps a drunken couple had shot each other just across the street. I was so sure that that's what it was that I turned out the lights. The police department was right across the alley and I was too frightened to go to the police. A detective came over after the murders were discovered and asked if I knew anything unusual. I denied any knowledge. I've thought since that if I'd done something, I might have saved some of the children."

If Mrs Dawes' reaction seems an instance of the Kitty Genovese syndrome, it could be asked who in her position would have gone out into a dark night to check out what she thought might be mutual murderers - an unusual species, but rational thought tends to trail such incidents at a safe distance. For all she knew she might have confronted a madman running down the street waving a shotgun, and she cannot be blamed for not having run out to intercept him. Good Samaritans on occasion become Dead Samaritans for their trouble.

Less understandable is her failure to discharge a civic duty to throw as much light as possible as soon as possible on murders which overnight had turned her street into the fevered center of Alberta. Dunne had the opportunity to do some probing here since it was in his interest to shake her evidence leaving the time of death either up in the air or, better, as established by Davey whose evidence was already in hand when Dunne rose to cross-examine Dawes. She was a prime target for skillful cross-examination ("Do you customarily look at your clock when anything untoward happens?" "Where were you at the preliminary inquiry?" "The first trial?" and so on) but Dunne got up, asked her four questions which served to tie down 12:10 am as the time of death, and sat down with the Davey evidence well and truly squandered.

Not that the Crown's first-trial case had been fatally flawed by Anderson's inability to establish the time of death with exactitude, but now he had it since no one doubted that Dawes had looked at her clock and had heard the discharges of a shotgun rather than backfiring. He was able, after a fashion, to make something of it in his address to the jury:

"It would be my suggestion that there are certain factors that I am safe in assuming are proved more or less beyond dispute. The first would be that Ray Cook was murdered and is dead[1]. The second would be that he was shot by means of a shotgun, most likely while in bed, and the next would be that his body was placed in a greasepit, and I would feel rather safe in making the suggestion that the time of death must have been late Thursday night or early Friday morning. My learned friend dwelt on that point. The evidence of Dr Davey and the evidence of Mrs Dawes. It is true that Dr Davey was not able to locate the time precisely which is not difficult to understand the circumstances being what they were and the problems that confronted him. With regard to Mrs Dawes I would point this out: Mrs Dawes apparently resided on this truck route as my friend indicated it to be. Presumably she heard many trucks pass, but this was one indication from which the noise she heard came particularly to her attention and apparently disturbed her to some extent, and the Crown feels fairly safe in assuming that it is a reasonable inference for you gentlemen to draw, that that is the best time that can be established, the time as related by Mrs Dawes."

Dawes did not live on the truck route but a block off it, but that was a small point. Thanks in no small part to Dunne the time was fixed at 12:10 am, Friday, and it was now possible to inquire into the merits of the alibi.

***

---

[1] *That he was dead if he'd been murdered was well beyond dispute, but was he dead? Death was proved in the first trial - his stepbrother had been asked to examine the body in the funeral home and had been able to identify it from a scar on the left thumb - but not in the second in which, in a spirit of comity, Dunne conceded the point.*

What now follows is Cook's account of his movements from the time he left home driving his father's station wagon until daybreak. It was corroborated in all essential details by his two alibi witnesses, Wilson and Mitchell, and after setting out the account we will examine its - and their - credibility. The account is an amalgam of trial testimony and cellblock notes.

Leaving his father standing in front of the house, Cook left for Edmonton at 10:30 pm, arriving at Frankie's Cafe, an all-nighter on Edmonton's South Side at about 1 am. He went in for cigarettes and ran into Black Jack Mitchell, a penitentiary acquaintance. They had coffee, chatted for half an hour or so and Cook left. He drove to downtown Edmonton where he stopped at another greasy spoon, the Pig 'n' Whistle on Jasper Avenue. He went in for cigars and on the way out ran into Sonny Wilson, another acquaintance from his penitentiary days which by now were a scant 55 hours behind him.

Wilson was on his way to meet a friend who was to join him in the resumption of Wilson's career of B&E. Cook drove Wilson to the intended meeting place, but the friend failed to show. Wilson then invited Cook to fill in for the no-show. Cook was reluctant to do so, going so far, he said, as to offer Wilson $50 if he would abandon the plan. Wilson was not to be dissuaded and, with a heavy heart, Cook decided to throw in with him, more as something to do to kill the balance of the night than because he himself wanted to get back in harness this soon. He had other plans, among them the Impala. He had the wherewithal in hand and did not need whatever petty proceeds he could expect to recover from a B&E. The usual arrangement in such enterprises is that the man whose score it is, the master mind whose half-baked plan is to kick in some flimsy momma and poppa confectionery, takes the lion's share, normally about 75% in a two-man operation even though the risks have been shared equally. Cook however told Wilson he could have all of whatever they got.

They drove back to the South Side sizing up business establishments along the way and finally settled on Cosmo Cleaners, "Mr Suede", a drycleaner specializing in suede garments. They drove to the rear of the one-storey building, parked the station wagon in the alley and made their way onto the roof by way of a stairway to an adjacent roof. They made their way inside through a ventilator shaft. Wilson rifled a cash drawer of $30, and a desk drawer from which he obtained a cheap ring. On the way out the front door Wilson grabbed up a car coat. Cook took him back to the north side and then drove back to the South Side to the Myhaluk residence where he slept in the car for a couple of hours until the house stirred. He went inside and it was then he told Lea Myhaluk whatever he told her to account for his no longer wearing the blue suit.

***

The alibi bears signs of having been concocted to meet an exigent situation ("You could tell the Warden that Bob Cook's life is in the balance" is how MacNaughton put it to the Prince Albert lawyer, anticipating the lawyer might encounter some difficulty getting in to see Wilson), the kind of thing Cook would fabricate, B&E being most of what he knew. First and last it was weighed in the balance of credibility and found wanting. For example, Mr Justice Locke of the Supreme Court of Canada was quoted in *The London Free Press* of October 6, 1960 as interrupting Arthur Maloney's argument to observe "it was a new kind of alibi to say you were committing a crime in one place at the time a crime was being committed in another. It's pretty feeble."

His Lordship's observation suffered from a different infirmity - inanity - since the defense of alibi does not prescribe what the person relying on it be doing or not be doing at B while the crime with which he is charged is being committed at A. He has merely to prove that he was at B at the material time. Had Cook chosen to say he was committing murder in Edmonton at the material time, and had he been able to prove it, it would have operated as a perfect alibi defense to the charge he had committed murder in Stettler. Cook was due to be disabused of any naive supposition he might have nursed that the higher he went in the court system, the better his chances for an intelligent hearing. Far from being feeble, Cosmo Cleaners is seen on reflection to have been the best Cook could have done, to have been the most plausible. His alibi was an assertion he was in Edmonton doing what he always did, doing what he did best when he wasn't stealing cars.

***

The defense could have hoped for a better witness than Black Jack Mitchell. He had a lengthy criminal record which the Crown used to undermine his credibility, and he had spent the better part of the night in question in a South Side beer parlor and was, by the time he reached Frankie's Cafe around midnight, "a little high." He was vague as to the time of Cook's arrival at the cafe and indeed as to the day of the week, although he seemed to remember "it was the day of the Patterson-Johansson fight" - whenever that was. In all not a sterling alibi witness, but the defense didn't have that many and he was called in both trials. Twice over he said his faltering piece following which he disappeared into obscurity, probably having done more harm than good. *If* he saw Cook, he could only have seen him when Cook said he did meaning the alibi was true, but Cook's two convictions attest to Mitchell's failure to persuade two juries. His evidence was easily dismissed.

Before the first trial, Main employed a private investigation agency to check out (perhaps after first finding) Mitchell who gave the two interviewing investigators a written and signed statement. In it Mitchell stated he saw Cook "after my release" (on June 18) and before "the date I heard about his trouble on the radio." In the statement he said he could not remember precisely when he saw Cook or where.

He told the investigators that he thought he'd seen Cook in Frankie's Cafe, after a week-long binge, either late Thursday night or early Friday morning, but he didn't want that information in the signed statement because he was uncertain of it. He was, however, certain he'd seen him.

His statement to the investigators rings truer than do those he gave on the stand when his memory had improved (or had been nudged) to the point where he was now able to state categorically that it *was* Frankie's. The defense might have been wiser to go with a repeat of the struggle to remember he'd experienced when talking to the investigators rather than allowing him to color his testimony with doubtful detail intended to lend veracity to it. The fact he was now certain about something he'd been uncertain about seven weeks earlier probably registered with the jurors as the enhanced evidence it was.

That should not have been the end of it however for the evidence of the Cosmo break-in jointly by Cook and Wilson could not be as readily dismissed as Mitchell's floundering attempt to reach back into an alcoholic fog. The details of the break-in were intricate enough, and if there was at least rough coincidence between the Cook and Wilson accounts of it, then prima facie a case was made. If Cook said a, b, c, and d and Wilson said a, b, c and d then, unless they had managed to get together in a shameless attempt to pull the wool over the eyes of Justice

- they may have thought she'd slipped her blindfold - there might be something to what each said[1].

***

The external walls of a prison are meant to be impregnable from the inside just as the internal walls are intended to separate one part of a prison population from another, one class of offender from another, but which never do. They are sieves, models of porosity, constant challenges to men with the time to do so to get through them with 'kites' and with the contraband commodities of prison commerce. Thus when Oliver Durocher clubbed Cook and received for his trouble 42 days in Prince Albert's hole, supposedly without access to writing materials or a courier, he nevertheless managed to get a kite to Cook warning him he hadn't seen the last of him - a threat Durocher felt he could make with impunity from the safety of the hole, and which Cook dismissed with good-natured contempt.

Anderson never offered any evidence - there was none - that Cook and Wilson had managed to communicate in Fort Saskatchewan over the month or so they were in residence there together, whether by kite, cooperative guards or trustee-inmates. To Anderson it was just a fact of prison life that prisoners wishing to communicate with each other would find a way to do so, as indeed they would. He explained it to the first-trial jury: "It was then suggested that between the time of that event, the [Cosmo Cleaners] breaking and entry, and the time of giving evidence, Wilson and the accused had no means of communication. Well I would suggest to you, gentlemen, that if I mentioned the 'grapevine' or the 'underground railway', you would know what I mean. It *[sic]* exists I think without a doubt. We have evidence of the fact that the accused and Wilson shared the accommodation of the same provincial institution on one occasion because Wilson saw the accused on that occasion at the same institution."

[1] *If Wilson managed to communicate all the details of the alibi break-in to Cook for regurgitation by him, he did so with remarkable thoroughness, leaving little to chance. Appended to a pre-trial note, Cook to Main, are two sketches, one of the Cosmo roof, one of the interior. There are 24 details in the two sketches which were checked and found to accord with what is there. If anything, they are too detailed since there seems to be more than a B&E man might be expected to observe in the course of a heist. Still, the sketches exist.*

It was hard to argue with this, although perhaps for reasons other than those which Anderson saw as unassailable, but the fact is that before Wilson was shipped off to Prince Albert to begin another term for B&E, his time in Fort Saskatchewan waiting for the time for appeal to expire overlapped with Cook's time waiting for the start of the first trial. They had at least 30 days of coextensive time during which, Cook acknowledged, he saw Wilson a number of times. From his B Block cell, he periodically saw Wilson going from A Block to B for his twice-weekly showers. During those brief encounters, it is doubtful Wilson managed to communicate to Cook many of the details of the Cosmo break-in (there was never any question of Wilson having participated in the break-in, the only question being was Cook with him?), leaving only either the grapevine or the underground railway as a means of communicating back and forth. The latter, however, thitherto used only for getting slaves out of the ante-bellum South, had fallen into disuse, but it may be that it had been re-commissioned inside the Fort and the possibility that it was used by Cook and Wilson to thwart the ends of justice should not be overlooked.

Would Wilson have been prepared to go down the primrose path of perjury as a not inconsiderable favor to Cook? If so, it would not have been because of the claims of friendship since neither claimed the other as a friend. There was nothing more between them than the loose fraternity forced upon them by past joint confinement in Saskatchewan Penitentiary; they knew each other, nothing more. For Anderson that was enough. The fact spoke for itself, and what it said was that a bond had been forged between Wilson and Cook strong enough that Wilson, even though there was nothing in it for him and well knowing the narrow view the courts took of perjury, would lie as a matter of casual course for a casual acquaintance. In for a penny, in for a pound. What difference did it make to the likes of a Wilson?

None. Wilson broke into Cosmo Cleaners and Cook did not; that much was clear. Or was it? What had been crystalline in its clarity, became clouded in the course of Anderson's peroration to the second-trial jury: "Here is a man who comes out of jail, two years away, spends an hour with his family and rushes back to join his friends in Edmonton. Here is a man who leaves his family for two or three hours. They have gone off to BC to set up a business in which he hopes to participate and within a matter of two or three years *[sic]* there he is, breaking and entering a business establishment in Edmonton, jeopardizing the whole BC venture, if it ever existed."

From here Anderson went on seemingly to concede that such was Cook's depravity, he stole a car in broad daylight in order to recover a cache of - what else? - stolen money. What Anderson meant is not as accessible as what he said. As with Bowden, he seemed to be conceding that Cook *had* broken into Cosmo. He seemed to be saying that Cook had left his family for two or three hours, implying he'd come back to them at the end of that time, when nothing suggests he had unless of course it was to kill them. On the other hand, *they* had left *him* by having gone off to BC pursuant to a plan which did not exist. "Two or three years" was a slip of the tongue where he meant to say that within two or three hours of leaving his family, he was breaking into Cosmo Cleaners. But if he meant that, Anderson was conceding the alibi.

He was not conceding the alibi. Anderson is perhaps best understood by recognizing he was a man who would attempt to have the jurors believe six impossible things before breakfast. Thus, not only was the alibi false, those elements in it which cast Cook in the worst light were true even though they were false. Thus not only was Cook an ingrate insensitive to the emotional needs of his family (as was seen in his fleeing for the fleshpots of Edmonton after an hour spent with them after a two-year absence), he had killed them which was to carry ingratitude to a quite unacceptable level. Not only had he jeopardized the plans to buy a garage in BC by courting arrest for the Cosmo B&E, there were no such plans. Not only had he jeopardized the non-existent plans to buy a garage in BC by courting arrest by breaking into Cosmo, he hadn't broken into Cosmo.

Not only was Cook a man who stole a car to use to recover his stolen money, he lied when he said he had, but, make no mistake, he was a car thief. Moreover he hadn't recovered any stolen money; he lied about that as well. But, make no mistake, had it existed it would have been stolen. About the only thing he had not lied about was having stolen a shotgun from some hardware store but, make no mistake, he would have lied about that as well had he been asked. Mass murder was beginning to appear to be the least of his transgressions. It was Anderson at his best.

***

Whether by underground railway, speaking in tongues or mental telepathy, clandestine communication goes on in prison and the question is was Wilson able to get to Cook with sufficient detail about the Cosmo break-in to make Cook's account of it believable? It would not have been a one-way street; Cook had to get information to Wilson, for example information as to certain contents of the station wagon. Face-to-face conversations were impossible given their prison situations, but kites were not, and it is possible Wilson could have communicated to Cook in writing the entire scenario of a break-in Cook did not have a part in starting with Wilson's meeting with someone at the Pig 'n' Whistle, at that point substituting Cook.

There are a dozen factors to be juggled and weighed, and in the end nothing more can be said than that it seems, to this analyst at least, that the story of Cook's participation in the break-in was not a fabrication; there were too many details which could have been known to Cook, not from getting them from Wilson, but only from having been on the Cosmo roof that night. But whether the Cook and Wilson accounts stood or fell together, there were things the defense could have done to shore them up.

It occurred to Cook what could be done. On December 13, 1959, three days after the first conviction, Cook wrote Main:

"I've got a kind of statement here I am going to try and get signed by the guards who were in charge to the effect it would have been impossible for me to have coached or contacted Sunny and Mitch in any way. Maybe its too late for any of that as I don't know a thing about how an appeal works, could you let me know. I never even had a suspision that are witnesses wouldn't be belived, when you think that I couldn't have got in touch by any means its impossible it could all be fabracated."

He followed with a note to Main in which he wrote:

"I have talked to the Warden Mr Holt and two of the guards in charge under him. When I came down here early in July I was under a special set of rules which were set down by Mr Holt and carried out by a Mr Ducgan & a Mr Van Sickle. I was not allowed to talk or mix atall with any of the other prisnors. I was watched at all times by at least one guard while out of my cell. Even while taking my weekly shower or walking in the center of the prison corrider for excersize. The only time I wasnt under close observation was at night in my cell. Nobody was allowed to come near my cell to talk to me at any time. Mr Holt, Mr Van Sickle and Mr Ducgan do say that to the best of there knolage there rules where carried out. To the best of there knolage I could not have contacted Sunny Willson who was in a differnt block or Jack Mitchell who was not in here at any time I was.

"They agree that while they were on duty these were the conditions and to the best of there knolage they were carried out. I was thing this would be pretty important to our case. I told them I was going to try and get you to come out here soon as you can to see me and would talk to them about it at that time. Thank You. Bob"

It has the ring of truth. For one thing it's highly unlikely he did not talk to Holt, Dougan and Van Sickle since, if he did not, the untruth would have readily been uncovered by Main. For another, it cannot be doubted that given who he was, and given the manhunt of a scant four months earlier, a special set of rules, probably unlike any seen before in the history of penology, would have been promulgated to ensure there were no more slip ups of *any* kind. No chances, the DAG had decreed, were to be taken with Cook, and none were. The RCMP, among others, were not amused by what he'd put them through.

It is not known whether Main adopted what seems in retrospect to have been a valuable suggestion, but in any case Dunne took over the defense and appeared not to appreciate that the alibi would be supported, perhaps beyond cavil, if it could be proved through the mouths of Holt, Dougan and Van Sickle that Cook and Wilson were not able to communicate with each other. The evidence of the Cooks, Wilsons and Mitchells of the world jurors can dismiss out of hand and are probably most often right in doing so. They are the men, lesser breeds without the law, who jimmy the business premises of the jurors, steal their cars, stick them with an intolerable tax burden to maintain the prison system which coddles them by way of preparing them for premature release.

Less easily dismissed would have been the evidence of the pillars of that system. Had the warden and two of his senior guards taken the stand to say it was categorically impossible for Wilson and Cook to have communicated to the extent necessary to impart all the details of the Cosmo break-in, no kites, no trustees scurrying back and forth with more details, no late night rap sessions after lights out, no nothing, it would have faced the jurors with an awkward dilemma: acquit Cook or brand Holt, Dougan and Van Sickle as men unfit to run a daycare center much less a prison housing about 600 men.

***

When he came home with his father on Thursday evening, Cook told the first-trial court, following a lunch of sandwiches and coffee with his parents he got up to leave[1]. Ray accompanied him to the station wagon standing at the front curb where they stood and chatted for a few minutes. Ray took his money from his wallet and handed the wallet to Cook for Cook's use of the station wagon registration certificate and driver's license. Ray then, Cook said, "mentioned a few other things. One I think is about the tools that were in the car. There was a toolbox in the car. He mentioned about not to forget to change that over. He told me don't leave it in the station wagon, and he told me...." Main cut him off and moved on to the next questions.

Cook's reference to a toolbox marked the entrance into oral evidence of the subject, but not the entrance of a toolbox itself. Such a box sat in the courtroom throughout the first trial without anyone referring to it and without, therefore, the marking of it as an exhibit. The jurors retired to deliberate with no idea of the toolbox's purpose, or even if there was one. Somewhat similarly in the second trial when the same toolbox sat throughout the Crown's entire case without Anderson once referring to it.

This all gets rather complex, but it is necessary to wade through it. The toolbox was to prove late in the second trial to have been found by Roach in the trunk of the Impala, but Anderson, who knew in the second trial what first-trial defense witnesses had had to say about *a* toolbox (although they were not necessarily talking about the one in the courtroom since it had not been marked as an exhibit in the Crown's first-trial case) he did not *now* have Roach identify the one sitting in front of him as large as life (and as it was to prove to Cook twice as ugly) as the one he'd taken from the Impala. When Anderson closed his second-trial case, once again the toolbox sat there with no one having either the slightest idea why it was there, or even much interest in it.

A way of getting into Cosmo Cleaners from its roof was to pry off a grate from a vent structure. Cook, Wilson said under oath, suggested

[1] *The one RCMP photograph of the sink cabinet on the east wall of the kitchen shows a number of coffee cups, appearing to be stacked for washing in the morning. The number cannot be made out, nor did the police count them. It might have been significant. Daisy had earlier served coffee to Jim and Leona Hoskins, and if there were four cups stacked, Cook's account of a warm homecoming over coffee and sandwiches doesn't cut it. If there were five (suggesting two cups from the Hoskins visit were re-used by her and Ray plus a clean one for their new guest) or seven (she splurged for the occasion and got down two clean ones for Ray and herself) it does. The fact of the cups being stacked suggests preparations for bed were peaceful.*

that Wilson go down to the station wagon to look for something to jimmy the grate, and at this point the jurors might have looked on knowingly since Cook would have a better idea of what was in the station wagon, and since it was Wilson's job, it might be expected that he would be giving the instructions. Nevertheless, nothing loath, Wilson dutifully descended to the station wagon to see what he could find. He struck a match to illuminate the toolbox which was sitting in the cargo area and, finding nothing suitable, returned to the roof where a board found somewhere was used to pry the grate off.

In direct examination by MacNaughton in the second trial, Wilson was asked whether he could identify the toolbox in the courtroom, and he was able to say only that he had seen one "the very same". MacNaughton didn't get from him that he'd seen it in the station wagon, which is where he had to have seen it otherwise his evidence was pointless. The reader should perhaps be reminded at this point that when MacNaughton questioned Wilson about the toolbox, the Crown's case was closed which meant that the Crown was no longer in a position to make whatever use of the toolbox might have been its purpose in bringing it into court. The toolbox had not been identified as having come from the station wagon, and there was no reason for MacNaughton to attempt to have Wilson identify it since, so far as evidence against Cook was concerned, it did not exist[1]. That is (and the point is important) the Crown had not established where it came from.

Cook's evidence in the first trial (which he was to repeat in the second) was that when he took delivery of the station wagon from Ray, the toolbox was in it, and he had transferred it to the Impala at Hood Motors just as Ray had reminded him to do.

When Anderson closed the Crown's case, it was now up to Dunne to produce defense witnesses, if any, to answer that case. But before doing so, Dunne unwittingly handed Anderson the means of sealing Cook's fate. When Anderson said, "The Crown's case is closed my Lord", Dunne was immediately on his feet:

---

[1] *Prior to closing his case Anderson had shown the toolbox to Bell expecting Bell to be able to say he'd seen it before (thus identifying it) since it was in the trunk of the Impala which Bell had searched for liquor. Bell however was not able to say he'd ever seen it and thus it was entered as an exhibit for later identification by whoever could say where it had come from. That of course would have been Roach since he'd removed it from the trunk on Saturday evening, but Anderson closed his case without asking Roach anything about it.*

"Just a minute. Before my friend closes his case, there is one exhibit I will need Sergeant Roach to identify sir. It is in for identification only."

THE COURT: "Mr Anderson?"

MR ANDERSON: "I have no objection my Lord."

MR DUNNE: "Call Sergeant Roach please."

SERGEANT THOMAS ROACH recalled on his former oath, cross-examined by Dunne.

THE COURT: "Mr Dunne?"

"Sergeant Roach, we did have put in as an exhibit [for identification] this large black object. Would you examine it please?"

"This was in the trunk of the 1959 Chevrolet Impala. It is a toolbox."

"That is when *[sic]* and where you first saw it?"

"At Stettler on the evening of the 27th of June, 1959."

"On Saturday evening?"

"Saturday evening."

"When you searched the car?"

"Yes."

"And found the other objects?"

"That is right. That is right."

"Whereabouts was that located in the trunk?"

"As near as I can recall it was under some of the clothes and that garment bag in the corner."

"I see. Now may I just ask now sir for that to be entered as an exhibit?"

THE COURT: "Yes. Mr Anderson?"

344

MR ANDERSON: "No objection my Lord."

Taking into account the preliminary inquiry, the first trial and his evidence prior to his being re-called in the second trial, Roach had described six times what he had found in the trunk of the Impala, yet only now, for the first time, did he mention finding the toolbox there. It was unusual and is difficult to explain, but so too was the presence of the toolbox in the courtroom. In any case, it was now marked as an exhibit which meant that defense witnesses who might know something about it could be cross-examined on it by Anderson where that avenue had been closed to him with the closing of his case.

It is also difficult to divine Dunne's reasoning behind having Roach identify the toolbox, but the attempt must be made: since Roach had found it in the Impala, unless Cook put it there when he was at home on Saturday evening, he had taken it with him in the station wagon on Thursday evening and had transferred it to the trunk of the Impala when he made the Hood Motors deal on Friday afternoon, meaning it had been continuously in the station wagon from the time of his leaving Stettler on Thursday night through to the time of the Impala transaction. Had been in the station wagon, that is, at the time of the Cosmo break-in. If Wilson was able to identify the toolbox (which the jury now knew had been taken from the Impala) as the one he saw in the back of the station wagon by the light of a flickering match, Cook was proved to have been at Cosmo Cleaners. Something like that.

If that was Dunne's reasoning it was sound enough except Dunne can be taken to have known (since it was in the first-trial transcripts) that Cook's own evidence of the removal of the toolbox from the Impala trunk contradicted Roach's. He should therefore have steered clear of asking Cook anything about the toolbox although he could not now prevent Anderson from doing so when the time came for the cross-examination of Cook. In other words, he ought not to have had the toolbox marked as an exhibit since it put Anderson in the position of tying Cook to his first-trial evidence which he could then contrast with Roach's, elicited by Dunne, on the same subject. Nevertheless he plowed on:

"Did you do anything else while you were at home that you can recall?"

"I do believe, and I am not - that I took some tools out of the Impala, but I am not sure of that, and put them on the bench in the garage."

It is not certain that Dunne knew what he wanted, but what he had was the unimpeachable Roach telling of finding the toolbox in the trunk on Saturday evening, and the all-too impeachable Cook telling of removing it from the trunk on Saturday evening[1] before Roach had ever seen the Impala, and never were the twain likely to meet. Given the choice between Roach and Cook was, for the jurors, to be given no choice at all.

Having gotten himself into it (although he may not have recognized that he had, such were the wanton vagaries that were a hallmark of the *Cook* trials), Dunne had to make the most of Wilson. He now had to get from Wilson that *that* toolbox was the selfsame toolbox he had groped through in the back of the station wagon. Nothing less than positive identification would now do. With all the respect due MacNaughton, this was not the time for examination in this vital area by junior counsel, yet Dunne turned Wilson over to him. "I am showing to you Exhibit 77. Do you recall having seen that article before?" and letting it go at "I have seen one the very same, sir" was not good enough, but that is what it got. MacNaughton was entitled to his day in the sun, but this was not that day.

When I interviewed Wilson, he told me that when he was pawing through the toolbox, the sleeve of his jacket picked up a grease stain. He happened to be wearing the jacket when he was brought from Prince Albert as a defense witness at the second trial. He pointed the stain out to Dunne, thinking Dunne would be able to use it to tie him to the toolbox as could have been done with, say, sophisticated spectrographic analysis. It may be defense resources did not permit such analysis; in any case Dunne ignored Wilson and ignored the means of conclusively proving that Wilson had been in the back of the station wagon behind Cosmo Cleaners.

***

With the toolbox now marked and Wilson's inadequate "one the very same" out of the way, the stage was set for Anderson's cross-examination of him. Such was the tension in the courtroom when he got up to do so, observers have told me, you could have heard a bomb drop as Thurber's Squawks Magraw said in another dramatic situation. When

---

[1] *Cook said tools but may have meant to say toolbox. The distinction may be important. The police photographs do not show a toolbox on a bench.*

I interviewed Anderson, he told me the thing which stood out most prominently in his memory was the alibi evidence. He remembered it all: Cosmo's proprietor, Hyman Estrin, a forthright and winning witness, the rope used by the thieves to lower themselves inside from the roof, the amount of cash taken, the ring, the car coat, Wilson (whom he remembered as Myhaluk) going down to the station wagon to look for a pry - he remembered all of it including his thinking the alibi was "airtight" (his word) after Wilson had given his evidence in chief.

He remembered the toolbox, although he could not tell me why it had twice been brought to court, nor why he had not employed it in his case in either trial. Each time he'd closed his case, he said, he had no idea of the contents of the toolbox, nor had "the RCMP guy" sitting with him in the second trial. When he cross-examined Wilson he ran him through the Pig 'n' Whistle meeting, the drive to the South Side, the break-in. Then, he told me, on a whim because he did not believe that Wilson had gone down off the roof to look for a pry, he asked him to step out of the witness box, go to the exhibit table and open the toolbox. 'Whim' suggests that Anderson still had no idea what was in the toolbox, but also suggests he knew Wilson was going to find something in there other than a feather duster:

"What is in it?"

"Hammer."

"Just put all the tools on the table. A hammer, screwdriver, wrench, screwdriver, wrench, big screwdriver, putty knife, wrench, pliers, wrenches, screwdrivers, pliers, wrench, pliers, wrench, wrench, another wrench, wrench, wrench, chisel, wrench, pliers, something, saw, file, wrench, something. Just to make this brief, are there any more screwdrivers in there?"

"Yes sir."

"Pick them all out will you?" "How many is that, no, that you just picked up?"

"Three."

"I see. How many more, two more?"

"Two more."

"Another one, another one, another one, another one. All right, that is enough thank you. You couldn't find a tool in this car to open this grate?"

"No sir. Not what I wanted sir."

"Not what you wanted out of this group?"

"No sir. I had lit a match and...."

"What did you want? What kind of tool did you want?"

"Something I could use like a tire iron is what I anticipated."

"You said a screwdriver or wrench didn't you?"

"Yes sir."

"The screwdriver, it wouldn't do?"

"No sir, that was probably at the bottom of the case."

"None of these tools would do for your job?"

"I was only in the car a couple of minutes sir."

"All I said was none of these tools would do that job you wanted it for?"

"I am not sure sir."

"Thanks."

So much for the alibi. MacNaughton tried ineffectively on re-examination to undo the damage, to stem the tide, but the floodgates were open releasing a torrent of screwdrivers. Until he questioned Wilson, Anderson told me, he was sure he had a loser, but as screwdriver after large screwdriver was taken from the box and laid on the table before the riveted jurors, the effect "was like an electric switch had been thrown in the courtroom." Dunne's efforts over six days had been turned back on him in as many minutes by Anderson's skillful use of the exhibit Dunne had made his own on a risky premise whose dangers he did not appreciate. He appreciated them now. The atmosphere in the courtroom may have been electric in a general sense, but at the defense table and in the prisoner's box it had about it the icy chill of death.

So much for the alibi indeed, but overlooked or lost sight of in all this were a handful of facts which demanded further examination if the story were to be complete: Cosmo had been broken into, Wilson was there, and the premises were searched for fingerprints. No one was called to say what the results of the search were. If prints were found, they should have been those fitting the Crown's case: Wilson's but none of Cook's. Such results would not have been conclusive in disproving the alibi, but would have pried open the door leading to the inference that it was false a little wider, and the Crown's failure to use such evidence, if it existed, can only be put down to oversight.

There is no need to dwell on the implications of a print of Cook's having been lifted, but as a contribution to completing the story, reference must be made to a quantity of oral and documentary extra-trial and post-trial evidence in the research material which too is inconclusive, but is unmistakably suggestive of the fact that the RCMP was holding the Cosmo break-in in reserve intending (working through the city police because of jurisdictional considerations) to charge both Wilson and Cook with Cosmo in the event Cook was acquitted of murder.

"That's the most important piece of evidence we've heard yet," said the King, rubbing his hands, "so let the jury - "

"If any one of them can explain it," said Alice, (she had grown so large in the last few minutes that she wasn't a bit afraid of interrupting him), "I'll give him sixpence. I don't believe there's an atom of meaning in it."

The jury all wrote down on their slates, "She doesn't believe there's an atom of meaning in it," but none of them attempted to explain the paper.

"If there's no meaning in it," said the King, "that saves a world of trouble, you know, as we needn't try to find any."

Alice's Adventures in Wonderland

CHAPTER 21

THE SECOND NEWSPAPER

The salient characteristic of a good part of the physical evidence which played a part in the Cook trials was its ability to materialize or vanish at will as if some psychic dimension enconjured from the intoxicating philosophy of the New Age hovered over the case extruding some things and swallowing others. Examples of things materializing were of course the Ross shirt, the orphaned Demon, eight fingerprints which made their way into RCMP records but not into RCMP testimony, a pillbox which popped in and out like a Cheshire Cat depending on the witness of the moment, a hodge-podge of shotgun shells, although that, like much else, was arguable. Were they there before? It was an angle which bore thinking about, as Frank Dunne said, addressing another problem.

Some things merely underwent puzzling transformations. Thirty-four dollars became enough for Cook to pay MacNaughton $40 and still have $92 left over when he reached the PMH. Sunday became Saturday. Two single-barreled shotguns turned into two shotguns, one single-barreled and one a toss-up as to the number of barrels - if it was even a shotgun; Sproule, who had examined it carefully, said it was, but Gurney, who owned it, had a different opinion. Some things appeared to depend on the eye of the beholder, the array of guns on the garage wall for example: at one moment there were three, then one, then two, then no guns at all - a shimmering mix of shotguns, rifles, .22s dancing in and out of the psychic dimension.

A psychic dimension began to seem attractive as a possible journey's end for a congeries of improbable things: Ray Cook's old Long Tom, Bob Cook's two white shirts, the lockplates from the shattered Demon and as many as four fragments of its stock, a shopping bag full of Cook's clothes and hobby stuff, maybe $4100, maybe "another long-barreled gun, a single-barreled gun which was there in the house which I was told where it came from", Beeching said, although no one ever told him - or anyone else - where it went to. Nor, for that matter, was anyone other than Beeching (the court for example) told where it came from.

Yet there had to be an explanation not quite as *outre* as things being last seen harmonically converging on an astral plane where they formed up ranks before disappearing through a crystal into a solstitial sunrise, probably escorted by an angel if not a choir of them. Incisive and powerful as New Age thinking is, it has yet to find much of a place in the courts or in analysis of the work of the courts, and it was time for the spirit of sober inquiry to re-assert itself and acquit itself. Sober inquiry hadn't been able to do much with the second Long Tom or the Demon's lockplates but there was one more chance since something else had turned up missing. The scruffy little house at the corner of 52nd Street and Railroad Avenue had struggled - and, on the face of it had failed - to contain everything that should have been in it since a newspaper, *The Calgary Herald* of Friday, June 26, too had vanished.

This last inquiry (there were to be no more questions which hadn't managed to percolate to the top when the Cook evidence was being worried in court) was not hampered by a total lack of evidence such as had attended the search for, say, the shopping bag. There were some facts informing the inquiry, although not as many of them as one could have hoped for:

First, the Cooks were subscribers to *The Calgary Herald*. It was delivered daily (except Sunday) by Wayne McAlister who picked up his papers from the bus depot and reached the Cook house on his paper route each day at about 6:30 pm.

Second, the Friday edition was delivered (as was Saturday's) at the usual time and deposited in its usual place: inside the outside door of the sun porch.

Third, while the Saturday paper was undisturbed and photographed by Sproule on Sunday morning, the Friday paper was missing from the porch; it had either been slipped from beneath Saturday's paper sometime after 6:30 pm on Saturday, or it had been removed between the time of its delivery and McAlister's arrival at 6:30 pm on Saturday. Before, that is, Cook's arrival from Camrose a half-hour later than McAlister.

And last, "three newspapers" (the RCMP's description) were found in the greasepit, only one of them identified: the issue of *The Herald* of Wednesday, June 24. It cannot be said that the other two were, say, complete editions for each of two days, nor even that they were copies of *The Herald*. It seems permissible to assume they were. Is it equally safe to assume that one of the unidentified papers was the issue of *The Herald* of Friday, June 26? If so, the argument to be developed in this chapter leads to a conclusion which doesn't sit that well with the fact that Cook was put to death by the judgment of 'a court of competent jurisdiction.'

***

If the Friday paper was not in the pit, then a further assumption is warranted: it had been removed from the house since there was no evidence, testimonial or photographic, that the police found newspapers (apart from the Saturday paper) anywhere else in it. If so, then in the 41 hours between the delivery of the paper on Friday evening and the arrival of the police on Sunday morning, the only people known to have been in the house who could have removed it were the police themselves (Roach's two visits) and Cook. While police methods in the Cook investigation are not immune from criticism, no one ever suggested they removed evidence from the scene of the crime.

Leaving Cook as the only person who could have taken it from the house. But if he took it (necessarily when he left the house on Saturday evening), then it should have been found in the Impala and it was not, although it may be that the police merely failed to notice it when they searched the car. But why would Cook take a newspaper with him? It seems probable there were things on his mind other than catching up with the news - cruising Main Street in a convertible among them - but if he wanted to, then why not take Saturday's as well as, or instead of, Friday's? On balance and resorting to common sense - occasionally an aid of last resort - everything points to the Friday newspaper not having been removed from the house.

If Cook merely wanted newspaper to be used, say, to soak up blood, why take the bottom paper from a two-paper stack of them? If it is objected that he did not necessarily take it from beneath the Saturday paper, that he could have removed the paper shortly after its delivery to the house (that is, when it was the only paper in the porch), then the objection is answered by pointing out that Cook was not in or near the house from the time of the paper's delivery - 6:30 pm on Friday - until his return to Stettler at 7 pm on Saturday by which time the Saturday paper had been delivered.

In another context, Anderson suggested the possibility that Cook "may have been to that residence more than the twice we are presently aware of," and in doing so flew in the face of the all the prosecution's evidence to the contrary which accounted for Cook's every waking minute (there were no sleeping ones) from the time he reached an Edmonton car dealer at 8 am Friday until he arrived home on Saturday evening.

With an exception: since Cook had about two hours between the time he took delivery of the Impala at Hood Motors and his meeting with Feth and Teeple in Camrose - time not accounted for by Crown witnesses - he could have gone to Stettler and removed the Friday paper, and it may be that Anderson had this in mind as the occasion of a third visit to the house. If one wished to believe that Cook made the 210 mile trip Edmonton to Stettler to Camrose in two hours (including the 80 miles between Stettler and Camrose in about half an hour; speeds hovering around 160 mph would explain the later failure of the Impala transmission), she would have been welcomed as a valuable member of the prosecution team. But it seems unlikely and we can, therefore, safely sum up: if he took the Friday paper, he took it from beneath Saturday's on Saturday, but the evidence suggests he did not.

***

In the two trials there was one question about the Friday paper put to one witness: Constable Sproule. After Sproule had identified his photograph of the Saturday paper, Dunne asked him if there was any sign of Friday's, and when Sproule said he could not recall, Dunne moved on to another subject. There was nevertheless a glimmer of recognition in the defense camp of the significance of the Friday paper, in particular in Dave MacNaughton who had a better grasp of it than did either of his seniors. The preliminary inquiry transcript bears his annotation "Where was Friday's paper?" opposite the transcription of Sproule's identification of his porch photograph. It was not a bad question. It was more than that: it was a question demanding an answer.

Working from the transcript, MacNaughton prepared a memorandum: a list of names of various Crown witnesses as headings, and beneath each of them the questions he felt Main should address to them in the forthcoming trial. Under the heading "Milkman" (whose name happened to be Marvin Burton Larson) MacNaughton wrote "Question him about whether he saw a paper when he went into the porch." Larson had been to the house between noon and 12:30 pm on Saturday, and said in the preliminary inquiry that "I never seen any bottles and I figured they must be still away so I left." Whether Main read the memorandum is not known although it was found in his papers. In any case, although Larson was called by the Crown in the first trial, Main elected not to cross-examine him, about anything, leaving a void which swallowed up MacNaughton's insight. The opportunity to question the milkman who had not seen any bottles on Saturday morning as to whether he had also not seen the Friday newspaper was lost permanently; Larson died before the second trial.

Later in the memorandum MacNaughton entered the heading "Howard" which was confusing since there had been no witness by that name, either given name or surname, at the preliminary inquiry, nor was there to be at either trial. There were no questions which MacNaughton thought should be put to "Howard", but there was, under that heading, some information for Main: "There was a newspaper boy on Saturday night. The papers came into the bus depot at approximately six o'clock. He would be at the Cook house at approximately 6:30 or 6:45. He advised that he did not see any other paper when he left the Saturday night *Calgary Herald*. Wayne McAlister... delivered the paper on Friday and I will be in touch with him" - an intention confirmed in MacNaughton's letter to Main of October 13, 1959 in which he wrote, "I am trying to ascertain from both the paper boy and the RCMP if the Friday paper was found", and in which he wrongly identified as *The*

Albertan the paper he'd previously (in the memorandum) identified correctly.

MacNaughton was not called upon to explain how the paper boy could be expected to know whether the Friday paper was found in the house after the murders (he could at most have known whether it was there when he delivered Saturday's paper), or the suggestion that Wayne McAlister had delivered the Friday paper, but that some "newspaper boy" other than McAlister had delivered Saturday's and had informed MacNaughton in advance of his interviewing McAlister that "he did not see any other paper."

When I talked to McAlister, I showed him MacNaughton's memorandum. He too was confused by it and agreed that MacNaughton seemed to be talking about two paper boys. McAlister was emphatic: no one shared his newspaper route with him, not "Howard", not anyone. He had, he told me, told MacNaughton "that I did not see any other paper when I left the Saturday night *Calgary Herald*", but he was not called as a defense witness to give that evidence. It could not have been readily ignored. If McAlister was right in saying he did not see another newspaper in the porch when he delivered Saturday's, and if one could infer from that that he did not see Friday's because it was not there (and not merely that it might have been there but he didn't happen to notice it), then MacNaughton's question became more insistent: where was Friday's paper? No less significantly, when had it been taken from the porch and by whom?

McAlister was 13 at the time of the first trial, old enough to understand the oath and the penalty for violating it (although not old enough to be allowed to remain as a spectator in the preliminary inquiry courtroom from which he was ejected), and his evidence would have been received had he been called. It might have been dismissed, but it should at least have been weighed. He may have been only 13, but he was also a hard-nosed businessman[1] whose business was delivering papers and taking note of factors which might affect his receiving payment for them when

---

[1] *He was also a cold-blooded one in the engaging way of some 13-year-olds. McAlister was at Buffalo Lake with his family on Sunday when he heard the news from Stettler - news which froze the town and its district and its province in an attitude of disbelief but which didn't faze the pragmatic McAlister. Mass murder is one thing, but business is business. He told me that when he heard it on the radio, "the first thing that went through my mind was 'Goddamn it! they owe me thirty-five cents.' " The Public Trustee never settled up when he was winding up the Cook estate, and McAlister remains unpaid for six issues of* The Calgary Herald, Monday, June 22 to Saturday, June 27, *all of which he delivered to the Cook residence.*

the time came to 'collect' - as we knew it when the writer was also delivering *The Calgary Herald*. He knew what he had seen on Saturday, or more particularly what he had not seen, and what he had not seen was Friday's paper lying in the porch because, he said, it was not there.

***

At this point the reader is asked to join me in an act of faith and assume that one of the three newspapers found in the pit was Friday's. If it was, then the pace of the argument begins to quicken starting from the fact that two of the three newspapers (excluding Wednesday's) were found two bodies - to put it crassly - from the bottom of the pit. In other words, Friday's newspaper was thrown in the pit before five of the victims were, meaning five bodies were thrown in the pit sometime after 6:30 pm on Friday. This left, as opportunity for Cook to have done so, only the one hour he was in the house on Saturday.

Fair enough; if he went to the porch on Saturday evening and grabbed Friday's paper from beneath Saturday's and threw it into the pit before anything else thrown in on Saturday, well, murderers do things those among us who are not murderers find beyond comprehension. But then, picking it up at this point, the argument of the proponents of Cook's guilt *must* run as follows: there were only two periods which in which he could have attempted concealment of the crime: in the hours immediately after the murders before he left for Edmonton where he was seen at a car dealership at 8 am, and in the hour he spent in the house Saturday evening before leaving for Main Street and apprehension by the RCMP.

He cannot have carried all the bodies to the greasepit on Friday morning since the Friday paper (the assumption still holding) was found under five of the bodies. Therefore, he came back to the house on Saturday evening and carried five more bodies to the garage after first throwing Friday's paper on top of the two bodies tumbled into the pit early on Friday morning. He saw no use for the Saturday paper which was left lying in the porch throughout all the bloody ablutions going on in the house.

He now had to clean up the blood left by three of the five bodies (the two adults were killed on the bed where no cleanup was possible, but the two girls and the youngest boy had evidently fled as far as the livingroom) but didn't do much of a job of it. He did a better job on the fingerprints (which admittedly could have been done on Friday morning but it seems improbable since there were still bodies to be moved), wiping down the entire house removing all but some smudges and two identifiable prints - ten if one has regard to the isolated and anonymous memorandum in the Cook file in the National Archives. All the materials found on the bed in the master bedroom - the clothing, the parts of the shotgun, the mailbag, the "jumble' that Roach saw on Saturday night and which Sproule photographed on Sunday morning - were thrown there on Saturday evening since the bodies of the adults had to have been moved off the bed first; the bodies of Ray and Daisy, in that order, were the last to be thrown into the pit.

He interspersed transporting and dumping the five bodies with gathering up eight blankets, two sheets, two chenille bedspreads, four pillows, a pillowcase, a chenille housecoat, five tires, two wheel rims (one reddish, one red), a crown gear, a set of tire chains, some hubcaps, a pair of rubber boots, two bread wrappers, "a towel or two", a leather strap, a man's grey sock, a couple of toy holsters and revolvers[1], a car floor mat, a can of tire patching, a broken handled shovel, a crumpled beer carton, two deflated inner tubes, Wednesday's newspaper, some pieces of the shattered stock of the Demon, a crumpled icing sugar box, an Export cigarette tobacco package, some pop bottles and a quantity of unidentified material suggesting a plastic garbage pail seen on the landing had been emptied of its contents, and threw them all into the pit, mixing all of them indiscriminately with the bodies. The receptacle measured 28 inches wide, 52 inches long and 56 inches deep - not quite 48 cubic feet. He then replaced the planks and covered them with grimy cardboard.

It was now time to get rid of the blue suit, which he did, hiding it in a place where he probably felt it would never be found and might not have

---

[1] *We have seen that at the motel party on Wednesday night Cook had produced proudly and somewhat incongruously considering the circumstances - a bunch of drunken ex-cons sitting around talking about blowing safes with homemade nitroglycerine - a toy holster and revolver he'd made for his nine-year-old brother Jerry. We have also seen it was probably left in Eddie Read's truck - the evidence is murky to say the least - and the fact that two sets were found in the greasepit appears to be only coincidence. There were three small boys in the family, all of them either cops or robbers, and as such they - or two of them - would have been armed to the teeth.*

been but for some first-rate police work. But before he hid the suit, in addition to removing fingerprints, he spent a minute or two washing wallpaper in the back bedroom and then wiped up as much blood as he could from the living room floor and furniture. He then went downstairs, washed up, cleaned his fingernails so thoroughly as to leave not a microscopic trace of blood, stole some of Gurney's clothes, went upstairs and put on a change of clothes, loaded two suitcases and a metal box in the trunk of the Impala, and then sat down to relax and have a beer, doubtlessly drained by his demanding endeavors and feeling he'd earned a ten-minute break. He did all this in the space of an hour. Truly a whirling Dervish, he had filled most of those unforgiving minutes with sixty seconds' worth of distance run, probably whistling while he worked. The cleanup alone invites awe. Seven maids with seven mops couldn't have accomplished in half a year what Cook carried off, along with everything else, in a little hour by way of covering his tracks to seven bodies.

***

No other argument is consistent with Cook's guilt if the Friday paper was in the pit, but it seems to want for something, credibility perhaps, together with some indication from the advocates of Cook's guilt as to where Friday's paper was if not in the greasepit: elsewhere in the house? in the Impala? blowing in the summer winds down Railroad Avenue? They might wish to consider the merits of the counterargument: brevity and simplicity. Someone came to the house in the dark hours of Friday night-Saturday morning to finish what he'd left undone in the dark hours of Friday morning.

Yet we don't know that Friday's *Herald* ended up as a rough shroud for Gerry and Patrick, the two oldest of the three boys. If the critical importance of the question is acknowledged, the whole of the case against Cook can be seen to turn on the balance of the probabilities brought to bear on that lone question: in light of the evidence and the contributing probabilities (he took it to the Impala, he didn't take it to the Impala; he took it from beneath Saturday's paper, he didn't take it from beneath Saturday's paper and so on) is it *probable* that Friday's paper was in the pit?

The question cannot be sloughed off as merely a trivial matter of indecisive probability in an inconsequential backwater of the evidence - the treatment it got (if as much) at the hands of everyone concerned. If this is an accurate analysis, then legal scholars will someday puzzle over the fact that the pre-eminent murder trial in Alberta's ninety-year history could have been and should have been resolved (which is not to say solved, but would have been to hand it back to the RCMP) by recourse to the civil law standard of proof being applied to MacNaughton's innocuous question: Where was Friday's paper? If it could not be said categorically that it was *not* in the pit, Cook was entitled to acquittal.

Wednesday's was in the greasepit; Saturday's was in the porch. The quadrumvirate is neatly completed by concluding that Thursday's and Friday's preceded their mid-week companion into the makeshift sepulchre. Those who sat in judgment might have been persuaded to this view had it been forcefully argued; at some point inference in the direction indicated by common sense becomes unavoidable by, as Main characterized them, "reasonable men, ordinary everyday people." At the very least they would have retired to deliberate saying to themselves (having been forced by defense argument to say to themselves), "Maybe that damn paper *was* in the pit. Where does that leave us?" Where it would have left them was having to thread their way through the minefield of their own reasonable doubt if in spite of it they were going to return bearing a guilty verdict.

***

Forgetting probabilities, we can only speculate on the difference it might have made had Beeching, standing beside the pit notebook in hand as the contents of the pit reached floor level, made the single entry (just before the entry "Body No. 6"): "newspaper, June 26." Suppose, that is, that since it appeared to the police important enough to note that the newspaper immediately under Ray's body was Wednesday's, it was equally important to note that the two covering Gerry and Patrick were Thursday's and Friday's. Knowing their condition would have helped too; were they saturated in such a way as to suggest they'd been used to blot up pools of blood? Little things; things trained investigators might have been expected to notice even if at first blush they didn't contribute as persuasively to the case against Cook as, say, a blood-saturated suit.

If so, if Beeching had made the telling entry, then he would have counted himself lucky that no one thought to ask him two or three questions along the lines of the following: "Was Friday's paper in the greasepit Staff Sergeant?" "Quite so. Were there bodies on top of it?" "How many?" "Are you suggesting then, Staff Sergeant, that Cook gathered up five bodies and moved them to the greasepit on Saturday evening after first throwing in the Friday paper?" "No? When then? After the wedding dance at the Avenroy?" "But wouldn't that indicate that Teeple, Feth and Beasley, who never said anything about having been in Stettler with Cook, were accessories after the fact of murder?"

But the questions were never asked and the counterargument was never argued. The counterargument could have been set up by the defense by first demonstrating the absurdity of the Crown's position even though (since the defense went first in the concluding arguments to the jury) the defense could not know how far Anderson might go in miring himself in that absurdity. Anderson talked in terms of the killer's "frantic frenzy", having in mind all he assumed the killer had done in the immediate aftermath of the murders on Friday morning, but it was as nothing compared to the hour-long frenzy we have looked at which necessarily follows from the supposition that the Friday paper was in the pit.

The paper in the pit stands up, but the whirlwind frenzy doesn't, and the Crown should have been forced to stand and admit that had it taken the time to think the matter through, ridicule was its lot. It never hurts to destroy the prosecution in advance of the prosecution's first opportunity to destroy itself. There is always the chance it might waken to the dangers inherent in the logical consequences of it position and maintain a politic silence in the face of them. Anticipating such a silence, defense counsel should have adopted Riley's practice and been ready with all the questions about the newspapers the jurors would ask themselves - surprised as they may have been to find out that those - or any others - were the questions they would ask themselves since it is clear unanswered questions didn't form part of the lightweight baggage carried into either jury room.

But having failed to recognize that proper handling of the Friday paper was as close to proof of their case as they were going to get, both Main and Dunne were silent on the subject throughout the trials and during their closing addresses. Having nothing to answer, Anderson too was silent. Like Alice, Justices Greschuk and Riley seemed to find not an atom of meaning in the missing newspaper. They too were dumb. What would an explanation for the paper have been worth to them had they not been saved a world of trouble by finding not so much as an atom? Alice's sixpence? It would have been cheap at twice the thirty-five cents still owed McAlister.

In the beginning you will recall also that I advised this is what is known as a circumstantial case. I think it is not too unlike something of a jigsaw puzzle. The prosecution provides the pieces as best we are able, and it is the responsibility of the jury to sort them out and put them together.

J. WALLACE ANDERSON, QC
Address to the second trial jury

CHAPTER 22

THE SUITCASES AND THE STRONGBOX

Anderson's grab-bag approach to prosecution - roughly "here are the pieces; see what you can make of them" - is not one widely employed in the criminal courts. Nevertheless it had a certain aptness in the circumstances if seen as having been necessitated by Anderson's own development of the case against Cook. In general terms, the case was something of a grab-bag of unruly evidence replete with inconsistencies, gaps, improbabilities, contradictions, evidence that showed Cook to be a murderer, innocent, a madman, naive, a liar, careless beyond belief, a not very sophisticated professional criminal. What better way to deal with the whole mess (which was not entirely of Anderson's making; the RCMP, the defense lawyers and the judges had done their share) than to dump it in the laps of the bemused jurors with a challenge to make some sense of it?

"In the beginning," Anderson informed the jurors, he had advised them that this was what was known as "a circumstantial case." They had not anticipated that in the end, darkness and chaos would still reign on the face of the deep; that they themselves would have to illuminate the evidence and vest it with form; they would have been forgiven had they wondered whether their oath had stuck them with the responsibility of shaping the Crown's case for it. This school of prosecution raised a question as to who was doing the proving of the case beyond a reasonable doubt, or even whether that was any longer seen as required. But pettifogging legalities were swept aside in the rush of Anderson's approach which proved quite serviceable.

As quoted in this chapter's epigraph, Anderson was referring to his entire case against Cook. The approach could have been cobbled together specifically to cope with the problem of the suitcases - one of the more difficult in the case - although Anderson did not view it as one to be isolated and dealt with in its own terms before fitting it into the larger picture. Still, the evidence relating to the suitcases was before the jurors (although not all of it, as we shall see), and they could have isolated the problem, and perhaps have 'solved' it. The guilty verdict should have meant that they had managed "to sort out the pieces and put them together," but it is doubtful, given the magnitude of the problem and the amount of time devoted to deliberation by each jury, that they did so or even attempted to.

Or that they were capable of doing so; it cannot be supposed that a jury is a rational animal capable of sustained rational thought. If anything in the evidence against Cook called for the best the jury could bring to it by way of analytic power, the suitcase problem was it. But jurors have "little or no training in consecutive thought. They will be largely if not entirely swayed by emotion. But remember that in all probability they do not think so. The less training or capacity for reasoning they have, the more certain it is they will pride themselves on being susceptible only to strict logic and impervious to mere emotion"[1]. It was thus a case of there being no analytic power to be wheeled up and unlimbered. At most a desultory swipe would have been taken at it before moving to the business at hand: reach a decision and get out of there[2]. Wretches hang that jurymen may dine, as Pope observed in a moment of cynicism.

[1] *Sir (later Mr Justice) Malcolm Hilbery:* Duty and Art in Advocacy *(Stevens, London, 1946).*

[2] *The jurors were sequestered throughout the first trial. One of them was reported to have pressed for a quick decision in order to bring an end to the enforced celibacy of 11 days.*

Even had they been capable of bringing strict logic to bear on the problem, it would not have yielded to it, and it may be that mere emotion would have been the best instrument after all. The evidence of the suitcases is as consistent with innocence as with guilt, and is not really consistent with either in the sense of one totally excluding the other. The best guess is that if the jurors thought about it at all, they would have assumed that if someone wished to take the time to worry the pieces into the semblance of a picture, it would be the one contended for by the Crown. In the meantime, whatever the suitcases said, it could not be allowed to interfere with the central question they were called upon to decide: was he guilty? Their emotions parading as logic would tell them whether he was. What did a melange of unsatisfactory evidence about something as inconsequential as a couple of nondescript suitcases, and the time they were removed from the house, have to do with it?

Perhaps nothing; the jurors may have been right to cut through the evidence in order to get at the verdict. But later observers, including the writer, cannot let the suitcases go as easily, for they leave the persistent impression that just maddeningly beyond cognition they contain the key to the case. The usual box of jigsaw puzzle pieces - to finish with Anderson's metaphor - carries an implied warranty that the pieces will make up into the picture on the box, but there is no such warranty here since there is no clearly defined picture. Or rather there are two - allegorical depictions of guilt and of innocence, with the pieces randomly interchangeable and capable of being made up into either. They are a puzzle without a solution, a puzzle made by and for the inmates of Charenton. But here, below, are the pieces; the reader is invited to do something with them. Being handed neat little packets of pieces will make less frustrating the impossibility of assembling them into an elegant picture, and to that end a system of headings and sub-headings has been employed.

***

As groundwork, only one fact and a restatement of Cook's explanation of it are required. The fact was that the suitcases and the strongbox were found in the trunk of the Impala on Saturday evening by Sergeant Roach, after Cook drove to the Detachment at the request of Constable Braden. Cook's explanation was that when he was having a beer in the kitchen on Saturday evening, he spotted the suitcases sitting on the floor and the strongbox on the table, thought that his family had forgotten them when they left for BC, and put them in the trunk thinking to take them along when, after they phoned him early in the coming week to tell him where they were, he went out to BC to bring them back.

When he first heard this, Main may have wondered at the fate that had thrown him together with a man who could carry implausibility to heights that would have intimidated men less audacious - or witless - than Cook. Who had ever left on a trip forgetting the suitcases packed for it? Who would think - or say he thought - that anyone would? Who would think - or say he thought - that someone coming home from a trip would need for the return trip the suitcases they had rather carelessly forgotten when they left on it? Not to mention - going and coming - a little metal box containing all the family's valuable and not-so-valuable papers? To think they had forgotten it when they left implied the belief that there was some reason - who could conceive it? - they would want to take it with them. And, finally, who could stickhandle this nonsense past six no-nonsense men of affairs?

***

The questions are disarmingly simple:

(1) WHAT WAS PACKED IN THE SUITCASES AND THE METAL BOX?
(2) WHEN WERE THEY PUT IN THE IMPALA?
(3) WHY WERE THEY PACKED, WHEN, AND BY WHOM?

(1) WHAT WAS PACKED IN THEM?

What were they first of all? They were two cheap black suitcases described only as a "larger one" and a "smaller one," and a little tin box, green, of the type that New York ward bosses used to hoard their meagre savings in. It was unlocked; its little tin key had long since been lost, as they invariably are. It was Roach who called it a strongbox, according it a grandeur to which it was scarcely entitled. Locked, it might have defeated a four-year-old bent on pilfering pennies.

The reader by now should not be particularly surprised to learn that it is not known with any reasonable degree of certainty what was in the suitcases. In investigating the scene of a crime, the police undoubtedly have to exercise their judgment as to what is important and what is not as evidence of the crime they are unraveling. We have seen that Sproule skimmed over the guns in the basement as being of no particular importance, and Beeching's inventory of what was removed from the greasepit suggested that he made decisions on the spot that A deserved being listed while B did not. This may be explained in part by understating the obvious: it cannot have been pleasant to stand beside the pit making a note of every blood-soaked blanket as it came from the pit, and it may have seemed that "some blankets[1] " would serve as a sufficient description, just as did "three papers." It was a matter of judgment. As it was, back at the Detachment, when Roach opened the suitcases. There was a "whole bunch of junk" (as Dunne later called it) in them, and it must have seemed to Roach that it would be sufficient to get an accurate inventory of the major items, and a rough idea of what appeared to be minor and of no particular significance.

His trial evidence was of a piece. The major items more or less came through, as it were, on all three occasions, but to know as exactly as possible what was in the suitcases it was necessary to collate Roach's evidence from one hearing to the next, and to supplement it with the evidence of other witnesses, Ray Cook's sister-in-law Lucy, for example, who was able to identify certain personal family items. Putting it all together made it possible to establish that what were dismissed as "miscellaneous articles" at one trial included among many other things a veritable horde - or hoard - of old electric shavers. Only when the contents were laid out in their entirety, as it were, would it be possible to reach a tentative characterization of them as either (a) clearly the sort of stuff one would pack for a next-day departure on a trip; or (b) who in their right mind would pack this junk for a next-day departure on a trip?

The Large Suitcase

Four complete pairs of children's pyjamas
Four Tex-made percale sheets in original cellophane
Portrait of Daisy Cook's sister
Photograph album with snapshots
Pants Hanger
Two group photographs
Two (three?) unidentified portraits
Unidentified plastic object

---

[1] *The count shown on p.358 is accurately derived from other sources.*

Lady's brown purse containing: lady's Timex wristwatch, two dentist's receipts, date book, earrings, quantity of sales slips, comb and Kleenex

The Small Suitcase

Thermos bottle
Man's grey dress shirt, 14½ - 33
Small black camera
Renown alarm clock
Gillette safety razor
Memo pad
Shaving cream
Green lighter
Toothbrush
Hair dressing
Razor blades
Shaving brush
Schick electric razor
Sunbeam electric razor
Electric razor, make not stated

It was a mixed bag, for which 'packed' is a description as loose as the packing itself must have been.

The Strongbox

The little box contained just about what such boxes usually do: a handful of papers of some intrinsic worth, and a mass of papers kept because no one had taken the trouble to weed them out. The Royal Bank passbook which was in the box when Roach removed it from the Impala was taken from the box and entered as a separate exhibit:

Five children's birth certificates
Special Welder's Certificate
Tax notice and tax receipt
Four group life policies, expired
Envelope containing Ray's mother's will
Marriage license
Certificate of marriage
Two optometrist's receipts
Children's Immunization and Weight records
Two report cards - Gerald Cook

Certificate of Proficiency, Department of Industries and Labor
Three letters addressed "Dear Mom and Dad" and signed "Bob"
Pink financial responsibility card
"large bundle of documents, most of them bills, receipts and so forth"[1]

(2) WHEN WERE THEY PUT IN THE IMPALA?

There were two answers, Cook's: Saturday evening when as his last act in the house he took the suitcases from the kitchen floor and the box from the kitchen table and loaded them into the Impala; and the Crown's: Friday afternoon at Hood Motors when he transferred them from the station wagon to the trunk of the Impala.

In addition to Roach, there were nine people apart from Cook able to say what they had seen or had failed to see or had not seen in the station wagon or the Impala at a given time - ten if one includes Sonny Wilson. To say that Wilson could say what was in the station wagon on Friday morning is to concede provisionally the truth of the alibi. I have included him in the ten for what his evidence may be worth, and, starting with him, have taken them chronologically from the time of Cook's arrival in Edmonton early on Friday morning - either in time to break in to Cosmo Cleaners with Sonny Wilson or in time to visit South Park Motors at 8 am - and ending with Braden, who searched the Impala trunk on Saturday evening before Roach did.

Albert Victor ("Sonny") Wilson (Cook's alibi witness, who said Cook took part in the Cosmo Cleaners break-in)

Since no defense witnesses were called at the preliminary inquiry, Wilson gave evidence only at the trials. At the first trial he had been preceded on the stand by Constable Jack Bell, a defense witness, who said that he'd seen suitcases in the Impala trunk on Saturday evening during the Camrose liquor search which, if true, meant they had been in the station wagon, and had therefore been taken from the house by Cook on the night of the murders. So damaging was Bell's evidence to the defense that Main found himself in the impossible position of having to use the evidence of one of his witnesses, Wilson, to discredit the evidence of another, Bell, and to do so without expressly disowning Bell. He asked Wilson:

"Did you have an opportunity to see inside of the station wagon?"

[1] *Sergeant Tom Roach, second trial.*

"Yes sir."

"Could you tell us what was in it?"

"A toolbox and a plastic clothes bag."

"Anything else?"

"No sir."

"I am showing you [the suitcases]. You say you didn't see anything like that?"

"No sir. There was nothing else in the inside."

On cross-examination, Anderson had Wilson confirm that he had seen a toolbox in the station wagon (it can only be guessed why he would do this since it was not in the Crown's interest to have Wilson confirm what he had just told Main), but did not ask him whether he had seen anything else. Wilson was Main's last witness so that when he stepped down the defense witnesses had reached stalemate and the jurors were left with a choice: suitcases in the Impala trunk (Bell) against no suitcases in the Impala trunk (Wilson). Put another way, Camrose police officer against three-time and counting loser.

In light of his first-trial evidence, Bell once again became a Crown witness at the second trial, so Dunne was able to treat him as the enemy. He was unable to shake Bell on the suitcases, but he did succeed in exposing Bell as a less than reliable observer of the remaining contents of the Impala trunk and thus, by implication, not a witness one would wish to go to the wall with on the presence or absence of the suitcases. It was imperative that MacNaughton bolster what Dunne had been able to do with Bell by getting from Wilson that there were no suitcases in the station wagon. Wilson was also a witness one would not wish to go the wall with:

"Did you by any chance have a period to examine the inside of the station wagon?"

"Yes sir."

"Can you give the court an explanation of this Mr Wilson?"

"Well, I went in the car looking for a screwdriver or a tire wrench that I could remove the grating with and there was no implement heavy enough in the car."

"Could you give the contents of the car to the court as you noticed them?"

"There was a plastic bag with a zipper and a folding seat, I believe it is called a folding seat, the last seat of the station wagon, and there was a tool kit. I don't recall anything else."

"I am showing you [the suitcases], rather large items, did you see these items in the station wagon?"

"No sir, I did not.

"I am showing to you...a green metal box."

"I never saw that before sir."

"You never saw it and did you have to search rather diligently for this pry that you were after?"

"I looked underneath the seats and in the tool kit. There wasn't - there was nothing of any sort that I could . . . ."

"I am showing you [the black toolbox], do you recall having seen that article before?"

"I have seen one the very same sir."

We know that when Anderson got up to cross-examine Wilson, the suitcases were forgotten as an extravagant supply of screwdrivers were lifted from an inexhaustible box, but he could have done nothing with the suitcases in any case; Wilson was not about to admit that he had seen them where he had told MacNaughton he had not. But what Wilson had seen - a garment bag as well as the toolbox - suggested that as well as Wilson's getting to Cook the multifarious details of the Cosmo break-in, Cook had to have been getting to Wilson what was in the station wagon, since there was in fact a garment bag in it as well as the toolbox.

Peter Myhaluk (Father of Jimmy Myhaluk, who was released from Saskatchewan Penitentiary the same day as Cook and rode the bus with him back to Edmonton)

After breakfast at Myhaluk's on Friday morning - the morning of the torn suit - Cook offered to drive Peter and his wife Lea downtown, which he did. He and Jimmy Myhaluk then returned to the South Side and Hood Motors, where Cook began to negotiate the Impala deal.

Myhaluk gave evidence as a Crown witness at the preliminary inquiry and both trials. However, Dunne - knowing Bell had been subpoenaed as a Crown witness and knowing what he would say about what he'd seen in the Impala - was the only one who asked Myhaluk what he had seen in the station wagon when, presumably sitting in the back seat, he had ridden in it from South Edmonton to downtown Edmonton:

"Did you have a look at the inside of that station wagon?"

"Well, I was inside of the station wagon."

"You were inside it?"

"Yes."

"Did you notice whether there was any luggage in it?"

"No, there was not any luggage in the car."

With well enough in hand, Dunne should have left it alone, but he went on to ask "You say there was no luggage in it?" leaving it open to Myhaluk to reply, "No, I did not see any luggage in the car" which is subtly different from his categorical "There was not any luggage in the car." Dunne elicited an answer open to the interpretation that there may have been luggage, but if there was Myhaluk didn't happen to see it. It is the mark of experienced counsel to recognize when he has the answer which will do it, to know when it cannot be improved upon and to quit at that point.

Lea Myhaluk (Peter Myhaluk's wife)

She too was called as a Crown witness at the preliminary inquiry and both trials. With her husband, she had been driven to downtown Edmonton in the station wagon. No one asked her what she had seen in it.

Jimmy Myhaluk (Cook's buddy and "a good thief")

Myhaluk was called by the prosecution at the preliminary inquiry and ended by being declared a witness hostile to it. He was not, therefore, called to give evidence at either trial; the Crown could not distance itself enough from Jimmy Myhaluk who had had ample opportunity to observe the contents of the station wagon and the alleged transfer of the suitcases from it to the Impala. He could have been called by the defense to throw in against Bell in the second trial, but the defense lawyers wisely decided against him. He was not a witness to grace a case whatever his evidence.

Leonard Amoroso (The salesman with whom Cook negotiated the deal for the Impala)

The Hood Motors salesman said at the preliminary inquiry that while Cook was transferring his belongings from the station wagon to the new Impala, he, Amoroso, was in the office speaking to the credit manager about the cracked windshield on the station wagon - for which Cook had given him $50 to cover until Cook could make an insurance claim the following Monday - and to see whether GMAC's insurance man had arrived to place coverage on the Impala. When he came out, Cook had gone. Amoroso was asked whether he could remember anything he might have seen in the station wagon. He could not.

He was not questioned at the first trial about the contents of the station wagon, but told Anderson when the suitcases were produced to him that he did not recall having seen them. Anderson therefore had given Dunne what he wanted, and Dunne did not make the mistake of cross-examining Amoroso about the contents of the station wagon. In such circumstances witnesses tend to become fearful and start hedging on previous testimony: "Well, I'm not sure; I don't remember seeing any suitcases," leaving it open to the jurors to infer suitcases should they choose to do so.

Ricky Feth (One of the teenagers who rode with Cook from Camrose to Whitecourt and back)

Feth too was a three-time Crown witness. He was with Cook in the Impala for about 22 hours, during which the trunk lid was open on at least three occasions: when the beer purchased in Camrose was being put in the trunk; when Cook stopped on the way to the Avenroy dancehall to lend his jack to some army cadets who had a flat tire; and when Cook drove two or so miles from the dancehall to cache the beer in a ditch. Only at the second trial was Feth questioned about the contents of the trunk. He told Anderson that when Cook came out of the

Arlington Hotel with two cases of beer, he, Feth, got out of the car and opened the trunk "Not all the way sir, just a little bit, just opened it enough" so it wouldn't lock again. He didn't see inside the trunk when the beer was put in, nor when Cook stopped to take out the jack or to cache the beer. He told Dunne that he "didn't notice nothing."

Lorraine Beasley (the 15-year-old who spent a memorable 22 or so hours riding in the Impala)

Beasley was not called to give evidence in the *Cook trials*, but she was interviewed by the RCMP who were sure Cook was carrying a gun in the glove compartment of the Impala and wanted confirmation from her: "The RCMP kept asking me if I had had a look in the cubby hole because he had a gun in there and they wanted to know whether I'd seen it. There was no gun. I was in and out of that cubby hole a dozen time - cigarettes...." They did not question her about the suitcases.

Homer Teeple (One of the teenagers who rode with Cook from Camrose to Whitecourt and back)

The evidence of Teeple paralleled that of Feth. Teeple "didn't believe" he ever looked in the trunk.

Constable Richard John Bell (The Camrose police officer who stopped Cook on Friday afternoon, had coffee with him and his passengers early Saturday morning, and stopped Cook for questioning when they returned to Camrose on Saturday afternoon)

The reason for Main's calling Bell as a witness for the defense in the first trial may only be guessed at from the thrust of the direct examination. He got from Bell evidence of the U-turn incident, the idle chatter over coffee at the highway cafe, the suspected beer purchase, and agreement with Main's description of the Impala as being a car inviting attention - all of them inconsistent with the supposed demeanor of a man who had killed seven people a few hours before Bell first saw him. All, with the exception of the U-turn, were also previously obtained from Feth and Teeple, witnesses less deadly than Bell would prove to be. Bell told Main nothing that did anything more than reinforce what the jurors had already heard from Feth and Teeple, which was reason enough for calling Bell if that were all Bell was going to say. It didn't hurt to have at least one policeman giving evidence of a sort in Cook's favor.

Or at least it didn't until Anderson cross-examined him. Anderson came out of left field with his first question: "Have you any idea how far it is from Camrose to Stettler?" Bell answered, "I don't know," which might have accounted for why he so casually said someone might be down to Stettler later to serve a summons on Cook when he invited Cook to get out of Camrose.

The only way to account for Anderson's next question is to assume that it too was out of left field, or that he knew what the answer was going to be:

"When you searched the car the accused was driving, do you recall what you observed being in it?"

"In the trunk of the car there was two suitcases and a small metal box."

There was no follow-up by Anderson, suggesting either that he didn't appreciate what he had or, more probably, that he knew exactly what he had and, unlike Dunne, knew when to quit. What he had was the means of showing that Cook had taken the suitcases and the strongbox on Thursday night / Friday morning, knocking into a cocked hat Cook's story of having idly noticed them on the kitchen floor on Saturday evening and, probably ruminating fondly on his parents' forgetfulness in leaving them behind, having loaded them for the trip to BC. He was nothing if not strangely inventive.

Bell came late in the day to the realization that he had seen the suitcases and the box in the Impala trunk. As a Crown witness at the preliminary inquiry he related to the prosecutor, Scotty Macdonald, everything he was to tell Main at the first trial about his three encounters with Cook. Where Main saw in them a construction favorable to Cook, Macdonald either saw its negative obverse or he merely wanted from Bell what would have been gaps in the narrative without Bell's evidence. Neither Macdonald nor Main asked Bell whether Bell had looked in the trunk and, to be fair to him, he cannot be expected to have supplied an answer to a question that wasn't asked.

Being interviewed by the police however is a less structured setting than a magistrate's court, and when the RCMP interviewed Bell on Sunday, June 28, he did not mention having searched the trunk of the convertible - information which, one might think, one cop would see as being of interest to another, however trivial the offense being investigated by Bell was compared to the one that had prompted the RCMP to talk to him.

Having told Anderson at the first trial about the trunk search, Bell couldn't help but mention it to the RCMP, for the first time, when they interviewed him again on April 6, 1960, i.e. between the two trials - when they evidently were still engaged in "working up" the case against Cook. Notes in the Solicitor-General's file on the case[1] say, "In this statement [Bell] said that when checking the trunk he noticed two suit cases and a green metal box and he described them in some detail. He added that he had not seen the suit cases and green metal box which were entered as exhibits [and] did not believe he could identify them as being the ones he saw in the trunk of the car. He mentioned that Constable Starchesky *[sic]*, who was present during the search, had opened the two suitcases."

Bell did not mention Starcheski in the first trial, but he told the second that Starcheski had been present during the search. He said nothing about Starcheski having opened the suitcases - an interesting omission. True to what he had told the RCMP, he was not able to identify the suitcases and strongbox in court as being those he had seen in the Impala. They looked, Bell said, "much the same," but for Anderson's purposes this meant they were the same. Bell's identification was as positive as Anderson required because, for Bell to have seen two suitcases and a metal box in the same trunk where, four hours later, Roach saw a different two suitcases and metal box, was to ask too much of coincidence. Therefore the suitcases and the strongbox had been put in the station wagon immediately after the murders. Cook's story was dead, to be followed shortly by its chronicler.

Not that it mattered, but Bell's power of observation stopped short of the other contents of the trunk. He did not remember seeing the green plastic garment bag, which was stretched out full-length and partially over the suitcases when Roach removed them from the Impala. He did not remember seeing a grey car coat, several shirts and a checkered windbreaker. He did not remember whether the spare tire was in an upright position and to one side, or flat and concealed in a well. He did not remember seeing the black toolbox, which was scarcely smaller than the small suitcase. Away from the contents of the trunk (apart from the suitcases and the strongbox) the accuracy of Bell's recollection was little better: asked the color of Cook's grey and pink shirt, he remembered it as white. It will be remembered Bell had sat with Cook for, at a guess, half an hour or so on Friday night-Saturday morning having coffee.

Charlie Starcheski (A Camrose police officer)

---

[1] *"Notes on* Cook Case*," Solicitor-General, Capital Case file, National Archives.*

Starcheski was a constable on the Camrose police force and was present when the Impala was stopped and searched by the police on Saturday afternoon. According to the "Notes on Cook Case" quoted above, Bell informed the RCMP on April 6, 1960 that Starcheksi had searched the two suitcases that day. Also according to the Notes, "Constable Starchesky *[sic]* . . . upon being interviewed, could not recall having checked the contents of the suit cases and in fact could not recall having seen the suit cases at all."

It may of course be the case that ten months after the event, Starcheski genuinely couldn't remember seeing (not to mention searching) the suitcases when in fact he had done one or both. Memory falters. But it seems probable that the details of his involvement in the Cook case, however peripheral, would tend to linger in memory for something longer than ten months, particularly when the definitive trial was still in the future. And it seems unfortunate that Dunne didn't interview Starcheski and call him as a witness for the defense. He had looked in the same trunk as Bell had and could not remember seeing suitcases, where Bell had not only seen them, but also had seen Starcheski searching them.

(According to Ricky Feth's second trial testimony, it was Bell and Constable (later Chief) Duff Franklin who had stopped them, rather than Bell and Starcheski. When I interviewed him, Feth thought it might have been all three. Franklin was not called as a witness. Interviewed in 1977, Franklin could not recall whether or not he had gone out to the street when the Impala was stopped, and could not recall having seen any suitcases. However, he did recall having seen "a green tackle box" with papers in it, though he could not remember where. At one point in the interview he thought he had seen it "upstairs" (where the police offices were), and at another that he had seen it in the trunk, even though he could not remember having gone out to the car.)

Constable Allan Eugene Braden (The Stettler police officer who stopped Cook on Saturday evening and brought him in for questioning on what became the false pretenses charge)

Where Braden had been instructed by Roach merely to bring Cook in, Braden followed good police practice and asked Cook to open the trunk. At the preliminary inquiry, Braden testified to having seen "some clothing," and at both trials, to having seen clothing and a green box. That's all he remembered, saying nothing about the garment bag, the toolbox or the suitcases. In the second trial Dunne got Braden to agree that the car was white with red upholstery and was "pretty conspicuous" - a fact that over the course of two trials was to become as well established as any. Dunne never thought it worth while to ask Braden whether he had seen the two suitcases in the trunk - suitcases that were, in the context of a trunk search, about as conspicuous as the car itself. But Braden's evidence was in any case immaterial to the enquiry as to the time of the suitcases having been placed in the trunk; even had he seen them - and remembered having done so - his saying so would not have supported Cook's account over Bell's or vice versa.

However, Braden's seeing only clothing and the small green strongbox in a trunk containing two large suitcases said something about his powers of observation; it said they were at best faulty. That fact could have been driven home by Dunne on the premise that it never hurts for defense counsel to impugn police powers of observation, no matter how inconsequential their evidence of what they saw or, in Braden's case, failed to see. Rather than ignoring the unseen suitcases in favor of establishing the color of the upholstery, Dunne could have tied down that Braden's trunk search had failed to reveal the presence of two suitcases. Dunne could then have asked what, if anything, that might say about Bell's claim to have seen suitcases (which he did not open up to search for the liquor he claimed to be searching for) in the same trunk, at a time when it was imperative that the defense show the suitcases not to have been there. What was in question here was nothing less than the infallibility of the police - or so the defense argument would run. To attack Braden would have been to set up an attack on Bell.

***

Sonny Wilson said he did not see any suitcases when, in the middle of the night Thursday/Friday, he searched the back of the station wagon when it was parked behind Cosmo Cleaners. Peter Myhaluk said there was no luggage in the station wagon on Friday morning when Cook drove him and his wife and son to downtown Edmonton. Leonard Amoroso had no recollection of having seen suitcases in the station wagon at Hood Motors in Edmonton on Friday afternoon. Charlie Starcheski informed the RCMP that he had not seen, much less searched, any suitcases in the Impala trunk in Camrose on Saturday afternoon, but he was not called upon to disclose that information in a trial court. Jack

Bell informed two such courts (but not the preliminary inquiry court), that he had seen suitcases in the Impala trunk on Saturday afternoon.

The box score seemed to favor Cook, but Bell won. Sonny Wilson of course was not believed - the station wagon had never been behind Cosmo Cleaners. Peter Myhaluk was ignored. Leonard Amoroso had contributed nothing one way or the other, although the probabilities could be seen as having contributed more to the defense than to the prosecution. His failure to see any suitcases indicated that there weren't any, rather more than that there were and he had merely failed to notice them. Starcheski's information to the RCMP flatly contradicted Bell's information to the same police force: where Starcheski said that he had not searched any suitcases, had not even seen any suitcases in the Impala trunk, Bell said that he saw Starcheski searching them.

For the Crown's purposes, Bell's evidence was to be preferred (which is to assume that the RCMP shared its Starcheski intelligence with Anderson; it may not have done so - an oversight), and Starcheski was not put to the trouble of being called as a Crown witness. But nor, for that matter, was he called by the defense - a particularly inexcusable omission after Main, in the first trial, had learned too late that his own witness Bell was to give evidence that would drive another nail home in Cook's none-too-figurative coffin.

If Bell could have been made to repeat on the witness stand what he had told the RCMP - that he had seen Starcheski searching the suitcases - and had Starcheski been called to refute that evidence under oath, Bell's own evidence of having seen the suitcases in the trunk would at best have been highly questionable. Had Bell stood firm, it would then have been an interesting enquiry as to why a town constable, either Bell or Starcheski, had lied to an RCMP investigator. But Bell's evidence was not impugned, and thus was accepted over Cook's contradictory account. Bell's seeing the suitcases in the Impala on Saturday afternoon made it possible to trace them back to the station wagon on Friday morning, and to fix Cook with lying about having taken them when he backed the Impala up to the garage door on Saturday evening.

Taking them on Saturday didn't make much sense, but insofar as there was any, it had to be found in Cook's reason for having done so: the folks would need them on returning from BC when he drove out to pick them up. Flimsy as it was, as reasons go, it is not possible to think of another; but neither is it possible to think of any reason for his having taken them early Friday morning in the immediate aftermath of murder

- unless, as Greschuk invited the jury to consider as a possibility, his taking the suitcases was intended as part of fostering the appearance of the family's having left on a vacation. If missing bedclothes might seem weak as evidence of a family's having left on vacation, the absence of suitcases seems marginally better. Yet would Cook, or anyone else in that situation, reason that the police would walk away from a field of carnage, having noticed that suitcases weren't strewn on it and deduced that the family was probably off on its annual two weeks in Aculpulco? In Greschuk's curious view, they might, and if the jury was prepared to buy that Cook had, then that explained the presence of the suitcases in the trunk of the Impala when Bell searched it.

But however unsatisfactory Cook's explanation, it must surely be seen as preferable to Greschuk's 'appearance-of-vacation' hypothesis; it leaves Saturday as the probable time when he put them in the trunk, and at the same time accounts for the Impala's being backed up to the garage door in full view of all the daylight traffic on Railroad Avenue. The fact that a witness testified that the car was backed in rather than drawn in frontwards suggests a loading of the trunk at that time - with the suitcases and the strongbox - and the unloading of the toolbox, which Cook said he took into the garage but which Roach said he found in the trunk (where, nevertheless, it was not seen either by Braden or by Bell). The possible significance of the car's orientation was not remarked on. When all the vexing facts are factored in, they amount to this: there was some reason for Cook's taking them on Saturday afternoon and some circumstantial evidence of it, but there was neither reason nor evidence - apart from the necessary implication of Bell's evidence - for his taking them on Friday morning if he was fleeing the scene of his crime.

When Bell's testimony unexpectedly indicated that Cook took the suitcases on Friday morning, Anderson was able to show that once again Cook had lied although not for any discernible reason. Anderson did not appear to be himself persuaded to the 'vacation' hypothesis - he did not argue it during his address to either jury - which left him with nothing to explain Cook's inexplicable action. Yet the merely inexplicable was not something to stay Anderson's hand. He provided the jury with a single piece of the jigsaw puzzle - Bell's evidence - "as best [he was] able." If the jury could sort it out and match it with a plausible reason for Cook's having taken the suitcases at the time of the murders, as Bell's evidence proved he did, well and good. And if it couldn't, well that too was well and good.

***

It is doubtful that the police, picking their cautious way through the mounting evidence of slaughter at the Cook house on Sunday, made much of the fact that there weren't all that many suitcases lying around. But long before Monday morning when they interrogated Cook, Beeching and Roach realized that the suitcases Roach had taken from the trunk of the Impala on Saturday evening were significant, in a way they could then only guess at. During the Monday interrogation, Beeching first asked Cook the time of his arrival home on Thursday and was informed that "It must have been 6 - after 6." The latter was literally true; it was, as we have seen, about 9:30 that evening. Beeching then asked him: "What suitcases did you have with you when you came home?" and Cook answered, "One big one and one small one." This was literally untrue. When Ray picked him up on Thursday evening, he was of course walking, and in any case had no suitcases with him. When he returned home on Saturday evening in the Impala, if he was to be believed, rather than bringing suitcases with him, he picked them up.

Beeching returned to the suitcases mid-way through the interrogation:

"How do you account for the children's pyjamas being in that suitcase?"

"Whose - mine? When I took the suitcases from the house I didn't think they were going to use both of them."

There Beeching left it, and there in the brief compass of two questions and two answers, Beeching left the problem of the suitcases beyond any possibility of solution. There were only two suitcases in question, yet Beeching appeared satisfied to have Cook bringing two home with him - probably on Thursday, although the day wasn't tied down - and taking at least two ("when I took the suitcases") when he left the house on a day the interrogation did not establish. Moreover, he was content to let Cook account for the presence of children's pyjamas in one of the suitcases (or were they Cook's pyjamas? - "Whose - mine?) with a confused explanation for taking the suitcases: he took two, leaving behind none, because he thought his family would need only one. It was not interrogation to inspire confidence, or to find its way into a manual of police techniques of doing such things.

It was nevertheless enough to alert Cook to the potential peril posed by being unable to satisfactorily explain the presence of the suitcases in the Impala. He had five months between the date of his arrest and the first trial to think about the problem, and to decide that the simple truth of the matter would not serve at the trial. He therefore concocted a fabrication out of whole cloth, reducing it to writing perhaps as a way of lending it substance. It is found only in a surviving segment of a longer note: "Mom told me to take the two suite cases that were in the basement as I'd need someplace to put the clothes I was going to buy in Edmonton. They were going to get a good set Friday morning."

This might have served, had it not failed to account for the strongbox (about which Beeching never questioned him; it is not known whether it was on view when Cook was shown the large suitcase containing the pyjamas) and but for the fact that the 'empty' suitcases to be taken in order to hold the new wardrobe were full of junk. He therefore abandoned it and went with the 'forgetful parents' explanation in court, which is not, of course, necessarily to say that he abandoned it in favor of the truth.

The note's compelling interest lies in its presumably artless indication of the point of origin of the suitcases as "the basement" rather than the kitchen floor. He had gone to the basement, on Saturday evening, to wash up and to grab Gurney's jacket on the careless supposition that it was his. It seems probable that the suitcases would have been kept in the basement, that the kitchen floor was not their normal repository, but then who brought them upstairs? Cook, his note inadvertently drawing attention to their point of origin? Daisy, beginning her preparations for the family's departure for BC on Friday or Saturday? Little green men emerging from a UFO? And, if Cook, why? It was a case in which one guess was as good as another.

***

For Mr Justice Greschuk, the question was not were the suitcases ever in the station wagon, as they would have to have been in order to be transferred to the Impala where they were later seen by Bell, but rather, as he said to the jury, "*When* were the suitcases placed in the station wagon?" [emphasis added] The question had a narrow choice of answers: it had to have been either Thursday evening when, he said, he left for Edmonton with his family alive and well and living where they had always lived; or Friday morning when, searching desperately for anything that would serve to dupe the police, his eyes lit on the suitcases (but where: in the basement? the kitchen?) and his cunning mind hatched the cool stratagem of removing both them and the bedclothes - in Greschuk's view of the evidence - to the station wagon.

But the question of whether he had placed the suitcases in the station wagon at all was of course in issue, a matter for the decision of the jury, and it is probable that Greschuk's putting the question as he did was merely an unfortunate error - although it was one that left the items' being placed in the station wagon on Friday morning as a *fait accompli* in the minds of the retiring jurors. The case was not immune from such errors; criminal trials rarely are, and thus the right of appeal in all such instances. Here the error was recognized by Main and urged as a ground of appeal, but it was not dealt with by the appellate court, which, as we have seen, set aside the first-trial conviction on another ground.

In his charge to the second jury Mr Justice Riley did not repeat Greschuk's error, but in dealing with trademark brevity - sixteen lines of transcript - with the problem of the contents of the Impala trunk - liquor, suitcases, toolbox, strongbox, clothing, garment bag, spare tire - and who saw what and when, Riley made two errors of his own. Each of them was nothing more than a slip of the tongue, and neither of them was of any discernible consequence in influencing the jury[1]. In any case neither found its way into the Notice of Appeal. The charge to the jury was a prime example of Riley's slipshod approach to the handling of facts - components of a criminal trial not without their own peculiar importance.

(3) WHY WERE THEY PACKED, WHEN AND BY WHOM?

The question cannot be answered in its own terms if by packing one thinks in terms of preparation for a trip; that much seems clear from the nature of the contents which suggest not that someone was getting ready for a departure from Stettler by packing three electric razors, a safety razor, a shaving brush, shaving cream and razor blades - erring, one would think, on the side of excess no matter how manic the compulsion to shave - but rather that the suitcases had served the mundane purpose of catch-alls for a superfluity of household articles for which there was no other storage space - some of it of current value (the children's pyjamas, the new sheets), some of it family keepsakes to be brought out on family occasions, if then (the portraits and photographs), the bulk of it junk of the type which, when they became popular in later years, would with luck have been finally disposed of in a garage sale.

---

[1] *He referred to Gurney as a "boarder" when he was a roomer only, and to "a black suitcase" being removed from the trunk, which was technically true but only half the picture - not even that.*

If that much is conceded, then the most probable answer to the rest of the question is indicated: they were 'packed' by Daisy over a period of weeks and months as a way of getting overflow possessions out of sight - a use to which suitcases otherwise used once a year are often put. When the time comes for the annual departure for London and Paris, they are retrieved from the basement, emptied of their contents and packed in the conventional sense. On their arriving home, the suitcases revert to their former homely estate and the process of accretion of junk in them is resumed.

But to agree that Daisy went to the basement and brought the suitcases to the kitchen for packing them in the morning she did not live to see, is to say nothing of Cook's reason for placing them in either the station wagon or the Impala - whichever it was. The explanation for each is found either in the Greschuk hypothesis or in Cook's account respectively, the inadequacies of both of which we have examined. Or it is to be found in some third set of facts the nature of which has yet to occur to anyone and is not now likely to.

It may be that the search for a rational explanation in response to these questions is misplaced - that everything that took place in the Cook household after the murders was a concatenation of irrational events, stemming from and in keeping with the quintessentially irrational act of murder, and that we will have to let it go at that. The two "suite cases" thus join the shotgun and the Ross shirt, to name two, among those fractious exhibits in *Regina v. Cook* that obdurately refuse to yield up convincing answers.

Do you suggest that a sergeant of the RCMP who is in charge
of this investigation would come in here and make a mistake of
those dimensions?

J. WALLACE ANDERSON, QC, *Cross-examination, second
trial,Robert Raymond Cook.*

CHAPTER 23

THE STRANGER THEORY AND STUTTERING OLIVER

Lawyers who would not accept elevation from private practice to the
bench of a superior court are as rare - if not as valued - as spotted owls.
Even rarer are those who make it and do not discover that on occasion
the pressures of a criminal trial are more than they anticipated. Theirs is
the responsibility to guide the uncertain process, and theirs the blame if
the process goes off the rails. The liberty of a man who may be innocent
is in the balance, and there was a time when lives were thrown into it as
well. When, in that time, the balance tipped in favor of society, a
moment dreaded by most trial judges had arrived. A black cap was
donned and the prisoner, in shock, ordered to stand the better to hear
words he could not credit as applying to him, words which would round
his little life with a sleep in a manner fully as barbaric as any he might
have visited on his innocent victim.

All the pressures were present in the 11 days of Cook's first trial, and
they seemed to take their toll on Mr Justice Peter Greschuk who took his
duties seriously indeed and who was thought by some observers to grow
more sallow and haggard as the trial ground on, and to be nearing
exhaustion as he approached the end of his five-hour charge to the jury.
Rumors of retaliation against him if the verdict went against Cook
(probably groundless but perhaps not), the resulting extraordinary
security measures taken in the courtroom, the near certainty of having to
pass the death sentence - the whole hypertense ordeal cannot have
contributed much to Greschuk's equanimity, and may explain why,

towards the end of the charge, he stumbled wearily into a statement of the jury's duty which on a surface reading appears unexceptionable but is found on analysis to be doubtful as a statement of law. "If," he admonished the jurors, "you believe that an unknown killer or killers perpetrated the killings, or if you are left in reasonable doubt as to whether an unknown killer or killers perpetrated the killings, then I say to you you must give the benefit of that reasonable doubt to the prisoner and you must acquit him."

His statement is seen to be made up of two parts. The first treats of the belief of the jurors in the guilt of an unknown killer or killers, but with no direction from the trial judge as to what was required of them if they harbored that belief. The second part may be seen as having sent the jurors off in hot pursuit of a wild goose. Cloistered in the jury-room, they were to weigh the evidence against someone other than Cook. If he jurors reasonably doubted that the guilt of the unknown killer had been proved - by whom is uncertain - the benefit of that doubt was to be conferred on Cook, the forgotten man for the moment in an inquiry in which he played no part, but now the beneficiary of the finding in it. The verdict brought out of the jury room would take roughly the form of finding Cook innocent because the jurors had not found anyone else guilty and, in the vernacular, everyone would walk.

It may be guessed he meant to say that if the jurors admitted there was a reasonable possibility that a stranger was the killer, it could not be said Cook's guilt had been proved beyond a reasonable doubt - a realm which does not admit of reasonable alternate possibilities or what the law of circumstantial evidence calls any other rational explanation. It is probable that the jurors, men whose sophistication did not lie in dissecting legal subtleties, were oblivious to what Greschuk had said, but it must have been otherwise with Main who was hearing the heart of his defense - the stranger theory - effectively gutted, to scramble a metaphor. What the jurors heard was if they thought it was a stranger, Cook was a free man. They none of them thought it was a stranger.

It is possible to see the incubation of the theory as early as the early stages of the preliminary inquiry the transcript of which bears Main's marginal annotations - "Any check of known crim. who were or had been in Stettler during the last 4 days?"; "Did P/C Braden receive any instructions to pick up and question strangers or known criminals on Sun. 28 June?" among others. It appears that early on Main had wisely decided not to rely on the supposition that the Crown would not be able to prove its case; he would reinforce its weakness by introducing the reasonable possibility of stranger as perpetrator. Nor was it a mere stratagem on Main's part; throughout he genuinely believed that the perpetrator would be found to be a "known criminal" other than Cook - as well-known a known criminal as Stettler boasted.

Believing in his client's innocence as Main did[1], by definition he believed in the guilt of someone else. But his view was a curiously limited one for an experienced criminal lawyer and former criminal court magistrate before whom every known variety of criminal had appeared at one time or another[2]. To Main, only a criminal of a particular stripe was capable of the savagery of the Cook murders.

There was far from an overwhelming body of evidence to suggest it - and indeed the evidence of it was signally short of whelming - nevertheless Main ought to have reckoned with the possibility that someone other than a known criminal - someone indeed other than a criminal - was entirely capable of slaughtering the Cook family. No one was exempt. Any resident of Stettler, anyone familiar with the Cook household although such familiarity was not essential, anyone an intimate of Ray and Daisy Cook's, anyone, in a word, was a possibility, but Main could not conceive of it and throughout he focussed as much of his attention as could be spared from staving off the Crown's case to "jailbirds and hoodlums" - the quaint words Main employed to delineate the class in which the killer of the Cooks would be found.

For Main therefore where else would the mantle of suspicion fall but on Stuttering Oliver Durocher who was a jailbird and hoodlum as if to the manor born. Durocher was one of nature's ignoble men. Brave beyond any telling of it when he was sneaking up behind Cook with an 18" steel pipe, on the street and away from the protection of a handful of hulking cohorts to whom he attached himself in the prison hierarchy he was anything but.

[1] *Unlike Dunne, he was cautious about sharing his belief and would not admit it to me. His widow Marjorie told me there was never any question in Main's mind.*

[2] *Among them Cook who, in December, 1951, was sentenced by Main to a year for car theft and six months concurrent for dangerous driving - sentences which were to be subsumed in the eighteen-month sentence imposed by a Calgary magistrate for B&E in the following month. Main would not have remembered that his notorious client of 1959 had appeared before him eight years earlier as a 14-year old car thief, and both died without realizing that they had met in former incarnations: Main as magistrate and Cook as car thief. In 1951 each to the other was a faceless cog in the system. It was otherwise in 1959-60. The ironies were such that the catalysts of the profound affection which grew between them were mass murder and Cook's pending death.*

Durocher's hatred of Cook was built up of various elements. There was probably a racial component (Durocher was a native) and rivalry between boxing cliques, but the chief element was one deriving from a situation which did credit to Cook, but which he could not bring himself to disclose at a time when he needed all the credit he could get: on the stand fighting for his life. Durocher was straight but with a bisexual bent - a homosexual dimension is often forced on heterosexual men by the particular pressures of a penitentiary - and he pined after a recently admitted inmate whom we shall call Baird, young, fair and virginal as these things are measured by the men who nurse those passions. The Bairds of a prison community are fair game for its Durochers, and Baird sought the protection of Cook, himself not of that propensity but willing to take the part of a potential underdog. He took Baird under his wing as it were; he feared no one, not certainly Stuttering Oliver. Cook had come between him and the object of his affections, and he tried to kill him.

Surprisingly, Durocher telegraphed his intentions towards Cook in advance of the corridor attack. The deputy warden of Saskatchewan Penitentiary, John Henry Weeks, told Wally Anderson of some of the surrounding circumstances when Anderson questioned him as to whether he had been an eye-witness to the attack which Anderson was seeking to discount: "This Durocher came up to my office and he told me that he was looking for a guy and he was going to get after him you see, so I got an officer and I put an officer on his tail, watch him around, you see, but during, you know, you have got six hundred fifty men running loose out in the prison there, you have got a lot of men to look after and he slipped by him somehow and then he got into this corridor." When the dust of Weeks' syntax had settled, the message MacNaughton (and Main before him) wished to convey was as firmly implanted as it would ever be: so much did Durocher hate Cook that nothing including the annihilation of Cook's family was too much by way of exacting his revenge for having been deprived of Baird's love.

It wasn't much, but it was the only card the defense in either trial saw itself as having to play and they played it for what they saw as its worth, (Dunne to a lesser extent than Main) missing the real worth of Durocher which was to show Cook in the favorable light he deserved. To play the Durocher card, they had to get him somewhere in the vicinity of Stettler. First prove opportunity. The defense was not entirely alone in wondering about Durocher. The public was already beginning to stir uneasily since from the first days of the investigation it all seemed too cut and dried. *The Calgary Herald* of July 11, 1959 in a manhunt story reported that "Local rumor also had it that a cellmate of Cook's in Prince Albert - since released and now working in northern Alberta - had beaten up on him in the penitentiary." Northern Alberta could have meant anywhere, but it least had him in the right province for defense purposes. But where was he on June 25? It is not known, but it was known (although not to the defense or the prosecution in the first trial, but perhaps to both in the second) that on June 24 he was very probably in Edmonton, having arrived there on the same day as Cook.

Penitentiary Service policy was to provide a prisoner being released with prepaid fare to the point of his arrest - in Durocher's case Brandon, Manitoba with a further destination, Winnipeg (at his expense) shown on his release documents. It was in the Crown's interest to show that wherever he ended up, Durocher at least departed the penitentiary heading easterly so far as penitentiary records indicated, but Anderson didn't appear to take the Durocher threat seriously, and he elicited no evidence in either trial to show that far from skulking around Stettler awaiting his opportunity, he had probably gone to Winnipeg - or at least Brandon. It was left to Mr Justice Riley to establish - or to think he'd established - that Durocher had gone to Winnipeg:

THE COURT: "Well, Mr Weeks, I wonder if you would help me on a couple of points if you could. Where was Durocher's home town?"

"Edmonton is his home town, yes."

"Do you know when he was discharged?"

"He was discharged on the 23rd of June."

"The same day as Cook?"

"Yes."

"Thanks ever so much."

"But he went in a different direction."

"Where did he go?"

"He went to Winnipeg."

"He went to Winnipeg."

But it appeared he didn't unless, as may have happened, he went to Winnipeg and almost immediately redoubled his tracks to Saskatoon and went on to Edmonton. The first inkling Main had that Durocher had gone to Edmonton either directly from Prince Albert or via Winnipeg occurred when Main was no longer actively involved in the defense. It came to light during Anderson's cross-examination of Cook in the second trial:

"Now, this note Durocher sent you didn't contain any suggestion whatsoever of personal harm to anyone other than you, did it?"

"No sir, it didn't say he was going to go after my father or mother or anything."

THE COURT: "Well, why are you pursuing that; the evidence is that Durocher went to Winnipeg."

COOK: "He didn't go sir."

MR ANDERSON: "We were told by Mr Weeks that Durocher planned to go to Winnipeg."

COOK: "Yes sir, but...."

THE COURT: "Weeks' evidence was more definite than that. Weeks said he went in the other direction."

MR ANDERSON: "Thank you my Lord. What about that?"

"COOK: "Well sir, I know he didn't go to Winnipeg."

"Well, tell us how you know."

"Because my lawyer enquired, Mr Main, of a Joe Spurling."

"Well, I don't know how far you can go with these enquiries. Do you know of your own personal knowledge whether he went to Winnipeg or not?"

"I know from what other people told me."

What would have been double hearsay - Cook telling the court what Main had told Cook he'd been told by Spurling - prompted Anderson to cut Cook off, leaving intact the Weeks evidence that Durocher had gone to Winnipeg which, for Durocher, was not a bad place to be thought to be when some lawyers for whom he bore no malice, who he didn't even know, were attempting to make of him the prime suspect in what he would have styled a serious murder beef.

***

Durocher was of little or no concern to the RCMP prior to the first trial, but for reasons known to them only, they decided to have a look at him between the two trials. On April 20, 1960, they found and interrogated him in Edmonton and got from him the surprising admission that he *had* been in Edmonton on June 24, 1959 and from his mother the claim that he had spent the night June 25-26 in her home. They could confirm only, from a hotel register, that he was in Edmonton at least for the period June 30 - July 2. The lines of communication between the RCMP and Anderson appear to have broken down since here was information - Durocher's admission, his mother's claim and the hotel register - which, had the RCMP seen fit to share it with Anderson, Anderson would then have been duty bound to disclose to the court to counter the Weeks evidence which appeared clearly to be mistaken. Moreover - a small boon for the defense - it would have corroborated the truth of Cook's evidence of what Main had told him he'd been told by Spurling, hearsay though it was.

It is inconceivable that Main would not have told Dunne what he'd been told by Spurling. The RCMP's information on Durocher being in Edmonton [1], had it been relayed from the RCMP to Dunne via Anderson (as it ought to have been) would merely have confirmed what Dunne already knew or should have known from Main. If Dunne had been serious about Durocher, he would have called Spurling (and the RCMP, had Anderson relayed the Edmonton information to him) in order to get Durocher about 600 miles closer to the scene of the crime they wished to accuse him of (without actually saying so) than if he'd been in Winnipeg. Still not close enough, but being eased in the right direction.

---

[1] *I will forego comment about "some RCMP guy" sitting in court with Anderson and remaining silent in the face of the Weeks evidence which he knew to be seriously misleading. See p. 341*

But Dunne was never as serious about Durocher as Main had been, except as Durocher formed part of the wispy band of criminals released with Cook any or all of whom could be considered, in Dunne's view, as Cook's good companions from the penitentiary bent on robbing him of his life's savings, one of whom - the doubly motivated Durocher?- wiped out Cook's family into the bargain. This was as close as Dunne got to a coherent theory.

***

Life was not kind to Stuttering Oliver Durocher - the very epithet is cruel and it has been too easy to follow suit. There is not much to be said in his favor insofar as his life brushed against Cook's, but what little is known should be recorded here. Were posterity to try him for the Cook murders he would be acquitted; the desperation on the defense side showed when Durocher was picked either as a murderer or as a man the jury might buy as a murderer *in absentia*. I asked Walter Bilton about him and the defense theory. He and Bilton were professional colleagues, Bilton as a long term guard at the Fort and Durocher as an inmate who came and went with routine frequency whenever he pulled a deuce less: "Stuttering Oliver? Hell no! A big bull around the jail but nobody on the street. Windsor Chalifoux and him; they were a pair. But Stuttering Oliver? Christ, he wouldn't kill anybody."

His life was bracketed between pre-natal despair and drugs. It ended in squalor by drug overdose on Vancouver's Skid Road and started in squalor with all the bright promise offered by being born in a rural ghetto in the grip of a raped and defeated heritage from which there was no direction open to him but straight down. Not surprisingly he took it and in due course began a lifelong shuffle through his mandatory role as part of the disproportionate percentage of native Canadians in prison populations. Like Cook he could not rise above the circumstances which life throws up to ensnare its bemused participants, although Cook at least tried when it no longer mattered, when the chance to do so was no longer there.

One man doesn't lay open another man's skull with a length of steel pipe out of some momentary pique; Durocher unquestionably hated Cook. Yet there may have been something between them stronger even than hatred: an identity of interest in the face of the common enemy.

Durocher told someone who knew them both (who related it to me) that he was prepared to appear in court to give his version of what had happened in the corridor attack and the reason for it (he had disclosed it to the RCMP in Edmonton, omitting nothing not excluding the Braid involvement) if doing so would help Cook. Well, perhaps. One would like to give Durocher at least that much.

***

In the end the Crown's chief argument against the stranger theory - a stranger would not have known of the existence of the greasepit - succeeded in destroying the theory, but it depended upon a fact which could not be proved: that the planks which closed it in were in place and completely concealed (by one or more of the seven pieces of flattened cardboard which littered the floor) when the stranger first came onto the landing outside the kitchen door looking for a place to hide the bodies. If the presence of the pit was concealed, then, the Crown implied, only someone who knew what lay beneath the cardboard knew that that was the one place in the house where the bodies could be hidden. This is not to say a stranger could not have discovered the presence of a concealed pit just as the police would do - by lifting a piece of cardboard not knowing what was beneath it - but the court was not dealing in remote possibilities, and all in all a non-stranger was persuasively indicated. Cook, the jurors did not need reminding, was not a stranger to the garage.

That the greasepit *was* concealed when the killer first came into the garage is indicated by a startling fact which was not recognized by anyone involved in either the investigation or the trials. Yet it can now be seen as critically important in weighing up the likelihood of the pit being concealed against that of it standing wide open when the killer-cum-stranger first burst wild-eyed from the kitchen door panic-stricken and looking desperately for a place to hide the bodies - to add a touch to Anderson's "frantic frenzy." And if the fact bore on the question of whether the pit was open or not at that time, by the same token it was relevant to the question of whether the killer *was* a stranger.

Criticizing the police and the courts for their failure to recognize the obvious is more satisfying if the critic himself hasn't failed in exactly the same way, yet the sobering fact is that I have lived with the Cook evidence for a number of years and only during the last re-write of the present chapter and thanks in no small part to a friend bringing to bear on the photographs his experience as a city police detective, did the startling and previously unrecognized fact leap out from the photographs: *the greasepit was not a greasepit.* Late in the day as it was, on realizing that the strangest thing about the stranger theory was that it carried within itself the seed of its own destruction, there was nothing for it but to trudge back to square one. Proving any part of the Crown's case for it was never a cardinal concern of the present study, yet reasoning from the indisputable fact that whatever it was it was not a greasepit achieved that result.

It is advisable to pause at this point and set out the premises upon which proof of the defense's stranger theory depended. *If* the killer was a stranger to the Cook household, then either (a) the pit was open when he first burst into the garage looking for a place to hide the bodies (Main's theory); or (b) if the pit was closed and concealed when the killer first came into the garage, then he had in some manner or other learned of its existence either just before the murders (if he was one of Dunne's forty footpads since, having trailed Cook from Prince Albert, they had only been in town about as long as he had), or well in advance of the murders as a matter of general knowledge in Stettler that Ray Cook had a greasepit. This was Dunne's theory which was easy enough to propound until one recognized the facts upon which it depended and began to work through its inherent flaws. Chief among those facts was that it was not what it was called and what it looked like: a greasepit. How is that known and how and why did it matter?

***

Functional and utilitarian though they were, greasepits are now banned - something to do with gasoline fumes accumulating in them. Older readers will remember them as being centrally located in garage floors where vehicles could conveniently be parked over them to permit stand-up access to the vehicle's underside. It will be seen in the police diagram of the garage floorplan Plate 32 that the pit (as it must now be called) was located hard up against the small landing at the kitchen door. Whatever its purpose, it was not intended that vehicles should be driven over it for servicing. It will also be seen that the planks had to be in place if a vehicle was to be driven, at an awkward angle, into the garage and over the pit. Only then could the planks be removed to permit a double-jointed mechanic to slither and insinuate himself into a pit almost impossible of access. Access to the left side of the vehicle was similarly impossible because of the landing.

Whatever its use - a root cellar perhaps, although the basement diagram shows a small room designated as a root cellar - it clearly did not stand open while Ray drove vehicles in and out as it could have done had it been centrally located. Since the oil-stained cardboard shows that he was constantly using the garage, the pit could not be left open and indeed was very probably permanently unused. That being the case, no wild-eyed stranger came bursting through the kitchen door to be confronted by a yawning pit.

It is certain that the pit was concealed when the police first came into the garage which is to say only that concealed or not when the killer was looking for - or remembering - a place to hide the bodies, he covered up the pit afterwards. Readers will notice that the police photograph (Plate 13) was posed. It was not taken as the police first removed cardboard before opening the pit and is therefore worthless as evidence of the condition of the garage before the discovery of the bodies. Why after the removal of the bodies the police would replace the planks and then stand over them holding cardboard while photographs were taken is police procedure not easily apprehended by the layman.

***

If the stranger theory was to stand any chance at all in the first trial, Main had to do what he could to show, in the absence of evidence one way or the other, that the pit was probably open at the time of the murders. He was thrown back on possibilities, and thus invited the jury to infer "that Mr Ray Cook may have been using that greasepit during the few days or so before his death for the purpose of fixing up that half-ton truck, and the greasepit may have been opened and unconcealed on Thursday night at the time [Ray and Daisy Cook] retired to bed." The argument came uncomfortably close to saying anything is possible, and so it is, but as an underpinning for the formidable task of turning the jury away from Cook and towards some unknown known criminal it failed to accord with what has been belatedly recognized as the fact of the pit's character. Main's failure to recognize that the pit was not a greasepit spared him from having to reason from that fact to the pit's being closed and concealed at the time of the murders (as will be argued shortly), and thus from having to shoot down his own stranger theory.

For his part, Dunne dealt with the problem of concealment by forgetting the forty footpads for the moment in favor of someone else, although it's hard to say who - perhaps all the residents of Stettler. Ray Cook, he reminded the jurors, was a mechanic. As such he would be aware of the hazards of carbon monoxide and would therefore leave the large door open when he was working on a vehicle. Anyone strolling by on Railroad Avenue could be taken to have spotted the open greasepit even though (although Dunne did not say this and was doubtlessly unaware of it) it would be completely concealed by a vehicle parked over it even from an observer standing, say, in the driveway. Even had the pit been located centrally in the floor, the chances of total concealment were good depending on how far forward and how far rearward respectively the pit and a vehicle were positioned.

It was a start if not much of a one given the pit's location in the garage floor, but then Dunne's argument becomes difficult to follow. He now stressed that there was a complete lack of evidence as to whether the pit was open or not, which was true, and lapsed into possibility to which the same lack of evidence applied: "It is entirely possible that at the time this offense was committed, the greasepit was open with either the half-ton parked over it or nothing parked over it." Had Dunne known it, he was saying to the jurors that if the half-ton was in the garage at the time of the murders, then the killer had backed the truck out, but only after first replacing the planks (which were necessarily not in place when the killer first came into the garage, otherwise he could not have discovered the pit) since the truck could not be moved otherwise. He then removed the planks again and began to carry the bodies from the house.

(The point can be made clearer if it is reiterated that the *only* time the pit would be open was when a vehicle was parked over it, and that a vehicle could be moved into or out of the garage *only* when the pit was closed. It would have been much easier to recognize that it was not a greasepit, with which recognition would come the realization that a vehicle in the garage and the pit did not go hand in hand; there was no connection between the two except that a vehicle parked in the garage in the normal manner (i.e. pulled straight ahead) would bar access to the pit. If the half-ton was in the garage at the time of the murders, and if someone knew of the closed-in pit beneath it, then he would have had to back the truck out to gain access. In that context, the ignition key to the half-ton being found in the jacket of the blue suit takes on heightened interest.)

So much, for Dunne, for the concealment problem. Without pausing for breath (there is no paragraph break in the transcript indicating the reporter heard it as all one subject) Dunne covered the entire subject of Ray's intention to buy a garage business in ten lines and, now with a paragraph break in the transcript, returned again, to cover in 14 lines, the "something like 40 or 60" criminals who had been released on the same day as Cook, but now with the emphasis on motive rather than on such inconsequential matters as how they would know of the pit's existence.

When Dunne proferred his "possibility for a motive for somebody else", the jurors now had the Railroad Avenue strollers pitted against 40 or 60 thugs, the former with no known motive but with probable knowledge of the pit, the latter with motive but with no knowledge of the pit unless, *en masse* and that afternoon since they had just followed Cook into in town, they had cased the garage. If they hadn't, then neither group was sufficient in and of itself, but that presumably was a problem for the jurors. Dunne was hopeful that somewhere in there they'd find a promising stranger. One was reminded of Anderson's jigsaw puzzle.

If the pit was not a greasepit, what is the upshot? Simply that the killer was not a stranger to the Cook household; the Crown had it partly right. But did that necessarily eliminate everyone but Cook as a suspect? Only if it could be shown that it was not possible for anyone else to know of the pit's existence - which was to take in a wide circle. It was to take in the entire world save Cook if one wished to put a fine point upon it. There were for starters Durocher on the one hand and 40 or 60 known criminals (Durocher among them) on the other, but no one but Main and Dunne respectively took them seriously. But what of Ray's neighbors, his friends, customers of his moonlighting mechanic activities, and others? But both Main and Dunne (and Anderson and Greschuk for that matter; Riley was above concerning himself with trifles) were afflicted with tunnel vision. 'Stranger' meant to them stranger to Stettler, where all that needed to be demonstrated by the defense was that he was a stranger only in the sense of no one knowing his identity, not that he was a stranger to Stettler and to the Cook household who happened fortuitously to come upon an open pit just when he most needed it.

***

Dunne concluded his address to the jury by asking, "Can you be satisfied with so many things left unanswered?" - a not unreasonable question. Riley, like some lordly potentate carelessly throwing alms to the deserving poor, then said to Dunne, "You did very well" - something a judge might say to an articling student if he wished to give him a patronizing pat on the head, but perhaps inappropriate from one man to another equal to him in terms of service in the courts. Dunne thanked him and sat down. Anderson was next, to be followed by Riley before the jury, after six-and-a-half days, came into its own.

To read Dunne, then Anderson and then Riley is to experience a mounting sense of unreality. It is necessary in reading these pages to constantly remind oneself that the sum of them wasn't a nightmare from which one could return at will to the real world - as Cook could not do. In the real world, one supposed, murder trials were conducted with scrupulous care by conscientious and intelligent men as if *their* lives depended on how they did it; by men who, in those days, never allowed themselves to forget the awful consequences of error; by men not prepared, if they could avoid it, to rely on the courts of appeal to undo error knowing that those courts too would have their complement of Rileys.

It was necessary to remind oneself that the transcripts were the real world - a reflection of it - the world in which Cook sat transfixed and afraid, watching his life made hostage to harrowing ineptitude by men who would have inspired unease had they been charged with something as trivial as the responsibility for reaching a decision in the elimination round of a noon black cat show.

CHAPTER 24

THE SUPREME COURTS

Like Death, the law of diminishing returns is a fell sergeant strict in its arrest, and any further analysis of the evidence which convicted Cook would be to invite its ill-tempered and short-sighted intervention. The time has come to leave the evidence behind, however reluctantly since one is never far away from the feeling that one more reading of a given segment of testimony (or one more look at a photograph) might disclose something never seen before.

My intention has been to arm the reader with the information which convicted Cook, and the assumption throughout has been that if it was set out fairly, keeping back and downplaying nothing, it would end with the Crown's case convicting itself whether or not Cook was convicted or exonerated in the process. Special pleading is ultimately self-defeating, as is an excess of editorializing; nevertheless the text has been accompanied by what may have struck the reader as just such an excess, but there has been no help for that since my deeper intention has been to take no chances and to see the Crown's case convicted.

Cook may indeed have been guilty but the proof of it didn't come out of this process. I have not been kind to Wally Anderson, the chief architect of the process, and I regret that (he received me with warmth and courtesy), but it seemed to me that his occasional flights from elementary coherence were part of an unworthy process by which Cook was being deprived of his life. It was thought the least of lives being subjected to the ultimate degradation was deserving of better. It seemed to me that Cook needed an advocate where Anderson could look after himself.

Short of having had the opportunity to observe the demeanor of witnesses - an important lack but not a fatal one - readers are now as well informed as was any juror (and as a matter of fact, to risk immodesty, a lot better informed), and are in a position to decide whether on this evidence Cook was proved to a moral certainty (which is what the courts sometimes call it when they wrestle yet again with the problem of defining when doubt is reasonable and when it is not) to be guilty of murder. Nothing now remains but to chronicle the last weeks of his life and to record the sad struggle of a handful of people to save it. We will pause however to first consider some numbers which are a measure of the remarkable differences between two trial courts seized of *Regina v. Cook*, and then to consider his last day in the second of those courts and, briefly, his appeals.

***

The numbers are revealing. The question they raise is what happened between the two trials such that the second was only about half as long as the first? For in exact court sitting time taking into account all recesses and adjournments, the second trial took only 22.9 hours, or 51.3% of the first trial's 44.6 hours. Yet the second trial went through 52 witnesses to the first's 46. The remaining numbers are commensurate: Greschuk's charge to the jury was 9.7 times longer than Riley's - 4.8 hours to 0.5. Anderson devoted 2.3 times as much time to his address to the first-trial jury as he did to the second: 78 minutes to 34 minutes. Main's address was 2.7 times as much as Dunne's: 4.0 hours to 1.5 hours. The first-trial jury took exactly three times as long to reach its verdict as did the second.

By the time the second trial was due to begin - almost a full year after Cook's arrest - the intense public interest in the murders and in the man already convicted of them was inevitably subsiding. It was felt Cook had been granted a new trial only because of some obscure legal technicality or other, and it is not too much to say it was widely felt that with the minor flaw of the first trial rectified, the second trial would again end in conviction. There was a form of schizophrenia abroad in the land however because it was also widely felt that Cook was innocent. By the time of the second trial there was a sense of old hat to the case; nothing was likely to be revealed in it which wasn't already known, and one could no longer look forward to a mystery being unfolded day by day. *Regina v. Cook* was no longer capable of shouldering other stories out of the headlines, no longer newsworthy enough to merit an 'extra' by *The Red Deer Advocate* when Cook was convicted the second time. Indeed, Red Deer no longer saw it as its story the way it had jealously regarded the first trial.

It was to be expected that interest would wane as well within the judicial system. There is a distinct sense pervading the second-trial transcripts of men going through the motions, of now doing a tiresome job rather than a star turn with the eyes of the world upon them[1]. It is best seen in Anderson's performance in each trial. In comparing Greschuk's five-hour charge to the jury to Riley's half hour, or Main's four-hour address to Dunne's hour-and-a-half, the fact they were different men must be taken into account; it happens sometimes that A will be more long-winded than B in saying the same thing or even less. It could be said for example that Greschuk overdid it just as it could be argued that Riley's half hour was all that was needed for an adequate summing up, difficult as it is may be to conceive how justice to the case could be crammed into 30 minutes. But what does one make of the fact that in the first trial Anderson devoted over twice as much time to his concluding address as he found it necessary to do in the second? Or that his opening of the case in the first trial takes up 14 pages of transcript, where in the second he was able to lay it out in nine?

Simply that the court system, Anderson included, had tired of Cook and was anxious to have done with him with as little further ado as possible consistent with justice being done. In the appeal from the first trial, Mr Justice J. A. Macdonald, while concurring in the decision to grant a new trial, said that "Such a course is regrettable as the trial took many days." Whether or not they were influenced by Macdonald's sour stricture, Anderson, Dunne and Riley between them managed to cut those many days almost in half in the second trial.

If the first trial's length is taken as having been adequate to fully and fairly consider evidence of this complexity, then however one views the

---

[1] *Or so they may have imagined. If so, they weren't far wrong. In its early stages the case was widely reported in the US, and even an Australian newspaper carried one or two stories. Certainly the eyes of Canada had been on them.*

numbers, whatever allowances are made for the variables, the second trial can only be seen as an exercise by men convinced of Cook's guilt - give them that - but performed perfunctorily and with waning enthusiasm since they knew going into the second round that they were no nearer to the answers to key questions than they had been in the first when they failed signally to provide them. They knew he was guilty; they merely didn't have the airtight proof of it. The Ross shirt of course was the premier example with the shotgun close behind. If the shirt did not accuse Cook of murder so much as it accused someone else of murder (and the RCMP of incompetence) or at least said that Cook could not be convicted without some *one* thing being known about where it came from and who owned it, rather than their hands being stayed, they took a half-hearted swipe at the problem hoping the chips would fall in the desired direction. Fortune smiled on the Crown and they did.

***

Throughout the second trial therefore the auguries for Cook were not good, and its last act opened as inauspiciously for him as things had gone to that point. At 2 pm on Tuesday, June 28, 1960, Mr Justice Riley prefaced his charge to the jury by apologizing for having "contacted *[sic]* quite a severe case of the flu", an affliction, he understood, which beset some of the jurors as well, it being "pretty hard in a crowded courtroom that is not too well ventilated to escape the germs." Thus Cook was faced with seven men some of whom were miserable with "severe" influenza - noses running, sinuses swollen, heads throbbing, feverish, chilled, bodies all aching and wracked with pain - not a group one would normally look to to give the evidence the impartial and painstaking analysis it required if the court - Riley and the jurors combined - was to reach a true verdict.

As Cook braced himself for the coming ordeal, he clearly feared the worst since he had long since lost what little confidence he had ever had in Dunne, and had formed an antipathy towards Riley more pronounced than his pronounced dislike for Greschuk, which was a little surprising since Riley's avuncular manner was far more effective in concealing *his* antipathies than Greschuk had ever managed, particularly towards Main. Not that Cook was influenced by mere appearance, being by now well able to assess for himself the virulent lack of sympathy behind Riley's.

Cook was not disabused of his antipathy as he watched Riley add to a reputation little in need of it by the celerity of his charge to the jury: 30 minutes from end to brusque end. He then watched the jurors retire, some of them wondering whether they would live long enough to decide whether Cook would live or die.

The charge comprised 23 pages of transcript. The first 12 are given over to Riley's exposition of the duties of the jurors and the applicable law (with the notable omission of the circumstantial evidence rule), and in the following 10 pages - perhaps 10 minutes in delivery - he reviewed the evidence, skimming over it and touching on some highlights, somewhat like Newton stopping on the strand to pick up a smoother pebble or prettier shell than the ordinary while the great ocean of truth lay all undiscovered before him.

For Riley, as we have seen, it all came down to the blue suit; the rest was so much dross cluttering up the picture of the self-evident. The suit was nothing less than the key to the whole case: "My own concluding observation is simply this: that the key to this whole foul affair may well be found in the blue suit. The conclusion is almost inescapable that the person who was wearing that suit and who placed it under the mattress was the person who did the killing." No one would dispute that the conclusion was inescapable, just as this late in the game no one was about to take the time to wonder whether what the conclusion meant to Riley and what it actually meant were one and the same thing.

The last page of the 23-page charge was devoted to reviewing the defenses advanced by Dunne, tacked on almost as a pro forma afterthought which later invited the comment from the office of the federal Solicitor General that it was "difficult to escape the conclusion that the Trial Judge's presentation of the case for the defense was somewhat brief and general[1]." It was also - although the functionary in the Solicitor General's office was too polite to say so - supercilious, an insult to Dunne and a gratuitous violation of the minimum respect the court owed to Cook, versed in the criminal arts though he was.

At 2:30 pm the jury retired to attend to the first order of business: the choosing as their foreman a clothing salesman named Henry Singer. Immediately on the jury withdrawing, Riley turned to counsel to ask for their comments on his charge to the jury - a standard practice. There then followed an exchange between Riley, Anderson and Dunne somewhat reminiscent of the blind men fumbling their way around the

---

[1] *"Memorandum for the Cabinet", November 7, 1960, National Archives, Ottawa.*

elephant, at the end of which it was finally agreed that Riley had overlooked mentioning alibi as one of the defenses advanced by Dunne. As it happened, he *had* mentioned it: the single word "Alibi" enumerated as one of the four defenses[1]. When the three had agreed nevertheless that he hadn't, Dunne commented that he didn't think it mattered that the trial judge had overlooked alibi, suggesting either that he had thrown in the towel at this point or really wasn't aware of what was going on. A minute or two earlier, when invited by Riley to comment on the charge, Dunne, although believing it to be the case that the alibi defense hadn't received even the one-word reference Riley had given it, declined the invitation, which was to say Riley's presumed omission of alibi was not important enough to Dunne to warrant his drawing it to Riley's attention.[2]

Having forgotten he'd mentioned alibi, Riley decided to withdraw to his private chambers to "check [his] notes", returning four minutes later to instruct the bailiff to bring in the jurors. He told them both Anderson and Dunne had drawn to his attention that he'd neglected to deal with alibi, where in fact Anderson had correctly said he'd dealt with it while wondering whether he'd dealt with it properly - in the nature of things difficult to do by devoting one word to it - and Dunne had drawn to his attention only that Riley's presumed omission of alibi as a defense didn't matter. The notes he ostensibly retired to check presumably said 'alibi', otherwise why make notes? But why then return to the courtroom to say they didn't?

[1] *The other three: first, the case hadn't been proved beyond a reasonable doubt; second, "the doctrine of circumstantial evidence" - with no explanation by Riley of what the doctrine was; and third, "the possibility," as Riley put it, "or even probability that the act was done by a stranger." They were stock defenses available on the Crown's evidence whatever Dunne chose to do or not to do with them. The alibi was the one which had stood the best chance of successful development. Riley's one-word dismissal of it and Dunne's dispirited lack of objection under the misapprehension that it hadn't rated even that one word were an echo of the whimper with which Cook's world was ending.*

[2] *Readers learned in the law will learn with interest that Dunne argued that Anderson had contended that Cook was in possession of Ray Cook's wallet which had been recently stolen, and this therefore imported in favor of the defense the doctrine of recent possession: that if the man in possession could give a reasonable explanation as to how he had come into possession, not knowing the property was stolen, he was entitled to acquittal. But Anderson had gone even further than that: he said that not only was Cook in possession of stolen property knowing it was stolen, the reason he knew it was stolen was because he had stolen it. He said this of course only as an essential part of a rather larger case; stolen property wasn't his primary concern. Cook, Dunne said, had given a reasonable explanation, but the record doesn't record an acquittal. Nor does it record a conviction. Nor, however, does it record a charge of possession of stolen property.*

No great matter; with everything cleared up to the general satisfaction of everyone, Riley now turned to the alibi defense - 15 lines in the transcript, a minute at most: "Gentlemen of the jury, I am sorry to bring you back but counsel have drawn to my attention that I omitted to deal with alibi. Now the law on alibi is this: that if the evidence of an alibi raises a reasonable doubt in your minds as to the accused's guilt, then the accused is entitled to the benefit of that doubt even if you are not satisfied of the truth of the alibi. If on the other hand you totally disbelieve the alibi you may if you choose infer the guilt of the accused and further infer a measure of corroboration of the evidence given by witnesses for the prosecution. Now in this case there is no doubt that the drycleaners were broken and entered. You have the evidence of Mr Estrin; you have emphasis placed on that by defense counsel this morning. The point is was Cook along? You have the evidence of Sonny Wilson; you have the evidence of Jack Mitchell, all of which sort of back [sic] up the accused's story of his movements that night. That is all I have to say to you now."

He had not exactly "scrupulously laid out all the evidence both pro and con stripped of all its non-essentials and properly related to the matters requiring factual decision[1], " but it was something, and with it the jurors retired for the last time.

They returned 25 minutes later with their verdict. Allowing, say, two minutes for each time they shuffled in and out of the courtroom, the polling of them on each of two occasions when they returned, and allowing two minutes for the selection of a foreman, they spent exactly 30 minutes considering the evidence - exactly the time Riley had spent instructing them. A pleasing symmetry if a fearful one for Cook.

Riley sentenced Cook to die on Tuesday, October 11, 1960, increased the jurors' daily stipend from $6 to $21 (costing the state an extra $630), and at 3:17 pm retired to his chambers to nurse his flu. Cook meanwhile retired to the death cell at the Fort to nurse what remained of his life: 139 days.

***

[1] *Annotation, (1952-53) C. R. Vol. 15, 190, A. E. Popple, "Summing-up the evidence in a criminal case."*

On September 15 the Appellate Division of the Supreme Court of Alberta dismissed the appeal, noting that "with respect to the directions of the learned trial judge in his charge to the jury, these must be considered as a whole and not piece-meal, as pointed out in the leading authorities. When so viewed the directions are in our unanimous opinion adequate in the circumstances of this case, notwithstanding that his directions on the defence of alibi are open to criticism [1]."

Riley's direction on the alibi defense was open to more than criticism; it was open to wholesale condemnation as a travesty. The question was did it lie in the mouth of the court to say the charge when considered as a whole was adequate when the heart of the defense (not that Dunne appeared to recognize it as such) had been destroyed by being dismissed first in a single word and then in a handful of them which were a measure of the contempt Riley had for it, and as such tacit permission for the jury to ignore it?

Remembering Dr J. Donovan Ross's pronouncement on the security measures at the PMH, this was the second time in the Cook saga when a deceptively simple concept - adequacy - took on peculiar dimensions, and something patently inadequate was tailored to fit a politically expedient model of the adequate. For had the court of appeal had the courage to recognize Riley for what he was - a superficially involved inebriate who masked his shallowness and viciousness behind a well-

---

[1] *It is true the charge must be considered as a whole, and in that regard interested readers are referred to a decision of the Supreme Court of Canada:* Ruest v. The King, *(1952-53) C. R. 63 per Rand, J. at 70. But the Appellate Division cannot have referred to* Rex v. McKenzie, *(1932) 58 C.C.C. 106 - a decision of the British Columbia Court of Appeal remarkably similar to the* Cook *case on the facts of the alibi defense, in which the appeal was allowed on the grounds of the judge's inadequate summing-up on that defense. "[The two independent alibi witnesses] may have been either mistaken or dishonest, but a careful presentation of all the evidence was necessary for the jury in a difficult task." (per Macdonald, J. A. at 120.) Nor can the Alberta court have referred to* Azoulay v. The Queen, *(1952-53) C. R. 181 (S.C.C.) per Taschereau, J. at 182: "The pivotal questions upon which the defence stands must be clearly presented to the jury's mind." Reading Riley's charge "as a whole" does little to cure the inadequacy of that portion relating to the pivotal question of alibi.*

See also Popple, op.cit. at 190: "A jury has the right to expect from the trial judge something more in his summing-up than a mere repetition of the evidence. They have a right to expect his trained legal mind will employ itself in stripping the testimony of its non-essentials and in presenting the evidence to them in its proper relation to the matters requiring factual decision and directed also to the case put forward by the prosecution and the answer of the defense, or such answer as the evidence permits."

polished veneer of bonhomie - and his charge "considered as a whole" an invitation to convict issued with his formidable blessing, it might have stopped the slide of the administration of justice into disrepute, but would have had a politically unacceptable result: a third trial.

Riley had come close to forcing such a result, but there was an out. After administering its irritated rebuke, the court of appeal scuttled for a section of the *Criminal Code*, finding refuge there in a section which permitted the five justices to rule unanimously that, regardless, there was "no substantial wrong or miscarriage of justice", and with that they washed their hands of the appellant.

On dismissal of the appeal Dunne applied to the trial division of the court for an order postponing the execution date to November 15 to permit the appeal to the Supreme Court of Canada to be prepared and, should the final appeal be dismissed, to permit time to prepare an appeal for executive clemency. On October 4, a five-man bench heard the appeal, sat on it overnight and dismissed it the following day without reasons, Mr Justice Cartwright dissenting from the opinion of his brothers, among them Mr Justice Locke who, while hearing Maloney, savaged what was left of the alibi defense by reasoning that if Cook claimed to be in Edmonton committing one crime, this probably meant he was in Stettler committing a different one.

The courts were now finished with Cook; they could do nothing more for him or to him. He had come a long way on the fearful path they had charted for him since the distant day in Stettler when he had been charged with the murder of his father. He had traveled it with courage and with dignity, earning the respect of the men charged with maintaining his life until the time came for them to assist in taking it. In doing so, he ensured it would not be easy for them.

CHAPTER 25

THE SOLICITOR GENERAL

Hope springs eternal through the shattering of it and nowhere more than
in a death cell where the shattering of it is the most devastating. After
the second conviction Cook lived through the mind-numbing experience
of being told of the defeat of his last chances in the courts, and then
through the six weeks leading to the last chance of all which lay with a
distant body of men: the Diefenbaker cabinet. Effectively it lay with
Diefenbaker. If the Chief said nay to the death penalty in a given case,
nay it was.

He hated capital punishment - a failing of most lawyers since they know
how the system works - but nine times a death warrant was laid before
him, and nine times he signed it with, as he told Alan Hustak, a
trembling hand. "You'll never know," he told Hustak, "how it feels to
have to sign the warrant", and he reflected on signed warrants being
taken by a secretary from his desk to start their journeys to distant
sheriffs each preceded by a telegram confirming its existence. The
moment one was lifted from his desk and disappeared through the door,
he recalled in the Hustak interview, there was no force on earth which
could be interposed between the waiting man and the waiting gallows.

In all then, from the point of view of the waiting man, a better man than,
say, the governor of Texas to be making the decision. Cook would know
from Main that there would be no rubberstamping the verdict which had
wound its way up through three court levels, but neither was

commutation a foregone conclusion. Diefenbaker was a politician charged by conscience with leading the country away from a fixation with hanging born of the Dark Ages. That some condemned men richly deserved to be hanged was not the point, but the country could not see it, and the country was not Diefenbaker's personal fiefdom however much he might have been inclined to view it as such in the heady days of 1958. Attention must be paid to such countries[1], and Diefenbaker was caught between his conscience and the demands of politics. A delicate balancing act was called for: commutation where there was the slightest justification for it without making a mockery of what was, after all, the law. Diefenbaker was not a man to mock the law.

He advanced the cause of abolition beyond any previous highwater mark and the country snarled but subsided. Prior to Cook, 32 times during Diefenbaker's regime death sentences came before his cabinet for review, and 26 times reasons sufficient to warrant commutation were found - reasons rarely apparent to the country. He exhibited political courage of a high order since his party's natural constituency knew the death penalty was the only effective deterrent to murder and the only fitting punishment for those murderers who were undeterred. Nothing exercised the man in the street quite as much as the threat of having this last protection against being murdered in his sleep taken from him by a haggle of lawyers skilled in casuistry and little else, and by academics with no experience of life outside the ivory towers, down in the mean streets where she is lived.

The odds in Cook's favor were thus about seven in eight, good odds but there had to be something the cabinet could point to as a reason for extending the royal prerogative of mercy. Not much was required so pronounced was Diefenbaker's antipathy to hanging - some redeeming feature in Cook's background or character, a jury's recommendation of mercy, a 3-2 split in the court of appeal or the Supreme Court of Canada - but none of these were present.

Cook's best hope lay in the cabinet taking the time to review the evidence which, effectively, was for someone else to take the time to

---

[1] *If not, fortunately, to the government's back benches. Some now-forgotten Calgary back-bencher in the first Mulroney government was quoted in the 1985 capital punishment debate as favoring "hanging them often and hanging them high." This probably meant he favored hanging as many men as possible, preferably after they'd been found guilty of something, rather than cutting a man down and hanging him again, although one can't be sure. He stopped short of calling for a display of severed heads on pike poles, perhaps with a nice regard for the image of Calgary then planning the forthcoming Winter Olympics.*

review the evidence and hand his or their recommendation to the cabinet. It was to introduce the Solicitor General's Department into what was now a race against time since there would be no postponement of the execution date beyond November 15. Two senior officials in the Department, T. D. McDonald and R. R. Price were assigned and the review, starting from ground zero, began. Before it was finished, Price and McDonald knew as much - and very probably more - about the case as anyone thitherto involved with the probable exception of the police.

They did not act on the supposition that the Supreme Court of Canada might allow the appeal and that therefore nothing need be done unless and until the final appeal was turned down. Indeed, even before the Alberta court of appeal announced its decision on September 16, Price and McDonald had asked Riley and Anderson for reports, and they already had in hand those of Greschuk following the first trial, and of Dr J. P. S. Cathcart the psychiatrist who, as we have seen, interviewed Cook after the first conviction.

The Cathcart report, a 3500-word document, might very well have brought Price and McDonald up short since clearly Cook had found himself a champion. It unintentionally reveals as much of Cathcart's character as it does of Cook's, and he comes through in its pages as a compassionate man, casually idiomatic, warm and informal. Some excerpts will show something of each of the two men:

"Prisoner resumed where I had interrupted. 'Why would anyone leave a shirt there? I have a theory someone came into the house and after the murder they wouldn't want to have blood on them and would take their clothes off and put on...(but I didn't catch all the details of this item) but would leave the shirt on till he removed the bodies to the pit and then put on his own clothes and possibly put on some of Dad's things. And the shells and the gun. Dad had no reason to have a gun; he wasn't a hunter and no one had ever seen him with a gun. And the shells found - if this fellow took shells out of his pocket, he would throw them in the dresser....' (I am wondering if prisoner's theory doesn't represent some of his own actions, but if so he is awfully plausible, yet doesn't seem to be acting the part."

"[Cook produced] the snapshots - several, including the whole family - father, mother and step-siblings *[sic]*. Seemed to take normal pride in showing me them and particularly in speaking about the kids and his father. He himself was not included in any of the groups - probably he had taken the snaps."

"I asked prisoner how he felt when Sgt. Roach, RCMP, told him about the murder on Sunday morning *[sic]* in the cell. 'It was like the end of the world - I don't know how to explain it - it's still hard to believe they are gone and to be charged on top of that. You got no idea how that can hurt. It wasn't until I got to Ponoka that the horror of it all hit me. The whole public jumped on me with both feet - I read the papers and I admit it's my fault I escaped from Ponoka. Everybody got panicky then and before the trial I was accused of about everything - even that I wanted to murder the Magistrate. They didn't look for anyone else but me. I'm afraid I'm getting rid of a lot of this bitterness on you doctor.' (Sounds off hand like a pretty genuine comment to me.)"

"At most times, the prisoner seems to act like a wholesome kid and particularly when he is discussing music and singing, has several favorites on the radio[1]. 'Well, I did have some chums - yes, some of them going straight. Hoskins, I used to have a good time with him - used to go on double dates together. No, I don't have a bad temper - just once - an argument in the pen. An Indian came up behind me and hit me right there (points to the right temple region scar.) I was pretty mad then - they took me to the hospital and put stitches in the scalp.' He tells the story almost humorously, says he didn't lay a complaint against the Indian, merely told him never to try that again. 'I don't hold grudges but I get into a lot of arguments.' (Gosh, it's getting harder and harder to see this fellow a wholesale murderer of his own folks.)"

"Further comments by prisoner merely accent the father as a kindly, forgiving person and 'if my father were alive, that's how he would feel about it. My dad always said don't cry over spilt milk and fight like hell while you're fighting, but afterwards shake hands - that's my way.'"

"After I had more or less made up my mind that there might be some truth behind this chap's story, I spoke to the Acting Assist. Warden Kennedy whom I knew from previous visits and he told me there was a strong opinion after the trial that the jury could have been as prejudiced as the young fellow claims, and even in jail amongst those who have come in contact with Cook - most think he isn't guilty, and the prisoner's lawyer, Mr Main, is reported to have expressed great surprise at the jury's findings."

***

[1] *"Blueberry Hill" was the favorite according to Lila Larson.*

412

Still in advance of the scheduled date of the Supreme Court appeal, Price prepared a "Condensed Summary " of the second-trial evidence. In 55 legal-size pages, typewritten and single-spaced, the evidence of 52 witnesses - including Cook's - was summarized. The summary was prefaced with a tabulation of his criminal record and concluded with a couple of notes concerning personal matters: "There is some indication he was spoiled when quite young" and "It also appears that he was extremely well treated by his stepmother."

It was an accurate summary of the evidence as far as it was able to go, but time had not permitted the fine-tooth comb, logic-chopping, side-by-side comparison of all the evidence of all the witnesses at all the court hearings that has gone into the preparation of this study, and accordingly Price, through the clock's fault and none of his own, was not able to pinpoint those areas where Constable A had confidently said black only to have Corporal B with equal confidence inform the court that white was the case, or where Constable A had said blackish at the first trial and whitish at the second. But within the constraints imposed upon him by the headlong rush of days, his efforts were a beacon in the slough of despond that the criminal investigation and judicial systems had proved themselves to be in *Regina v. Cook*. For example, alone of all the people who had looked at the Ross shirt and wondered about it, Price brought to it something other than resignation or stupefaction. Alone of all the people in any way involved in Cook's fate he asked where were the other two white shirts?

His opinion of Riley was revealed in a single, restrained comment: "I may say that my impression from the charge is that the Jury would have no doubt whatsoever that the trial Judge felt that the accused was guilty and might possibly have concluded, from the brief way in which the defence's arguments were dealt with, that the problems raised by the defence, while referred to in the charge as deserving their 'serious consideration', did not seem to commend themselves to the trial Judge as serious obstacles to the position of the Crown."

***

The denial of the final appeal by the Supreme Court of Canada on October 5 meant to McDonald and Price a redoubling of their efforts in

413

the remaining six weeks as they gathered as much information as they could unearth on Cook's antecedents, upbringing, character, prison behavior, possible motives. There was a blizzard of memoranda: October 17: McDonald to Price; October 26: McDonald to Solicitor General; November 2: Price to McDonald; November 7: Price to Solicitor General; November 7: Solicitor General to the cabinet; November 7: Solicitor general to the cabinet; undated: author unidentified to the Solicitor General.

In the end they ran out of time, but they had learned enough to know there were questions needing answers which, while they remained unanswered, mandated something other than the death of Cook. They prepared for the signature of the Minister of Justice a recommendation to His Excellency the Governor General in Council that "the death penalty be commuted to a term of life imprisonment in the Saskatchewan Penitentiary."

It is curious, but until that moment I had never realized what it was to destroy a healthy, conscious man. When I saw the prisoner step aside to avoid the puddle, I saw the mystery, the unspeakable wrongness, of cutting a life short when it is in full tide.

GEORGE ORWELL, "A Hanging"
Collected Essays

Here's the way I figure it. I am going to be 18 in a few days and its just about time to smarten up. If I get into trouble again, don't write me or anything, just forget I am your son. Dad, Im really sincere this time. I mean everything I say for if I get into another jam, it will go on and on until I kick the bucket in a pen or some dirty provincial jail, but if things work out the way I plan, I'll be home for Christmas.

ROBERT RAYMOND COOK
Letter to his father, July, 1955

CHAPTER 26

THE STORAGE ROOM

On December 11, 1959, Mr Justice Peter Greschuk ordered Cook to be hanged on April 15, 1960 - a date far enough in the future to allow an appeal to be heard in the Alberta court of appeal and the execution to proceed if the appeal failed and the right of appeal to the Supreme Court of Canada was abandoned. Had he been hanged as first scheduled, eyebrows might well have been raised since Good Friday fell on that date in 1960. Of all the days in the Christian calendar which Greschuk could have chosen, only Christmas and Easter Sunday would have been more inappropriate. It can only be understood as pure inadvertence or, more probably, because he counted on the appeal process extending beyond the fateful day. If the latter, it was still a curious and dicey choice; the worst could have come to the worst, for Greschuk not to mention Cook, and had it happened it would have offended religious sensibilities beyond being mollified by whatever explanation might have been offered by whichever spokesman was chosen to make the embarrassed attempt. But the worst was prevented from coming to the worst for on March 24 the court of appeal ordered that Cook be tried a second time.

Main wrote Cook to give him the good news[1] and Cook, never happier now that he'd been handed back his life, sat down to contemplate the future. First a new trial with a new judge; he had escaped Greschuk. Acquittal was assured because of the Cosmo Cleaners alibi. Then three or more likely three-and-a-half years for Cosmo Cleaners - a small price to be paid for the gift of life Cosmo would finally prove to be. Who would have thought when they were on that roof in the middle of the night...? Then a new start with a job, a girl (who had "become rather special" to him; we will meet her) and a family. He had been given one more chance to smarten up, and this time...*this* time....

But he had not reckoned with Harold W. Riley who he had seen once in his life, during a routine court appearance before the first trial when Riley was taking the criminal arraignments. Nor had he reckoned with the court of appeal and could not anticipate that when he appeared before the same panel a second time, the three judges who had rescued him from the trial result orchestrated, as he saw it, by Greschuk, would cut and run with the rest of them leaving swirling in their wake a confused picture of when the conduct of a criminal trial adds up to a substantial wrong or miscarriage of justice and when it does not.

***

In September, 1988 a new correctional institution (having some of the attributes of a jail) opened on the south-eastern outskirts of the town of Fort Saskatchewan replacing the old jail (which had few of the attributes of a correctional institution) which had stood on the town's western

---

[1] *See p. 23*

boundary since 1914. The new jail, if one may call it that, is state of the penological art: bright, clean, well-designed, attractive within the limits imposed by its function, and costly. It is a credit to its Californian designers and a humane testament to emergence from the Dark Ages represented by the prison it replaced. When Cook wrote his father in July, 1955 with his uncanny forecast of the place if not the manner of his death, he knew the run of dirty provincial jails almost as well as he knew penitentiaries. He had never seen the Fort before July, 1959, but he might as well have been coming home.

Not that the old Fort was inordinately dirty; it wasn't. Men with not all that much to do swiped endlessly and listlessly at its corridors and tiers with damp grey mops, their minds anywhere but on what they were doing, but they kept it as clean as massive institutions ever get. From time to time Department of Public Works painters moved in to add a coat of paint to everything certifiably inanimate, and when they were finished the moppers resumed their desultory swiping.

With his second conviction Cook was returned to the same death cell, one of two, he had occupied following the first. The "Condemned Cells" (so styled in the original blueprints) were located at the north end of a basement corridor which ran almost the entire length of the prison's south wing. The two cells were separated by the ominously-named "Preparation Room" where men on their way to the scaffold were given their last change of clothing - dungarees, open-necked shirt, carpet slippers - before being led through a doorway to a short flight of steps leading up to the exercise yard where the gallows waited, floodlit, foursquare and patient against the night sky.

Before Cook, 27 men and one woman left the Preparation Room to keep their appointment in Samarra. Men walked if they were capable of it, were supported if they were not, or were dragged fighting for their lives - a miserable prize which the executioner was sure to win. Florence Lassandra proved capable of nothing, neither of walking unaided or aided, nor of struggle. In the Preparation Room she fainted in abject terror and was carried from it strapped to an innocent chair brought hurriedly from the kitchen and hanged with her. So far as is known, it was not a moment in the history of capital punishment much cited in Parliament in support of the practice.

***

His choices limited, Cook settled in to make what he could of his final 106 days which were later extended by 34 days to allow for appeals. He wrote letters, pored over the evidence trying to worry it into the form he thought it should take in argument before the court of appeal, talked to his guards and played cards with them, listened to a battery radio (there were no 110 volt outlets), and read; he came too late in life to an appreciation of reading. (He took a crack at general relativity theory and threw the book aside with a good-natured admission of defeat.) He kept his cell tidy and clean and himself well-groomed. He conferred with counsel, received a handful of approved visitors, counted the remaining days and, as he had done before in the PMH, looked around for a means of escape.

It is thought that there were three escape attempts, but it has been possible to authenticate only one of them, and I shall deal with it later. As interesting as one of the two merely rumored attempts is, involving as it reputedly did the complicity of a civilian guard[1] - one of the death watch 'baby sitters' - number codes of Folger-Adam keys being couriered to Edmonton, mid-night 'meets' scheduled and not kept between a key maker from Edmonton and Cook's inside man, knowing the location of the three doors which had to be unlocked before he gained access to a 'freedom door' - a door which led to the outside world - all the elements of a first-rate story were there except the proof of it, and I reluctantly decided that it could not be included as an instance of Cook's refusal to say die.

The RCMP may not have been aware of any cloak and dagger escape attempts being mounted inside the prison, but they were ever vigilant against the possibility that some of Cook's hare-brained cohorts might try something from the outside. Even before the first trial the rumors had begun to fly, and by letter of November 9, 1959 from the Edmonton City Police, the RCMP were apprised that "two well-known criminals, James Andrew MYHALUK and Vincent Daniel MARRESE" were in possession of "several pistols and revolvers" believed to be the proceeds of a sporting goods store robbery in Edmonton. Myhaluk had "stated his intention of engineering a second escape attempt by Robert COOK" and had "made a vow that COOK will never hang."

The telegraphing of Myhaluk's intentions has the ring of braggadocio in

---

[1] *A guard's complicity on this scale, if it occurred, suggests that Cook wouldn't have experienced insuperable difficulty in receiving prohibited communications from other parts of the prison if it mattered to him to do so. From, e.g., Sonny Wilson - the question explored in Chapter 20.*

the presence of an informer, but hollow as the threat undoubtedly was, it was taken seriously. The police could safely assume escape was uppermost in Cook's mind, and they could not safely ignore the possibility that abetting escape might well occur to the Myhaluks and Marreses in Cook's circle of acquaintances. Hare-brained was indeed the word for them; prisons are even harder to break into than to escape from, and death cells within a prison close to impossible, but with their experience of him, the police attitude towards Cook verged on paranoia. If Myhaluk and Marrese came at the prison some night with their several pistols and revolvers blazing, they could expect a reception in kind.

***

Main's letter to Cook informing him of the success of the appeal was his last official act, as it were, before he stepped aside in favor of Dunne. But he did not divorce himself from Cook's fate; neither his sense of professional obligation nor his ever-deepening personal regard for Cook would permit it. He was in less than robust health, but on October 6 he was able to write and sign on behalf of his law firm a 1500-word letter to Leon Balcer, the Solicitor General. In it he advanced his stranger theory for the last time, touched on some of the important points of evidence, contended that Cook could not have received a fair trial "anywhere in Western Canada" given the hysteria following the escape, and pointed out the complete lack of violence in Cook's record.

He closed with the quaint but literally correct third-person construction still employed by law firms having their roots in another time: "...both our Mr Main and our Mr Dunne cannot rid their minds of the uneasy feeling that perhaps this young man has been improperly convicted. We would respectfully request that you take this matter up with the commutation authorities." The lawyer in Main would not let him go further than this cautious urging, and he was right not to do so since the clamor from a soapbox is rarely heard in the back row of an assemblage where the decisions are being made.

There was a cabinet shuffle just at the time Balcer received Main's letter, and on October 11 W. J. Browne replied to Main as the new Solicitor General: "Your representations will receive full consideration in the course of the study that is being given this case prior to a final decision by the Governor-in-Council whether to commute the sentence or to allow the law to take its course." Browne or, more probably either Price or McDonald, had read Main's letter carefully and in Browne's reply he asked about Main's reference "to a large single-barrelled shotgun. Will you please let me know whether this reference is correct?" It wasn't; Main had meant to refer to the Demon and he promptly wrote Browne to that effect, closing with congratulations on his "recent appointment to the responsible office of Solicitor General of Canada." Any little edge.

***

In the chapter of his book *They Were Hanged* [1] dealing with the *Cook* case, Alan Hustak writes, "Through the summer of 1960 the government was besieged with at least a thousand letters from throughout North America pleading for clemency in the *Cook* case. However, a memorandum sent by the Department of Justice to the cabinet deliberately ignored the petitions and pleas in Cook's favor: 'A number of letters [the memorandum read] have been received, one criticising the practise of commutation generally and in the *Cook* case in particular' it acknowledged, 'and the others (4) in favor of Cook.'" I have not been able to substantiate the numbers quoted by Hustak, but if a thousand pro-Cook letters were received and only five brought to the attention of the cabinet, there would appear to have been some deliberate misrepresentation going on with a vengeance.

But there is no reason to think vengeance or misrepresentation had any part in Ottawa's deliberations (emphatically to the contrary when one thinks of the exceptional efforts of Price and McDonald), and it is probable that the truth lay somewhere between the memorandum's five and Hustak's thousand, rather closer to the former than to the latter. A tabulation of the letters received for and against commutation is found in the capital case file in the National Archives showing fifteen for commutation and two against, one of the two being one Eldon Woolliams, at the time a Progressive Conservative MP from Calgary.

The tabulation fails to record however a letter to the Solicitor General from another Progressive Conservative MP from Calgary, a Douglas Harkness. In Harkness the quality of mercy was strained beyond

[1] *Toronto: J. Lorimer, 1987.*

420

forbearance when it came to Cook, and in registering his opposition to commutation he delivered himself of an opinion based on facts known only to him: "...this man has previously escaped from a mental home and terrified a family to the extent to where *[sic]* they moved away." To his credit, Harkness was not suggesting these alone were grounds sufficient to justify hanging Cook.

The tabulation does record two petitions in favor of commutation, but it is known there were four carrying a total of 310 signatures from points as distant as Vancouver and Coho, Alaska and, closer to home, from High River and Stettler.

No government ever buckled in the face of a 310-signature petition. It is a small number as petitions go; that many names can be obtained in an afternoon on a petition advocating repeal of the second law of thermodynamics if signing will get rid of the person at the door. But if the number cannot be said to betoken a groundswell of opinion in Cook's favor, it is nevertheless significant in the notorious circumstances of the case. There were few places in Canada where Cook's name and the excessively bloody nature of the crime were not known. In putting their signatures to a paper bearing that name they knew what they were doing. They were asking for mercy for a man they knew had been proved in a court of law to have shown none to his father, a defenseless woman and five small children. But in doing so they were not pointing to extenuating circumstances justifying commutation since there were none to point to. Rather, they were averring their belief in Cook's innocence (at that a form of extenuating circumstance), saying flatly that the courts were wrong, whether or not they thought it through in those terms.

Ironically, some of the signatories are known to have been proponents of capital punishment. But they were in favor of capital punishment only if a man was *really* guilty as distinct from merely having been proved to be beyond a reasonable doubt as, for example, Cook had been. They rendered meaningless the concept of proof to the criminal law standard and substituted their own which they could not have put into words and so, unaware of the anomaly in their thinking, they signed in this instance. But God help the next man if he really did it as distinct from merely having been proved to have done it.

***

421

The petitions were chiefly the work of three people: Edith and John Larson and their daughter Lila. As an out-of-control 14-year old, Cook had been sent by child welfare authorities to the Larson's farm 30 or so miles northwest of Edmonton where he remained for a few months until the Larsons sold their farm and moved, eventually settling in Surrey, BC. The foster care arrangement had been temporary from the start; the farm was listed for sale prior to Cook's arrival.

The Larson interview notes are clogged with phrases - "kind", "full trust in him", "couldn't have been more pleasant, more understanding", "a very vibrant person, a lot to give to life", "he was just one-hundred percent", "I never saw a mean streak in him", "such a good worker", "performed all tasks cheerfully" - which are cloying and perhaps a little suspect as if the Larsons were contributing to his posthumous redemption by coloring and warming their memory of him. Still, they are the phrases, and the fact is they seriously considered adoption and would have proceeded with it had Daisy - an interesting inversion of what might have been expected - not put a stop to it.

If Cook as Goody Two-Shoes sounds too good to be quite true, or anywhere near it, the Larsons never felt they'd been hoodwinked by him. It is true the senior Larsons never saw him at work under a dashboard explaining to the impressionable Lila the intricacies of hot-wiring (a little vainglory at that age in the presence of an attractive girl is acceptable), but they were not children; they knew why he was with them. The Cook they saw, the Cook who came through in the interviews, was just as genuine, neither more nor less, as the Cook self-destructing on the shoals of petty crime both before and after they knew him. They of course knew in advance they were taking on a severely troubled 14-year old who, in his own mind, was a tragic figure: dumped by his father in favor of some red-headed Jezebel at age 12, orphaned at 13 (as he was to tell a penitentiary officer), soon to be jailed at 14½. They were not prepared for what they got: an infectious personality, someone with the gratitude of a pint-sized Blanche Dubois eagerly overreacting to the kindness of strangers.

Their apprehension in later years was that the criminal pattern would have been broken had they been permitted to adopt him, and when they weren't he reverted to the pattern temporarily interrupted by their kindness. But it never seemed to them to be a pattern which left unchecked would lead to murder. When they thought back on the bloody events in Stettler it was never with the chilling realization that there but for the grace of God (which the Cook family could have used) went John, Edith and Lila Larson. They knew - take it or leave it - that he was innocent. Adoption would have meant a distancing from Stettler. It would have averted his physical proximity to the annihilation of his family by a person or persons still unknown, and his resulting ensnarement by a conjunction of condemnatory circumstances.

On the morning the Larsons were to say goodbye to their farm, a child welfare officer arrived to take Cook. It was the same man (a Mr. MacNaughton, later an RCMP officer) who had brought Cook to them and had promptly turned around and driven away with his charge since John Larson had taken an instant dislike to him. Edith Larson's judgment prevailed over that of her husband, the disappearing car was caught five miles down the road and Cook was brought back. Now with the Larsons on the point of leaving Alberta for good, MacNaughton told them he was prepared to send Cook to them when they were re-settled. Goodbyes, most of them tearful, were said and once again they watched a receding car carrying a young Robert Raymond Cook towards Edmonton. John Larson's better judgment now told him his wife's had been vindicated.

Pending the possibility of again placing Cook with the Larsons, MacNaughton did not want to institutionalize Cook and he now placed him on the Henry Stucke farm a few miles east of Edmonton where Cook lasted until he and a new-found friend stole a neighbor's car and lit out for the Territory - in their case the whole of the United States which Cook had targeted as his future theater of operations. They made it, but only just. They were arrested fleeing through North Dakota, returned to Edmonton and sentenced to the juvenile institution at Bowden. Cook was at last well and truly institutionalized and the rest was explosive history.

Cook kept in touch with the Larsons by letter for a time following their parting, but the flow of letters gradually dried up probably, John Larson thought, "because he was ashamed of the trouble he was getting into." Contact had been lost for a few years when the Larsons heard the Sunday evening broadcast telling of Cook's arrest and the charge of murder. Lila Larson's memory of the night is vivid: "I was in North Surrey when I heard it. I screamed and ran outside into the orchard. I was hysterical, crying. I sat down on the grass, unable to move. I couldn't think. Dad came out and held me. He said, 'That's our Bob.' The next morning I picked up the phone, quit my job and flew back to Edmonton."

Her doing so was the first full measure of her devotion which never wavered while Cook lived. Her remarkable efforts started on the day of her arrival in Edmonton and stopped on the afternoon of the day of his death. She wrote letters to everyone she could think of who might be able to help including the Prime Minister, the Governor General, the Premier and the federal Solicitor General. She raised what money she could for the defense. She organized petitions. She attended each day's session of each trial, traveling to and staying in Red Deer for the first trial so that Cook would know there was one person in the packed courtroom "in his corner." Her constancy so impressed Main that he arranged with court officials for a seat to be reserved for her in the front row of the Red Deer courtroom, a favor he was to repeat in Edmonton even though it was now Dunne's trial.

She took a job at a medical clinic to maintain herself and lost it, she thought, "probably because of my association with Bob." She supplied him with books ("I couldn't keep him in books. I tried, but he devoured everything. Mostly law books, books concerning writing") and delivered messages for him.

She may have been an unwitting go-between in the escape attempt we have looked at briefly - the evidence suggests she was. She preserved his notes and poems ("written on Kleenex, serviettes and so on that were smuggled out to me by that French Canadian guard") most of which were stolen from her when she was away in Alaska on a brief vacation, giving some perplexed people in Coho only dimly aware of Cook, if at all, a chance to sign her petition. She conferred endlessly with Main, and with Dunne whom she did not like. She saw a private investigator but could not meet the cost of the private investigation she thought might unearth something missed by the RCMP. She arranged his introduction to a Lutheran pastor, and Sunday after Sunday she visited him at the Fort.

Access to death cells was jealously guarded. Prison officials had access of course, as did the chaplain, senior police officers if they had good reason, certain members of the immediate family and defense counsel. There the list ended. The rules governing access admitted of no exceptions, and it is left to the reader to decide what it says about each of them that an exception was made in Cook's case in favor of Lila Larson.

She started with Main. "Main phoned the Warden. I rented a car - a Pontiac Laurentian - and drove out to the Fort and saw Holt [the

424

Warden.] He was very gracious. Through the lawyer's phone calls and so on, I finally arrived at Short's home, a big stone house on the South Side. He gave me some kind of paper to take to Holt." Holt had sent her to the Sheriff. As Sheriff, it was Allan Short's responsibility to arrange all the details of a judicial execution - a responsibility he hated. At the time he had no opinion one way or the other as to Cook's guilt (he came later to seriously question the conviction), and it may be he saw Larson's request as a harmless opportunity for him to alleviate the agony of a condemned man who, to him, was only a man he was responsible for having hanged when the time came with a minimum of bureaucratic fuss. He could help Cook by turning a blind eye to the rules, and he did so, responding to Larson's request as graciously as Holt had. He gave her the paper she had to have.

"Holt said to me, 'How good is your stomach? Can you go to this death row?' I said yeah. It bothered me but I wasn't going to let that show." Nor did she; she was as strong as Cook himself, a woman apart. She was the girl who had "become special" to Cook. Walter Bilton, a senior guard, struggled to remember her 17 years later: "Who was she? She came from a good family. She was a lovely little girl, a good looking girl." Indeed who?

***

As the narrowing days closed in on him and his chances crumbled one by one, he never allowed himself to lose hope nor his cheerful comportment in the presence of the babysitters, the lawyers and others, although he could not conceal flashes of bitterness from Lila Larson. He was never content to leave the fight entirely to others. Two weeks after the Supreme Court of Canada dismissed his final appeal, he wrote a moving letter to the Solicitor General. The spelling (which was constantly improving) is his, but some of the terminology suggests he had help, perhaps from a babysitter:

"Dear Sir: I have the honour of writing to make a personal appeal that the royal prerogative of mercy be granted in my case. My appeal Sir is not one of mercy for a crime but for time wich will reveal beyond doubt innocence. I respectfully put it Sir, that when the facts replace the unaswerd questions and infernce the err of this confiction will be proved. Sir, I firmly believe that the truth will out, to me its just a question of time, time wich I respectfully and hopefully request be granted through commuting my sentence of death. The circumstances in this case in wich guilt was inferd I have truthfully explained as far as my knowledge of them went. I volunteered to take a lie detector test or anything wich will prove if I have told the truth or not. I know of nothing more I can do, Sir, but request that my sentence be commuted and patiently await the truth wich I feel must come out. I have every confidience that you will give this matter youre most carefull consideration. Thank you most sincerely."

For every Riley enmeshed in Cook's fate, cosmic justice required there be a counterpoise of decency, and it found one in the Solicitor General, William J. Browne. He replied to Cook on October 31: "Dear Mr Cook: I wish to acknowledge your letter of October 20, 1960 requesting the sentence of death imposed upon you as a result of your conviction for the murder of Raymond Albert Cook be commuted to imprisonment.

"I can only let you know that, in accordance with the practise, all matters relevant to the question whether or not your sentence should be commuted will be painstakingly considered by me and reviewed by the Cabinet prior to a final decision being taken by the Governor-in-Council."

In the circumstances it was all he could say; to have held out any hope, however slight, would have been cruelly inappropriate and Browne appears to have been too considerate a man to have done so. While it was broadly true all matters relevant to commutation would be - and were - considered, it was also probably true that one which had no relevance whatever to Cook's case also entered into the cabinet's painstaking deliberations. That at least was the more or less responsible speculation of the time. It was the matter of one Robert McCorquadale.

***

McCorquadale had been sentenced to death for the sexual assault and murder of a ten-year old girl in the basement of Scarboro United Church in Calgary. A few weeks prior to the scheduled date of Cook's execution, McCorquadale's sentence had been commuted without the cabinet's reasons being disclosed - they never are - but in fact because

McCorquadale by then was certifiably and visibly a gibbering idiot for whom the gibbet might have seemed an appropriate destination if only as a matter of word play. But it was deemed otherwise, an essential of capital punishment being that the man about to be killed appreciate that he is about to be killed - or put to sleep as some readers may prefer. And so, with commutation, McCorquadale was transferred from the condemned cells in Lethbridge Provincial Gaol to the 'disassociation' cells reserved in Saskatchewan Penitentiary for sexual offenders.

The indicators suggest he was insane at the time of the murder and during his trial, and if so he ought not to have been tried much less convicted, but that is another story - one which ended with McCorquadale hanging himself in solitary confinement, using a belt for the purpose. Long-term inmates have a way of knowing everything that goes on in the joint, and one of them told me that to prevent suicide McCorquadale's belt had been taken from him long before he was thrown (they're always thrown) into the hole. Then, more or less inexplicably, "a belt belonging to one of the bulls" had followed the cordially hated skinner into solitary. Like Mormons, penitentiaries have a way of taking care of their own.

A woman scorned hath no fury like Calgary's when its uncomplicated idea of justice is frustrated by bleeding hearts who insist on asking questions first and shooting, if they shoot, afterwards. The city came close to volcanic eruption when the news of the McCorquadale commutation broke. A combination of factors - the brutality of the rape-murder, the victim's age, her attractiveness and utter helplessness, McCorquadale's personality which even other pedophiles would have found repellent, the violation of church sanctuary[1] - made the case the most intensely felt in the city's recent memory, and now it was being deprived of the only form of retribution capable of assuaging its towering anger. The political enormity of what it had done - of what it could not avoid doing given McCorquadale's deteriorating mental state - was borne in on the Diefenbaker cabinet on a tidal wave of editorial outrage and ferocious letters to the editor. The message was not lost on a cabinet for which to lose a Calgary was to lose the world.

[1] *He violated it twice. McCorquadale returned to the scene of his crime a week or so after it. He was spotted lurking in the church basement by the writer's aunt, the late Mrs Dorothy Wilson, who was alone in the church preparing for a forthcoming afternoon tea. No description of McCorquadale had been published - the police were as yet clueless - but Mrs Wilson knew intuitively who it was. With great presence of mind she calmly phoned the police without alerting McCorquadale. The $5000 reward posted for information leading to his arrest and conviction was paid to her.*

It cannot be stated definitely that the fevered feedback from Calgary weighed in the deliberations on Cook's fate. Put at its least however, Cook's chances cannot have been enhanced by it however conscientiously the cabinet (effectively Diefenbaker) may have attempted to focus on the merits of the case before it to the exclusion of all else. To some observers - Frank Dunne and Allan Short among them (with Dunne having a source close to Diefenbaker) - such objectivity was too much to expect of the political animal. Those I asked heard my questions with a knowing look. For them it was almost beyond argument that the imperative of preventing a repeat of the political cost of the McCorquadale commutation entered into the Cook deliberations if only subconsciously.

I mentioned the possibility to Alan Hustak who, being a reporter, decided to ask someone he knew who might know. He phoned Diefenbaker and informed him that it was rumored extraneous considerations, political in nature, had been allowed to influence the Cook decision. The Chief exploded and a vehement denial came spluttering into the room in which I happened to be sitting with Hustak. To suggest as much, to suggest he of all people would see a man go to the gallows for his, Diefenbaker's, cynical political advantage was, he said, "sinister."

His indignation fell short of being entirely convincing. Diefenbaker may not have seen the document reproduced in Plate 44, but he cannot have been unaware of the deep-seated unease among the senior law officers which led to its preparation - carefully considered preparation without question. It cannot be thought, that is, that Browne would sit at the cabinet table and not make known to his colleagues and his prime minister that Price and McDonald, the latter the Assistant Deputy Minister of Justice, felt hanging Cook could well haunt the conscience of the Diefenbaker cabinet and the country in years to come.

Diefenbaker's committed opposition to capital punishment has been noted. On 26 of 32 occasions prior to Cook he had found a reason for a pretext in the guise of a reason to commute. Now however he found a reason not to extend the royal prerogative of mercy, and he found it in the face of a recommendation to the contrary made after close study of the case by the men charged with the responsibility of advising their minister in accordance with whatever was indicated to them by their review of the evidence and all related circumstances - Riley's charge to the jury for example, and Riley's report to the Solicitor General.

It may be that Browne disagreed with the recommendation of Price and McDonald, but nor can it be thought that that recommendation did not reach the cabinet table. Yet it was rejected, and if one were to ask why there are two schools of thought. The first school pointed to the magnitude of the crime and asked what choice the government really had? He had been proved guilty, there were no extenuating circumstances, and the public could not be expected to understand the questions which had exercised McDonald and Price. To ask the public to do so would be a form of second-guessing the courts which could not be permitted. The second school impatiently dismissed the entire workings of the justice system and turned its sinister gaze towards Calgary.

***

E. E. Buchanan, "Buck" to everyone on the right side of the law who knew him, was a 31-year veteran of the RCMP when he retired in 1950 as second in command in the Lethbridge Subdivision with the rank of Senior Staff Sergeant. In 1951 he was asked by the provincial Attorney General to take on a new career as Superintendent of Prisons for the province. As such, in 1954 Buchanan took the decision to do away with the exercise yard (shown on old blueprints prepared in a more courtly time as "Courtyard II") as the site of Fort Saskatchewan executions, and to construct an indoor facility. (The same decision was taken for Lethbridge Provincial Gaol.) There were a handful of reasons for it, chief among them - so far as the Fort was concerned - the fact that there was visual access to the exercise yard from some of the cells on the upper tiers in A Block, and from high on nearby grain elevators where townspeople could - and did, some of them - strain for a view of a form of violence that television can only dream of.

It had long been recognized what the effect of an execution was on any part of a prison population which witnessed what it was not meant to see: it served as a *casus belli* in the powder keg which all prisons become in the hours leading up to an execution. It had been the practice to unfurl tarpaulins from the roof of A Block blocking the offending windows but, in Buchanan's view, there had to be a better way.

Indoors, out of sight of the inmates locked into their cells for the night (although far from out of mind) was clearly better if indoors was possible, and it proved to be. A ground level room at the extreme south end of the south wing lent itself to the purpose. The room, a drygoods storage room for the nearby kitchen, would serve as the "Execution Chamber" - so designated on the blueprints now drawn up by the engineers in the Department of Public Works. To prisoners and staff however it was never anything but the Storage Room.

Immediately beneath it was a room identical in size which became the Autopsy Room. Here the prison physician would monitor the dying heartbeat, and three of the six coroner's jurors would see what they had to see before they could set their hands to a document attesting, in Cook's case, to Cook having died "from a fracture dislocation of the spine and severance of the spinal cord as a result of judicial execution in accordance with the sentence imposed by a Court of Competent Jurisdiction."

In the concrete floor of the Autopsy Room, a concrete Death Pit (a name bestowed on it on the blueprints by some no-nonsense draftsman or engineer evidently not much given to euphemism), five feet square and four feet deep was installed immediately beneath the trapdoors set overhead in the concrete floor of the Execution Chamber - the Autopsy Room's ceiling. The distance from the trapdoors to the floor of the Death Pit was 16 feet. In the floor of the pit a drain would allow the foul substances excreted on violent death to drain away, encouraged by a pail of water to be kept close at hand. Or would have had the drain called for by the blueprints been installed. For whatever reason it was not, although a galvanized pail was kept in the pit for years after Cook.

To anyone with an appreciation for good industrial design, the trap door release mechanism was a finely engineered guarantee that nothing would go wrong; it was designed to work when it was called upon to work. No less important, it was unthinkable that there could be any chance of the doors being accidentally released - by someone stumbling or fainting and collapsing against the release lever for example - and to prevent this a locking device had to be released by the hangman before the lever could be pulled. But the locking device was itself locked with a second locking device so that three distinct and well-rehearsed operations were required of the hangman before, with the third of them, the black boilerplate doors opened swiftly and silently[1] and rid

---

[1] *The downward swing of the doors was arrested by padded rails. There was therefore no appreciable sound other than a satisfying click as spring-loaded holdback catches caught and held the doors at the bottom of their travel.*

themselves of their burden. The mechanism was tested and tested again to ensure it would work without chance of misadventure.

***

By November, 1954, construction was completed and all was in readiness. The stage was set, but for six years no actor strode onto it. In the meantime, the demands of an antiquated and overcrowded prison being what they were, the Execution Chamber could not be allowed to stand unused. The lever and its mount were removed and stored, The trapdoors were covered with a piece of battleship linoleum set into the matching linoleum surrounding the opening, and once more kitchen trustees came and went with gallon cans of stewed tomatoes and sacks of onions. The Storage Room had come again into its own.

But it would never again be merely a nondescript room in an out-of-the-way corner of the prison. It was still that, but now with a double purpose: the one dull and utilitarian, the other deadly.   The physical manifestations of the second purpose were now nowhere strongly in evidence, but they were there. Inmates could try and ignore the four-foot square of linoleum set in linoleum, figuratively distancing themselves from it with gallows humor ringing as hollowly as did the floor itself as they staggered across it lugging cases of kitchen supplies, feeling the ominous spring beneath their feet as the trapdoors sagged slightly for all the rigidity of their construction, but they could not forget it.

Even more difficult to ignore was the apparatus overhead: a two-inch bar bent in the shape of a Flying W (it could almost have served as a branding iron) bolted tightly to the concrete ceiling. At the bottom of each of its flattened v's, a U-bolt was affixed. Through one of these the rope would be threaded before either running over to a ring fixed on a nearby wall, or being tied to the second U-bolt - I was told both; I did not see a ring. The second U-bolt (apart from its possible use as the place to tie the end of a single rope) was on standby should events ever conspire to bring two men there at one time[1].

In 1974 the Storage Room was converted to a library, but the gallows machinery, sans lever, remained in place where it had been in all the years following construction. The U-bolts were now hidden by a dropped acoustic tile ceiling where for 20 years they had openly advertised a purpose at egregious odds with the warehousing activities going on below - with most other forms of activity when one stopped to think of it.

Indoor-outdoor carpet was laid but now with no cutout showing the location of the trapdoors. Nothing gave the location away except a slight yielding underfoot, easily undetected if it was not expected. It was still an execution chamber however, for all it masqueraded as a library. Prisoners sitting there on a Sunday afternoon reading the gentle essays of Elia were sitting in a room whose primary purpose was the infliction of death.

After the prison was abandoned in September, 1988 and until it was razed in 1991, only an act of imagination could paint in the rope which had hung there briefly through the tests of November 14, 1960 until, at about 12:20 am, November 15, its employment was at an end and Cook's body was cut down with the razor sharp knife kept in readiness for the purpose. No one wanted to be standing by the Death Pit sawing at a rope with a dull blade, nor, for that matter, for any other reason, but until the stretcher went up the stairs and out to the waiting truck the business was not over.

Imagination was not required of a group of sightseers who, in May, 1989 toured the now-closed prison. A picture in *The Edmonton Journal* of May 14, 1989 shows a group of 24 in the Storage Room, men, women and six children one of whom appears to be about three years old. They are contemplating a hangman's noose which had been installed to lend authenticity to what a crude, hand-lettered sign on the back wall identifies as "The Hanging Room." Some of them, most noticeably two women and an enthusiast in a baseball cap all beaming in the direction of the noose, are clearly enjoying themselves to an extent which might be thought to be out of keeping with the setting. It would be too much

---

[1] *Double hangings have occurred twice in Alberta's history, both in Lethbridge Provincial Gaol and both on the same day, December 18, 1946, when four German prisoners-of-war were executed for the murder of a fellow POW who had espoused some anti-Nazi views to a class he was teaching in the Medicine Hat POW camp. The four were preceded on the same day by a fifth man, one Donald Sherman Staley who, like McCorquadale, had killed a little girl in Calgary.*

to assume they were entertained with visions of men about to die dancing in their heads - which may have had room for them - and it is more probable they were excited by the prospect of their pictures appearing in a newspaper.

The three-year-old too is gazing at the noose, one foot twisting behind the other and her fist held wistfully against her mouth - the classic attitude of children who find the ways of adults beyond human understanding. Her mother has given her an image which she can carry and cherish all her life, but she is too young yet to appreciate it. For the moment, the noose is something which obviously belongs in a playschool playground, something from which she should be swinging before plopping shrieking with laughter into the friendly sandbox below. What in the world is it doing here?

In the accompanying 200-word story, *The Journal* managed eight factual errors (and one spelling mistake and one typo) - about par for any story having anything to do with the *Cook* case which has generated its own mythology. However, a 1990 dramatization of the case produced by CKUA, an Edmonton radio station, carried off the prize without serious competition. In a 30 minute *tour de force*, it crammed in 28 errors of fact. Even Riley's report to the Solicitor General had not achieved as much.

***

On my first visit to this part of the prison I had not been informed that I was now entering the infamous Storage Room although seeing it was the purpose of the visit. As I walked onto the unseen trapdoors not knowing I was doing so, and was bidden by the Deputy Warden to "stop here; flex your knees", with the icy recognition of where I stood, a place I had long thought of without being able to imagine it, I was swept by a sensation which seemed to me would be as close as anything I would ever know to the black fear which Cook, brave as he was[1], would have known, and I stepped back quickly onto the concrete floor, away from the terrible steel anomaly concealed in it. It would be some moments before the

[1] *He denied being afraid - see Appendix B. One of the coroner's jurors told me that he noticed a slight trembling of Cook's hands pinioned behind his back, and another that of all the men he'd seen hanged, Cook was the bravest.*

process of coming to terms with it began. It would continue through three subsequent visits to check details of the Storage Room, escape routes and other matters, and it continues yet through the calls for the return of the noose by unspeakable politicians of the moment playing to the fearful.

The proximity to a working scaffold was, it seemed to me, made more unnerving by the incongruity of its setting. It was as if it was the more threatening, if that was possible, because of the seeming innocence, the deceptiveness of this not unpleasant room - carpeted, pastel walls, trees and lawn visible through the single, sunlit window. Since 1954 it had led a double life, only one of them officially sanctioned as it were. There were no blueprints reading "library" nor, earlier, had there been any designating the room as storage space for canned goods. But the 1954 blueprints had been specifically drawn up for the design of a "chamber" for the workmanlike inflicting of death, neither more, neither less. It had served that purpose well when demand was made of it on one occasion only: a black, cold November midnight not noticeably relieved by sunlight or birdsong streaming in at the window.

He had died here, the victim of the Faustian bargain by which the nation had given up its soul in return for the right to execute its Robert Raymond Cooks, its Guy Paul Morins and Donald Marshalls of that day (and, be it admitted, its Clifford Olsons and Paul Bernardos of that day) without having to answer to conscience. The story, begun 23 years earlier on a sere, sun-bleached day in Hanna, had ended here with brutal swiftness a few inches from where I stood, a few hundred feet from where the traditional black flag had been run up the prison flag pole. More precisely, it had ended a few precisely calculated feet beneath this floor just short of the floor of the aptly named Death Pit. There was too, one supposed, a certain aptness, a searing irony to be found in the fact that the story's final chapter had started a few feet short of another death pit.

EPILOGUE

I have purposely omitted a discussion of Cook's religious conversion being unqualified to offer any opinion - assuming one is called for - on its genuineness. As a non-believer, I saw myself as running the risk of dismissing it as a foxhole conversion without having the credentials to pronounce on it in any way. Being unqualified to have an opinion however rarely operates as a bar to having one, and mine is that it was genuine. If a man's last words are a call for forgiveness of those who have trespassed against him, as much as one can do is grant him the moment and stand back in silent and contemplative respect.

It is nevertheless too important a question to merit nothing more than a cop-out, and I have decided to include as an appendix the moving account of the late Reverend George Rode of Cook's last hours which will be to furnish readers with better information and insight than I can give them.

But to know the kingdom of God is not necessarily to want to go there just yet, and he believed also in keeping his powder dry. One of the guards who took an arm for the long walk was Pete Patrick, a large - a very large - heavy-set man who reminded me of Toar in the great days of the original "Popeye" strip. On the morning following the execution, Tom Holt, the Warden, asked Patrick to accompany him on an inspection of the death cell. They found that the heavy mesh screen that enclosed the small window opening onto the old exercise yard had been completely cut through with the exception of a single strand by which it remained suspended in place. The integrity of the bars beyond the screen was yet to be violated. Holt, Patrick told me, turned pale.

APPENDIX A

THE STATEMENT

The following is the "EXTRACT FROM REPORT OF A/SGT. ROACH DATED JULY 7, 1959." - Cook's statement. It is an exact word-for-word reproduction of the Extract except for the numbering of the questions which has been added for ease of reference. Minor punctuation and typing errors have been corrected.

At 10:30 AM 29/6/59 Robert COOK was warned and questioned by Staff/Sgt. Beeching and Sgt. Roach. He was given the official warning and upon acknowledging that he understood he was asked the following questions and made the following answers:

Q.1   You have been arrested on a charge of murder and you appeared before Mag. Biggs at 10:15 AM and at that time the charge was formally read to you and you were remanded for 30 days to Ponoka Mental Hospital. Have you anything to say in answer to the charge?

A.   Just didn't do it - that's all - that's all I've got in the world - what would you think I want to hurt them for?

Q.2   Do you wish to say anything else?

A.   No.

Q.3   During Saturday evening June 27/59 you were in the police office and you were questioned by Sgt. Roach as to the whereaboutsof your parents and the children and you told him they had gone to B.C. to buy a garage business. Have you anything to say to this?

A.   That's right, that's right - that's where they were supposed to be when I left them last. That's where they were supposed to go. When I left them I gave them some money. I gave them all the money I had then except for $100 and they were supposed to leave the next morning.

436

Q.4   Do you wish to make a statement?

A.   The only statement I can make is that I had nothing to do with it at all.

Q.5   Where did you get the money you gave to them?

A.   That's kind of hard to answer. I got it out of all the places I was charged with and some that I was not charged with.

Q.6   How much did it amount to?

A. $4100.00.

Q.7   When did you get out of the penitentiary?

A.   The 23rd.

Q.8   When did you arrive back in Stettler?

A.   I came here - I got out Tuesday (counts on fingers) Thursday afternoon.

Q.9   When did you go home?

A.   8 O'clock Thursday - about an hour after that - 2 hours after that.

Q.10   What took place when you got home.

A.   Just - nothing - talking and Mom made some coffee and talking about getting a garage.

Q.11   When did you leave?

A.   That's what I say about 8:30 or 9.00 O'clock.

Q.12   That same Thursday evening?

A.   Yes.

Q.13   Where did you go?

A.   To Edmonton.

Q.14	Did you go alone?
A.	Yes.
Q.15	How did you go?
A.	In my car.
Q.16	Whose car?
A.	My Dad's.
Q.17	How did you get it?
A.	He gave it to me.
Q.18	Where did you go as soon as you got to Edmonton?
A.	To Jimmy MYHALUK's I think.
Q.19	Was he at home?
A.	Yes. I had to wait for a while. I had to wait in front of his house before he came out to see him *[sic]*.
Q.20	What time did you get there?
A.	God - (thinking) 2 or 3:00 O'clock.
Q.21	What time did he come out?
A.	About one hour after that.
Q.22	What did you do then?
A.	Just rode around for a while and then went back to the house.
Q.23	By we whom do you mean?
A.	Jimmy and I.
Q.24	Can we go back to you and the visit at home on Thursday evening?
A.	Yes.

438

Q.25   How did you get from Edmonton to your home?

A.   A fellow drove me.

Q.26   Who was that?

A.   A guy by the name of Eddie REID.   *N.B. Later changed this to being Walter William Berezowski who drove him in Eddie Reid's truck.*

Q.27   Where does he live?

A.   Gee, I don't know.

Q.28   Has he a record?

A.   Yes.

Q.29   Is his home at Edmonton?

A.   Yes he is working there.

Q.30   How long has he been out?

A.   I don't know.

Q.31   Why did he not drop you right at the house?

A.   I wanted him to drop me at the Cafe. I knew my dad was at work.

Q.32   Wouldn't your mother have welcomed you?

A.   She sure would. I wanted to wash up a little before I went to the house.

Q.33   What time did you arrive in town?

A.   About - it must have been after dinner sometime.

Q.34   What time did you go home?

A.   As soon as he came off work.

Q.35   What time would that be?

A.   It must have been 6 - after 6.

Q.36   What suitcases did you have with you when you came home.

A.   One big one and one small one.

Q.37   Did you have anything else?

A.   No.

Q.38   Then what were you wearing?

A.   I was wearing tan slacks and a light coat.

Q.39   I suggest to you you were wearing the suit you [sic] made in
        prison.

A.   No - I had it with me but I wasn't wearing it. I had changed
        over. I changed my clothes after I got there.

Q.40   Where did you change?

A.   In the Club Cafe.

Q.41   Do I understand you changed there from the tan slacks to the
        present suit?

A.   No the other way around.

Q.42   You changed from the prison suit into the slacks.

A.   Right.

Q.43   What did you do with the prison suit?

A.   Gave it to my dad.

Q.44   Why?

A.   He was going to Vancouver and had no proper clothes and the
        suit wasn't in bad shape and it fit him good, about the same
        size as I am.

Q.45   If you went home soon after 6:00 and left around 9:00 O'clock
        were there any visitors to the home?

A.   No.

Q.46   How do you account for having your father's wallet in your possession?

A.   Because of the driver's license and the registration of the car.

Q.47   Why did you need that?

A.   To drive the car to Edmonton.

Q.48   Where were your parents going?

A.   To B.C.

Q.49   Who was going to look after the kids?

A.   We were supposed to take them to B.C. I was supposed to go here. I was going to check back here on Tuesday or Wednesday and I was to wait right here, that's why I came.

Q.50   Who knew you had given money to your father?

A.   Nobody, I guess.

Q.51   How do you account for the children's pyjamas being in that suitcase?

A.   Whose - mine? When I took the suitcases from the house I didn't think they were going to use both of them.

Q.52   I suggest to you that you did not go home until your father came downtown for you after 9.00 O'clock.

A.   No, no. It was later than that - I say earlier.

Q.53   There were visitors at your house at 9 O'clock.

A.   Yes.   My dad and I were in the hotel drinking beer. Maybe Mum was home.

Q.54   Were you drinking with anyone else in the bar?

A.   No.

Q.55   Which hotel?

A.   The one, not the one on Main Street - the one down towards the skating rink.

Q.56   When did you go in there?

A.   I don't know - I know I am all mixed up in these times.

Q.57   Was the family in bed when you left Thursday?

A.   (Thinking) No.

Q.58   This money you gave your father was it all cash?

A.   Yes.

Q.59   How big a stack?

A.   (Shows about two inches)

Q.60   What did he do with it?

A.   Took it into the bedroom with him and took it with him when he went to B.C.

Q.61   But he didn't go to B.C.

A.   I know.

Q.62   Did you tell him where you got the money

A.   No I did not. He no doubt knew where I got the money. He doesn't ask questions like that.

Q.63   Is you father an honest man?

A.   Yes.

Q.64   Would he deal with stolen money?

A.   Well in a case like that when I got the money and I gave it to him he wouldn't. He knows it had been a long time and as far as he and I were concerned I had paid for that money.

Q.65   When you went to gaol the last time your father said he would
        have nothing more to do with you.

A.   Oh no he didn't. That's as wrong as you can ever get. When I
        went to gaol last time he sent me money and came to see me
        and everything. I got letters steady all the way through.

Q.66   Isn't it true that you have a very bad temper?

A.   No.

Q.67   I suggest to you it is.

A.   I'd say I haven't. I don't get mad very easy.

Q.68   Where were you keeping that $4100?

A.   When I came out of the Bowden Treasury Branch I put that -
        the money - I got out of that and other money I already had in
        a can and buried it.

Q.69   12 telephone poles from where?

A.   (very indignant and angry) No.

Q.70   Where did you bury it?

A.   What's the use to say any more on that.

Q.71   Why?

A.   I just don't want to say any more.

Q.72   Did you tell your father and mother where you buried it?

A.   They knew it was at Bowden, but didn't know where.

Q.73   You say you relationship with your father was very friendly.

A.   I didn't say very.

Q.74   How was it? How would you describe it?

A.   Well it couldn't be any better relationship.

Q.75   Someone killed him.

A.   I know that. You think it was me - you all do. I can tell you
        right now if I can ever get my hands on that guy there will be
        something going on too. He never did anything in his life. A
        man with a softer heart you never saw. If you want to ask him
        [sic] for anything you'd get it[1]. (very emotional - right arm
        shaking and on the verge of tears.)

Q.76   Did he have any enemies?

A.   He's not the kind to make enemies. He is too friendly - too
        nice.

Q.77   Why did someone kill him?

A.   I don't know.

Q.78   Did you black out Thursday night?

A.   No - I didn't kill him. I don't give a shit what you say.
        (still very emotional - voice raised.)

---

1 *There are three slightly different versions of this part of A..75 one of them
presumably accurate: "If you went and asked him for anything, you'd get it."*

APPENDIX B

The following is extracted from a document written by the late Reverend George Rode, then of Grace Lutheran Church and one of the two pastors who accompanied Cook to the Storage Room, written on the day following the execution. Reverend Rode told me how he and Reverend W. A. Rumsch, then of Redeemer Lutheran, went to an all-night coffee shop after the execution, sleep of course being out of the question. He then went home and wrote "Four Hours to Midnight." The ring Cook was allowed to wear had been given to him by Lila Larson. At Cook's request it was returned to her.

"FOUR HOURS TO MIDNIGHT"

It was Monday, November 14 at 8 pm when we arrived at the prison. The iron gates were closed but not locked. We opened them and drove through to the small parking lot near the front entrance of the main building. The place was quiet; there was no indication on the outside that in four hours a man would be hanged, convicted of the murder of his father. We had come to see Robert Raymond Cook.

Inside the main door the Deputy Warden asked us to wait a moment. He opened a drawer in his office and looked at the personal effects of the prisoner - all his possessions in a small brown envelope. He selected a gold signet ring, then led the way downstairs to the death cell. He unlocked the steel door which opened into a small corridor. A guard was stationed near one end where the wall was of steel mesh and through which you could look into the death cell. The door was opened and we walked into the seven by eight room with a small L to one side in which a toilet and wash basin were located.

Robert rose from the small cot - the only piece of furniture - and took the ring from the Deputy Warden. It was something he cherished and he wanted to wear it. He shook our hands. If he was nervous, he failed to show it; a smile came easily to his eyes and lips. He seemed to be in remarkably good health; there was little prison pallor, he was clean-shaven, his dark eyes were bright and his hand shake was firm - like that of a man in training for an athletic contest.

445

"Glad you are here," he said, "won't you sit down?" and he pointed apologetically to the cot. We had to make room, for a number of books were already spread out: the RSV, Luther's Small Catechism, a new testament and others. On the floor lay a number of novels. Cook had read much in prison, much of it the Scriptures and the Catechism.

Pastor Rumsch said, "Robert, one of the first things I want to ask you is if you are ready to proceed with what we talked about earlier today - your baptism." He indicated he would like to be baptised: "I am absolutely sure now" he said. "Even three days ago I was not sure. I believed, but somehow the assurance wasn't here," and he pointed to his heart. I recalled having spoken to him in July about this very matter. He wanted to know at that time if a person can actually be certain that he has faith. "I think I believe" he said at the time, "but I'm not sure." Now there was no doubt in his mind. "I know what baptism is and I am sure that through it I receive the assurance that my sins are forgiven. This is why I have no fear. "You know," he continued, "you may not understand, but I am kind of looking forward to...to this...." The word death however did not fall from his lips.

***

Pastor Rumsch had brought along a small bowl and a towel. We needed water. He went over to the sink and Robert had to ask the guard outside to turn on the water. There were no taps or light switches in the room; everything was controlled from outside. There was no organ, no congregation singing, but the service was one of the most moving I have ever witnessed.

Following the baptism we talked about various things. Robert reflected on some of his experiences as a professional boxer... [there follow here two paragraphs of a handful of things that Cook reminisced about which suggest the fantasizing of a mind under extreme stress since it is highly doubtful some of them occurred]. And so he reminisced - occasionally a trace of nervousness showed through; he would open up his NT which he carried in his hand [and] point to a passage he had marked. Now he turned to John 5:30: I can of mine own self do nothing: as I hear, I judge: and my judgment is just;... "I cannot understand it, but God's judgment is true."

He turned quickly to Rumsch. "Say, did you get the matter of my eyes straightened out?" He had willed his eyes to the eye bank and wondered whether Rumsch had made the necessary arrangements. Pastor Rumsch reached into his pocket and showed him the document - all it required was the doctor's signature. He seemed to be pleased. "What will they do with the remains?" Pastor Rumsch explained that he thought it was the procedure to forward the body to the University Hospital.

***

Occasionally he would reach for a package of tobacco and begin to roll a cigarette. Each time the guard offered him a tailor-made cigarette. It was handed through the mesh followed by a match.

At no time was he reluctant to talk about his faith or his fate. He wondered why others who had confessed to murder had their sentences commuted while he, convicted on circumstantial evidence, was going to hang. "It's wrong, Bob, terribly wrong" said the guard, "I just cannot understand it."

He reflected on God's providential care. "If I had gone after my first conviction, I would not have gone as I am going now. But there was a new trial and then (pointing to Pastor Rumsch) you came. Now I am able to go as a Christian. The Lord works in wonderful ways."

"We began walking the floor again - it was now after 10. He wondered whether he could receive the Lord's Supper. Pastor Rumsch assured him that he could, but suggested it be done later. We sat down on the bed again, and Rumsch asked him if he would like to have something read to him. "Sure, I'd like that. Rumsch took out a book of Lenten sermons - "Crowds Around Calvary" - and began reading one of the meditations.

After a few minutes the guard interrupted: "Say, would you like some coffee? I have some of my own here but I cannot give it to you, but if I talk to them upstairs, they might bring some down." He spoke into the intercom asking for three cups of coffee. The coffee was brought down shortly; it was hot and sweet. Robert apologized that we might not like the coffee that way but added: "Boy, it sure tastes good to me tonight."

***

He combed his dark hair out of his eyes and turned to the question of the Lord's Supper. It was now past 11 o'clock. Pastor Rumsch took out the Catechism and once again reviewed the section on Holy Communion. "This is the part I find most meaningful" said Robert as he pointed to Part II of Luther's Catechism: "Given and shed for you for the remission of sins, namely that in the Sacrament forgiveness of sins, life and salvation are given through these words. For where there is forgiveness of sins, there also is life and salvation." We went through each part carefully and then through the order of private communion. Again he showed a deep understanding of what Holy Communion is. "In it I receive the forgiveness of sins. "You know," he added, "I think in Holy Communion we come as close to God as we can come in this world. I would like to receive it."

***

The communion was over and he walked around a bit again. "I guess the Lord won't hold it against me if I indulge in a cigaret." Again the guard offered him one. Then the match. "This is the last match I'll be able to give you Bob." A little smile - "Yes, I guess I won't be needing any after this." He smoked the cigaret and then went to the sink and asked for some water. He put some on his comb to slick back his hair. Then he washed his face. It was now about 12 minutes to midnight. He shivered a bit. "This is not because I am cold;" he said, "I used to feel like this just before a fight - and again after, when I won."

"Clang" - the opening of the metal door sounded like a cannon in my ear. "Amen, this is it" said Robert Cook.

The door opened and the Warden stepped in. "You've been a good boy." "I'd like to shake your hand sir." They shook hands. The hangman, a short, heavy man with thick glasses and a beret on his head took Robert's right arm and fastened a heavy strap to it just above the elbow. He reached for the other arm. "Just a minute please, I'd like to shake hands with these gentlemen. He shook Rumsch's hand first and said cheerfully: "Thanks, and I'll see you again." Then we shook hands. "God's grace keeping me faithful, we shall meet again" I said. Then the other arm was pulled behind his back, the strap fastened to it, one guard took each arm and the last walk began.

First went the Warden, beside him the prison chaplain, an RC priest who wanted to be there. Then Rumsch followed, then I, and directly behind me so that occasionally I felt his toe on my heel walked Robert Cook between two prison guards. As we left the cell I noticed that the cell guard was fighting to hold back tears. We walked down the corridor. We walked up ten concrete stairs to the room above. Members of the RCMP were standing at attention. The room was absolutely bare. At the far end there was a black metal square on the floor - the trapdoor. On the wall to one side was a black hood, and waiting in readiness, the rope.

Robert was led directly to the center of the trapdoor. Pastor Rumsch and I took our positions directly in front of him, less than five feet away. A leather strap was placed around his legs just below the knees.

"Our Father who art in heaven...." Hardly audible, the prisoner joined in. The black hood was placed over his head and the noose tightened. "Hallowed be Thy name; Thy kingdom come...." The lever was pulled. There were several gasps in the room.

We went down to the room below. Already the doctor was in front of him, stethoscope in hand. Only the breathing of those who stood by could be heard. One man in a grey suit began to sway; two others stepped forward to steady him. At 12:18 the doctor removed the ends of the stethoscope from his ears. He looked at the others and said to no one in particular, "This man is dead."

And so died Robert Raymond Cook. He had found life in a death cell and, having found how to live, he knew how to die.

449

Errata

P.103   In the Welty case, the Weltys - husband and wife - were the victims of one O'Shea who was subsequently found not guilty by reason of insanity. He is presently confined in a mental institution. The author wishes to apologize to the Welty family for any distress caused by this error.

P.417   Read "26 men and one woman".